The Little Big
VEGETARIAN BOOK

The Little Big Vegetarian Book
was created and produced by McRae Books Srl
Borgo Santa Croce, 8 – Florence (Italy)
info@mcraebooks.com
www.mcraebooks.com
Publishers: Anne McRae and Marco Nardi

Text by the Editors of McRae Books
Photography: Lorenzo Borri, Mauro Corsi, Leonardo Pasquinelli, Gianni Petronio,
Walter Mericchi, Stefano Pratesi, Studio Marco Lanza
Food Styling: Arianna Cappellini, Francesco Piccardi
Home Economist: Benedetto Rillo
Translation: Osla Fraser, Ailsa Wood
Editing: Helen Farrell
Indexing: Ellie Smith
Art Director: Marco Nardi
Layout: Adina Stefania Dragomir, Sara Mathews, Filippo Delle Monache
Repro: Pica, Singapore - Fotolito Toscana, Florence

The Publishers would like to thank:
Bellini Più, Montespertoli (Florence); Bitossi Ceramiche, Montelupo Fiorentino (Florence);
Ceramiche Virginia, Montespertoli (Florence)

ISBN 88-89272-33-3

Printed and bound in Italy by Grafiche Industriali, Foligno

The recipes defined as ***Vegan** in this book exclude all dairy products (butter, eggs, milk, cheese,
and yogurt) and honey. For complete reassurance, check the packaging on individual products
to be certain of their suitability for your diet.

The Little Big
VEGETARIAN
BOOK

McRae Books

CONTENTS

SNACKS

CROSTINI WITH PEAS AND ZUCCHINI

Serves: 6	
Preparation: 15'	
Cooking: 30'	
Level of difficulty: 1	

- 2 zucchini/ courgettes, cut in small cubes
- 1 cup/100 g fresh garden peas
- 2 tbsp butter
- 2 tbsp all-purpose/ plain flour
- 1 cup/250 ml hot milk
- salt and freshly ground black pepper to taste
- ¼ tsp freshly grated nutmeg
- 1 large egg yolk, lightly beaten
- ½ cup/60 g freshly grated Parmesan cheese
- 6 slices whole-wheat/wholemeal bread

Cook the zucchini in a pot of salted, boiling water for 5–10 minutes, or until tender. • Drain well, reserving the cooking water. Pat the zucchini dry on paper towels. • Return the cooking water to a boil and cook the peas for 5 minutes, or until tender. • Drain well. • Preheat the oven to 400°F/ 200°C/gas 6. •

This springtime snack is loaded with vitamins, minerals, and fiber.

9

Butter a baking sheet. • Cook the butter and flour in a small saucepan over low heat for 1 minute, stirring constantly. • Remove from the heat and pour in half the hot milk. Return to the heat and warm until the mixture thickens. Gradually add the remaining milk, stirring constantly. Season with salt, pepper, and nutmeg. • Cook for 5 minutes, stirring constantly, to make a creamy sauce. • Remove from the heat and mix in the egg yolk. • Add 2 tablespoons of Parmesan, the peas, and zucchini and mix carefully. • Arrange the slices of bread on the prepared sheet. Bake for 5 minutes. • Spread the topping on the lightly toasted bread and sprinkle with the remaining Parmesan. • Bake for 7–10 minutes more, or until crisp and toasted. • Serve hot.

NEAPOLITAN CRÊPES

P repare the crêpe batter and set aside to rest. •
Sauté the onion in the oil in a large frying pan
over medium heat for about 5 minutes, or until
golden. • Add the tomato, eggplants, and olives.
Season with salt and pepper. • Cook for 15–20
minutes, or until the tomato has broken down and
the eggplant is tender and cooked. • Meanwhile,
cook the crêpes, stacking them up in a warm
oven.• Spoon the vegetables and Mozzarella onto
the crêpes, covering a quarter of the surface of
each one. • Fold each crêpe in four and arrange
them on a serving dish. • Serve warm.

Serves: 4

*Preparation: 15' +
time to prepare
crêpes*

Cooking: 25'

Level of difficulty: 2

- **12 crêpes
  (see page 956)**
- **1 small onion, thinly
  sliced**
- **2 tbsp extra-virgin
  olive oil**
- **1 large firm-ripe
  tomato, finely
  chopped**
- **2 eggplants/
  aubergines, finely
  chopped**
- **½ cup/50 g black
  olives, pitted and
  chopped**
- **salt and freshly
  ground black
  pepper to taste**
- **10 oz/300 g fresh
  Mozzarella
  (preferably made
  from water-buffalo
  milk), cut into small
  cubes**

EGGPLANT TORTILLAS

S lice the eggplant into four thick slices. • Place on a grill pan and cook for about 5–7 minutes on each side, or until soft. Chop coarsely. • Fill each tortilla with the eggplant, salsa, Mozzarella, tomatoes, and basil. Tuck in the edges of the tortillas and fold to enclose the filling. • Lower the flame slightly beneath the grill pan. Grill the filled tortillas for 2–3 minutes on each side. • Serve hot.

Serves: 4
Preparation: 15'
Cooking: 25'
Level of difficulty: 2

- 1 large eggplant/ aubergine
- salt and freshly ground black pepper to taste
- 4 tbsp extra-virgin olive oil
- 4–8 tortillas
- 4 tbsp Spicy Tomato Salsa (see page 50)
- 8 oz/250 g Mozzarella cheese, sliced
- 2 tomatoes, thinly sliced
- 2 tbsp coarsely chopped basil

CROSTINI WITH MUSHROOM CREAM

Serves: 4

Preparation: 30' + 30' to chill

Cooking: 10'

Level of difficulty: 1

- 10 oz/300 g white mushrooms, finely sliced
- 2 cloves garlic, finely chopped
- 4–6 tbsp extra-virgin olive oil
- 2/3 cup/150 g fresh creamy cheese (Robiola, cream cheese)
- salt to taste
- 4–8 slices toasted bread

Sauté the mushrooms and garlic in 2 tablespoons of oil in a frying pan over medium heat for 7–10 minutes, or until the mushrooms are tender and the cooking juices they release have evaporated. • Transfer the mushrooms to a food processor or blender with the cheese and enough of the remaining oil to make a smooth cream. • Season with salt and refrigerate for 30 minutes. • Spread the cream over the toasted bread and serve.

LENTIL AND SPINACH TOASTS

*Vegan

Serves: 4–8

Preparation: 15'

Cooking: 25–35'

Level of difficulty: 1

- 2 cups/200 g Puy lentils
- 2²/₃ cups/650 ml vegetable stock
- 1 large onion, coarsely chopped
- 4 tbsp extra-virgin olive oil
- salt and freshly ground black pepper to taste
- 4 tomatoes, peeled and coarsely chopped
- 1 lb/500 g spinach, tough stems removed, chopped
- 2 tbsp balsamic vinegar
- 8 slices toasted bread, crusts removed
- 1 clove garlic, peeled

Place the lentils in a large saucepan with the stock. Bring to a boil over medium heat and simmer for 30 minutes, or until tender. Drain and set aside. • Sauté the onion in 2 tablespoons of oil in a large saucepan for 5 minutes, or until softened. Season with salt. • Add the tomatoes and cooked lentils and sauté for 3 minutes. • Add the spinach and cook for 3–4 more minutes, or until the spinach is wilted. • Beat the remaining oil and vinegar in a small bowl. Season with salt and pepper. Rub the toast all over with the garlic. • Arrange the toast on serving dishes and spoon the lentil and spinach mixture over the top. • Drizzle with the oil and vinegar and serve.

Thought to lower cholesterol levels, spinach is best eaten when raw or lightly cooked.

15

CARROT AND OLIVE CROSTINI

P rocess the carrots and olives in a food
   processor or blender until smooth. • Add the
oil and season with salt and pepper. Taste before
adding the salt; the olives are already quite salty.
• Spread the olive and carrot paste over the bread
and serve. • If liked, toast the bread before
spreading with the olive and carrot paste.

16

*Vegan

Serves: 4–6

Preparation: 10'

Level of difficulty: 1

- 3 large carrots, peeled and chopped
- 1 cup/100 g pitted and chopped black olives
- 2 tbsp extra-virgin olive oil
- salt and freshly ground black pepper to taste
- sliced firm textured bread, to serve

MUSHROOM TOASTS

Serves: 4

Preparation: 20'

Cooking: 15–20'

Level of difficulty: 1

- 1¼ lb/600 g fresh porcini mushrooms
- 1½ tbsp butter
- 4 tbsp extra-virgin olive oil
- ½ white or mild red onion, finely chopped
- 2 cloves garlic, finely chopped
- 1 tbsp finely chopped thyme or parsley
- salt and freshly ground black pepper to taste
- ½ cup/125 ml vegetable stock (see page 945)
- 1 long loaf firm-textured white bread, toasted

Remove any grit or dirt from the mushrooms, rinse quickly under cold running water, and pat dry with paper towels. • Separate the stalks from the caps and dice only the firm, unblemished stalks. Chop the caps coarsely. • Heat the butter and oil in a large frying pan over medium heat and sauté the onion, garlic, and thyme for 5 minutes. • Add the mushrooms and season with salt and pepper. Cook for 5 minutes, stirring constantly. • Gradually stir in enough stock to keep the mixture moist but not sloppy. Cook for 8–10 minutes, or until the mushrooms are tender. • Spread each toast with a generous helping of the mushroom mixture and serve.

FAVA BEAN AND CHEESE BRUSCHETTE

Cook the fava beans in a large pot of salted, boiling water for 5–10 minutes until tender. • Drain and transfer to a large bowl. Add 1 tablespoon of oil, lemon juice, dill, salt, and pepper. • Toast the bread on both sides until golden and crisp. Drizzle with the remaining oil. Spoon the bean mixture onto the bruschette. • Top with the Camembert and broil (grill) for 2–3 minutes, or until the cheese is melted. • Serve hot.

Serves: 2

Preparation: 5'

Cooking: 10–15'

Level of difficulty: 1

- 4 oz/125 g frozen fava/broad beans, thawed
- 2 tbsp olive oil
- 1 tbsp fresh lemon juice
- 1 sprig dill, finely chopped
- salt and freshly ground black pepper to taste
- 2–4 slices firm-textured bread
- 3 oz/90 g Camembert cheese, sliced

PECORINO CHEESE WITH FRESH PEARS

Serves: 4

Preparation: 5'

Level of difficulty: 1

- 8 oz/250 g Pecorino cheese (young or aged, as preferred)
- 2–4 tasty ripe eating pears, preferably organic
- 2 tbsp fresh lemon juice

Rinse the pears thoroughly under cold running water. If using organic pears, leave the peel on – they make the dish so much tastier. • Cut the pears in half or in wedges, depending on their size. Drizzle with the lemon juice to stop them from turning brown. • Slice the cheese and place the pears and cheese on a serving dish.

FLATBREAD WITH GARLIC AND HERB CHEESE

Prepare the flatbread dough. Knead and divide into 4 pieces. Shape each piece into a ball.
• Chop the parsley, celery leaves, and basil in a food processor. • Add the garlic, salt and pepper, and 2–3 tablespoons of oil and chop until smooth.
• Place the goat's cheese in a large bowl and stir in the ground herbs to make a soft green cream. Add the lemon juice, if liked. • Roll out each piece of dough to about 6–7 inches (15–18 cm) in diameter. • Cook on a cast-iron griddle until bubbles appear on the surface. • Spread each flatbread with herb cheese, season with pepper, and serve.

Serves: 4

Preparation: 20'

Cooking: 35'

Level of difficulty: 2

- $^{1}/_{2}$ **quantity Italian flatbread dough (see page 207)**
- 1 bunch parsley
- 4 tender celery leaves
- 1 large sprig basil
- 3 cloves garlic, finely chopped
- salt and freshly ground black pepper to taste
- 2–3 tbsp extra-virgin olive oil
- $^{3}/_{4}$ cup/180 g soft goat's cheese
- 1 tbsp fresh lemon juice (optional)
- 1 tbsp butter

GARBANZO BEAN SNACKS

Vegan

Serves: 6

Preparation: 5'

Cooking: 8–10'

Level of difficulty: 1

- 4 cups/600 g garbanzo bean/ chick pea flour
- 2 quarts/2 liters water
- ³/₄ cup/180 ml extra-virgin olive oil
- salt and freshly ground black pepper to taste

Preheat the oven to 400°F/200°C/gas 6. • Set out a large nonstick roasting pan. • Sift the flour into a large bowl and make a well in the center. Use a wooden spoon to gradually stir in enough water to form a thick pouring batter. • Add the oil and season with salt and pepper. • Pour the batter into the pan, filling to a depth of ¹/₄ inch (5 mm). • Bake for 8–10 minutes, or until a thin crust forms on the surface. • Transfer to a serving dish and season with pepper. • Serve hot.

FLATBREAD WITH CAPRINO AND WILD SALAD GREENS

Serves: 6–8

Preparation: 20' + 20' to rest

Cooking: 10'

Level of difficulty: 2

- **1 quantity Italian flatbread dough (see page 207)**

TOPPING
- **6 oz/180 g mixed wild salad greens (dandelion, cress, arugula/rocket)**
- **6 tbsp extra-virgin olive oil**
- **1 cup/250 g Caprino (soft Italian goat's cheese)**
- **salt and freshly ground black pepper to taste**

Prepare the flatbread dough. Knead and divide into 8 pieces. Shape each piece into a ball. • Topping: Wash the salad greens and dry well in a salad spinner. Chop coarsely. • Transfer to a large bowl and stir in 4 tablespoons of oil. Season with salt and pepper. • Roll out each piece of dough to about 6–7 inches (15–18 cm) in diameter. • Cook on a cast-iron griddle until bubbles appear on the surface. • Spread the flatbread with the goat's cheese and top with the salad greens. • Drizzle with the remaining oil and serve immediately.

Caprino is a soft, fresh Italian goat's cheese. Substitute with another fresh, creamy cheese.

CROSTINI WITH GARBANZO BEAN PURÉE

S oak the garbanzo beans overnight in a large bowl of cold water with the baking soda. Drain and rinse well. • Transfer to a pressure cooker with the 1/2 cup (125 ml) of water and cook for 10 minutes. • Open the pressure cooker and add the sesame oil, lemon juice, and a pinch of salt. Top up the water if necessary. • Close and cook for 10 minutes more. (If you do not have a pressure cooker, cook the beans in a large pan of lightly salted water for 1 hour, or until tender. Drain the beans and add the sesame oil, lemon juice, and a pinch of salt.) • Chop the garbanzo beans in a food processor until smooth. Add the garlic, paprika, and parsley and mix well. • Spread the garbanzo bean mixture over the toast and serve.

*Vegan

Serves: 4–8

Preparation: 25' + time to soak beans

Cooking: 20' (or 1 h)

Level of difficulty: 1

- 3 1/2 cups/350 g dried garbanzo beans/chick peas
- 1 tsp baking soda/ bicarbonate of soda
- 4 tbsp sesame oil
- juice of 2 lemons
- salt to taste
- 1 clove garlic, finely chopped
- 1/8 tsp mild paprika
- 1 tbsp finely chopped parsley
- 8 slices wholewheat/wholemeal bread, toasted

FRESH CHEESE AND ZUCCHINI BAGUETTE

Heat a grill pan over medium heat and arrange the zucchini slices on top. Season with salt and pepper. Cook until the zucchini are tender on both sides, about 10 minutes. • Cut the baguette in half lengthwise. • Place the baguette halves on the grill pan until lightly toasted. • Spread with the goat's cheese and arrange the tomatoes, Provolone cheese, and zucchini on top. Season with salt and pepper. • Press the two halves of the baguette together to make a sandwich.

Serves: 2

Preparation: 15'

Cooking: 15'

Level of difficulty: 1

- ½ zucchini/
  courgette, thinly
  sliced lengthwise
- 1 tbsp extra-virgin
  olive oil
- salt and freshly
  ground black
  pepper to taste
- 1 long French-style
  baguette
- ½ cup/125 g fresh
  creamy goat's
  cheese
- 2 tomatoes, thinly
  sliced
- 6 oz/180 g smoked
  Provolone (or
  other) cheese,
  thinly sliced

BELL PEPPER CROSTINI

Vegan

Serves: 4

Preparation: 20' + 4 h
to marinate

Cooking: 10–15'

Level of difficulty: 2

- 1 red bell pepper/ capsicum
- 1 yellow bell pepper/ capsicum
- 1 clove garlic, finely chopped
- 4 leaves basil, torn
- 2 tbsp pitted black olives, coarsely chopped
- 4 tbsp extra-virgin olive oil
- salt and freshly ground black pepper to taste
- firm-textured bread for the crostini (French baguette or Italian ciabatta are ideal), sliced and toasted

Broil (grill) or roast the bell peppers whole until the skins are blackened. • Wrap them in a paper bag for 5 minutes, then remove the skins and seeds. Rinse carefully and dry on a clean cloth. • Slice the bell peppers into small, thin strips and place in a large bowl. Add the garlic, basil, olives, oil, salt, and pepper and marinate in the refrigerator for 4 hours. • Spread the bell pepper mixture on the freshly toasted bread and serve.

TOASTED BREAD
WITH BLACK TUSCAN KALE

Vegan

Serves: 4

Preparation: 5'

Cooking: 15–20'

Level of difficulty: 1

- 1 head black Tuscan kale, washed, stalked, and coarsely chopped
- 4 large slices firm-textured bread, such as Italian ciabatta or French loaf
- 1–2 cloves garlic, peeled and whole
- salt and freshly ground black pepper to taste
- 6 tbsp extra-virgin olive oil

Cook the kale in salted, boiling water in a large deep saucepan for 15–20 minutes, or until tender. • Toast the bread and rub it with the garlic. • Arrange the kale on the toasted bread. Season with salt, pepper, and a generous drizzling of oil.

If you can't find Tuscan kale, substitute with spinach. Cooking time will be 5–10 minutes less.

SOUTH AMERICAN CORNMEAL SNACKS

Preheat the oven to 400°F/200°C/gas 6. • Oil a baking sheet. • Mix the cornmeal, cheese, salt, and enough water in a large bowl to make a soft dough. • Knead for 2–3 minutes until smooth. • Cover the dough with a kitchen cloth and let rest for 5 minutes. • Brush a griddle or cast-iron frying pan over medium heat.
• Cook the dough in the frying pan for 3–4 minutes on each side, or until the south american cornmeal bread are soft inside but have formed a golden crust on the outside. While cooking, keep separating the south american cornmeal bread from the griddle or pan, or they will stick. • Keep warm while you cook the remaining dough. • Serve warm.

These cornmeal snacks come from the Andes. Serve with cheese, tomato, or other toppings.

30

Serves: 6–8

Preparation: 20'

Cooking: 25'

Level of difficulty: 1

- 3⅓ cups/500 g finely ground cornmeal
- 1¼ cups/150 g freshly grated firm cheese (such as processed Mozzarella)
- 1 tsp salt
- 2 cups/500 ml water

PANCAKES WITH WALNUTS, PECORINO, AND APPLE

S ift both flours, baking powder, and salt into a medium bowl. • Beat in the eggs, butter, and milk until creamy. Season with salt and pepper. • Heat a lightly oiled griddle or small crêpe pan and add 4 tablespoons of batter, tilting the pan so that the batter covers the bottom in an even layer. • Cook on one side until the bubbles that form in the pancake look dry. Use a spatula to turn the pancake and cook until the other side is golden brown. • Place the pancake in a warm oven and cook the rest of the batter. You should get 12 pancakes. • Place a pancake on a serving dish and cover with a layer of apple, walnuts, and cheese. Drizzle with $1/2$ tablespoon of honey and cover with another pancake. Repeat the layering process and top with a third pancake. Garnish with Pecorino, walnuts, and honey. • Serve immediately.

Serves:	4
Preparation:	10'
Cooking:	20'
Level of difficulty:	1

- 1$1/3$ cups/200 g all-purpose/plain flour
- 1 cup/150 g whole-wheat/wholemeal flour
- 2 tsp baking powder
- $1/2$ tsp salt
- 2 large eggs, lightly beaten
- salt and freshly ground black pepper to taste
- 4 tbsp butter, melted
- 1$1/2$ cups/375 ml milk
- 2 Granny Smith apples, cored and thinly sliced
- 5 oz/150 g Pecorino Romano cheese, thinly sliced
- 6 tbsp honey, warmed
- 1 cup/125 g walnuts, hulled and lightly toasted

TUSCAN TOMATO PÂTÉ

Sauté the garlic in 4 tablespoons of oil in a large saucepan over low heat for 2 minutes. • Add the 7 oz (200 g) of tomatoes and half the basil. Season with salt and pepper. Cook for about 15 minutes, or until reduced by half. • Remove from the heat and mix in the bread. • Line an 8 x 9-inch (20 x 23-cm) baking pan with waxed paper. • Pour the tomato mixture into the prepared pan. Cover with plastic wrap (cling film) and refrigerate for 30 minutes. • Process the remaining 3 tomatoes with the remaining oil, 2 tablespoons of water, the rest of the basil, salt, and pepper until smooth. Pour into a small saucepan and warm over low heat. Add the agar-agar and continue to cook, stirring constantly, for 5 minutes. Remove from the heat and let cool. • Pour the tomato and agar-agar sauce over the chilled tomato mixture. Refrigerate for 30 minutes. • Turn on the broiler (grill) to the high setting. Turn out the pâté and slice into squares. Broil for 2–3 minutes. Transfer to a serving dish and garnish with remaining basil.

*Vegan

Serves: 4

Preparation: 25' + 1 h to chill

Cooking: 25'

Level of difficulty: 2

- 1 clove garlic, finely chopped
- 7 tbsp extra-virgin olive oil
- 7 oz/200 g peeled plum tomatoes, coarsely chopped
- 4 sprigs basil, torn
- salt and freshly ground black pepper to taste
- 8 oz/250 g day-old bread (preferably saltless), cut into small cubes
- 3 tomatoes, finely chopped
- 3 tbsp water
- 1 tsp agar-agar
- 1 small bunch basil, torn, to garnish

PARTY
FOOD

SPICED YOGURT DIP

Sauté the garlic, turmeric, and salt in the ghee in a small saucepan over medium heat for 2–3 minutes, or until the garlic is lightly cooked. • Add the yogurt, $1/2$ teaspoon paprika, and cilantro to the pan and cook for 5 minutes. • Let cool. • Sprinkle with the extra paprika and chopped cilantro to garnish. • Serve chilled or at room temperature with tortilla chips, crackers, pappadams, or toast.

Serves: 4

Preparation: 10'

Cooking: 10'

Level of difficulty: 1

- 1 clove garlic, finely chopped
- $1/2$ tsp ground turmeric
- $1/2$ tsp salt
- 1 tbsp ghee (clarified butter)
- 1 cup/250 ml thick plain yogurt
- $1/2$ tsp cayenne pepper
- 1 tsp finely chopped cilantro/ coriander
- cayenne pepper, to garnish
- chopped cilantro/ coriander, to garnish

POTATO NESTS WITH CORN AND PEAS

Serves: 4

Preparation: 30' + time to make mashed potato

Cooking: 20'

Level of difficulty: 2

- 3 tbsp butter
- 3 egg yolks, lightly beaten
- 2 lb/1 kg mashed potato (with butter, milk, and nutmeg)
- 1 carrot, cut in small dice
- 3 oz/90 g canned corn
- 4 oz/125 g hulled/shelled peas
- salt and freshly ground black pepper to taste

Preheat the oven to 350°F/180°C/gas 4. • Mix 2 tablespoons of butter, 2 egg yolks, and the mashed potato in a large bowl until well blended. • Spoon the mixture into a pastry bag fitted with a plain tip. Squeeze out 8 rings (or "nests") onto a lightly buttered baking sheet. Brush with the remaining beaten egg yolk. • Bake for 10–12 minutes, or until golden. • Cook the carrot, peas, and corn in salted, boiling water for 5 minutes, or until tender. • Drain well, toss in the remaining butter and season with salt and pepper. • Spoon into the potato nests and serve.

EGGPLANT AND GARLIC DIP

Preheat the oven to 400°F/200°C/gas 6. •
Prick the eggplants all over with a fork and
place them on a baking sheet. • Bake for 1 hour,
or until softened. • Scoop out the flesh with a
spoon and mash with a fork in a medium bowl.
• Mix in the garlic, tahini, lemon juice, and salt.
• Garnish with the parsley. • Serve with triangles
of toasted bread.

*Vegan

Serves: 4	
Preparation: 20'	
Cooking: 1 h	
Level of difficulty: 1	

- **2 large eggplants/ aubergines**
- **2 cloves garlic, finely chopped**
- **2 tbsp sesame seed paste (tahini)**
- **juice of 1 lemon**
- **salt to taste**
- **1 bunch parsley, finely chopped**

FRESH VEGETABLE RAITA

Serves: 4

Preparation: 20' + 1 h to chill

Level of difficulty: 1

- ½ cucumber, diced
- 1 small onion, diced
- 1 boiled potato, diced
- 3 tomatoes, diced
- 3½ oz/100 g radishes, finely chopped
- 2 stalks celery, finely chopped
- 1¼ cups/310 ml thick creamy yogurt
- salt and freshly ground black pepper to taste
- 1 sprig parsley, to garnish

P lace the cucumber, onion, potato, tomatoes, and celery in a medium bowl. Stir in the yogurt. Season with salt and pepper. • Chill in the refrigerator for at least 1 hour. • Garnish with the parsley and serve with toast or fresh bread.

FRESH VEGETABLES WITH THREE DIPS

Serves: 6

Preparation: 15'

Level of difficulty: 1

DIP 1

- 1 cup/250 ml mayonnaise
- 1 clove garlic, finely chopped
- freshly ground white pepper

DIP 2

- ¾ cup/180 ml extra-virgin olive oil
- 3 tbsp balsamic vinegar
- salt and freshly ground black pepper to taste

DIP 3

- 1 cup/250 ml plain yogurt
- juice of ½ lemon
- 2 scallions/spring onions, sliced

TO SERVE

- 10 oz/300 g cherry tomatoes
- 5 oz/150 g scallions/spring onions
- 7 oz/200 g fennel
- 7 oz/200 g celery
- 8 small carrots
- 8 radishes

Dip 1: Mix the mayonnaise with the garlic in a small bowl. Season with pepper. • Dip 2: Beat the oil and balsamic vinegar in a small bowl. Season with salt and pepper. • Dip 3: Mix the yogurt, lemon juice, and scallions in a small bowl. Season with salt and pepper. • Cut the cherry tomatoes in half. Trim the scallions. Cut the fennel into wedges. Remove any tough filaments from the celery and cut into long pieces. Scrape the carrots and cut into long sticks. Rinse and peel the radishes. • Arrange the vegetables on a large serving dish. • Serve immediately with the dips.

Use any in-season vegetables to create this colorful platter.

FOCACCIA WITH CHERRY TOMATOES AND BASIL

Prepare the focaccia dough and set aside to rise. • Preheat the oven to 400°F/200°C/ gas 6. • Oil a rectangular baking pan about 10 x 15 inches (25 x 38 cm) in size. • When the rising time has elapsed, use your fingertips to press the dough into the baking pan. • Place the tomatoes on top, cut side up, pressing them into the dough. Drizzle with half the oil. Season with salt and pepper. • Bake for 15–20 minutes, or until the focaccia is golden. • Drizzle with the remaining oil and garnish with the basil. • Let cool, then cut into triangles. • Serve hot or at room temperature.

Vegan

Makes: one (10 x 15-in/ (25 x 38-cm) focaccia	
Preparation: 30'	
Rising time: 1 h 30'	
Cooking: 15–20'	
Level of difficulty: 2	

- 1 quantity Focaccia Dough (see page 954)
- 12 oz/350 g cherry tomatoes, cut in half and seeded
- 2–4 tbsp extra-virgin olive oil
- salt and freshly ground black pepper to taste
- fresh basil, to garnish

CORN ON THE COB WITH BUTTER

C ook the corn in a large pan of salted, boiling water for 5–10 minutes, or until the corn is tender. The cooking time will depend on how fresh the ears of corn are. • Drain well and place in a heated serving dish. • Melt the butter over the corn and season with salt and pepper. • Serve hot.

Serves: 4–6

Preparation: 10'

Cooking: 5–10'

Level of difficulty: 1

- **4–6 very fresh ears of corn, silk and husks removed**
- **4–6 tbsp softened butter, chopped**
- **salt and freshly ground black pepper to taste**

ZUCCHINI FLOWER BITES

Serves: 4

Preparation: 25'

Rising time: 1 h 30'

Cooking: 10–12'

Level of difficulty: 2

- ¹/₂ **quantity Pizza Dough (see page 952)**
- **4 tbsp extra-virgin olive oil**
- **6–8 cherry tomatoes, sliced**
- **6 zucchini/ courgette flowers**
- **salt to taste**
- **1¹/₂ oz/45 g Parmesan cheese, flaked**
- **1 tbsp finely chopped thyme**

Prepare the pizza dough and set aside to rise. • Preheat the oven to 425°F/220°C/gas 7. • Oil a baking sheet. • When the rising time has elapsed, knead 1 tablespoon of oil into the dough. • Roll out on a lightly floured surface to ¹/₄-inch (5-mm) thick. Use a pastry cutter to cut out 1¹/₂-inch (4-cm) rounds. • Place a slice of tomato on each piece of dough. • Place the small pizzas on the baking sheet. Let rise for 15 minutes. • Clean the zucchini flowers and chop finely. Place a little on each pizza. Season with salt and drizzle with the remaining oil. • Bake for 10–12 minutes, or until golden and risen. • Sprinkle with the Parmesan and thyme. • Serve hot or at room temperature.

BANANA AND YOGURT CHILE DIP

B eat the cream with an electric mixer at high speed until thick. • Mash the bananas in a medium serving bowl. • Carefully stir in the yogurt and cream. • Season with salt and the finely chopped chile peppers, reserving a little to garnish, and stir well. • Chill in the refrigerator for at least 1 hour. • Garnish with the reserved chile pepper. Serve with tortilla chips, potato crisps, pappadams, or toast.

Serves: 4–6

Preparation: 15' + 1 h to chill

Level of difficulty: 1

- $1/2$ cup/ 125 ml heavy/ double cream
- 2 ripe bananas
- generous $3/4$ cup/ 200 ml thick plain yogurt
- salt to taste
- $1/2$ small red chile pepper, seeded and finely sliced
- 1 small green chile pepper, seeded and finely sliced

BAJI'S SOUR CREAM AND YOGURT DIP

Serves: 4

*Preparation: 20' + 1 h
to chill*

Cooking: 5–10'

Level of difficulty: 1

- 1 carrot, peeled
- 1 small cucumber,
  peeled and finely
  sliced
- 1¾ tsp salt
- 1 cup/250 ml plain
  yogurt
- ½ cup/125 ml
  sour cream
- 1 clove garlic,
  finely chopped
- ¼ tsp freshly
  ground black
  pepper
- 1 shallot, finely
  chopped
- 1 tbsp finely
  chopped parsley
- ¼ tsp paprika
- ½ tsp ground
  cumin seeds

Cook the carrot in a large pot of salted, boiling water for 5–10 minutes, or until tender. • Drain, let cool, and grate finely. • Sprinkle the cucumber with 1 teaspoon of salt in a colander. Let drain for 5 minutes. • Beat the yogurt and sour cream with the remaining salt in a medium bowl. Add the garlic and season with pepper. • Rinse the cucumber and drain well. Mix the carrot, shallot, and cucumber (reserving 4 slices to garnish) into the yogurt. Refrigerate for 1 hour. • Sprinkle with the parsley, paprika, and cumin. Garnish with the reserved cucumber and serve with tortilla chips, potato crisps, pappadams, or toast.

SPICY TOMATO SALSA

P lace the tomatoes, onion, garlic, jalapeno peppers, red pepper flakes, and cilantro in a medium serving bowl. • Add the lime juice and oil and season with salt and pepper. • Chill in the refrigerator for at least 1 hour. • Serve with tortilla chips, potato crisps, fresh bread, or toast.

*Vegan

Serves: 6

Preparation: 10' + 1 h to chill

Level of difficulty: 1

- 3–4 large ripe tomatoes, peeled and finely chopped
- 1 red onion, finely chopped
- 2 cloves garlic, finely chopped
- 2 pickled jalapeno peppers, finely chopped
- ½ tsp red pepper flakes, or more, to taste
- 2 tbsp finely chopped cilantro/ coriander
- juice of 1 lime
- 2–4 tbsp extra-virgin olive oil
- salt and freshly ground black pepper to taste

BLACK BEANS IN MANGO SAUCE

Place the beans in a large saucepan with enough water to cover and bring to a boil over low heat. Remove from the heat and let soak for 2 hours. • Drain. Pour in the boiling water and add the bay leaves. Bring to a boil and simmer over low heat for 1 hour 15 minutes, or until the beans are tender. • Drain and discard the bay leaves. Let cool completely. • Mix the beans, mango, lemon and orange juices, maple syrup, and cilantro in a large bowl. Season with salt and pepper. • Drizzle with the lime juice and refrigerate until ready to serve. • Serve with freshly made tortillas.

52

*Vegan

Serves: 6–8

Preparation: 20' + time to soak beans

Cooking: 1 h 20'

Level of difficulty: 1

- 8 oz/250 g dried black beans, soaked overnight and drained
- 1 quart/1 liter boiling water
- 4 bay leaves
- 10 oz/300 g mango, peeled and cut into cubes
- 1 tbsp lemon juice
- 1 tbsp orange juice
- 1 tbsp maple syrup
- 3 tbsp finely chopped cilantro/ coriander
- salt and freshly ground black pepper to taste
- 1 tbsp fresh lime juice
- wheat tortillas, to serve

ASPARAGUS AND ORANGE CROSTONI

Serves: 6–8

Preparation: 30'

Cooking: 30'

Level of difficulty: 2

- 3 lb/1.5 kg fresh asparagus, trimmed
- 1 orange
- 12 slices firm-textured bread, toasted
- 3 egg yolks
- ⅔ cup/150 g butter, cut in small pieces
- salt to taste

Cook the asparagus in a large saucepan of salted, boiling water for 8–10 minutes, or until tender. • Drain well and cut off all but the most tender part of the stalks. • Squeeze the orange and set the juice aside. Cut half the zest into thin strips. Blanch in a pot of boiling water for a few seconds. Drain. • Place the asparagus on the toast. • Beat the egg yolks with a few pieces of butter, salt, and 1 tablespoon of water in a double boiler over barely simmering water. • As soon as the butter begins to melt, add the rest a little at a time, so that it is gradually absorbed, taking care that the sauce never boils. • When the sauce is creamy, add more salt and, very gradually, the orange juice, stirring carefully all the time. • Remove from the heat and stir in the orange zest. • Spoon the sauce over the crostoni and serve.

EGGPLANT AND YOGURT DIP

Serves: 4–6

Preparation: 20' + 1 h to cool and chill

Cooking: 1 h

Level of difficulty: 1

- 3 large eggplants/ aubergines
- 2 cups/500 ml thick plain yogurt
- 2 cloves garlic
- 4 tbsp extra-virgin olive oil
- 2 tbsp fresh lemon juice
- salt and freshly ground black pepper to taste
- thinly sliced tomatoes, to garnish

Preheat the oven to 400°F/200°C/gas 6. • Prick the eggplants all over with a fork and place them on a baking sheet. • Bake for 1 hour, or until softened. • Let cool completely. • Cut the eggplants in half lengthwise and scoop out the flesh with a spoon. Squeeze out any excess water with a fork. • Process the eggplants in a food processor or blender with the yogurt, garlic, oil, lemon juice, salt, and pepper until smooth. • Transfer to a serving dish and chill in the refrigerator for at least 30 minutes. • Garnish with the tomatoes. • Serve with pita bread or toast.

ONION, CHEESE, AND OLIVE TRIANGLES

Prepare the pizza dough and set aside to rise. • Peel the onions and slice thinly. • Cook the onions with the water, 2 tablespoons of oil, and the thyme and rosemary in a large frying pan over medium heat for 5–10 minutes, or until all the liquid has evaporated. • Season with salt, remove from the heat, and let cool. • Preheat the oven to 425°F/220°C/gas 7. • Oil a large baking sheet. • When the rising time has elapsed, roll the dough out about $1/8$-inch (3-mm) thick and cut into triangles. • Spread the cheese, olives, and onion mixture on each triangle. Season with pepper and drizzle with the remaining oil. • Transfer the triangles to the baking sheet and bake for 10–12 minutes, or until the pizza dough is golden. • Serve hot or at room temperature.

These tasty little treats are perfect to serve at cocktail parties with wine or other drinks.

56

Serves:	6
Preparation:	35'
Rising time:	1 h 30'
Cooking:	20–25'
Level of difficulty:	2

- 1 quantity Pizza Dough (see page 952)
- 4 medium red onions
- ¾ cup/180 ml water
- 4 tbsp extra-virgin olive oil
- 1 tbsp finely chopped thyme
- 1 tbsp finely chopped rosemary
- salt and freshly ground black pepper to taste
- 1¼ cups/310 g fresh creamy cheese (goat's cheese, Mozzarella, Stracchino)
- 4–6 tbsp pitted black olives

SMALL RICOTTA AND ZUCCHINI PIZZAS

Prepare the pizza dough and set aside to rise. • Cut the zucchini and their flowers julienne-style. Sauté the zucchini, zucchini flowers, and scallion in the oil in a large frying pan over high heat for 5 minutes. Season with salt and pepper, remove from the heat and let cool. • Beat the Ricotta, eggs, and thyme in a large bowl. • Preheat the oven to 400°F/200°C/gas 6. • Roll the dough out thinly on a lightly floured surface. Divide into six equal parts and line six 4-inch (10-cm) tartlet pans. Let rise for 15 minutes. • Mix the zucchini into the Ricotta mixture. Spoon the mixture evenly into the pans. • Bake for 10 minutes. • Lower the temperature to 350°F/180°C/gas 4 and bake for 10 minutes more, or until golden. • Garnish with the pistachios and the reserved flowers and serve.

Serves: 6

Preparation: 30'

Rising time: 1 h 45'

Cooking: 25–30'

Level of difficulty: 2

- ^{2}/3 **quantity Pizza dough (see page 952)**
- **14 oz/400 g young zucchini/ courgettes, preferably with flowers**
- **1 scallion/spring onion, finely sliced**
- **2 tbsp olive oil**
- **salt and freshly ground black pepper to taste**
- **1^1/4 cups/310 g Ricotta cheese**
- **2 eggs**
- **1 tbsp finely chopped thyme**
- **^{1}/2 cup/50 g chopped pistachios**

BITE-SIZED NEAPOLITAN PIZZAS

Serves: 6–8

Preparation: 45'

Rising time: 1 h 45'

Cooking: 15'

Level of difficulty: 2

- 1 quantity
  **Pizza dough
  (see page 952)**
- 1 cup/250 ml olive
  oil, for frying
- 1²/₃ cups/400 g
  **Tomato Sauce,
  store-bought or
  homemade
  (see page 951)**
- 1 cup/125 g
  **freshly grated
  Parmesan cheese**
- 2 tbsp finely
  chopped basil
- 1 tsp dried oregano

Prepare the pizza dough and set aside to rise. • When the rising time has elapsed, knead the dough again until smooth and elastic. • Divide into 12 pieces and shape into balls. Cover with a cloth and let rise for 15 minutes. • Roll the dough balls out on a lightly floured surface into ¹/₄-inch (5-mm) thick rounds. The edges should be slightly higher than the center. • Heat the oil in a large frying pan to very hot. • Fry the pizzas in small batches until golden, spooning the oil over them. This will help them swell up. • Drain well on paper towels. • Cut a slice into the sides of the pizzas and spoon in the tomato sauce. Sprinkle with the Parmesan, basil, and oregano and serve hot.

ASPARAGUS AND GOAT'S CHEESE MINI QUICHES

Serves: 4–8

Preparation: 30'

Cooking: 30–35'

Level of difficulty: 2

- 7 oz/200 g large asparagus stalks, coarsely chopped
- 1 clove garlic, lightly crushed but whole
- 2 tbsp extra-virgin olive oil
- salt and freshly ground black pepper to taste
- 1 lb/500 g frozen puff pastry, thawed
- 4 eggs
- 1¼ cups/310 ml milk
- 2 small forms semi-matured goat's cheeses

Cook the asparagus in a large pan of salted, boiling water for 5–10 minutes, or until crunchy-tender. • Drain and cut off the tough part of the stalk. Chop the remaining stalks coarsely. • Sauté the chopped asparagus with the garlic in the oil in a large frying pan over medium heat for 5 minutes. • Season with salt and pepper. Discard the garlic. • Preheat the oven to 400°F/200°C/gas 6. • Butter eight 4-inch (10-cm) high-sided mini cake or flan pans. Line the bottom and sides with the pastry. • Spoon the asparagus evenly into the pastry bases. • Beat the eggs and milk in a large bowl until frothy. Season with salt and pepper. Pour the mixture over the asparagus. • Cut the goat's cheeses horizontally to make 8 rounds. Place a cheese round in each pie. Season generously with pepper. • Bake for 20 minutes, or until golden. • Let stand for 10 minutes before serving. • If not serving immediately, reheat a little in the oven.

SPRING LEEK SALAD

Prepare the leeks at least 1 hour before you will need them. Wash under running water to rinse away any dirt. • Cook the leeks in a large pot of salted, boiling water with 1 tablespoon of oil for 5–10 minutes, or until tender. Drain and let cool. • Slice the leeks in half lengthwise. • Mix the onion, bell peppers, cucumbers, capers, and tomatoes in a large salad bowl. Drizzle with the remaining oil and vinegar. Add the parsley and oregano. Season with salt and pepper. • Arrange the watercress, arugula, and spinach on individual serving dishes. Place a layer of sliced leeks on top of each one and spoon the bell pepper mixture over the top. • Serve immediately.

*Vegan

Serves: 6

Preparation: 25'

Cooking: 5–10'

Level of difficulty: 1

- **12 young leeks**
- **6 tbsp extra-virgin olive oil**
- **1 red onion, finely chopped**
- **3 bell peppers, mixed colors, seeded, cored, and finely chopped**
- **4 pickled gherkins, finely chopped**
- **½ cup/100 g salted capers, rinsed and chopped**
- **2 tomatoes, chopped**
- **2 tbsp vinegar**
- **1 tbsp finely chopped parsley**
- **1 tbsp finely chopped oregano**
- **salt and freshly ground black pepper to taste**
- **4 oz/125 g watercress**
- **4 oz/125 g arugula/rocket**
- **2 oz/60 g spinach**

ARUGULA AND CREAMY CHEESE PIZZAS WITH WALNUTS

Serves: 6–8

Preparation: 20'

Rising time: 1 h 45'

Cooking: 10–15'

Level of difficulty: 2

- 2 quantities
  Pizza Dough
  (see page 952)
- 10 oz/300 g cherry
  tomatoes, thinly
  sliced
- 7 oz/200 g fresh
  creamy cheese
  (Robiola, goat's
  cheese, cream
  cheese)
- 2 tbsp extra-virgin
  olive oil
- salt to taste
- 1 bunch arugula/
  rocket
- about 20 walnuts,
  coarsely chopped
- 1 tbsp balsamic
  vinegar

Prepare the pizza dough and set aside to rise. • Preheat the oven to 425°F/220°C/gas 7. • Oil a large baking sheet. • When the rising time has elapsed, divide the dough into 16 pieces and shape into balls. Roll the dough balls out on a lightly floured surface into rounds. Transfer the rounds to the prepared baking sheets, placing them well apart. • Let rise for 15 minutes. • Arrange the tomatoes on the pizzas. Spoon some of the cheese over each one, drizzle with the oil, and season with salt. • Bake for 10–15 minutes, or until the dough is golden. • Wash and dry the arugula and shred finely. • Place the arugula and walnuts on top. • Drizzle with the balsamic vinegar and serve warm.

LIGHT AND AIRY FILLED CORNMEAL FRITTERS

D ough: Sift the flour, cornmeal, baking powder, and salt into a large bowl. Mix in the eggs and milk to make a thick batter. • Drop spoonfuls of the batter into a hot lightly-oiled frying pan. The batter will spread and swell up. Cook until golden brown on one side, then turn to brown the other side. Repeat until all the batter is cooked. • Filling: Place the cabbage in a large bowl with the goat cheese, oil, lemon juice, mustard, and salt. • Split the fritters in half horizontally. • Spread with the filling and put the top back on. • Serve warm or at room temperature.

Serves: 8

Preparation: 30'

Cooking: 10'

Level of difficulty: 2

DOUGH

- 2 cups/300 g all-purpose/plain flour
- ½ cup/75 g finely ground cornmeal
- 1 tsp baking powder
- ¼ tsp salt
- 2 eggs
- 1 cup/250 ml milk
- 2 tbsp extra-virgin olive oil, for the pan

FILLING

- 7 oz/200 g Savoy cabbage, finely shredded
- 1 cup/250 ml fresh creamy goat's cheese
- 1 tbsp extra-virgin olive oil
- 1 tbsp fresh lemon juice
- 1 tbsp mustard
- ⅛ tsp salt

MINI PIZZAS WITH SHALLOT AND HERB TOPPING

Prepare the pizza dough and set aside to rise. •
Soak the shallots in the water and vinegar for
15 minutes. Drain well. • Preheat the oven to
400°F/ 200°C/gas 6. • Oil a baking sheet. • Sauté
the shallots in 3 tablespoons of oil in a large frying
pan over high heat for 5 minutes. Season with salt,
pepper, and half the herbs and remove from heat.
• Roll the dough out thinly on a lightly floured
surface. Use a 2-inch (5-cm) cookie-cutter to cut
out rounds. Place on the baking sheet. Let rise for
10 minutes. • Spoon some shallots over each
pizza. Sprinkle with the remaining herbs and drizzle
with the remaining oil. Bake for 10–15 minutes, or
until golden. • Serve hot.

Vegan

Serves:	4–8
Preparation:	45'
Rising time:	1 h 40'
Cooking:	25–30'
Level of difficulty:	2

- 1 quantity
  Pizza Dough
  (see page 952)
- 12 shallots, finely
  chopped
- ½ cup/125 ml
  water
- ½ cup/125 ml
  white wine vinegar
- 5 tbsp extra-virgin
  olive oil
- salt and freshly
  ground black
  pepper to taste
- 1–2 tbsp dried
  mixed herbs
  (marjoram,
  rosemary, and
  thyme)

EASY POTATO KNISHES

Serves: 4–6

Preparation: 25'

Cooking: 1 h 10'

Level of difficulty: 1

- **6 large potatoes, peeled**
- **6 eggs, lightly beaten**
- **salt and freshly ground white pepper to taste**
- **6 tbsp potato starch**

Cook the potatoes in salted, boiling water for about 25 minutes, or until tender. • Preheat the oven to 350°F/180°C/gas 4. • Butter a large baking sheet. • Drain and transfer the potatoes to a large bowl and mash well until smooth. • Add the eggs, beating until well blended. Season with salt and pepper. • Stir in the potato starch. The mixture should be dry enough to shape into balls with your hands, adding more starch if needed. • Arrange the knishes on the prepared baking sheet. • Bake for about 45 minutes, or until golden brown. • Serve warm.

COCONUT FLATBREAD WITH YOGURT TOPPING

Coconut Flatbread: Sift the flour into a bowl. Stir in the coconut and enough water to make a smooth dough. • Dust your hands with flour and knead until smooth and elastic. Cover and let rest for 30 minutes. • Form the dough into a log and cut into 12–14 pieces. Shape each piece into a ball and roll out thinly on a floured work surface. • Heat a cast-iron griddle. Grease with a little oil and cook the flatbreads one at a time until lightly browned on each side. Oil the pan after cooking each one. • Keep the cooked flatbread warm in the oven . • Yogurt Topping: Mix the scallions and chile into the yogurt. Season with salt. • Spread the mixture over the flatbread and garnish with the reserved chile.

Serves: 6

Preparation: 20' + 30' to rest

Cooking: 25'

Level of difficulty: 2

COCONUT FLATBREAD
- 2 cups/300 g all-purpose/plain flour
- 1 cup/100 g unsweetened dessicated coconut
- 4–6 tbsp water

YOGURT TOPPING
- 3 scallions/spring onions, finely chopped
- 1–2 fresh red chile peppers, finely sliced (reserving a few slices to garnish)
- 1 cup/250 ml thick, creamy yogurt
- 1 tsp salt

FILLED BRUSSELS SPROUTS

Serves: 4–6

Preparation: 30'

Cooking: 25'

Level of difficulty: 1

- 1 lb/500 g fresh or frozen Brussels sprouts
- bunch of mixed fresh herbs (parsley, dill, basil, tarragon, marjoram)
- 1 tbsp white wine vinegar
- 1 clove garlic, finely chopped
- 3 tbsp butter
- 4 tbsp heavy/ double cream
- salt and freshly ground black pepper to taste
- 1 red bell pepper/ capsicum, seeded, cored, and cut into small pieces

Cook the sprouts with the herbs and vinegar in a large pan of salted, boiling water for 5 minutes. Drain well. • Coarsely chop one-third of the sprouts. Hollow the centers out of the remaining sprouts. • Sauté the garlic in half the butter in a large frying pan until pale gold. Add the chopped sprouts and cream. • Season with salt and pepper and cook, stirring often, for 10 minutes. • Place the hollow sprouts in a pan with the remaining butter. Season with salt and pepper and cook for 10 minutes. • Fill the sprouts with the cream mixture. Top each sprout with a small piece of bell pepper. • Serve hot or at room temperature.

PEA AND PECORINO RING

Serves: 6–8

Preparation: 30'

Rising time: 1 h

Cooking: 20'

Level of difficulty: 2

- 1½ tbsp active dry yeast
- ¾ cup/180 ml milk, hot
- 3⅓ cups/500 g all-purpose/plain flour
- ½ tsp salt
- 4 large eggs, lightly beaten
- 2 tbsp granulated sugar
- ¾ cup/180 g butter, cut up
- ¼ tsp freshly ground pepper
- 1¾ cups/215 g freshly grated Pecorino cheese
- 2 cups/200 g peas, lightly cooked

Mix the yeast and milk in a small bowl. Let stand for 15 minutes, until foamy. • Sift the flour and salt into a large bowl and make a well in the center. Mix in the yeast mixture, eggs, sugar, butter, and pepper to make a soft, elastic dough. • Add the Pecorino and peas and knead well. • Butter a 10-inch (26-cm) ring mold.

Substitute Parmesan for the Pecorino if unobtainable.

• Place the dough in in the ring mold. • Let rise in a warm place for about 1 hour. • Preheat the oven to 375°F/190°C/gas 5. • Bake for 25–35 minutes, or until well risen and golden brown. • Remove from the oven and let cool for 5 minutes before turning out onto a rack. • Slice and serve while still warm.

PUFF PASTRY VEGETABLE PARCELS

P reheat the oven to 350°F/180°C/gas 4. •
Lightly oil a baking sheet. • Cook the carrots
in a large pan of salted, boiling water for 5
minutes. Drain well. • Sauté the carrots, zucchini,
leek, onion, celery, salt, pepper, and oregano in
the oil in a large frying pan for 10 minutes. • Unroll
the sheets of pastry on a lightly floured surface.
Use a sharp knife to cut into 16 rectangles
measuring about 3 x 4 inches (8 x 10 cm). • Divide
the vegetable filling and cheese among eight of the
rectangles, placing them in the center of each
piece. Brush the edges of the pastry with the egg
and cover with another rectangle of pastry,
pressing down on the edges to seal well. Use the
knife to make cuts in the tops of the pastries so
that steam can escape during cooking. • Place the
parcels on the prepared baking sheet. • Bake for
15–20 minutes, or until golden brown. • Serve hot
or at room temperature.

Serves: 6–8

Preparation: 30'

Cooking: 30–35'

Level of difficulty: 1

- 8 oz/250 g carrots, cut in small cubes
- 10 oz/300 g zucchini/courgettes, cut in very thin slices
- white of 1 large leek, thinly sliced
- 1 medium onion, finely chopped
- 1 stalk celery, finely chopped
- salt and freshly ground black pepper to taste
- 1 tsp dried oregano
- 2 tbsp extra-virgin olive oil
- 14 oz/400 g frozen puff pastry, thawed
- 4 oz/125 g Emmental or Cheddar cheese, cut in very small cubes
- 1 egg, beaten

RICE AND ZUCCHINI TARTLETS

Serves: 6
Preparation: 35'
Cooking: 40–45'
Level of difficulty: 1

Preheat the oven to 350°F/180°C/gas 4. • Oil a six-hole muffin pan. • Dough: Sift the flour and salt into a large bowl. Mix in the milk, water, and oil. • Shape into a ball. • Filling: Bring the milk and salt to a boil in a medium saucepan. • Add the rice and cook until tender. • Remove from the heat. • Sauté the shallot in the oil in a large frying pan until softened. • Add the zucchini and cook for 5 minutes. Season with salt. • Blanch the zucchini flowers in a large pot of salted, boiling water for 5 seconds. Drain. • Stir the zucchini mixture into the rice. • Add the eggs, Parmesan, marjoram, and nutmeg. Season with pepper. • Roll the dough out thinly. Cut out rounds to line the pans. Fill with the rice mixture and top with a zucchini flower in the center. Dot with butter. • Bake for 15–20 minutes, or until golden. • Serve warm.

DOUGH

- 1⅓ cups/200 g all-purpose/plain flour
- ⅛ tsp salt
- 6 tbsp milk
- 3 tbsp water
- 3 tbsp extra-virgin olive oil

FILLING

- 1 quart/1 liter milk
- ¼ tsp salt
- ¾ cup/150 g rice
- 1 shallot, chopped
- 2 tbsp olive oil
- 4 zucchini/courgettes, cut into small rounds
- salt and freshly ground black pepper to taste
- 6 zucchini flowers, carefully washed
- 2 eggs, lightly beaten
- ⅔ cup/80 g freshly grated Parmesan cheese
- ½ tsp dried marjoram
- ¼ tsp freshly ground nutmeg
- 1 tbsp butter, cut up

Serves: 6

Preparation: 25' + 30' to chill

Cooking: 12–15'

Level of difficulty: 1

- 1 quantity Short Crust Pastry (see page 958)
- 2 hard-boiled eggs, peeled and chopped
- 2 tbsp finely chopped parsley and marjoram
- 2 tbsp finely chopped marjoram
- 1 cup/250 ml mayonnaise

BOATS WITH HERB MAYONNAISE

Prepare the pastry and chill for 30 minutes. • Preheat the oven to 350°F/180°C/gas 4. • Oil about 12 small boat- (or other-) pastry molds. • Roll the pastry out and use it to line the molds. Prick well with a fork. • Bake for 12–15 minutes, or until golden brown. Turn out carefully onto a rack and let cool completely. • Place the eggs in a bowl and mix with the parsley, marjoram, and mayonnaise. • Fill the shells with the sauce. • Serve immediately before the shells have time to become soggy.

ZUCCHINI FLOWER FLATBREAD

Beat the garbanzo bean flour, water, and salt in a large bowl to make a thick batter. • Add the zucchini flowers and chives and mix well. • Lightly oil an 8-inch (20-cm) frying pan and warm over medium heat. • Pour the batter into the pan and cook for 5–7 minutes, or until golden brown. Turn carefully and cook the other side for 5 minutes, or until golden brown all over. • Serve hot.

*Vegan

Serves: 4

Preparation: 15'

Cooking: 15–20'

Level of difficulty: 1

- 1 cup/150 g garbanzo bean/ chick pea flour
- about 4 tbsp water
- 1/4 tsp salt
- 20 zucchini/ courgette flowers, cleaned and coarsely chopped
- 1 small bunch chives, finely chopped

CRISP MINI RÖSTI

P eel the potatoes and cut into very thin strips. •
Place the potatoes on a clean cloth and gently
squeeze out as much moisture as possible. The
more moisture you remove, the crispier the
finished rösti will be. • Heat $^1/_2$ tablespoon of oil in
a medium frying pan and add a quarter of the
potato to the pan. Press down on the potato with a
metal spatula so that the bottom turns crisp and
golden brown. Flip the rösti and cook the other
side. • Season the cooked rösti with salt and
pepper and serve hot.

Serves: 4–6
Preparation: 15'
Cooking: 20'
Level of difficulty: 1

- **4 large potatoes**
- **2–3 tbsp extra-
  virgin olive oil**
- **salt and freshly
  ground black
  pepper to taste**

MARINATED ZUCCHINI

Serves: 2–4

Preparation: 20'+
24 h to marinate

Cooking: 25'

Level of difficulty: 1

- 8 zucchini/
  courgettes
- 4 tbsp extra-virgin
  olive oil
- 1 cup/250 ml white
  wine vinegar
- 1 small red chile
  pepper
- salt and freshly
  ground black
  pepper to taste

Rinse the zucchini thoroughly under cold running water and dry well. Cut the ends off and slice into rounds. • Heat the oil in a large deep frying pan until very hot. • Fry the zucchini in batches for 6–8 minutes, or until golden brown all over. • Drain well on paper towels. • Transfer the zucchini to a deep serving dish. • Bring the vinegar and chile to a boil in a small saucepan. Pour over the zucchini. • Season with the salt and pepper. Cover and let marinate for 24 hours. • Serve at room temperature.

SWEET AND SOUR ONIONS

Place the onions in a saucepan with the raisins, oil, wine, vinegar, and sugar. • Season with salt and pepper. Add the bay leaf and pour in the water. Mix well and cook over medium heat until almost all the liquid has been absorbed and the onions are glazed. • Melt the butter over the onions and serve hot.

Serves: 6

Preparation: 15'

Cooking: 20'

Level of difficulty: 1

- 1 lb/500 g pearl onions, peeled
- ⅓ cup/60 g golden raisins/ sultanas, soaked in warm water and drained
- 4 tbsp extra-virgin olive oil
- 3 tbsp dry white wine
- 2 tbsp white wine vinegar
- 1 tbsp sugar
- salt and freshly ground black pepper to taste
- 1 bay leaf
- ½ cup/125 ml water
- 1 tbsp butter

GLAZED CHESTNUTS

Serves: 6–8

Preparation: 40'

Cooking: 50'

Level of difficulty: 3

- **2 lb/1 kg fresh chestnuts**
- **4 tbsp sugar**
- **²⁄₃ cup/150 ml vegetable stock + more if needed (see page 945)**
- **⅛ tsp salt**
- **3 tbsp butter**

Preheat the oven to 400°F/200°C/gas 6. • Make an incision in each chestnut. Place them on a baking sheet and bake for 15 minutes, or until the shells open slightly. • Remove from the oven and shell. Remove the skins. This should be easy but if the skins will not come away, blanch in boiling water for a few seconds. • Caramelize the sugar in a large saucepan over medium heat. Add the chestnuts and mix. Add the stock and salt. Cover and simmer over low heat for 30 minutes, adding more stock during the cooking time if needed. • When the chestnuts are tender and have absorbed all the stock, add the butter, and mix gently. • Serve hot.

QUICHES & SAVORY PIES

CRUSTY EGGPLANT AND TOMATO QUICHE

Prepare the pastry and set aside to chill. •
Place the eggplant in a colander and sprinkle
with salt. Let drain for 30 minutes. • Rinse the
eggplant under cold running water and gently
squeeze out any excess moisture. Lay the slices
out on a clean cloth to dry. • Heat the oil in a large
frying pan until very hot. Fry the eggplant in small
batches for 5–7 minutes, or tender. Drain well on
paper towels. • Preheat the oven to 400°F/
200°C/gas 6. • Cook the potatoes in lightly
salted water for 12–15 minutes, or until tender.
• Sprinkle the tomatoes with salt and place cut-
side down in a colander to drain the liquid. • Roll
the dough out on a floured surface to fit a 10-inch
(25-cm) pie dish, covering the edges. • Arrange
the vegetables on the pastry and sprinkle with the
bread crumbs. • Beat the eggs in a medium bowl
and season with salt. Pour over the vegetables.
• Bake for 20–25 minutes, or until the dough has
risen and is lightly browned. • Serve hot or at
room temperature.

Serves: 4–6

*Preparation: 45' +
time to make pastry
and degorge
eggplant*

Cooking: 40–50'

Level of difficulty: 3

- **1 quantity Short Crust Pastry (see page 958)**

- **1 large eggplant/ aubergine, thinly sliced**
- **1 tbsp coarse salt**
- **2 cups/500 ml olive oil, for frying**
- **2 potatoes, peeled and thinly sliced**
- **8 cherry tomatoes, halved**
- **3 eggs**
- **salt to taste**
- **4 tbsp fine dry bread crumbs**

ASPARAGUS IN A CRUST

Preheat the oven to 400°F/200°C/gas 6. •
Butter a baking sheet. • Trim the tough bottom
parts off the asparagus. Cook in salted, boiling
water for 5–10 minutes, or until crunchy-tender.
Drain and chop coarsely. • Sauté the asparagus in
the butter in a large frying pan over medium heat
for 5 minutes. Season with salt and pepper. •
Unfold or unroll the pastry into a rectangle (reserve
a little to decorate). • Place the asparagus in the
center with the cheese and parsley. • Brush the
edges of the pastry with the egg yolk. Fold the
pastry over the filling, pressing the edges to seal.
• Place on the baking sheet seam-side down.
Brush with the remaining egg yolk and decorate
with the reserved pastry. • Bake for 25–30
minutes, or until golden. • Serve warm.

Serves: 4

Preparation: 40'

Cooking: 35–45'

Level of difficulty: 2

- **14 oz/400 g asparagus stalks**
- **1 tbsp butter**
- **salt and freshly ground black pepper to taste**
- **12 oz/350 g frozen phyllo pastry, thawed**
- **4 oz/125 g Taleggio or Cheddar cheese, diced**
- **2 tbsp finely chopped parsley**
- **1 egg yolk, lightly beaten**

FETA AND SPINACH PIE

Serves: 4

Preparation: 35'

Cooking: 50'

Level of difficulty: 2

- **4 scallions/spring onions, thinly sliced**
- **3 tbsp extra-virgin olive oil**
- **2 lb/1 kg spinach, blanched and chopped**
- **salt and freshly ground black pepper to taste**
- **8 oz/250 g Feta cheese, diced**
- **2 oz/60 g dill, finely chopped**
- **2 eggs, lightly beaten**
- **5 sheets frozen phyllo pastry, thawed**
- **4 tbsp butter, melted**
- **1 tbsp milk**

Preheat the oven to 400°F/200°C/gas 6. • Butter an 8-inch (20-cm) square pan. • Sauté the scallions in the oil in a large frying pan. • Add the spinach and sauté for 5 minutes. • Place in a large bowl and add the Feta, dill, and eggs. Season with salt and pepper. • Unfold or unroll one sheet of pastry and place in the pan. Mix the butter and milk in a small bowl and brush over the pastry. Place another sheet of pastry on top and brush with butter and milk. Spoon the filling into the pan.
• Top with the remaining three sheets of pastry, brushing each layer with butter and milk. • Cut the top of the pie with a knife. Brush with melted butter.
• Bake for 40 minutes, or until golden. Serve warm.

GOAT'S CHEESE AND VEGETABLE PUFF

Preheat the oven to 375°F/190°C/gas 5. •
Oil a 10-inch (25-cm) springform pan. • Grill the
eggplants in a grill pan until tender. • Broil (grill) the
bell peppers whole in the oven until the skins are
blackened all over. Wrap in paper for 10 minutes,
then remove the skins. Slice into long strips. Rinse

Use a barbecue or grill pan to create the charcoal
line effect on the eggplant and bell peppers.

carefully and dry
well. • Place the
goat's cheese in a large bowl with the egg, egg
yolks, garlic, and salt and pepper. Mix well with a
wooden spoon. • Roll the dough out on a lightly
floured work surface to fit the bottom and sides of
the pan. Make sure the edges are 1 inch (2.5 cm)
high. Prick all over with a fork. • Spoon the goat's
cheese filling into the pastry. • Arrange the
tomatoes, bell peppers, and eggplant on top.
Sprinkle with basil, if liked, and season with salt
and pepper. • Bake for 30–35 minutes, or until
the pastry is golden brown. • Serve hot or at
room temperature.

Serves: 6

Preparation: 45'

Cooking: 1 h

Level of difficulty: 2

- 8 oz/250 g
  eggplants/
  aubergines, thinly
  sliced
- 2 red bell peppers/
  capsicums,
  seeded, cored, and
  halved
- 1¼ cups/310 g
  fresh creamy
  goat's cheese
- 1 egg and 2 egg
  yolks
- 1 clove garlic,
  finely chopped
- salt and freshly
  ground black
  pepper to taste
- 8 oz/250 g puff
  pastry
- 10 cherry
  tomatoes, sliced
- 6 leaves fresh basil,
  torn (optional)

RICOTTA QUICHE WITH RAISINS AND PINE NUTS

Serves: 4–6

*Preparation: 45' + 30'
  to chill*

Cooking: 35–40'

Level of difficulty: 2

PASTRY
- 1⅔ cups/250 g all-purpose/plain flour
- ⅛ tsp salt
- 6 tbsp Ricotta fresh cheese
- 6 tbsp butter, softened
- 1 egg, beaten
- 3 tbsp white wine

FILLING
- 2 lb/1 kg scallions/spring onions
- ⅓ cup/60 g golden raisins/sultanas, soaked and drained
- ¼ cup/45 g pine nuts
- 8 tbsp cream
- 4 eggs
- salt and freshly ground black pepper to taste
- ⅛ tsp freshly grated nutmeg
- ⅔ cup/80 g freshly grated Parmesan cheese

Pastry: Sift the flour and salt into a medium bowl. Mix in the Ricotta, butter, and egg. Add the wine and knead briefly to make a smooth elastic dough. • Shape into a ball, wrap in plastic wrap (cling film), and refrigerate for 30 minutes. • Preheat the oven to 350°F/180°C/gas 4. • Butter and flour a 9-inch (23-cm) pie dish. • Filling: Blanch the scallions in salted, boiling water for 4 minutes. Drain and slice thinly. • Mix with the raisins and pine nuts in a large bowl. • Roll the pastry out on a lightly floured surface to fit the pan. Line the bottom and sides of the pan, trimming the edges to fit. Prick all over with a fork. • Spread the scallion mixture over the base. • Beat the cream and eggs in a large bowl until frothy. Season with salt and pepper. Mix in the nutmeg and Parmesan. Pour over the scallions and fold the edges of pastry in neatly. • Bake for 30–35 minutes, or until the pastry is golden brown. • Serve hot or at room temperature.

CHERRY TOMATO AND EGGPLANT SAVORY PIE

Pastry: Sift the flour and salt into a medium bowl. • Mix in the butter, egg, and half the Parmesan to make a smooth dough. Shape into a ball, wrap in waxed paper, and refrigerate for 30 minutes. • Preheat the oven to 400°F/200°C/gas 6. • Butter a 9-inch (23-cm) pie pan. • Roll the pastry out on a lightly floured surface to $^1/_4$ inch (5 mm) thick. Line the prepared pan with the dough, trimming the edges to fit. Prick all over with a fork. Refrigerate for 15 minutes. • Cook the eggplants in a grill pan for 10–15 minutes, or until tender. • Arrange the eggplant slices in the pastry base. Fill the gaps with the cherry tomatoes and olives. • Beat the eggs, cream, remaining Parmesan, basil, and mint in a large bowl. Season with salt and pepper. • Pour the mixture over the eggplants and tomatoes. • Bake for 20–30 minutes, or until the pastry is golden brown. • Serve hot or at room temperature.

Serves: 4

Preparation: 45' + 45' to chill

Cooking: 35–40'

Level of difficulty: 2

PASTRY
- 1 $^1/_3$ cups/200 g all-purpose/plain flour
- $^1/_3$ tsp salt
- 6 tbsp butter
- 1 egg, beaten
- $^3/_4$ cup/45 g freshly grated Parmesan cheese

FILLING
- 1 lb/500 g eggplants/ aubergines, sliced lengthwise in 4
- 5 oz/150 g cherry tomatoes
- 2 oz/50 g pitted black olives
- 3 eggs
- $^3/_4$ cup/180 ml cream
- 1 tbsp torn basil
- 1 tbsp torn mint
- salt and freshly ground black pepper to taste

Serves: 4

Preparation: 35' +
   time to make pastry

Cooking: 1 h 30'

Level of difficulty: 2

- 1 quantity Short-
  Crust Pastry
  (see page 958)
- 2 cloves garlic,
  lightly crushed but
  whole
- 3 tbsp extra-virgin
  olive oil
- 10 oz/300 g baby
  carrots
- 1 zucchini/
  courgette, thinly
  sliced
- white of 1 leek,
  thinly sliced
- 1 red bell pepper/
  capsicum, seeded,
  cored, and
  chopped
- 1 yellow bell
  pepper/capsicum,
  seeded, cored, and
  chopped
- salt to taste
- 4 tbsp vegetable
  stock
- 3 eggs
- 3/4 cup/180 ml
  cream
- 2 leaves fresh
  marjoram, finely
  chopped
- 1 fresh chile
  pepper, finely
  chopped

SPICY MIXED VEGETABLE BAKE

Prepare the pastry and chill in the refrigerator.
• Preheat the oven to 350°F/180°C/gas 4.
• Butter a 9-inch (23-cm) pie pan. • Roll the
pastry out on a lightly floured surface to 1/4 inch
(5 mm) thick. Line the pan with the dough,
trimming the edges to fit. Prick all over with a
fork. • Bake for 30
minutes, or until
lightly golden. • Sauté the garlic in the oil in a
large frying pan over medium heat until pale gold.
• Discard the garlic. Add the vegetables and
sauté over high heat for 3 minutes. • Season with
salt and cook for 15–20 minutes, adding the
stock. • Arrange the vegetables in the pastry
case. • Beat the cream and eggs until frothy.
Season with salt and add the marjoram and chile
pepper. • Bake for 25–35 minutes, or until
golden. • Serve hot or at room temperature.

Make sure not to touch your eyes after cutting the chile peppers.

RICH VEGETABLE QUICHE

Serves: 4

Preparation: 45' + 2 h 30' to chill

Cooking: 55'

Level of difficulty: 2

Pastry: Sift the flour and salt into a large bowl. Mix in half the Parmesan, butter, paprika, sugar, and egg yolks. Shape into a ball, wrap in plastic wrap (cling film), and refrigerate for 2 hours. • Sauté the vegetables in the oil in a large frying pan over medium heat for 5 minutes. Season with salt and pepper and add the oregano. • Oil a 9-inch (24-cm) pie pan. • Roll the pastry out on a lightly floured surface to 1/4 inch (5 mm) thick. Line the prepared pan with the dough, trimming the edges to fit. Prick all over with a fork. Refrigerate for 30 minutes. • Preheat the oven to 350°F/180°C/gas 4. • Beat the cream and eggs until frothy in a large bowl. Stir in the Ricotta and vegetables. • Pour the mixture into the chilled pastry base, smoothing the surface. Sprinkle with the remaining Parmesan. • Bake for 50 minutes, or until golden.

PASTRY
- 1 1/3 cups/200 g all-purpose/plain flour
- 1/4 tsp salt
- 3/4 cup/90 g freshly grated Parmesan cheese
- 6 tbsp butter, cut up
- 1/4 tsp paprika
- 1/2 tsp sugar
- 2 egg yolks

FILLING
- 1 onion, sliced
- 1 red bell pepper/capsicum, seeded, cored, and diced
- 1 zucchini/courgette, diced
- 1 eggplant/aubergine, diced
- 1 tomato, diced
- 2 tbsp extra-virgin olive oil
- salt and freshly ground black pepper to taste
- 1 tbsp finely chopped oregano or 1 tsp dried oregano
- 1/2 cup/125 ml heavy/double cream
- 1 egg
- 6 tbsp Ricotta cheese

VEGETABLE AND RICOTTA PIE

Serves: 4–6

Preparation: 30'

Cooking: 1 h

Level of difficulty: 1

- ½ onion
- 3 tbsp extra-virgin olive oil
- ½ yellow bell pepper, seeded, cored, and chopped
- ½ red bell pepper, seeded, cored, and chopped
- 1 small zucchini/ courgette, cut into sticks
- 4 oz/125 g eggplants/ aubergines, diced
- 10 cherry tomatoes, diced
- salt to taste
- 4 tbsp vegetable stock
- 8 oz/250 g frozen puff pastry, thawed
- ⅔ cup/150 g Ricotta cheese
- 4 tbsp freshly grated Parmesan cheese
- 1 egg yolk

Preheat the oven to 375°F/190°C/gas 5. • Oil a 10-inch (28-cm) pie pan. • Sauté the onion in the oil in a large frying pan over medium heat until softened. • Add the bell peppers, zucchini, and eggplants and sauté over low heat for 5 minutes. • Add the tomatoes and season with salt. Cover and cook over very low heat for 15 minutes, stirring occasionally, adding the stock if the mixture dries out. • Roll the pastry out to ⅛-inch (3-mm) thick. Line the prepared pan with the pastry. Prick all over with a fork. Cover with pie weights or dried beans. Bake for 15–18 minutes, or until lightly browned. • Discard the paper and beans. • Mix the vegetables, Ricotta, Parmesan, and egg yolk in a large bowl. • Fill the pastry case with the vegetable mixture. • Bake for 20–25 minutes, or until the filling has set. • Serve hot or at room temperature.

SAVORY PIE WITH RUSSIAN SALAD

Prepare the pastry and chill in the refrigerator.
• Preheat the oven to 350°F/180°C/gas 4.
• Butter a 9-inch (23-cm) pie pan. • Roll out the pastry on a lightly floured surface to ¹/₄ inch (5 mm) thick. Line the prepared pan with the dough, trimming the edges to fit. Prick all over with a fork. • Fill with pie weights or dried beans and bake for 20 minutes, or until lightly browned. • Cook the vegetables in salted boiling water until tender-crunchy. • Drain and let cool slightly. Dice the potatoes and carrots and coarsely chop the beans into short lengths (Reserve a few vegetables to garnish). • Mix the mayonnaise and vegetables in a large bowl. Spread over the pastry base. • Garnish with the reserved carrots and beans.

Serve this unusual pie as a centerpiece at a buffet-style party.

Serves: 6

Preparation: 30' + time to make pastry

Cooking: 30'

Level of difficulty: 2

- **1 quantity Short-Crust Pastry With Egg (see page 958)**
- **2–3 potatoes**
- **6 oz/180 g baby carrots**
- **6 oz/180 g green beans**
- **6 oz/180 g peas**
- **2 cups/500 ml mayonnaise**

ARTICHOKE AND FAVA BEAN QUICHE

Serves: 4–6

Preparation: 30'

Cooking: 45–55'

Level of difficulty: 2

- 1 quantity Short-Crust Pastry With Egg (see page 958)
- 1 scallion/spring onion, thinly sliced
- 4 tbsp extra-virgin olive oil
- 5 oz/150 g frozen fava/broad beans, thawed
- 6 oz/180 g frozen artichokes, thawed
- salt and freshly ground black pepper to taste
- 3 tbsp dry white wine
- 7 tbsp Ricotta cheese
- 3 eggs
- 1 tbsp finely chopped thyme

Prepare the pastry and chill in the refrigerator. • Preheat the oven to 350°F/180°C/gas 4. • Oil a 10-inch (25-cm) pie pan. • Sauté the scallion in the oil in a large frying pan over low heat for 5 minutes. • Add the fava beans and artichokes. Season with salt and pepper and sauté for 5 minutes. • Add the wine and cook for 10 minutes. • Beat the Ricotta, eggs, thyme, and salt and pepper in a large bowl. • Roll the pastry out on a lightly floured surface to 1/4 inch (5 mm) thick. Line the pie pan with the dough, trimming the edges to fit. Prick all over with a fork. • Arrange the vegetables in the pastry case and pour in the Ricotta mixture. • Bake for 25–35 minutes, or until golden brown. • Serve hot or at room temperature.

ZUCCHINI SAVORY PIE

Serves: 4–6

Preparation: 25' +
time to make pastry

Cooking: 45–50'

Level of difficulty: 2

Prepare the pastry and chill in the refrigerator.
• Preheat the oven to 350°F/180°C/gas 4.
• Oil a 10-inch (25-cm) pie pan. • Soak the
mushrooms in a little warm water for 15 minutes.
Drain and chop coarsely. • Sauté the zucchini and
mushrooms in the oil in a large frying pan over
medium heat for 10 minutes. Season with salt and
pepper and let cool. • Beat the eggs, Pecorino,
Parmesan, marjoram, zucchini, and mushrooms in
a large bowl. • Roll the pastry out to fit the pan.
Line with the dough, trimming the edges to fit.
Prick all over with a fork. • Spread the topping
over the base and sprinkle with the bread crumbs.
• Bake for 35–40 minutes, or until golden and set.
• Serve hot or at room temperature.

- **1 quantity Short-Crust Pastry (see page 958)**
- **1 oz/30 g dried mushrooms**
- **3 tbsp extra-virgin olive oil**
- **6 medium zucchini/courgettes, sliced**
- **salt and freshly ground black pepper to taste**
- **3½ oz/100 g Pecorino Romano cheese, flaked**
- **3 tbsp freshly grated Parmesan cheese**
- **2 eggs**
- **1 tbsp marjoram**
- **1 tbsp fine dry bread crumbs**

Serves: 4–6

Preparation: 25'

Cooking: 35–40'

Level of difficulty: 2

- 5 eggs
- 1 cup/250 g Ricotta cheese
- 5 oz/150 g Mozzarella cheese, diced
- 2½ oz/75 g Parmesan cheese, diced
- 5 tbsp milk
- ⅛ tsp freshly grated nutmeg
- salt to taste
- 1 lb/500 g frozen puff pastry, thawed

THREE CHEESE PUFF

Preheat the oven to 400°F/200°C/gas 6. • Butter and flour a 10-inch (26-cm) baking dish. • Beat the eggs, Ricotta, Mozzarella, Parmesan, 4 tablespoons of milk, nutmeg, and salt in a large bowl. • Divide the pastry in two; one piece twice as large as the other. Roll the large piece out thinly and line the pan. Prick all over with a fork. • Pour in the cheese filling. Roll out the remaining pastry and cut to fit the pan. Cover the pan, folding back the edges. Brush with the remaining milk. • Bake for 35–40 minutes, or until golden. • Serve hot or at room temperature.

TOMATO QUICHE WITH YOGURT

Pastry: Sift the flour into a bowl. Mix in the egg yolk, salt, pepper, and oil to form a smooth elastic dough. Shape into a ball, wrap in plastic wrap (cling film), and set aside for 1 hour. • Preheat the oven to 375°F/190°C/gas 5. • Oil a 9-inch (24-cm) springform pan. • Filling: Blanch the tomatoes in salted, boiling water for 30 seconds. Drain and peel. Remove the seeds and slice thinly. • Roll out the pastry on a lightly floured surface to $1/4$ inch (5 mm) thick. Line the prepared pan with the dough, trimming the edges to fit. Prick all over with a fork. Sprinkle with half the Emmental and cover with the tomatoes. • Beat the eggs with the milk, remaining Emmental, salt, and pepper. Pour the mixture over the pastry. • Bake for 30–40 minutes, or until set and golden brown. • Mix the yogurt, basil, and mint in a small bowl. Serve the quiche hot or warm with the yogurt sauce.

Serves: 4

Preparation: 30' + 1 h to rest

Cooking: 35–40'

Level of difficulty: 2

PASTRY
- 1²/₃ cups/250 g all-purpose/plain flour
- 1 egg yolk
- ⅛ tsp salt
- ⅛ tsp ground black pepper
- 2 tbsp extra-virgin olive oil

FILLING
- 1¾ lb/800 g firm-ripe tomatoes
- ¾ cup/90 g freshly grated Emmental (Swiss) cheese
- 3 eggs
- 4 tbsp milk
- salt and freshly ground black pepper to taste

TO SERVE
- 1 cup/250 ml plain yogurt
- 1 tbsp finely chopped basil
- 1 tbsp finely chopped mint

ITALIAN SAVORY PIE WITH ARTICHOKES

Serves: 4

Preparation: 30' +
time to make pastry

Cooking: 55'

Level of difficulty: 2

- **1 quantity Short
  Crust Pastry
  (see page 958)**

FILLING
- **2 tbsp fine dry
  bread crumbs**
- **4 artichokes**
- **2 tbsp finely
  chopped parsley**
- **1 clove garlic,
  finely chopped**
- **salt and freshly
  ground black
  pepper to taste**
- **4 tbsp freshly
  grated Parmesan
  cheese**
- **2 tbsp butter,
  melted**
- **2 tbsp extra-virgin
  olive oil**

Prepare the pastry and chill in the refrigerator.
• Preheat the oven to 375°F/190°C/gas 5.
• Oil an 8-inch (20-cm) pie pan and sprinkle with bread crumbs. • Divide the dough in two (one portion slightly larger than the other) and roll both pieces out on a lightly floured work surface to fit the pie pan. Use the larger piece to line the bottom and sides of the pan, leaving the edges overhanging the sides. Prick all over with a fork.
• Filling: Trim the stalks and cut the top third off the top of the artichokes. Remove the tough outer leaves by bending them down and snapping them off. Cut in half and use a knife to remove any fuzzy choke. Cut into thin wedges. • Steam the artichokes for about 15 minutes, or until tender.
• Place the artichokes in a bowl with the parsley, garlic, salt, and Parmesan. Drizzle with the butter and oil. • Spoon the artichoke mixture onto the pastry base. • Cover with the remaining pastry. Seal the pie by folding the overhanging edges in. Prick the surface with a fork. • Bake for 35–45 minutes, or until the pastry is golden. • Serve hot or at room temperature.

LEEK AND ALMOND QUICHE

Serves: 4–6

Preparation: 25' + time to make pastry

Cooking: 35–45'

Level of difficulty: 2

Prepare the pastry and chill in the refrigerator.
• Preheat the oven to 400°F/200°C/gas 6.
• Oil a 9-inch (24-cm) pie dish. • Beat the eggs, cream, milk, and salt in a medium bowl. • Roll the dough out very thinly on a lightly floured surface. Divide the dough in three. • Place one-third of the dough in the prepared dish, letting it overlap the sides. • Sprinkle with half the almonds and half the Parmesan. Cover with the second sheet of dough and sprinkle with the remaining almonds and cheese. Cover with the remaining sheet of dough. Top with the leeks and pour the egg mixture over the top. • Bake for 35–45 minutes, or until golden.
• Serve hot or at room temperature.

• 1 quantity Short Crust Pastry With Egg (see page 958)

FILLING
• whites of 3 leeks, thinly sliced
• 2 tbsp butter
• 2 tbsp water
• salt to taste
• 3 eggs
• 1/2 cup/125 ml tbsp cream
• 1/2 cup/125 ml milk
• 2/3 cup/60 g chopped almonds
• 2/3 cup/80 g freshly grated Parmesan cheese

JERUSALEM ARTICHOKE PIE

Serves: 6

Preparation: 30'

Cooking: 40–45'

Level of difficulty: 2

PASTRY

- 1½ cups/225 g all-purpose/plain flour
- ⅔ cup/100 g finely ground almonds
- ⅛ tsp salt
- ⅔ cup/150 g butter
- ½ cup/60 g freshly grated Parmesan cheese
- 3 tbsp water

FILLING

- 1½ lb/650 g Jerusalem artichokes, peeled and thinly sliced
- 1 clove garlic, finely chopped
- 2 tbsp extra-virgin olive oil
- salt and freshly ground black pepper to taste
- 2 eggs
- 5 tbsp cream
- ¾ cup/90 g freshly grated Pecorino cheese
- 1 tbsp sesame seeds

Pastry: Sift the flour and salt into a medium bowl. Add the almonds and cut in the butter. Add the Parmesan, and enough water to make a smooth dough. Shape into a ball and refrigerate for 30 minutes. • Preheat the oven to 350°F/180°C/gas 4. • Oil a 10-inch (26-cm) pie dish. • Roll the pastry out on a floured surface to fit the pan. • Place in the pan and bake for 10 minutes, or until golden. • Increase the oven temperature to 400°F/200°C/gas 6. • Filling: Sauté the Jerusalem artichokes and garlic in the oil in a large frying pan until tender. Season with salt and pepper. • Beat the eggs, cream, and Pecorino in a bowl. Season with salt and pepper. • Fill the pastry with the artichokes and egg mixture. Sprinkle with the sesame seeds. • Bake for 25–30 minutes, or until golden. • Serve hot.

VEGETARIAN STRUDEL

Serves: 4–6

Preparation: 35' + time to make pastry

Cooking: 40–45'

Level of difficulty: 2

- **1 quantity Short-Crust Pastry With Egg (see page 985)**

FILLING

- **1 clove garlic, chopped**
- **⅓ cup/60 g pine nuts**
- **4 tbsp extra-virgin olive oil**
- **1 lb/500 g zucchini/courgettes, grated**
- **salt to taste**
- **2 cups/500 g fresh Ricotta cheese**
- **⅔ cup/80 g freshly grated Parmesan cheese**
- **1 egg + 1 egg yolk**
- **6–8 leaves basil, torn**
- **1 quantity Pesto (see page 946)**

Prepare the pastry and chill in the refrigerator.
• Preheat the oven to 350°F/180°C/gas 4.
• Line a baking sheet with waxed paper. • Sauté the garlic and pine nuts in 3 tablespoons of oil in a large frying pan until pale gold. • Add the zucchini and sauté for 5 minutes, or until they have released all their liquid. Season with salt. • Mix the Ricotta, Parmesan, egg and egg yolk, basil, and salt in a large bowl. • Roll the pastry out very thinly on a lightly floured work surface into a large rectangle. • Spread with the Ricotta mixture, leaving a border of about ¾ inch (2 cm) around the edges. • Arrange the zucchini on top. Fold in the edges down the long side, then roll the pastry up from the short sides over the filling. • Transfer to the prepared baking sheet and shape it into a ring. • Brush with the remaining oil and bake for 30–35 minutes, or until golden. • Serve hot or at room temperature with the pesto on the side.

ARTICHOKE QUICHE

Serves: 4–6

*Preparation: 30' +
time to make pastry*

Cooking: 1 h

Level of difficulty: 2

- **1 quantity Short-Crust Pastry
  With Egg
  (see page 985)**

FILLING

- **6 artichokes**
- **1 shallot, finely chopped**
- **4 tbsp water**
- **2 tbsp extra-virgin olive oil**
- **salt and freshly ground black pepper to taste**
- **1 cup/250 g Ricotta cheese**
- **2 eggs**
- **1 tbsp finely chopped parsley**
- **$\frac{1}{8}$ tsp freshly grated nutmeg**
- **$3\frac{1}{2}$ oz/100 g Fontina cheese, diced**

Prepare the pastry and chill in the refrigerator.
• Preheat the oven to 400°F/200°C/gas 6.
• Butter and flour a 10-inch (25-cm) pie pan.
• Roll the pastry out on a lightly floured surface until very thin. Line the prepared pan with the dough, trimming the edges to fit. Prick all over with a fork. • Cover with waxed paper and fill with pie weights or dried beans. • Bake for 10 minutes, or until lightly browned. • Discard the paper and beans. • Filling: Trim the stalks and cut the top third off the top of the artichokes. Remove the tough outer leaves by bending them down and snapping them off. Cut in half and use a knife to remove any fuzzy choke. Cut into thin slices. • Stew the artichokes in a large saucepan with the shallot, water, oil, and salt for 10–15 minutes, or until the artichokes are tender. • Mix the Ricotta, eggs, parsley, nutmeg, and salt and pepper in a large bowl. • Fill the pastry case with the Fontina, the artichoke mixture, and the Ricotta mixture. • Bake for 25–35 minutes, or until golden. • Serve hot or at room temperature.

MINI QUICHES WITH BELL PEPPER SAUCE

Prepare the pastry and chill in the refrigerator.
• Preheat the oven to 400°F/200°C/gas 6.
• Oil four 4–5-inch (10–13-cm) tartlet pans. • Roll
the pastry out on a lightly floured surface. Cut out
four circles large enough to line the tartlet pans.
Prick all over with a fork and sprinkle with mustard
powder. • Sauté the scallions in the butter in a
large frying pan over low heat for 5 minutes.
Season with salt. • Cover and cook for 10 minutes.
• Remove the cover and cook until any cooking
liquids have evaporated. • Beat the eggs, Ricotta,
Parmesan, salt, and pepper in a large bowl. Add
the scallions and mix well. • Divide the mixture
evenly among the pastry cases. Sprinkle the top
with the parsley, mint, and paprika. • Bake for
20 minutes, or until golden and set. • Sauce:
Process the bell peppers with the cream in a food
processor or blender until smooth. Season with
salt. • Serve the quiches with the bell
pepper sauce.

Serves: 4–6

Preparation: 40'

Cooking: 35'

Level of difficulty: 2

- 1 quantity Short-Crust Pastry With Egg (see page 985)

FILLING

- 1 tbsp mustard powder
- 14 oz/400 g scallions/spring onions, finely chopped
- 4 tbsp butter
- salt and freshly ground black pepper to taste
- 3 eggs
- 1⅓ cups/310 g Ricotta cheese
- 6 tbsp freshly grated Parmesan cheese
- 1 tbsp finely chopped parsley
- 1 tbsp finely chopped mint
- ⅛ tsp mild paprika

SAUCE

- 2 red bell peppers/capsicums, peeled, cored, and seeded
- 3 cups/750 ml light/single cream
- salt to taste

BROCCOLI AND CARROT QUICHE

Serves: 6

Preparation: 30'

Cooking: 26–31'

Level of difficulty: 2

- 1 quantity Short-Crust Pastry With Egg (see page 985)

FILLING

- 8 oz/250 g broccoli
- 6 scallions/spring onions, coarsely chopped
- 2 carrots, thinly sliced
- 3 eggs
- 4 tbsp milk
- 2 tbsp heavy/double cream
- 3 oz/90 g Emmental cheese, sliced
- 1/8 tsp freshly grated nutmeg
- salt and freshly ground black pepper to taste

Prepare the pastry and chill in the refrigerator.
• Preheat the oven to 400°F/200°C/gas 6.
• Butter and flour a 9-inch (23-cm) pie dish. • Cook all the vegetables in salted, boiling water for 4–5 minutes. Drain well. • Roll the pastry out very thinly on a lightly floured work surface. Line the prepared pan with the dough, trimming the edges to fit.
• Arrange the vegetables on top. • Beat the eggs, milk, cream, Emmental, nutmeg, salt, and pepper in a large bowl. Pour the mixture over the vegetables. • Bake for 25–30 minutes, or until golden. • Serve hot or at room temperature.

122

SPINACH STRUDEL WITH FRUIT CHUTNEY

Preheat the oven to 400°F/200°C/gas 6. •
Butter and flour a baking sheet. • Rinse the
spinach (or Swiss chard) and cook with just the
water left clinging to its leaves for 5 minutes.
Cool and chop finely, squeezing out any excess
moisture. • Sauté the spinach with the garlic in 3
tablespoons of butter in a large frying pan over
medium heat for 5 minutes. Season with salt.
• Roll the pastry out very thinly in a large rectangle
on a lightly floured work surface. • Cover with the
spinach, Emmental, and chutney. Tuck the short
ends in and carefully roll the pastry and filling into
a strudel. • Transfer to the prepared baking sheet
and make several cuts in the top. Brush with the
beaten egg. • Bake for 30–35 minutes, or until
golden. • Serve immediately.

Serves: 4–6

Preparation: 30'

Cooking: 35'

Level of difficulty: 2

- 1 lb/500 g spinach or Swiss chard
- 4 tbsp butter
- 1 clove garlic, finely chopped
- salt to taste
- 1 lb/500 g frozen puff pastry, thawed
- 5 oz/150 g Emmental cheese, thinly sliced
- 1¼ cups/310 g fruit chutney
- 1 egg, lightly beaten

VEGETABLE STRUDEL

Strudel Dough: Sift the flour and salt into a medium bowl. Mix in the oil and enough water to make a firm dough. Knead until smooth and elastic. • Filling: Boil the asparagus, zucchini, and peas in a large pot of salted boiling water for 5 minutes. Drain well. • Sauté the onion in the oil in a large frying pan over medium heat until softened. • Add the par-boiled vegetables and mushrooms and cook for 5 minutes. • Add the parsley and season with salt and pepper. Let cool. • Add 2 eggs and mix well. • Preheat the oven to 350°F/180°C/gas 4. • Roll the dough out into a large rectangle on a lightly floured surface. • Beat the remaining egg in a small bowl and brush it over the pasta. • Spread the vegetable filling on the pasta leaving a 3/4-inch (2-cm) border around the edges. Starting from one long side, roll up the dough. Seal the ends by tucking them in. • Transfer the strudel to a baking sheet and glaze with the beaten egg. Bake for 20–30 minutes, or until golden brown. • Serve hot or at room temperature.

Serves: 4–6

Preparation: 45'

Cooking: 30–35'

Level of difficulty: 2

STRUDEL DOUGH
- 2 cups/300 g all-purpose/plain flour
- 1/8 tsp salt
- 3 tbsp extra-virgin olive oil
- warm water

FILLING
- 6 asparagus stalks, thinly sliced
- 4 zucchini/courgettes, thinly sliced
- 1 cup/125 g peas
- 1 onion, finely chopped
- 1 tbsp olive oil
- 1/2 oz/15 g dried porcini mushrooms, soaked in warm water for 15 minutes and drained
- 2 tbsp finely chopped parsley
- salt and freshly ground black pepper to taste
- 3 eggs

OLD-FASHIONED SPELT OR BARLEY PIE

Serves: 6

Preparation: 35' + 30' to chill

Cooking: 1 h 15'

Level of difficulty: 2

- 1 quantity Short-Crust Pastry With Egg (see page 985)

FILLING
- 3 cups/300 g spelt or pearl barley
- 1 quart/1 liter milk
- 4 tbsp butter
- 4 tbsp freshly grated Parmesan cheese
- 3 large eggs

Prepare the pastry and chill in the refrigerator. • Cook the spelt or pearl barley in the milk in a large saucepan over medium heat for about 40 minutes, or until tender. • Drain, reserving the milk. • Mix in the butter, Parmesan, eggs, and enough of the reserved milk to make a moist filling. • Preheat the oven to 350°F/ 180°C/gas 4. • Oil a deep 9-inch (23-cm) springform pan. • Line the base and sides of the prepared pan with the dough, trimming the edges to fit. • Fill the pastry case with the spelt mixture. • Bake for 30–35 minutes, or until golden brown. • Serve hot.

TOFU BAKE WITH WHOLE-WHEAT AND CARROT PASTRY

Preheat the oven to 400°F/200°C/gas 6. • Oil an ovenproof baking dish. • Place the zucchini and carrots in a colander. Sprinkle with salt and let drain for 15 minutes. • Squeeze out the excess moisture. • Mix the zucchini, carrots, and whole-wheat flour. Mix in the oil and enough water to make a dough. • Press the mixture into the bottom of a 10-inch (25-cm) oiled pie dish. • Mix the tofu, tahini, miso, basil, thyme, and onion in a small bowl. Spoon the topping over the base. • Bake for 40–45 minutes, or until firm to the touch. • Serve hot.

Vegan

Serves: 6

Preparation: 20' + 15' to drain

Cooking: 40–45'

Level of difficulty: 1

BASE

- 2 cups/200 g grated zucchini/ courgettes
- 1 cup/100 g shredded carrot
- coarse salt
- 2/3 cup/100 g whole-wheat/ wholemeal flour
- 2 tbsp extra-virgin olive oil
- water (optional)

TOPPING

- 8 oz/250 g tofu (bean curd), cut in cubes
- 3–4 tbsp tahini (sesame seed paste)
- 3–4 tbsp miso
- 4 leaves fresh basil, torn
- 1 tbsp finely chopped thyme
- 1 tbsp finely chopped onion

Serves: 4

Preparation: 50' + 30'
to chill

Cooking: 50–55'

Level of difficulty: 2

PASTRY

- 2⅓ cups/350 g all-purpose/plain flour
- ¼ tsp salt
- 2 eggs, lightly beaten with 1 tbsp olive oil

FILLING

- 1½ lb/700 g onions, finely sliced
- 4 tbsp extra-virgin olive oil
- 7 oz/200 g Swiss cheese, such as Gruyère, cut into small cubes
- 3 eggs, beaten + 1 egg yolk, beaten
- ½ cup/60 g freshly grated Parmesan cheese
- ½ cup/50 g finely chopped pitted black olives
- salt and freshly ground black pepper to taste

SAVORY PIE WITH ONIONS

Pastry: Sift the flour and salt into a medium bowl. Stir in the egg mixture. Knead until smooth and elastic. • Wrap in plastic wrap and refrigerate for 30 minutes. • Preheat the oven to 350°F/180°C/gas 4. • Oil a 9-inch (23-cm) pie dish. • Filling: Sauté the onions in the oil in a large saucepan until softened. • Roll the pastry out to ¼ inch (5 mm) thick and cut out two circles, one slightly larger. • Use the larger pastry circle to line the pie dish. • Cover with the Swiss cheese. • Beat the eggs with the Parmesan. • Stir in the onions and olives and season with salt and pepper. • Pour the filling into the pie and cover with the remaining pastry. Brush with the egg yolk. • Bake for 30–35 minutes, or until golden. • Serve hot.

PEAR PIES WITH CHEESE AND WALNUT SAUCE

Preheat the oven to 400°F/200°C/gas 6. •
Peel, halve, and core the pears (leaving the
stalks attached). Use a teaspoon to hollow out
some of the flesh. Reserve the flesh. • Brush the
pears with the lemon juice and place them cut-side
down on a baking sheet lined with waxed paper.

Change the cheeses to any combination that you already have in your refrigerator.

• Roll out the
pastry to a
1/8-inch (3-mm) thick. Prick all over with a fork and
cut out oval shapes a little larger than the pears.
• Place the pastry ovals over the pears. Trim off
the excess pastry, leaving enough to allow for
shrinkage during cooking. • Shape the pastry
offcuts into leaves and place next to the pear
stalks. • Brush the pastry all over with the milk.
• Bake for 15–20 minutes, or until the pastry is
golden. Remove from the oven and let cool
completely. • Finely chop the reserved pear.
• Cheese and Walnut Sauce: Process the Taleggio,
Gorgonzola, half the walnuts, the reserved pear,
brandy, cream, and paprika in a food processor or
blender until puréed. • Spoon the mixture into the
hollowed pears. • Sprinkle with the remaining
walnuts and serve.

Serves: 4
Preparation: 30'
Cooking: 15–20'
Level of difficulty: 2

- 4 soft, juicy pears
- juice of 1/2 lemon
- 7 oz/200 g frozen puff pastry, thawed
- 1 egg yolk, lightly beaten with 2 tbsp milk

CHEESE AND WALNUT SAUCE
- 5 oz/150 g Taleggio (or Fontina) cheese
- 2 oz/60 g Gorgonzola cheese
- 10 walnuts, shelled and finely chopped
- 1 tbsp brandy
- 1 tbsp heavy/ double cream
- 1/2 tsp paprika

FAVA BEAN QUICHE

Prepare the pastry and chill in the refrigerator.
• Preheat the oven to 400°F/200°C/gas 6.
• Set out a 10$\frac{1}{2}$-inch (26-cm) baking dish. • Chop
a third of the fava beans. Process the remaining
fava beans in a food processor or blender with the
Ricotta, cream, Parmesan, Tabasco, and salt and
pepper until well blended. • Roll the dough out and
use it to line the pan, letting it overlap the edges.
Prick with a fork. • Spoon in half the chopped fava
beans, the filling, and top with the remaining fava
beans. • Fold in the overlapping edges. Brush with
the beaten egg. • Bake for 30–35 minutes, or until
golden. • Serve warm.

Serves: 4–6

*Preparation: 30' +
time to make pastry*

Cooking: 30–35'

Level of difficulty: 2

- • **1 quantity Short
  Crust Pastry
  (see page 958)**
- • **10 oz/300 g
  fava/broad beans,
  lightly cooked**
- • **1$\frac{1}{4}$ cups/310 g
  Ricotta cheese**
- • **$\frac{3}{4}$ cup/180 ml
  single/light cream**
- • **$\frac{3}{4}$ cup/90 g freshly
  grated Parmesan
  cheese**
- • **2 drops Tabasco
  sauce**
- • **salt and freshly
  ground black
  pepper to taste**
- • **1 egg, lightly
  beaten**

TOMATO QUICHE

Serves: 4

Preparation: 15' +
time to make pastry
+ drain tomatoes

Cooking: 35–40'

Level of difficulty: 1

- 1 quantity Short Crust Pastry (see page 958)
- 4 large tomatoes, peeled, seeded, and cut into small cubes
- 4 large eggs
- ⅔ cup/150 ml milk
- salt and freshly ground black pepper to taste
- ⅔ cup/150 g heavy/double cream
- 5 oz/150 g freshly grated Gruyère cheese
- 2 cloves garlic, finely chopped
- 1 tbsp finely chopped parsley
- 4 leaves basil, torn
- 1 tbsp finely chopped thyme

Prepare the pastry and chill in the refrigerator. • Drain the tomatoes in a colander for 1 hour. • Preheat the oven to 400°F/200°C/gas 6. • Oil a à-inch (23-cm) pie pan. • Beat the eggs and milk in a large bowl until frothy. Season with salt and pepper. • Stir in the tomatoes, cream, cheese, garlic, parsley, basil, and thyme. • Roll the dough out and use it to line the pan, letting it overlap the edges. Prick with a fork. • Pour the filling into the pan. • Bake for 35–40 minutes, or until a toothpick inserted into the center comes out clean. • Serve hot or at room temperature.

BELL PEPPER SAVORY PIE

Serves: 6–8

Preparation: 10'

Cooking: 30–40'

Level of difficulty: 1

- **8 oz/250 g frozen puff pastry, thawed**
- **whites of 4 leeks, cut into small rounds**
- **2 red bell peppers/ capsicums, seeded, cored, and cut into small squares**
- **3 small red chile peppers, finely chopped**
- **3 tbsp butter**
- **1 tbsp water**
- **3 eggs, lightly beaten**
- **3/4 cup/180 ml light/single cream**
- **6 tbsp freshly grated Parmesan cheese**
- **1/4 tsp paprika**

Preheat the oven to 400°F/200°C/gas 6. • Butter a 10-inch (25-cm) springform pan. • Unfold or unroll the puff pastry on a lightly floured surface. Line the base and sides of the prepared baking pan, trimming the edges to fit. • Use a fork to prick the pastry all over. • Bake for 15–20 minutes, or until puffed and golden brown. • Cook the leeks, bell peppers, and chile in the butter and water in a medium saucepan over medium heat for 20 minutes. • Season with salt and remove from the heat. • Beat the eggs, cream, Parmesan, and paprika in a small bowl. Pour the beaten egg mixture into the bell pepper mixture, blending well. • Pour the mixture into the baked pastry base. • Bake for 15–20 minutes, or until firm to the touch. • Transfer to a serving plate and serve hot or at room temperature.

ZUCCHINI AND ARTICHOKE QUICHE

Serves: 4–6

Preparation: 30'

Cooking: 25–30'

Level of difficulty: 1

- 1 lb/500 g fresh or frozen puff pastry, thawed if frozen
- 1 clove garlic, lightly crushed
- 3 tender artichoke hearts, thinly sliced
- 3 zucchini/courgettes, thinly sliced
- 3 tbsp extra-virgin olive oil
- 2 tbsp water
- 6 tbsp fresh, creamy goat's cheese
- 4 tbsp Ricotta cheese
- 3 eggs, lightly beaten
- 2/3 cup/150 ml milk
- 4 tbsp light/single cream
- 1/4 tsp salt

Preheat the oven to 350°F/180°C/gas 4. • Butter a 10-inch (25-cm) quiche or pie pan. • Unfold or unroll the puff pastry on a lightly floured work surface. Line the base and sides of prepared pan, trimming the edges to fit. • Use a fork to prick the pastry all over. • Sauté the garlic, artichokes, and zucchini in the oil in a frying pan over low heat until the zucchini are lightly browned. • Add the water and cook over low heat until the vegetables are tender. • Discard the garlic. • Spoon the goat's cheese and Ricotta into the pastry base. Sprinkle the vegetable mixture on top. • Beat the eggs, milk, cream, and salt in a small bowl. • Pour the mixture over the vegetables. • Bake for 25–30 minutes, or until set. • Serve hot or at room temperature

Artichokes are a delicious winter vegetable. Choose plump heavy buds with tightly packed leaves.

SOUTHERN ITALIAN POTATO PIE

P repare the pastry and chill in the refrigerator.
• Preheat the oven to 350°F/180°C/gas 4.
• Butter a deep 10-inch (25-cm) springform pan.
Line with waxed paper. Butter the paper. • Roll the
dough out into a disk large enough to cover the
bottom and sides of the pan with the edges
overlapping. • Mix the potatoes, butter, milk, egg,
egg yolk, Parmesan, salt, and pepper in a large
bowl. Spoon the filling mixture into the pastry. Fold
the overlapping edges of the dough inward.
• Bake for 40–45 minutes, or until golden brown.
• Serve hot or at room temperature.

Serves: 6–8

Preparation: 15'

Cooking: 40–45'

Level of difficulty: 2

- • **1 quantity Short Crust Pastry With Egg (see page 958)**
- • **2 lb/1 kg potatoes, boiled and mashed**
- • **½ cup/125 g butter, melted**
- • **1 cup/250 ml milk**
- • **1 large egg + 1 large egg yolk**
- • **½ cup/60 g freshly grated Parmesan cheese**
- • **salt and freshly ground black pepper to taste**

MEDITERRANEAN CHEESE PIE

Serves: 6

Preparation: 20'

Cooking: 25–30'

Level of difficulty: 1

- 3 eggs, lightly beaten
- 2 cups/500 ml plain yogurt
- 1 lb/500 g Feta cheese, crumbled
- 2/3 cup/180 ml extra-virgin olive oil
- salt to taste
- 12 sheets frozen phyllo dough, thawed

Preheat the oven to 350°F/180°C/gas 4. • Line a 9-inch (23-cm) square baking pan with waxed paper. Brush with oil. • Mix the eggs, yogurt, Feta, and 4 tablespoons of oil in a large bowl until well blended. Season with salt. • Lay out the sheets of phyllo dough and cover with a damp cloth. • Place 4 phyllo sheets in the prepared pan, brushing each sheet with oil and allowing the dough to drape over the sides of the pan. • Spoon half the cheese mixture into the pan. • Cover with another 4 phyllo sheets, each brushed with oil, trimming to fit the pan. • Spoon the remaining cheese mixture into the pan. • Fold the overlapping dough over the top. • Cover with the remaining 4 phyllo sheets, each brushed with oil. • Prick all over with a fork. • Bake for 25–30 minutes, or until golden brown. • Serve hot or at room temperature.

FOUR CHEESE AND POTATO SAVORY PIE

Serves: 4

Preparation: 30'

Cooking: 15–20'

Level of difficulty: 1

- **8 oz/250 g boiled potatoes**
- **2 eggs**
- **4 oz/125 g Taleggio cheese**
- **2 oz/60 g Robiola cheese**
- **2 oz/60 g Crescenza cheese**
- **¼ tsp freshly ground pepper**
- **8 oz/250 g frozen puff pastry, thawed**
- **6 tbsp freshly grated Emmental cheese**

Preheat the oven to 425°F/220°C/gas 7. • Line an 11 x 8-inch (28 x 18-cm) baking dish with waxed paper. • Process the potatoes, 1 egg, Taleggio, Robiola, Crescenza, and pepper in a food processor until well blended. • Unfold or unroll the puff pastry on a lightly floured work surface. Line the base and sides of the prepared pan with two-thirds of the pastry, overlapping the edges. Prick all over with a fork. • Fill with the potato mixture and cover with the remaining sheet of pastry. Fold the overlapping edges in to seal the pie. • Prick the top with a fork. Brush with the remaining beaten egg. Sprinkle with the Emmental. • Bake for 15–20 minutes, or until golden. • Serve hot.

CHEESE AND CARROT SAVORY PIE

Pastry: Sift the flour and salt into a medium bowl. Cut in the butter until the mixture resembles bread crumbs. Stir in enough water to make a stiff dough. Shape into a ball, wrap in plastic wrap (cling film), and refrigerate for 30 minutes. • Filling: Process the carrots in a food processor or blender until smooth. Transfer to a large frying pan with 4 tablespoons of butter. Cook for 5 minutes over low heat, stirring constantly.
• Place the remaining butter and flour in a small saucepan over low heat. Cook for 1 minute, stirring constantly. • Remove from the heat and pour in half the hot milk. Return to the heat and cook until the mixture thickens. Gradually mix in the remaining milk, stirring constantly. Season with salt, pepper, and nutmeg. • Cook for 5–10 minutes, stirring constantly, to make a creamy Béchamel sauce.
• Add the Béchamel to the carrot mixture. Mix in the egg yolks and Parmesan. • Roll the pastry out into a $^1/_4$ inch (5 mm) thick sheet. • Preheat the oven to 375°F/190°C/gas 5. • Butter a deep 8-inch (20-cm) baking pan and sprinkle with flour.
• Put the dough in the prepared pan, trimming the edges to fit. • Beat the egg whites in a large bowl until stiff peaks form. Fold them gently into the carrot mixture. • Pour the mixture over the pastry base. • Bake for 45–50 minutes, or until a toothpick inserted into the center comes out clean.
• Turn out onto a serving plate. Serve hot or warm.

Serves: 4

Preparation: 45' + 30' to chill

Cooking: 56–66'

Level of difficulty: 2

PASTRY
• 1$^1/_3$ cups/200 g all-purpose/plain flour
• $^1/_4$ tsp salt
• $^1/_2$ cup/125 g butter
• 4 tbsp water

FILLING
• 1$^1/_2$ lb/750 g carrots, boiled and thinly sliced
• 6 tbsp butter
• 2 tbsp all-purpose/plain flour
• 1$^1/_4$ cups/310 g hot milk
• salt and freshly ground white pepper to taste
• $^1/_4$ tsp freshly grated nutmeg
• 4 eggs, separated
• $^2/_3$ cup/80 g freshly grated Parmesan cheese

TOMATO AND BASIL PUFF

Serves: 4

Preparation: 40'

Cooking: 15–20'

Level of difficulty: 1

- 1 lb/500 g tomatoes
- 1 bunch fresh basil
- 1 tbsp extra-virgin olive oil
- 8 oz/250 g frozen puff pastry, thawed
- salt and freshly ground black pepper to taste

CREAM SAUCE
- ²⁄₃ cup/150 ml single/light cream
- juice of ½ lemon
- 1 shallot, finely chopped
- 1 tsp finely chopped chives
- salt and freshly ground black pepper to taste

Preheat the oven to 350°F/180°C/gas 4. • Cut the tomatoes in half and squeeze out the juice and seeds. Use a sharp knife to slice the tomatoes thinly and lay them on kitchen towels to absorb any excess liquid. • Turn them over to drain the other side on a clean paper towel.
• Process half the basil with the oil in a food processor or blender until puréed. • Roll the dough out to ¹⁄₈ inch (3 mm) thick. Brush with the basil oil. • Arrange the tomato rings on top of the pastry and brush again with the basil oil. Season with salt and pepper. • Bake for 15–20 minutes, or until risen. • Garnish with the remaining basil.
• Cream Sauce: Beat the cream and lemon juice in a small bowl. Mix in the shallot and chives and season with salt and pepper. • Serve the puff hot or at room temperature with the cream sauce.

CAULIFLOWER QUICHE

Sift the flour into a large bowl. • Mix in the butter, almonds, Parmesan, and cinnamon. Add 1 egg white and stir to make a smooth dough. • Shape into a ball, wrap in plastic wrap (cling film), and refrigerate for 30 minutes. • Cook the cauliflower in a large pot of salted boiling water for 15 minutes. Drain well. • Preheat the oven to 350°F/180°C/gas 4. • Oil a deep 8-inch (20-cm) pie pan wit a removable base. • Roll the dough out very thinly on a lightly floured surface. • Line the bottom and sides of the pan with the dough, trimming the edges to fit. • Cover with aluminum foil and fill with dried beans or pie weights. • Bake for 15 minutes. • Remove from the oven and remove the foil with the beans or pie weights. • Beat the egg and cream in a large bowl. Season with salt. Stir in the cooked cauliflower until well mixed. • Spoon the cauliflower mixture into the baked pastry. • Bake for 15–18 minutes, or until set and lightly browned. • Serve hot or at room temperature.

Serves: 4–6

Preparation: 50' + 30' to chill

Cooking: 15–20'

Level of difficulty: 2

- ¾ cup/125 g all-purpose/plain flour
- 6 tbsp butter
- ½ cup/50 g finely chopped almonds
- 2 tbsp freshly grated Parmesan cheese
- 1 tsp ground cinnamon
- 1 egg + 1 egg white, lightly beaten
- 14 oz/400 g cauliflower florets
- 6 tbsp light/single cream
- ½ tsp salt

CHEESE AND POTATO PIE

Serves: 4–6

Preparation: 20'

Cooking: 30'

Level of difficulty: 1

- 3 lb/1.5 kg baking/floury potatoes
- 3 large eggs, lightly beaten
- 7 oz/200 g Provolone (or Cheddar) cheese, cut into small cubes
- scant ½ cup/50g freshly grated Parmesan cheese
- 2 tbsp finely chopped parsley
- salt and freshly ground black pepper to taste

Cook the potatoes in a large pot of salted, boiling water for about 20 minutes, or until tender.
• Drain and mash in a large bowl. • Mix in the eggs, Provolone, Parmesan, and parsley. Season with salt and pepper. • Lightly oil a large nonstick frying pan and place over medium heat. When the pan is hot, spread the potato mixture in the pan in an even layer, about 1 inch (2.5 cm) thick. Level with the back of a spoon. • Cook for about 5 minutes, or until golden and crispy underneath. • Turn the cake over by turning it out onto a plate and then sliding it back into the pan. • Cook on the other side for about 5 minutes, or until golden. • Serve hot.

PIZZA

GORGONZOLA AND ONION PIZZA WITH FRESH SAGE

Prepare the pizza dough and set aside to rise.
• Preheat the oven to 425°F/220°C/gas 7.
• Oil a 12-inch (30-cm) pizza pan. • When the rising time has elapsed, knead the dough for 1 minute, then use your fingertips to press it into the pan. • Drizzle with a little oil. Sprinkle with the sage and then the onion rings. Season with salt.
• Bake for 15–20 minutes. • Sprinkle the pizza with the Gorgonzola and bake for 5–10 minutes more, or until the cheese is bubbling and golden.
• Serve hot.

154

Makes: one (12-inch/
    30-cm pizza)

Preparation: 25'

Rising time: 1 h 30'

Cooking: 20–30'

Level of difficulty: 1

- 1 quantity
  Pizza Dough
  (see page 952)
- 2–4 tbsp extra-
  virgin olive oil
- salt to taste
- 2–3 tbsp finely
  chopped sage
- 2 large white
  onions, peeled and
  thinly sliced into
  rings
- 5 oz/150 g
  Gorgonzola
  cheese, crumbled

PIZZA WITH BELL PEPPERS AND PARMESAN

Makes: one (12-inch/ 30-cm pizza)

Preparation: 30'

Rising time: 1 h 30'

Cooking: 20–30'

Level of difficulty: 1

- 1 quantity
  Pizza Dough
  (see page 952)
- 1 onion, finely
  chopped
- 2 tbsp extra-virgin
  olive oil
- 10 oz/300 g bell
  peppers/
  capsicums,
  seeded, cored, and
  cut into thin strips
- salt to taste
- 1½ oz/45 g
  Parmesan cheese,
  flaked
- 1 cup/100 g pitted
  and chopped green
  olives
- 1 tbsp salt-cured
  capers, rinsed

Prepare the pizza dough and set aside to rise.
• Sauté the onion in the oil in a large frying pan over medium heat for 2–3 minutes. • Add the bell peppers. Partially cover and cook over low heat for 15 minutes, stirring often. Season with salt.
• Preheat the oven to 425°F/220°C/gas 7. • Oil a 12-inch (30-cm) pizza pan. • When the rising time has elapsed, knead the dough for 1 minute, then use your fingertips to press it into the pan. • Top with the bell peppers and cooking liquid. Sprinkle with half the Parmesan, olives, and capers. • Bake for about 20 minutes, or until lightly browned.
• Sprinkle with the remaining Parmesan and serve.

OLIVE AND ROBIOLA PIZZA

Prepare the pizza dough and set aside to rise.
• Preheat the oven to 425°F/220°C/gas 7.
• Oil a 12-inch (30-cm) pizza pan. • When the rising time has elapsed, knead the dough for 1 minute, then use your fingertips to press it into the pan. • Drizzle with 1 tablespoon of oil. • Bake for 15–20 minutes. • Remove from the oven and top with the tomatoes and season with salt. • Bake for 10 minutes. • Add the olives, gherkins, and Feta and drizzle with the remaining oil. • Serve hot.

Makes: one (12-inch/30-cm pizza)

Preparation: 20'

Rising time: 1 h 30'

Cooking: 25–30'

Level of difficulty: 1

- 1 quantity Pizza Dough (see page 952)
- 2 tbsp extra-virgin olive oil
- 2 large tomatoes, thinly sliced
- salt to taste
- 2 oz/60 g black olives
- 2 oz/60 g gherkins, sliced
- 3 oz/90 g Feta cheese, cut in small cubes

MUSHROOM CALZONE

Makes: one (12-inch/ 30-cm calzone)

Preparation: 25'

Rising time: 1 h 30'

Cooking: 45'

Level of difficulty: 1

- 1 quantity Pizza Dough (see page 952)
- 10 oz/300 g champignon mushrooms
- 1 clove garlic, finely chopped
- 1 tbsp finely chopped parsley
- 2 tbsp extra-virgin olive oil
- salt to taste
- ⅔ cup/150 g Ricotta cheese
- 2 tbsp freshly grated Parmesan cheese

Prepare the pizza dough and set aside to rise.
• Preheat the oven to 425°F/220°C/gas 7.
• Oil a 12-inch (30-cm) pizza pan. • Sauté the mushrooms, garlic, and parsley in the oil in a large frying pan over low heat until the mushrooms are tender. Season with salt. • When the rising time has elapsed, knead the dough for 1 minute, then roll it out to about 12 inches (30- cm) in diameter. • Spoon the mushroom mixture and Ricotta into the center of the dough. Sprinkle with the Parmesan. Fold over the dough and press the edges with your fingers to seal. • Bake for 25–30 minutes, or until lightly browned. • Serve hot.

PIZZA WITH MOZZARELLA AND OLIVES

Makes: one (12-inch/ 30-cm pizza)

Preparation: 20'	
Rising time: 1 h 30'	
Cooking: 25–30'	
Level of difficulty: 1	

- 1 quantity
  Pizza Dough
  (see page 952)
- 1¼ cups/310 g
  Tomato Sauce
  (see page 951)
- 5 oz/150 g
  Mozzarella cheese,
  thinly sliced
- ½ cup/50 g black
  olives
- 1 tbsp extra-virgin
  olive oil

Prepare the pizza dough and set aside to rise.
• Preheat the oven to 425°F/220°C/gas 7.
• Oil a 12-inch (30-cm) pizza pan. • When the rising time has elapsed, knead the dough for 1 minute, then use your fingertips to press it into the pan. • Spread with the tomato sauce and sprinkle with the Mozzarella and olives. Drizzle with the oil. • Bake for 20–30 minutes, or until the dough is lightly browned and the cheese is melted and bubbling.• Serve hot.

TOMATO PIZZA WITH PESTO

Makes: one (10 x 15-in/ 25 x 38-cm) pizza

Preparation: 25' + time to make pesto

Rising time: 1 h 30'

Cooking: 25–30'

Level of difficulty: 1

P repare the pizza dough and set aside to rise.
• Preheat the oven to 425°F/220°C/gas 7.
• Oil a 10 x 15-inch (25 x 38-cm) baking pan.
• When the rising time has elapsed, knead the dough for 1 minute, then use your fingertips to press it into the pan. • Drizzle with the oil and season with salt. • Bake for 25 minutes. Remove from the oven and sprinkle with the cheese. • Bake for 5 more minutes. • Drizzle with the pesto and add the tomatoes. • Serve hot.

- 1 quantity Pizza Dough (see page 952)
- 2 tbsp extra-virgin olive oil
- salt to taste
- 8 oz/250 g smoked cheese
- $^1/_2$ cup/125 ml Pesto (see page 946)
- 4 oz/125 g tomatoes, finely chopped

Makes: one (12-inch/
30-cm pizza)

Preparation: 25'

Rising time: 1 h 30'

Cooking: 25–30'

Level of difficulty: 1

- 1 quantity
  Pizza Dough
  (see page 952)
- 4 oz/125 g
  Gorgonzola
  cheese, diced
- 2 tbsp freshly
  grated Parmesan
  cheese
- 3 tbsp extra-virgin
  olive oil
- 4 oz/125 g canned
  pineapple rings
- 4 oz/125 g
  Mozzarella cheese,
  diced
- 2 cloves garlic,
  finely chopped
- freshly ground
  black pepper to
  taste (optional)

GORGONZOLA PIZZA WITH PINEAPPLE

Prepare the pizza dough and set aside to rise.
• Preheat the oven to 425°F/220°C/gas 7.
• Oil a 12-inch (30-cm) pizza pan. • When the rising time has elapsed, knead the dough for 1 minute, then use your fingertips to press it into the pan. • Sprinkle with the Gorgonzola and Parmesan and drizzle with 2 tablespoons of oil.
• Bake for 10–15 minutes. • Take the pizza out of the oven and arrange the pineapple rings on top. Sprinkle with the Mozzarella and garlic, drizzle with the remaining oil, and finish with a generous grinding of pepper, if using. • Bake for 10 minutes.
• Serve hot.

FILLED DEEP-CRUST PIZZA WITH GOAT'S CHEESE

Prepare the pizza dough and set aside to rise.
• Preheat the oven to 425°F/220°C/gas 7.
• Oil an 8-inch (20-cm) pizza pan. • When the rising time has elapsed, knead the dough for 1 minute, then divide it in two. • Roll the dough out on a lightly floured work surface into two thick rounds. Place one in the prepared pan. • Spread with the goat's cheese and garlic. Top with the remaining dough, pressing down lightly to seal. Set aside for 20 minutes. • Top with the tomatoes and olives and season with salt and pepper. Drizzle with the oil. • Bake for 25–30 minutes, or until risen and lightly browned.
• Serve immediately.

Makes: one (8-inch/ 20-cm pizza)

Preparation: 25'

Rising time: 1 h 30'

Cooking: 35–45'

Level of difficulty: 1

- 1 quantity **Pizza Dough (see page 952)**
- ⅔ cup/150 g fresh creamy goat's cheese (Caprino)
- 2 cloves garlic, finely chopped
- 15 cherry tomatoes, halved
- 15 black olives, pitted
- salt and freshly ground black pepper to taste
- 2 tbsp extra-virgin olive oil

PIZZA WITH EGGPLANT AND TOMATOES

Prepare the pizza dough and set aside to rise.
• Preheat the oven to 425°F/220°C/gas 7.
• Oil a 12-inch (30-cm) pizza pan. • When the
rising time has elapsed, knead the dough for
1 minute, then use your fingertips to press it into
the pan. • Mix the tomatoes, oil, oregano, and salt
and pepper in a small bowl. Spread the mixture
over the dough. • Bake for 20 minutes, or until
lightly browned. • Meanwhile, dredge the eggplant
in the flour. • Heat the oil in a large frying pan to
very hot. Fry the eggplant for 5–7 minutes, or until
tender. • Drain well on paper towels. • Remove the
pizza from the oven and sprinkle with the Ricotta
Salata. Cover with the eggplant and serve hot.

Makes: one (12-inch/ 30-cm pizza)

Preparation: 25'

Rising time: 1 h 30'

Cooking: 25–30'

Level of difficulty: 1

- **1 quantity Pizza Dough (see page 952)**
- **5 oz/150 g canned tomatoes**
- **2 tbsp extra-virgin olive oil**
- **½ tsp dried oregano**
- **salt and freshly ground black pepper to taste**
- **1 small eggplant/ aubergine, thinly sliced**
- **⅓ cup/50 g all-purpose/plain flour**
- **1 cup/250 ml olive oil, for frying**
- **1 cup/125 g freshly grated Ricotta Salata cheese**

THREE CHEESE PIZZA

Makes: one (12-inch/ 30-cm pizza)

Preparation: 25'

Rising time: 1 h 30'

Cooking: 25–30'

Level of difficulty: 1

- 1 quantity Pizza Dough (see page 952)
- 1 tbsp extra-virgin olive oil
- 1 tbsp milk
- 3½ oz/100 g Mozzarella cheese, diced
- ¾ cup/90 g freshly grated smoked Scamorza cheese
- ¾ cup/90 g freshly grated Fontina cheese
- salt and freshly ground black pepper to taste

Prepare the pizza dough and set aside to rise. • Preheat the oven to 425°F/220°C/gas 7. • Oil a 12-inch (30-cm) pizza pan. • Let rise for 1 hour, then knead the dough for 1 minute. Use your fingertips to press it into the pan. • Brush with the oil and milk and set aside for 30 minutes. • Bake for 20 minutes. • Remove from the oven and sprinkle with the Mozzarella, Scamorza, and Fontina. Season with salt and pepper. • Bake for 10 minutes, or until the cheese is golden and bubbling. • Serve hot.

CORNMEAL PIZZA WITH TOMATO AND RICOTTA

Prepare the pizza dough, substituting half the all-purpose flour with finely ground cornmeal. Set aside to rise. • Oil a 12-inch (30-cm) pizza pan. • After 1¹/₂ hours, knead the dough for 1 minute, then use your fingertips to press it into the pan. • Spread with the tomato sauce and let rise for 30 minutes. • Preheat the oven to 425°F/220°C/ gas 7. • Bake for 25 minutes. • Mix the Ricotta, basil, and salt in a large bowl. • Remove the pizza from the oven and spread with the Ricotta mixture. Drizzle with the oil. • Bake for 5 more minutes. • Serve hot.

166

Makes: one (12-inch/ 30-cm pizza)

Preparation: 25'

Rising time: 2 h

Cooking: 25–30'

Level of difficulty: 1

- **1 quantity Pizza Dough (see page 952)**
- **¹/₂ cup/125 ml Tomato Sauce (see page 950)**
- **1 cup/250 g fresh Ricotta cheese**
- **2 tbsp finely chopped basil**
- **1 tbsp extra-virgin olive oil**
- **¹/₈ tsp salt**

CHEESE, POPPY SEED, AND SAGE PIZZA

Makes: one (12-inch/ 30-cm pizza)

Preparation: 15'

Rising time: 1 h 30'

Cooking: 25–30'

Level of difficulty: 1

- 1¹/₂ quantities Pizza Dough (see page 952)
- 3 oz/90 g Mozzarella cheese, diced
- 4 oz/125 g Fontina cheese, diced
- ²/₃ cup/80 g freshly grated Parmesan cheese
- 6–8 sage leaves, finely chopped
- salt to taste
- 1 egg yolk, lightly beaten
- 4 tbsp poppy seeds

Prepare the pizza dough and set aside to rise.
• Preheat the oven to 425°F/220°C/gas 7.
• Oil a 12-inch (30-cm) pizza pan. • When the rising time has elapsed, knead the dough for 1 minute, then use your fingertips to press three-quarters of it into the pan. • Sprinkle with the Mozzarella, Fontina, Parmesan, and sage. Season with salt. • Shape the remaining dough into small balls. Place on the pizza. Brush with the egg and sprinkle with poppy seeds. • Bake for 10 minutes. Lower the oven temperature to 350°F/180°C/gas 4 and bake for 20–25 minutes more, or until lightly browned. • Serve hot.

BRIE AND POTATO PIZZA

Prepare the pizza dough, incorporating the mashed potatoes. Set aside to rise. • Oil a 12-inch (30-cm) pizza pan. • After 1 hour, knead the dough for 1 minute, then use your fingertips to press it into the pan. • Sprinkle with the Emmental, Brie, and the diced potatoes. Drizzle with the oil. Season with salt and rosemary and sprinkle with the Parmesan. Let rest for 30 minutes. • Preheat the oven to 425°F/220°C/gas 7.• Bake for 25–30 minutes, or until lightly browned. • Serve hot.

Makes:	one (12-inch/ 30-cm pizza)
Preparation:	15'
Rising time:	1 h 30'
Cooking:	25–30'
Level of difficulty:	1

- 1 quantity Pizza Dough (see page 952)
- 7 oz/200 g potatoes, boiled, 1/4 mashed, rest diced
- 2 oz/60 g Emmental cheese, diced
- 2 oz/60 g Brie cheese, diced
- 1 tbsp extra-virgin olive oil
- salt to taste
- 1 tbsp rosemary leaves
- 1/2 cup/60 g freshly grated Parmesan cheese

*Vegan

Makes:	one (12-inch/ 30-cm pizza)
Preparation:	15'
Rising time:	1 h 30'
Cooking:	25–30'
Level of difficulty:	1

- 1 quantity Pizza Dough (see page 952)
- 1 large potato, boiled and mashed
- 4 tbsp extra-virgin olive oil
- salt and freshly ground black pepper to taste
- 20 cherry tomatoes, halved
- 1 tsp dried oregano

CHERRY TOMATO PIZZA WITH HERBS

Prepare the pizza dough, incorporating the mashed potato and 2 tablespoons of oil. Set aside to rise. • Oil a 12-inch (30-cm) pizza pan. • When the rising time has elapsed, knead the dough for 1 minute, then use your fingertips to press it into the pan. • Preheat the oven to 425°F/ 220°C/gas 7. • Place the tomatoes on the pizza. Season with salt, pepper, and oregano. Drizzle with the remaining oil. • Bake for 20–25 minutes, or until golden brown. • Serve hot or at room temperature.

PIZZA MARGHERITA REVISITED

Prepare the pizza dough and set aside to rise.
• Preheat the oven to 425°F/220°C/gas 7.
• Oil a 12-inch (30-cm) pizza pan. • When the rising time has elapsed, knead the dough for 1 minute, then use your fingertips to press it into the pan. • Sprinkle the base with the grated Parmesan. Spread the tomatoes over the top and cover with the Mozzarella and garlic, if liked. Season with salt and pepper. • Bake for 15–25 minutes, or until golden brown. • For plain Magherita pizza, serve as it (the traditional recipe does not have garlic). For a modern version of this old classic, top the pizza straight from the oven with the arugula and flakes of Parmesan. • Drizzle with the oil and serve hot.

Makes: one (12-inch/ 30-cm pizza)

Preparation: 25'

Rising time: 1 h 30'

Cooking: 15–25'

Level of difficulty: 1

- 1 quantity
  Pizza Dough
  (see page 952)
- 2 tbsp freshly
  grated Parmesan
  cheese
- 12 oz/300 g
  canned tomatoes
- 6 oz/180 g
  Mozzarella cheese,
  thinly sliced
- 2–3 cloves garlic,
  thinly sliced
  (optional)
- salt and freshly
  ground black
  pepper to taste
- 1 small bunch
  arugula/rocket
- 2 oz/60 g
  Parmesan cheese,
  in flakes
- 2 tbsp extra-virgin
  olive oil

PIZZA WITH BUFFALO MOZZARELLA

Prepare the pizza dough and set aside to rise.
• Preheat the oven to 425°F/220°C/gas 7.
• Oil a 12-inch (30-cm) pizza pan. • When the
rising time has elapsed, knead the dough for 1
minute, then use your fingertips to press it into
the pan. • While the dough is rising, blanch the
tomatoes in boiling water for 1 minute. Drain and
slip off the skins. Slice thinly, removing as many
seeds as possible. • Place the tomatoes in a
colander and sprinkle with salt. Let drain for
15 minutes. • Slice the Mozzarella thinly and let
drain in another colander. • Place the tomatoes,
Mozzarella, and garlic on the pizza dough and
drizzle with the oil. • Bake for 15–25 minutes, or
until golden brown. • Serve hot, garnished with
basil, if liked.

Makes: one (12-inch/
30-cm pizza)

Preparation: 25'

Rising time: 1 h 30'

Cooking: 15–25'

Level of difficulty: 1

- **1 quantity
  Pizza Dough
  (see page 952)**
- **4–6 tomatoes**
- **salt to taste**
- **10 oz/300 g
  buffalo milk
  Mozzarella cheese**
- **1 clove garlic,
  finely chopped**
- **2 tbsp extra-virgin
  olive oil**
- **fresh basil, torn, to
  garnish (optional)**

WHOLE-WHEAT PIZZA WITH ONIONS AND RICOTTA CHEESE

Makes: one (12-inch/ 30-cm pizza)

Preparation: 25'

Rising time: 1 h 30'

Cooking: 15–25'

Level of difficulty: 1

DOUGH

- 2 (¹/₄-oz/7-g) packages) active dry yeast or 1 oz/30 g fresh yeast
- 1 tsp sugar
- ¹/₂ cup/125 ml warm water, + extra, as required
- 1²/₃ cups/250 g all-purpose/plain flour
- 1¹/₃ cups/200 g whole-wheat/ wholemeal flour
- ¹/₈ tsp salt

TOPPING

- 2 onions, thinly sliced
- 6 tbsp extra-virgin olive oil
- ¹/₈ tsp salt
- 2–3 tbsp water
- ³/₄ cup/180 g Ricotta cheese
- 1 tbsp each finely chopped parsley and marjoram (optional)

Dough: Dissolve the yeast and sugar in the water and set aside for 15 minutes, until foamy. • Sift both flours and salt into a large bowl. Mix in the yeast mixture and enough warm water to make a fairly stiff dough. Knead on a lightly floured work surface until smooth and elastic. • Shape into a ball, place in an oiled bowl, and cover with a cloth. Let rise in a warm place for 1 hour. • When the rising time has elapsed, knead the dough for 1 minute, then use your fingertips to press it into the pan. Set aside to rise for 30 minutes. • Preheat the oven to 425°F/220°C/gas 7. • Oil a 12-inch (30-cm) pizza pan. • Topping: Sauté the onions in 4 tablespoons of oil in a large frying pan. Season with salt and cover and cook over low heat until softened and golden brown. Add 2–3 tablespoons of water to prevent them from burning. • Prick the dough with a fork. Spread the Ricotta and onions on top and drizzle with the remaining oil. • Bake for 15–25 minutes, or until crisp and golden brown. • Sprinkle with the parsley and marjoram, if using, and serve immediately.

EGGPLANT PIZZA

Prepare the pizza dough and set aside to rise.
• Preheat the oven to 425°F/220°C/gas 7.
• Oil a 12-inch (30-cm) pizza pan. • When the
rising time has elapsed, knead the dough for 1
minute, then use your fingertips to press it into
the pan. • While the dough is rising, blanch the

Eggplants are full of fiber and should be eaten soon after purchase for the best flavor.

tomatoes in salted,
boiling water for 1
minute. Drain and peel. Remove the seeds and
slice thinly. • Sprinkle with salt, pepper, and
oregano. • Cook the eggplant in a grill pan for
about 5 minutes on each side, or until tender.
• Lay the tomatoes on the dough and drizzle with
the remaining oil. • Bake for 15–20 minutes.
Remove from the oven and add the eggplant
slices and Mozzarella. • Bake for 5–10 minutes,
or until lightly browned. • Serve hot.

---

*Makes: one (12-inch/
30-cm pizza)*

Preparation: 20'

Rising time: 1 h 30'

Cooking: 35–45'

Level of difficulty: 1

- **1 quantity
  Pizza Dough
  (see page 952)**
- **10 oz/300 g
  tomatoes**
- **salt and freshly
  ground black
  pepper to taste**
- **½ tsp dried
  oregano**
- **8 oz/250 g
  eggplants/
  aubergines, thinly
  sliced**
- **2 tbsp extra-virgin
  olive oil**
- **10 oz/300 g
  Mozzarella cheese,
  sliced**

OLIVE, RICOTTA, AND ESCAROLE PIZZA

Makes: one (12-inch/ 30-cm pizza)

Preparation: 25'

Rising time: 1 h 30'

Cooking: 30–35'

Level of difficulty: 1

- 1 quantity Pizza Dough (see page 952)
- 4 heads escarole
- 3 tbsp extra-virgin olive oil
- ⅔ cup/150 g Ricotta cheese
- 5 oz/150 g black olives
- 4 tbsp pine nuts
- 4 tbsp golden raisins/sultanas
- 2 tbsp salt-cured capers, rinsed
- salt and freshly ground black pepper to taste

Prepare the pizza dough and set aside to rise. • Preheat the oven to 425°F/220°C/gas 7. • Oil a 12-inch (30-cm) pizza pan. • When the rising time has elapsed, knead the dough for 1 minute, then use your fingertips to press it into the pan. • Cook the escarole in salted, boiling water for 5 minutes. • Drain, squeezing out excess moisture, and chop finely. • Sauté the escarole in 2 tablespoons of oil in a large frying pan over medium heat for 3 minutes. • Transfer to a large bowl and mix in the Ricotta, olives, pine nuts, raisins, and capers. Season with salt and pepper. • Spread the mixture over the dough and drizzle with the remaining oil. • Bake for 25–30 minutes, or until lightly browned. • Serve hot.

WHOLE-WHEAT PIZZA WITH VEGETABLES

B ase: Mix the yeast, $1/2$ cup (125 ml) of the water, and sugar in a small bowl. Set aside for 10 minutes, until foamy. • Sift the flours and salt into a large bowl. • Mix in the yeast mixture and enough remaining water to make a firm dough. • Knead until smooth and elastic, 5–7 minutes. • Shape into a ball, place in an oiled bowl, and cover with a clean cloth. Let rise in a warm place for 45 minutes. • Turn out onto a lightly floured surface and knead for 10 minutes. • Return to the bowl, cover with a clean cloth, and let rise for 45 minutes, or until doubled in bulk. • Preheat the oven to 375°F/190°C/gas 5. • Grease a 13-inch (32-cm) round pizza pan with oil. • Topping: Sauté the eggplant, garlic, and parsley in 4 tablespoons of oil in a frying pan over medium heat until the eggplant is lightly browned. • Add the zucchini and cook for 7 minutes. • Place the risen pizza dough in the prepared pan, pushing it outward with your fingertips to cover the bottom of the pan in an even layer. • Sprinkle the vegetable mixture, olives, Pecorino, and tomatoes on top. Drizzle with the remaining oil. • Bake for 25–30 minutes, or until the dough is cooked and the vegetables are tender. • Serve hot or at room temperature.

Makes:	one (13-in/ 32-cm) pizza
Preparation:	30'
Rising time:	+ 1 h 30
Cooking:	25–30'
Level of difficulty:	1

BASE

- 1 oz/30 g fresh yeast
- 1⅓ cups/310 ml warm water + more if needed
- 1 tsp sugar
- 2 cups/300 g unbleached flour
- 1 cup/150 g all-purpose/plain flour
- 1 cup/150 g whole-wheat/wholemeal flour
- 1 tsp salt

TOPPING

- 1 eggplant/ aubergine, cut in small cubes
- 1 clove garlic, finely chopped
- 1 tbsp finely chopped parsley
- 6 tbsp extra-virgin olive oil
- 5 oz/150 g zucchini/ courgettes, cut in small cubes
- 20 green olives
- 5 oz/150 g Pecorino cheese, diced
- 12 cherry tomatoes, halved

BREAD & FOCACCIA

FOCACCIA CAPRI-STYLE

Makes: one (12-in/ 30-cm) focaccia

Preparation: 25'

Rising time: 1 h 30'

Cooking: 25'

Level of difficulty: 1

- 1 quantity Focaccia Dough (see page 954)
- 4 tbsp extra-virgin olive oil
- 10–12 cherry tomatoes
- salt and freshly ground black pepper to taste
- 7 oz/200 g Mozzarella cheese, thinly sliced
- $1/8$ tsp dried oregano
- 8 leaves fresh basil, torn
- $1/2$ cup/60 g Ricotta Salata cheese, thinly sliced

Prepare the focaccia dough, kneading 1 tablespoon of oil in as you work. Set aside to rise (about $1^1/2$ hours). • Slice the tomatoes and place in a colander. Sprinkle with salt and let drain for 10 minutes. • Preheat the oven to 450°F/ 220°C/gas 7. • Oil a baking sheet. • Roll out the dough on a floured surface to make a 12-inch (30-cm) round. • Transfer the dough to the prepared baking sheet. Dimple the surface with your fingertips. • Bake for 20 minutes. • Remove from the oven and cover with the tomatoes and Mozzarella. Season with salt and pepper. Sprinkle with oregano and basil and drizzle with the remaining oil. • Bake for 5 minutes more. • Sprinkle with the Ricotta Salata and serve.

OLIVE AND THYME FOCACCIA

Prepare the focaccia dough and set aside to rise (about 1 hour). • Process the olives and a sprig of thyme in a food processor or blender until finely chopped. • Knead the olive mixture into the dough. Let rise for 30 more minutes. • Preheat the oven to 450°F/220°C/gas 7. • Oil a baking sheet. • Roll the dough out into a rectangle about 10 x 15 inches (25 x 38 cm) and place on the baking sheet. • Dimple the surface with your fingertips. Brush with the oil and water. Sprinkle with sea salt. • Bake for 30 minutes, or until golden. • Serve hot or at room temperature.

*Vegan

Makes: one (10 x 15-in/ 25 x 38-cm) focaccia

Preparation: 25'

Rising time: 1 h 30'

Cooking: 30'

Level of difficulty: 1

- 1 quantity Focaccia Dough (see page 954)
- 2 oz/60 g pitted green olives
- 1 small bunch fresh thyme
- 1 tbsp extra-virgin olive oil
- 1 tbsp water
- coarse sea salt to taste

Makes: one (10 x 15-in/
25 x 38-cm) focaccia

Preparation: 25'

Rising time: 1 h 30'

Cooking: 30'

Level of difficulty: 1

- 1 quantity
  Focaccia Dough
  (see page 954)
- 15–20 fresh sage
  leaves, finely
  chopped
- 2 tbsp extra-virgin
  olive oil
- coarse sea salt to
  taste

SAGE FOCACCIA

Prepare the focaccia dough, kneading the sage in as you work. Set aside to rise (about $1^1/_2$ hours). • Preheat the oven to 450°F/220°C/gas 7. • Oil a baking sheet. • Roll the dough out into a rectangle about 10 x 15 inches (25 x 38 cm) and place on the baking sheet. • Dimple the surface with your fingertips. Brush with the oil and sprinkle with sea salt. • Bake for 30 minutes, or until golden. • Serve hot or at room temperature.

PESTO FOCACCIA WITH ZUCCHINI

Prepare the focaccia dough and set aside to rise (about 1¹/₂ hours). • Preheat the oven to 450°F/220°C/gas 7. • Oil a 10 x 15-inch (25 x 38-cm) baking pan. • Cook the zucchini in salted, boiling water for 5 minutes, or until just tender. • Drain and season with salt and pepper. • Roll the dough out into a rectangle to fit the pan and place in the pan. • Dimple the surface with your fingertips. • Spread with the pesto on top. • Bake for 10–15 minutes, or until the dough is beginning to brown. • Arrange the zucchini on top of the focaccia. Bake for 5 minutes more. • Serve hot.

Vegan

Makes: one (10 x 15-in/ 25 x 38-cm) focaccia

Preparation: 25'

Rising time: 1 h 30'

Cooking: 25–30'

Level of difficulty: 1

- 1 quantity Focaccia Dough (see page 954)
- 3 zucchini/ courgettes
- 4 tbsp extra-virgin olive oil
- salt and freshly ground black pepper to taste
- ¹/₂ cup/125 ml Pesto (see page 946)

FOCACCIA WITH POTATOES AND OREGANO

Prepare the focaccia dough and set aside to rise (about 1 hour). • Oil a 10 x 15-inch (25 x 38-cm) baking pan. • Roll the dough out into a rectangle to fit the pan and place in the pan. • Let rise for 30 more minutes. • Preheat the oven to 450°F/220°C/gas 7. • Peel and thinly slice the potatoes. Arrange them in single layer on top of the dough. Season with salt and pepper and sprinkle with oregano. Drizzle with 4 tablespoons of oil. • Bake for 20–25 minutes, or until lightly browned. Drizzle with the remaining oil during baking to prevent the surface from drying out. • Serve hot.

Vegan

Makes: one (10 x 15-in/ 25 x 38-cm) focaccia

Preparation: 35'

Rising time: 1 h 30'

Cooking: 25–30'

Level of difficulty: 1

- 1 quantity Focaccia Dough (see page 954)
- 1 lb/500 g potatoes
- salt and freshly ground black pepper to taste
- 1 tsp dried oregano
- 6 tbsp extra-virgin olive oil

ONION FOCACCIA

*Vegan

Makes: one (10 x 15-in/
25 x 38-cm) focaccia

Preparation: 35'

Rising time: 1 h 30'

Cooking: 25–30'

Level of difficulty: 1

- 1 quantity
  Focaccia Dough
  (see page 954)
- 2 onions, thinly
  sliced
- 2 tbsp extra-virgin
  olive oil
- salt to taste
- 1/2 tsp each dried
  thyme and
  marjoram
  (optional)

Prepare the focaccia dough and set aside to rise (about 1 hour). • Oil a 10 x 15-inch (25 x 38-cm) baking pan. • Roll the dough out into a rectangle to fit the pan and place in the pan. • Let rise for 30 more minutes. • Preheat the oven to 450°F/220°C/gas 7. • Sauté the onions in the oil for 5 minutes. • Brush the dough with oil. Arrange the onion slices on top, season with salt, thyme, and marjoram, if liked. • Bake for 20–25 minutes, or until golden. • Serve hot.

WHOLE-WHEAT FOCACCIA WITH POTATOES AND OLIVES

Dissolve the yeast and sugar in $^1/_2$ cup (125 ml) of water then set aside for 15 minutes, until foamy. • Sift both flours and salt into a large bowl. Mix in the bran, potato, 2 tablespoons of oil, and the remaining water to make a smooth dough. Knead until smooth and elastic. • Let rise (about 1 hour) • Oil a 12-inch (30-cm) pan. • Roll the dough out to fit the pan and place in the pan. • Brush with the remaining oil and dimple the surface with your fingertips. Sprinkle with the olives and season with salt and pepper. Let rise for 30 more minutes. • Preheat the oven to 450°F/ 220°C/gas 7. • Bake for 15 minutes. • Lower the oven temperature to 350°F/180°C/gas 4 and bake for 25 minutes. • Serve hot.

Vegan

Makes: one (12-in/ 30-cm) focaccia

Preparation: 35'

Rising time: 1 h 30'

Cooking: 45

Level of difficulty: 1

- 1 oz/30 g fresh yeast or 2 ($^1/_4$-oz/ 7-g) package active dry yeast
- $^1/_2$ tsp sugar
- 1$^2/_3$ cups/300 ml warm water
- 2$^1/_3$ cups/350 g whole-wheat flour
- 1 cup/150 g all-purpose/plain flour
- sea salt and freshly ground black pepper to taste
- $^1/_3$ cup/50 g bran
- 1 medium potato, boiled and mashed
- 4 tbsp extra-virgin olive oil
- 5 oz/150 g black olives, pitted

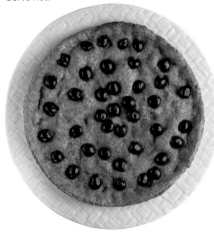

FOCACCIA WITH PESTO

*Vegan

*Makes: one (10 x 15-in/
25 x 38-cm) focaccia*

Preparation: 35'

Rising time: 1 h 30'

Cooking: 25–30'

Level of difficulty: 1

- 1 quantity
  Focaccia Dough
  (see page 954)
- ¾ cup/180 g Pesto
  (see page 946)
- 1 tbsp milk
- 2 tbsp extra-virgin
  olive oil

Prepare the focaccia dough, kneading the pesto in as you work. Set aside to rise (about 1 hour). • Oil a 10 x 15-inch (25 x 38-cm) baking pan. • Roll the dough out into a rectangle to fit the pan and place in the pan. • Let rise for 30 more minutes. • Preheat the oven to 450°F/220°C/gas 7. • Brush with the oil and milk. • Bake for 20–25 minutes, or until golden. • Serve hot.

GARBANZO BEAN FLATBREAD WITH RICOTTA AND OLIVES

Dough: Dissolve the yeast and sugar in 4 tablespoons of water and set aside for 15 minutes, until foamy. • Sift both flours and the salt into a large bowl. Mix in the yeast mixture, oil, and enough of the remaining water to make a stiff dough. Knead for 5–10 minutes, until smooth and elastic, then set aside to rise for 2 hours. • Oil four baking sheets. • Divide the dough in four and roll out thinly on a lightly floured surface. • Transfer to the prepared baking sheets.
• Topping: Spread with the tomato sauce (or chopped tomatoes) and season with salt. Let rise for 30 more minutes. • Preheat the oven to 450°F/ 220°C/gas 7. • Bake for 25 minutes.
• Remove from the oven and spread with the Ricotta. Sprinkle with the olives. Drizzle with the oil. • Bake for 5 more minutes. • Serve hot.

Makes: 4 focaccias

Preparation: 40'

Rising time: 2 h 30'

Cooking: 30'

Level of difficulty: 2

DOUGH
- ½ oz/15 g fresh yeast or 1 (¹/₄-oz/ 7-g) package active dry yeast
- ½ tsp sugar
- 1¼ cups/310 ml warm water
- 2²/₃ cups/400 g all-purpose/plain flour
- ¾ cup/125 g garbanzo bean/ chickpea flour
- ½–1 tsp salt
- 1 tbsp extra-virgin olive oil

TOPPING
- ½ cup/125 ml Tomato Sauce (see page 951) or chopped canned tomatoes
- salt and freshly ground black pepper to taste
- ½ cup/125 g Ricotta cheese
- 1 cup/100 g pitted black olives
- 1 tbsp extra-virgin olive oil

FOCACCIA WITH TOMATOES AND ZUCCHINI

Vegan

Makes: one (10 x 15-in/ 25 x 38-cm) focaccia

Preparation: 35'

Rising time: 1 h 30'

Cooking: 35–40'

Level of difficulty: 1

- 1 quantity Focaccia Dough (see page 954)
- 2 zucchini/ courgettes, thinly sliced
- 24 cherry tomatoes, cut in half
- salt and freshly ground black pepper to taste
- 3 tbsp extra-virgin olive oil
- ½ tsp dried oregano

Prepare the focaccia dough and set aside to rise (about 1 hour). • Oil a 10 x 15-inch (25 x 38-cm) baking pan. • Roll the dough out into a rectangle to fit the pan and place in the pan. • Let rise for 30 more minutes. • Preheat the oven to 450°F/220°C/gas 7. • Bake for 25–30 minutes, or until golden brown. •

Savor the combination of summer vegetables with freshly baked bread.

While the focaccia is in the oven, cook the zucchini and tomatoes in a grill pan until tender. Season with salt and pepper. • Place the grilled vegetables on the hot focaccia, drizzle with the oil, and dust with the oregano. • Serve immediately.

FOCACCIA WITH CHERRY TOMATOES AND BELL PEPPERS

Prepare the focaccia dough and set aside to rise (about 1 hour). • Oil a 10 x 15-inch (25 x 38-cm) baking pan. • Roll the dough out into a rectangle to fit the pan and place in the pan. Dimple with your fingertips. • Let rise for 30 more minutes. • Preheat the oven to 450°F/ 220°C/gas 7. • Arrange the tomatoes, bell pepper, pine nuts, and basil on the dough. Drizzle with the oil. • Bake for 25–30 minutes, or until golden brown. • Serve hot.

*Vegan

Makes: one (10 x 15-in/ 25 x 38-cm) focaccia

Preparation: 35'

Rising time: 1 h 30'

Cooking: 35–40'

Level of difficulty: 1

- 1 quantity Focaccia Dough (see page 954)
- 2 tbsp extra-virgin olive oil
- 1 tsp water
- salt to taste
- 12 cherry tomatoes, halved
- 1 red bell pepper, seeded, cored, and cut into strips
- 2 tbsp pine nuts
- fresh basil, torn, to garnish

VEGETARIAN FOCACCIA

Dissolve the yeast and sugar in the water and set aside for 15 minutes, until foamy. • Mix the flour, mashed potato, the yeast mixture, and salt in a large bowl to make a stiff dough. • Knead until smooth and elastic. Shape into a ball. • Place in an oiled bowl and let rise for 1 hour. • Preheat the oven to 450°F/220°C/gas 7. • Oil a baking sheet. • Season the zucchini and onions with salt. • Roll out the dough on the baking sheet. Dimple with your fingertips. • Place the onions on top of the dough. Drizzle with 1 tablespoon of pesto. • Bake for 20 minutes. • Add the zucchini and more pesto. Sprinkle with the pine nuts. • Bake for 20 minutes. • Drizzle with the remaining pesto and serve hot.

*Vegan

Serves 4

Preparation: 40'

Rising time: 1 h

Cooking: 40'

Level of difficulty: 2

- ½ oz/15 g fresh yeast or 1 (¹/₄-oz/ 7-g) package active dry yeast
- ½ tsp sugar
- ½ cup/125 ml warm water
- 1¹/₃ cups/200 g all-purpose/plain flour
- 3½ oz/100 g mashed potato
- salt to taste
- 6 oz/180 g zucchini/ courgettes, very thinly sliced
- 4 oz/125 g onions, very thinly sliced
- ½ cup/125 ml Pesto (see page 946)
- 2 tbsp pine nuts

CHEESE-FILLED FOCACCIA

Prepare the focaccia dough, kneading in 4 tablespoons of oil as you work. Set aside to rise (about 1 hour). • Oil a 10 x 15-inch (25 x 38-cm) baking pan. • Divide the dough in two and roll both pieces out to fit the pan. Place one piece in the pan. Spread with the cheese, leaving a 1/2-inch (1-cm) border around the edges, and cover with the remaining dough. Press down at the edges to seal. • Let rise for 30 more minutes. • Preheat the oven to 450°F/220°C/ gas 7. • Bake for 25–30 minutes, or until golden brown. • Serve hot.

*Vegan

Makes: one (10 x 15-in/ 25 x 38-cm) focaccia

Preparation: 35'

Rising time: 1 h 30'

Cooking: 20–30'

Level of difficulty: 1

- **1 quantity Focaccia Dough (see page 954)**
- **1 tsp salt**
- **6 tbsp extra-virgin olive oil**
- **1 cup/250 ml water**
- **1¼ cups/300 g Stracchino (or other fresh, creamy) cheese, melted with 1 tablespoon milk**

*Vegan

Makes: 16–20 rolls

Preparation: 45'

Rising time: 2 h 30'

Cooking: 18–20'

Level of difficulty: 1

- 1 oz/30 g fresh yeast or 2 (¼-oz/7-g) packages active dry yeast)
- 1 tsp sugar
- 1 cup/250 ml warm water
- 8 oz/250 g canned garbanzo beans/chick peas
- 5 cups/750 g all-purpose/plain flour
- 2 tsp salt
- 6 tbsp extra-virgin olive oil

GARBANZO BEAN ROLLS

Dissolve the yeast and salt in ½ cup (125 ml) of water and set aside for 15 minutes, until foamy. • Purée the garbanzo beans in a food processor with the remaining water. • Combine the flour in a large bowl with the salt, yeast mixture, purée, and 4 tablespoons of the oil. Knead until smooth and elastic. Shape into a ball and set aside to rise. • When the rising time has elapsed (about 1½ hours), transfer to a lightly floured work surface. Knead for 2 minutes. • Divide into 16–20 equal portions and shape into round rolls. • Smear a few drops of the remaining oil on each. • Use a serrated knife to cut a deep cross in the surface of each roll. • Transfer to two oiled baking sheets, keeping the rolls well spaced. Cover with a cloth and leave to rise for 1 hour. • Preheat the oven to 425°F/ 220°C/ gas 7 and bake for 18–20 minutes, or until golden.

VEGETABLE BREAD CROWN

Prepare the dough and set aside to rise (about 1 hour). • When the rising time has lapsed, roll the dough out to a sheet about $1/2$ inch (1 cm) thick. Cut out a 12-inch (30-cm) circle. • Butter a 12-inch (30-cm) springform pan. • Transfer the dough to the prepared dish. Knead the offcuts into a long rounded roll.

Serve this eyecatching bread to children as an after school snack or surprise your friends at supper.

• Brush the edge of the dough with egg yolk and stick the roll on top, pressing it firmly. • Make small cuts 1 inch (2.5 cm) apart along the edge. Cover with a cloth and let rise in a warm place for 1 hour. • Preheat the oven to 450°F/220°C/gas 7. • Sauté the bell peppers in 3 tablespoons of oil in a large frying pan over medium heat for 10 minutes, or until crunchy-tender. Transfer to a large ovenproof dish. • Sauté the zucchini and leeks in the remaining oil in the same frying pan over medium heat for 10 minutes, or until crunchy-tender • Cook the peas in salted boiling water for 10 minutes, until just tender.
• Transfer all the vegetables to the ovenproof dish with the peppers. • Warm the vegetables in the dish in a warming oven. Add the basil and soy sauce. Season with salt and pepper. Brush the bread with the remaining beaten yolk. • Bake for 35–40 minutes, or until risen and golden brown.
• Transfer to a serving plate and arrange the vegetables in the crown. • Serve hot or warm.

Makes: one (12-in/ 30-cm) loaf

Preparation: 40'

Rising time: 2 h

Cooking: 1 h 10'

Level of difficulty: 2

- 1 quantity **Bread Dough** (see page 954)
- 1 egg yolk, lightly beaten
- 3 bell peppers/ capsicums, mixed colors, weighing about 1½ lb/650 g, seeded, cored, and cut into strips
- 6 tbsp extra-virgin olive oil
- 1 lb/500 g zucchini/ courgettes, cut into rounds
- 3½ oz/100 g leeks, cut into rounds
- 1 cup/125 g hulled/shelled peas
- 5 leaves fresh basil, torn
- 1 tsp soy sauce
- salt and freshly ground black pepper to taste

FILLED BRIOCHE

Makes: one (11-in/
28-cm) brioche

Preparation: 45'

Rising time: 1 h

Cooking: 30'

Level of difficulty: 1

Dough: Dissolve the yeast with the sugar in 4 tablespoons of water and set aside for 15 minutes, until foamy. • Pulse the flour, butter, yeast mixture, 1 egg, and salt in a blender. Gradually trickle in the remaining water and milk to make a smooth dough. Cover and let rise for 30 minutes, or until doubled in size. • Butter and flour an 11-inch (28-cm) baking dish. • Filling: Mix the goat cheese, Mozzarella, garlic, and pepper in a large bowl. • Form the dough into small balls. Stuff with a teaspoon of filling and seal the dough around it. Place the balls of dough in the prepared dish. Let rise for 30 minutes. • Preheat the oven to 400°F/ 200°C/gas 6. • Brush with the beaten egg and milk. • Bake for 30 minutes, or until lightly browned. • Serve hot.

DOUGH
- 1 oz/30 g fresh yeast or 2 (1/4-oz/7-g) packages active dry yeast
- 1 tbsp sugar
- 1 cup/250 ml warm water
- 3 1/3 cups/500 g all-purpose/plain flour
- 1/2 cup/125 g butter
- 1 egg
- 1/8 tsp salt
- 2 tbsp milk

FILLING
- 2/3 cup/150 g soft goat cheese
- 3 oz/90 g Mozzarella cheese, diced
- 1 clove garlic, finely chopped
- freshly ground black pepper to taste
- 1 tbsp milk

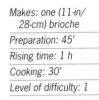

Makes: 9 flatbreads

Preparation: 30'

Cooking: 25'

Level of difficulty: 3

- ½ tsp active dried yeast
- 1 tsp salt
- 1¾ cups/430 ml warm water
- 5 cups/750 g all-purpose/plain flour
- scant 1 cup/225 g vegetable shortening, melted
- 2 tbsp extra-virgin olive oil
- 8 oz/250 g fresh creamy cheese (cream cheese, mascarpone, Crescenza, Robiola)

ITALIAN FLATBREAD WITH CHEESE

Dissolve the yeast with the salt in the water for 15 minutes, until foamy. • Sift the flour onto a clean surface and make a well in the center.
• Mix in the shortening and yeast mixture to make a dough. Knead the dough until smooth and elastic, adding the oil a little at a time as you knead.
• Divide the dough into 9 pieces. Shape each piece into a ball. • Roll out each piece of dough to about 6–7 inch (15–18 cm) in diameter. • Cook on a cast-iron griddle until bubbles appear on the surface. • Spread with the cheese. Fold in half and warm again on the griddle.

WHOLE-WHEAT BREAD

Dissolve the yeast and sugar in 4 tablespoons of water and set aside for 15 minutes, until foamy. • Sift both flours and salt into a large bowl. Mix in the yeast mixture and enough of the remaining water to make a stiff dough. Knead until smooth and elastic. Place in an oiled bowl, cover, and let rise for 1 hour. • Turn out onto a lightly floured surface and knead for 5 minutes. • Divide the dough into two equal portions and shape into long loaves. Sprinkle with flour and use a serrated knife to cut diagonal slashes about $^{1}/_{4}$ inch (5 mm) deep along the top of each loaf. Repeat, making slashes in the other direction to create a grid pattern. • Place the loaves on two baking sheets, cover with a cloth, and let rest for $1^{1}/_{2}$ hours. • Preheat the oven to 400°F/200°C/gas 6. • Bake for 40 minutes, or until risen and dark brown.

Vegan

Makes:	2 loaves
Preparation:	30'
Rising time:	2 h 30'
Cooking:	40'
Level of difficulty:	2

- 1 oz/30 g fresh yeast or 2 (¼-oz/ 7-g) packages active dry yeast
- 1 tsp sugar
- 1¼ cups/310 ml warm water
- 3½ cups/525 g whole-wheat/ wholemeal flour
- 2 cups/300 g unbleached white flour
- 1–2 tsp salt

CIABATTA (ITALIAN BREAD)

Makes: 2 loaves

Preparation: 40'

Rising time: 20 h

Cooking: 50'

Level of difficulty: 3

BREAD DOUGH

- 1 oz/30 g fresh yeast or 2 (1/4-oz/ 7-g) packages active dry yeast
- 1 tbsp warm water
- 3 1/2 cups/500 g + 2 tbsp all-purpose/ plain flour
- 1 cup/250 ml water
- 1/2 tsp natural or organic honey
- 1/2 cup/125 ml water
- 1 tsp salt
- 4 tbsp extra-virgin olive oil
- durum wheat flour, to dust

Dissolve the yeast in the water and set aside for 15 minutes, until foamy. • Sift the 3 1/3 cups (500 g) of flour into a large bowl. Mix in the yeast mixture and enough water to make a smooth dough. • Knead until smooth and elastic. Place in an oiled bowl, cover, and let rest for 18 hours. • Turn the dough out onto a surface. • Dissolve the honey in the water. Stir in the remaining flour and salt. Knead the honey mixture into the dough. Transfer to an oiled bowl, cover, and let rise for 30 minutes. • Shape into two ciabatta loaves. • Cover and let rise for 1 hour. • Preheat the oven to 425°F/ 220°C/gas 7. • Dust the loaves with durum wheat flour. Place on a baking sheet. • Bake for 10 minutes. Lower the oven temperature to 350°F/180°C/gas 4 and bake for 40 minutes more.

SPIRAL SAGE BREAD

Serves: 4–6

Preparation: 40'

Rising time: 2 h 30'

Cooking: 35–40'

Level of difficulty: 2

- **1 quantity Bread Dough (see page 954)**
- **1¼ cups/150 g freshly grated Pecorino cheese**
- **⅛ tsp salt**
- **10–12 leaves fresh sage, finely chopped**
- **7 oz/200 g Fontina (or other) cheese, thinly sliced**

Prepare the bread dough, kneading the Pecorino into the dough as you work. • Set aside to rise (about 1 hour). • Oil a deep-sided 12-inch (30-cm) baking pan. • Roll the dough out very thinly into a large rectangle on a lightly floured surface. • Cover with the sage and Fontina. Roll the dough up. Transfer the roll to the prepared pan and shape carefully into a spiral. Let rise for 1½ hours. • Preheat the oven to 400°F/200°C/gas 6. • Bake for 35–40 minutes, or until risen and golden brown. • Serve hot.

This deliciously flavored bread is scented with sage and filled with melted Fontina.

BLINI

Serves: 6–8

Preparation: 20' + 1 h 50' to rest

Cooking: 25'

Level of difficulty: 3

- **2 tbsp active dry yeast or ¹/₂ oz/ 15 g fresh yeast**
- **¹/₈ tsp sugar**
- **7 tbsp warm water**
- **1¹/₄ cups/310 ml milk**
- **4 tbsp sour cream**
- **4 tbsp unsalted butter**
- **3 large eggs, separated**
- **1 cup/150 g buckwheat flour**
- **1 cup/150 g all-purpose/plain flour**
- **¹/₂ tsp salt**

FILLING

- **1 lb/500 g white mushrooms**
- **2 tbsp butter**
- **1 tbsp finely chopped parsley**
- **2 tbsp fresh lime juice**

Dissolve the yeast and sugar in 4 tablespoons of water and set aside for 15 minutes, until foamy. • Beat the milk and sour cream in a measuring jug. Add enough cold water to make 2 cups (500 ml) of liquid. Transfer to a saucepan and warm over low heat. Add the butter and warm until the butter is melted. Let cool until warm. • Beat in the egg yolks. • Sift both flours and salt into a large bowl. • Stir in the milk and the yeast mixtures to make a smooth batter. Cover with a damp cloth and let rest for 90 minutes. • Beat the egg whites until stiff and fold them into the batter. • Let rest for 10 minutes, or until the batter is covered in bubbles. • Heat a small frying pan over medium heat. Lightly oil and spoon 2 tablespoons of batter into the pan. Turn after 2 minutes and cook on the other side for 2 minutes. • Stack the blini separated by sheets of waxed paper. Repeat until all the batter is used. The blini should be very thin. If the batter is too thick, thin it down with milk or water. • Filling: Sauté the mushrooms in the butter with the parsley for 10 minutes, or until tender. Drizzle with the lime juice. • Spread the filling mixture on the blinis and serve hot.

> *Blinis are a type of Russian pancake traditionally served during the week before Lent.*

213

OLIVE AND ROSEMARY BREAD

*Vegan

Makes one 12-in/
  30-cm ring loaf

Preparation: 30'

Rising time 1 h 15'

Cooking: 25–35'

Level of difficulty: 1

- 1 oz/30 g fresh
  yeast or 2 (¼-oz/
  7-g) packages
  active dry yeast
- 2 tsp salt
- 1½ cups/310 ml
  warm water
- 5⅓ cups/800 g all-
  purpose/plain flour
- 1⅓ cups/200 g
  whole-wheat/
  wholemeal flour
- ½ cup/125 ml
  extra-virgin olive
  oil
- 2 cups/200 g black
  olives, pitted
- 3 tbsp finely
  chopped rosemary

Dissolve the yeast and salt in ½ cup (125 ml) of water and set aside for 15 minutes, until foamy. • Sift the flours into a large bowl. • Stir in the yeast mixture and enough of the remaining water to make a firm dough. • Knead the dough until smooth and elastic,. • Shape into a ball, place in an oiled bowl, and cover with a clean cloth. Let rise for 45 minutes in a warm place. • Oil a 12-inch (30-cm) ring baking pan. • Knead the dough again, working in the olives and rosemary. • Place in the prepared baking pan. Cover with a clean cloth and let rise for 30 minutes, or until doubled in bulk. • Preheat the oven to 350°F/180°C/gas 4. • Bake for 25–35 minutes, or until lightly browned. • Cool for 15 minutes in the pan. • Turn out onto a rack and let cool completely.

RAISIN BREAD

Dissolve the yeast in 4 tablespoons of water and set aside for 15 minutes, until foamy. • Sift the flour and salt into a large bowl. Mix in the sugar, yeast mixture, and the remaining water to make a stiff dough. Knead the dough until smooth and elastic. • Let rest for 1 hour. • Preheat the oven to 400°F/ 200°C/gas 6. • Oil a baking sheet. • Sprinkle the raisins with flour. • Transfer the dough to a lightly floured surface and knead well. Incorporate the raisins and butter into the dough as you knead. • Divide the dough into 8 equal portions, sprinkle with flour, and shape into long rolls. • Place the dough on the prepared baking sheet, keeping them well spaced (their volume will double as they rise). Cover with a cloth and let rise for 30 minutes. • Bake for 20 minutes, or until lightly browned.

Makes: 8 rolls

Preparation: 30'

Rising time: 1 h 30'

Cooking: 20'

Level of difficulty: 1

- 1 oz/30 g fresh yeast or 2 (¼-oz/ 7-g) packages active dry yeast
- ⅔ cup/150 ml warm water
- 3 cups/450 g all-purpose/plain flour
- 1 tsp salt
- 2 tbsp sugar
- 3 tbsp butter, chopped
- 1⅓ cups/200 g dark raisins, soaked in warm water for 15 minutes and drained

PLAIN, ONION, AND SESAME BREADSTICKS

Sauté the onion in the oil for about 5 minutes, or until transparent. Set aside to cool. • Dissolve the yeast in 4 tablespoons of water for 15 minutes, until foamy. • Sift the flour and salt into a large bowl. Mix in the sugar, yeast mixture, and the remaining water to make a stiff dough. Break off one-third of the dough and knead the onion and oil mixture into it. Knead the remaining dough until smooth and elastic. Set aside to rise. • After about 1 hour, transfer the dough to a lightly floured work surface and knead for 2–3 minutes. • Divide the dough into portions about the size of an egg, then shape them into sticks about the thickness of your little finger. • Take one-third of the dough sticks (not the ones flavored with onion) and roll them in the sesame seeds. • Sprinkle all the dough sticks lightly with flour and transfer to three oiled baking sheets, keeping them a finger's width apart. • Cover with a cloth and set aside to rise for 1 hour. • Bake in a preheated oven at 450°F/220°C/gas 7 for 5–7 minutes. When cooked, the breadsticks will be well-browned but not too dark. • Let cool before removing from the sheets.

Breadsticks come from the old northern Italian city of Turin. They can be made in many flavors.

218

Serves: 4
Preparation: 30'
Rising time: 1 h 30'
Cooking: 20'
Level of difficulty: 1

- 1 medium onion, finely chopped
- 2 tablespoons extra-virgin olive oil
- 1 oz/30 g fresh yeast or 2 (¼-oz/7-g) packages active dry yeast
- 1 tsp sugar
- scant 1 cup/200 ml warm water
- 3½ cups/525 g all-purpose/plain flour
- 1 tsp salt
- 4 tbsp sesame seeds

FILLED BREAD WITH RICOTTA AND ZUCCHINI

Makes: one (7-in/ 18-cm) filled bread

Preparation: 40'

Rising time: 1 h 30'

Cooking: 45'

Level of difficulty: 2

- **2 quantities Focaccia Dough (see page 954)**

FILLING
- **²⁄₃ cup/140 g short-grain rice**
- **1 onion, thinly sliced**
- **4 tbsp extra-virgin olive oil**
- **4 zucchini/ courgettes, finely grated**
- **salt and freshly ground black pepper to taste**
- **²⁄₃ cup/80 g freshly grated Parmesan cheese**
- **²⁄₃ cup/150 g Ricotta cheese**
- **4 marjoram leaves**
- **¹⁄₈ tsp freshly grated nutmeg**

Prepare the focaccia dough and set aside to rise (about 1¹⁄₂ hours). • Preheat the oven to 425°F/220°C/gas 7. • Oil a 7-inch (18-cm) high-sided pan. • Cook the rice in salted, boiling water for 10 minutes. Drain well. • Sauté the onion in 3 tablespoons of oil in a large frying pan over medium heat for 3 minutes. • Add the zucchini and salt and cook for 5 minutes over high heat. • Add the rice and cook for 2 minutes. • Transfer to a large bowl and mix in the Parmesan, Ricotta, marjoram, nutmeg, salt, and pepper. • Roll the dough out and make three long strips, a 9¹⁄₂-inch (24-cm) round, and a 7-inch (18-cm) square.
• Lay the strips of dough inside the prepared pan, crossing over and hanging over the sides. Cover with the large round of dough, with edges overlapping. • Spoon in the filling and drizzle with oil. Fold the edges and strips into the center. Moisten the square piece of dough and place it on top. Brush with oil. • Bake for 25 minutes. • Turn out onto a baking sheet and bake for 10 minutes, or until golden.

RUSSIAN FILLED BREAD

Dough: Dissolve the yeast with the sugar in the milk for 15 minutes, until foamy. • Sift the flour and salt into a large bowl. • Mix in the yeast mixture, butter, and eggs to make a smooth dough. Knead on a floured surface until smooth and elastic. • Cover and let rise for 1 hour. Knead for 5–10 minutes. Cover and let rest for 30 minutes. • Line a baking sheet with waxed paper. Roll the dough out thinly in a large rectangle on the prepared sheet and cover with a cloth. • Filling: Toast the buckwheat in the oil in a large saucepan over medium heat for 5 minutes until it begins to crackle. • Add 1 cup (250 ml) of stock and the bay leaves. Cook for 10 minutes. • Add 3 tablespoons of butter. Season with salt and pepper and let cool. • Sauté the onion in 1 tablespoon of butter in a large saucepan over medium heat until transparent. • Add the cabbage and remaining stock. Cook for about 7 minutes, or until the liquid has evaporated. Season with salt and pepper and let cool. • Sauté the mushrooms in the remaining butter in a large frying pan over medium heat for 4 minutes. • Add the crème fraiche and cook for 3 minutes. Add the dill and remove from the heat. • Preheat the oven to 450°F/220°C/ gas 7. • Spread a layer of buckwheat over half the dough. Top with the cabbage and mushroom sauce. Fold the remaining pastry over the filling and seal the edges. Brush with the egg yolk. • Bake for 25–30 minutes, or until it sounds hollow when you tap the base. • Let cool slightly.

Serves: 8–10

Preparation: 45'

Rising time: 1 h 30'

Cooking: 1 h

Level of difficulty: 3

DOUGH

- ½ oz/15 g fresh yeast or 1 (¼-oz/7-g) package active dry yeast
- 1 tsp sugar
- 4 tbsp milk, hot
- 1⅔ cups/250 g all-purpose/plain flour
- 2 tsp salt
- 6 tbsp butter
- 2 large eggs, beaten

FILLING

- ¾ cup/125 g buckwheat
- 1 tbsp sunflower oil
- 1½ cups/375 ml vegetable stock (see page 945)
- 1 bay leaf
- salt and freshly ground black pepper to taste
- 8 tbsp butter
- 1 large onion, finely chopped
- 8 oz/250 g Savoy cabbage, shredded
- 8 oz/250 g mushrooms, sliced
- 8 tbsp crème fraiche
- 3 tbsp chopped dill
- 1 small egg yolk, lightly beaten with 1 tbsp water

SOUPS

COOL CREAM OF CARROT SOUP WITH SOUR CREAM

S auté the leek in the oil in a saucepan over medium heat for 8 minutes, or until softened.
• Add the carrots and potatoes and sauté for 2 minutes. • Sprinkle in the flour and mix to prevent any lumps from forming. • Pour in 1 cup (250 ml) of stock and stir well. • Pour in the milk and season with salt. Bring to a boil and simmer over low heat for 45 minutes. • Process the soup in a food processor or blender to make a smooth cream. • Let cool. • Ladle into soup bowls.
• Spoon a tablespoon of sour cream into the center of each bowl. Use a toothpick to "pull" threads of cream outward from the center.
• Garnish with the parsley and serve.

Serves: 4

Preparation: 30'

Cooking: 1 h

Level of difficulty: 1

• white of 1 leek, finely chopped
• 2 tbsp extra-virgin olive oil
• 10 oz/300 g carrots, diced
• 4 oz/125 g potatoes, peeled and diced
• 1 tbsp all-purpose/ plain flour
• 1 quart/1 liter Vegetable Stock (see page 945)
• ¾ cup/180 ml milk
• salt to taste
• 4 tbsp sour cream
• 1 tbsp finely chopped parsley

CREAM OF LETTUCE SOUP

Sauté the onions in the butter in a large saucepan over medium heat for 2–3 minutes, or until softened. • Add the lettuce. Season with salt and pepper and add the sugar. Pour in the water and simmer over low heat for 30 minutes. • Drain the lettuce, reserving the stock. • Process the lettuce in a food processor or blender until smooth. • Return the lettuce purée to the saucepan over low heat. Add the egg yolks and cream and mix well. Stir constantly for 5–10 minutes, or until the mixture thickens, adding enough reserved stock to make it smooth and creamy. • Ladle into soup bowls and garnish with the parsley and Parmesan. • Serve hot.

228

Serves: 6

Preparation: 10'

Cooking: 37–43'

Level of difficulty: 1

- **2 onions, finely chopped**
- **6 tbsp butter**
- **3 lettuces, coarsely chopped**
- **salt and freshly ground black pepper to taste**
- **½ tsp sugar**
- **1½ quarts/1.5 liters boiling water**
- **3 large egg yolks**
- **1¼ cups/310 ml heavy/double cream**
- **1 tbsp finely chopped parsley**
- **½ cup/60 g freshly grated Parmesan cheese**

WARM CARROT SOUP WITH MASCARPONE AND PARMESAN

Serves: 4

Preparation: 30'

Cooking: 30'

Level of difficulty: 1

- 1 lb/500 g carrots, peeled
- 1 sprig parsley, finely chopped
- 1 sprig thyme, finely chopped
- 2 bay leaves
- 5 whole black peppercorns
- 2 cloves garlic, 1 whole and unpeeled + 1 chopped
- 6 tbsp Vegetable Stock (see page 945)
- 1 tbsp olive oil
- 2 tbsp Mascarpone cheese
- 1 tbsp freshly grated Parmesan cheese
- ¼ tsp freshly grated nutmeg
- salt and freshly ground black pepper to taste

Preheat the oven to 300°F/150°C/gas 2. • Cook the carrots in a pan of salted, boiling water with the parsley, thyme, bay leaves, peppercorns, and whole garlic clove for 15 minutes, or until tender. Drain, reserving the stock and discarding the herbs and garlic. • Transfer the carrots to an oiled baking sheet and bake for 10 minutes. • Process the carrots with the remaining clove of garlic and stock in a food processor or blender until smooth. • Transfer the purée to a saucepan, add the oil and enough reserved stock to make a thick, smooth cream, and cook over medium heat for 5 minutes. • Stir in the Mascarpone, Parmesan, and nutmeg. Season with salt and pepper. • Ladle into soup bowls and serve warm.

CREAM OF PEA AND WATERCRESS SOUP

S auté the shallots in 2 tablespoons of butter and
the oil in a large saucepan over medium heat
for 1 minute. • Add the peas and watercress. Pour
in 1²/₃ cups (400 ml) of the stock and bring to a
boil. Cover and simmer over low heat for about
30 minutes. • Melt the remaining butter in a large
saucepan over low heat. Stir in the flour.. Gradually
add the remaining stock, stirring constantly.
Remove from the heat. • Process the peas and
watercress in a food processor or blender until
pureed. • Add the puree to the stock. Bring to a
boil, stirring constantly. • Stir in the cream and
season with salt. • Ladle into serving bowls and
sprinkle with the Parmesan. Garnish with the
crumbled egg yolk and croutons. Serve hot.

Serves: 4–6

Preparation: 25'

Cooking: 50'

Level of difficulty: 2

- **4 shallots, finely chopped**
- **4 tbsp butter**
- **1 tbsp extra-virgin olive oil**
- **2½ lb/1.25 kg fresh garden peas, hulled/shelled**
- **8 oz/250 g watercress, stalks removed**
- **1½ quarts/1.5 liters boiling Vegetable Stock (see page 945)**
- **3 tbsp all-purpose/ plain flour**
- **4 tbsp heavy/ double cream**
- **salt to taste**
- **½ cup/60 g freshly grated Parmesan cheese**
- **1 hard-boiled egg yolk, crumbled, to garnish**
- **croutons, to garnish**

CREAM OF SPINACH SOUP

Serves: 4
Preparation: 30'
Cooking: 1 h
Level of difficulty: 1

- 1 small onion, finely chopped
- 3 tbsp butter
- 14 oz/400 g young spinach leaves, tough stems removed and coarsely chopped
- 1 tbsp all-purpose/ plain flour
- 1 cup/250 ml milk
- 2 cups/500 ml Vegetable Stock (see page 945)
- salt to taste
- 2/3 cup/150 ml heavy/double cream
- generous 1/4 cup/ 40 g freshly grated Parmesan cheese
- 1 large egg

Sauté the onion in the butter in a large saucepan over medium heat for 3–4 minutes, or until translucent. • Add the spinach and cook for about 10 minutes, or until wilted. • Sprinkle in the flour and mix to prevent any lumps from forming. • Pour in the milk and stock. Season with salt. Simmer for about 40 minutes. • Transfer the soup to a food processor or blender and process until smooth. • Beat the cream, Parmesan, and egg in a small bowl. Add the mixture to the soup, stirring constantly, over medium heat until well blended and the soup has thickened slightly. • Serve hot.

*Vegan

Serves: 4–6

Preparation: 20'

Cooking: 30'

Level of difficulty: 2

- 2 tbsp extra-virgin olive oil
- 2 red onions, finely chopped
- 2 cloves garlic, finely sliced
- 1 fresh red chile pepper, seeded and finely chopped
- 2 medium potatoes, chopped
- 1 tsp cumin seeds, crushed
- seeds from 3 cardamom pods, crushed
- 4 black peppercorns, crushed
- 1 quart/1 liter Vegetable Stock (see page 945)
- 2 tbsp cream of coconut
- 1 tbsp finely chopped mint
- 2 tbsp finely chopped parsley
- 14 oz/400 g fresh spinach, coarsely chopped
- juice of 1 lime
- salt and freshly ground black pepper to taste
- 1 small red chile, thinly sliced

AROMATIC SPINACH PURÉE

Heat the oil in a large saucepan over medium heat. Add the onions, garlic, chile pepper (reserving some to garnish), and potatoes. sauté over low heat for 5 minutes. • Add the cumin, cardamom, and peppercorns. Cook for 5 minutes, stirring constantly. • Pour in the stock and bring to a boil. Simmer over low heat for 20 minutes. • Add the cream of coconut, mint, and parsley. Remove from the heat. Add the spinach and lime juice. Season with salt and pepper. • Process the mixture in a food processor or blender until smooth. Return the soup to the saucepan and reheat over low heat. • Ladle into soup bowls. Garnish with the reserved chile pepper and serve hot.

SHERRY MUSHROOM SOUP

Serves: 4

Preparation: 35'

Cooking: 30'

Level of difficulty: 3

- 4 tbsp butter
- 8 oz/250 g white mushrooms, cleaned and cut in small cubes
- 8 oz/250 g wild mushrooms, cleaned and finely chopped
- 2 cloves garlic, finely chopped
- 3 tbsp finely chopped parsley
- 1 cup/250 ml dry sherry
- salt and freshly ground black pepper to taste
- 1 quantity Béchamel Sauce (see page 948)
- 1⅓ cups/330 ml Vegetable Stock (see page 945)

Melt the 4 tablespoons of butter in a large saucepan over low heat. Stir in the white and wild mushrooms and cook for 10 minutes, stirring often. • Add the garlic, half the parsley, and sherry. Season with salt and pepper. • Cook for 3 minutes, then transfer half the mushrooms to a serving dish. Keep warm. • Stir the Béchamel sauce and half the vegetable stock into the mushrooms in the pan. The soup should be thick and creamy. Add more stock if it is too thick. • Cook for 3 more minutes then top with the remaining mushrooms. • Garnish with the remaining parsley and serve hot.

RICE AND PUMPKIN SOUP

P ut the pumpkin in a saucepan with the milk
and salt and cook for 10 minutes, or until the
pumpkin is tender. • Purée the pumpkin in a food
processor. • Place the purée in a heavy-bottomed
pan over very low heat and cook for about 5
minutes, stirring continuously with a wooden
spoon. Remove from heat. • In a large heavy-
bottomed pan, sauté the onion in the butter until
soft. • Add the pumpkin mixture and mix well.
• Pour the stock into the pumpkin mixture, and
when it returns to the boil, add the rice. Check the
seasoning and cook for about 15 minutes, or until
the rice is tender. • Sprinkle with the Parmesan
and serve hot.

236

Serves: 6

Preparation: 10'

Cooking: 30'

Level of difficulty: 1

- 3 lb/1.5 kg
  pumpkin, peeled,
  seeded, and cut in
  1-inch/2.5 cm
  cubes
- 2 cups/500 ml milk
- salt to taste
- 1 large onion, finely
  chopped
- 6 tbsp butter
- 1 1/2 quarts/1.5
  liters boiling
  Vegetable Stock
  (see page 945)
- 1 cup/200 g short-
  grain white rice
- 1/3 cup/45 g freshly
  grated Parmesan
  cheese

POTATO HERB SOUP

Serves: 4

Preparation: 20'

Cooking: 40'

Level of difficulty: 2

- 1 onion, finely chopped
- 2/3 cup/150 g butter
- 3 oz/90 g celery stalks, coarsely chopped
- 3 oz/90 g watercress, coarsely chopped
- 1 bunch parsley
- 1 quart/1 liter water
- salt and freshly ground black pepper to taste
- 2 lb/1 kg potatoes, peeled and cut in small cubes
- 2–4 leaves fresh basil, torn
- 4 tbsp sour cream

Sauté the onion in 6 tablespoons of butter in a large saucepan over low heat until lightly browned. • Add the celery, watercress, and parsley. Cover and cook over low heat for 5 minutes. • Pour in the water and season with salt. • Add the potatoes and cook for 30 minutes, or until the potatoes are tender. • Run through a vegetable mill or chop in a food processor until smooth. • Return to the saucepan over low heat and stir in the remaining butter. • Ladle into soup bowls and garnish with pepper, basil, and sour cream.

CARROT AND POTATO PURÉE

Sauté the onion in the oil in a large saucepan over medium heat for 5 minutes, or until tender. • Add the rosemary, leeks, carrots, salt and sauté for 5 minutes. • Add the potatoes and pour in with the vegetable stock. Cover and cook for about 20 minutes, or until all the vegetables are tender. • Discard the rosemary and process the mixture in a food processor or blender until smooth. • Season with salt and transfer to a heated serving bowl. Serve hot.

238

*Vegan

Serves: 4

Preparation: 15'

Cooking: 30'

Level of difficulty: 1

• 1 onion, finely chopped
• 3 tbsp extra-virgin olive oil
• 1 sprig rosemary
• 4 leeks, finely chopped
• 14 oz/400 g carrots, peeled and chopped
• salt to taste
• 2 large potatoes, peeled and chopped
• 1 quart/1 liter Vegetable Stock (see page 945)

SEMOLINA WHISKED IN STOCK

Mix the semolina, Pecorino, eggs, and parsley together in a bowl • Bring the stock to a boil in a large saucepan and gradually stir in the semolina mixture. • Simmer over low heat for 5–10 minutes, stirring often. • Transfer to a tureen or soup bowls and serve hot.

Serves: 4–6

Preparation: 20'

Cooking: 15'

Level of difficulty: 1

· 1²/₃ cups/250 g semolina
· 1 cup/125 g freshly grated Pecorino cheese
· 1 bunch parsley, finely chopped
· 2 eggs
· 2 quarts/2 liters Vegetable Stock (see page 945)

CREAM OF SCALLION SOUP

Serves: 4

Preparation: 20'

Cooking: 40'

Level of difficulty: 1

- 8 scallions/spring onions, very thinly sliced (reserve a few rings to garnish)
- 1 tbsp butter
- 3 cups/750 ml Vegetable Stock (see page 945)
- 1 cup/250 ml milk
- 1 tbsp cornstarch/ corn flour
- salt to taste
- ½ tsp freshly grated nutmeg
- 1 tbsp finely chopped parsley
- 4 tbsp freshly grated Parmesan cheese
- 2 egg yolks, lightly beaten

Sauté the scallions in the butter in a large saucepan over low heat until softened.
• Heat the vegetable stock and milk in separate saucepans. • Sprinkle the scallions with the cornstarch. • Gradually pour in the stock, alternating with the milk, stirring constantly.
• Season with salt and nutmeg. • Cook for 20 minutes over low heat, stirring often. • Add the parsley, Parmesan, and egg yolks, beating until just blended. • Cook for 5 minutes more and serve hot.

GREEK LEMON SOUP

Melt the butter in a large saucepan over low heat. Add the onion and cook over medium heat for 5 minutes until transparent. • Add the flour, zest of 1 lemon, stock, and milk, stirring constantly. Bring to a boil and boil for 5 minutes. • Add the lemon juice and season with salt and pepper. Let cool. • Strain the soup through a fine mesh strainer. • Ladle into serving bowls. Garnish with the yogurt and sprinkle with the remaining lemon zest. Serve at room temperature.

Serves: 4

Preparation: 15'

Cooking: 10'

Level of difficulty: 1

- 2 tbsp butter
- 1 onion, finely chopped
- 2 tbsp all-purpose/ plain flour
- zest and juice of 2 lemons
- 1 quarts/1 liter Vegetable Stock
- 2/3 cup/150 ml milk
- salt and freshly ground black pepper to taste
- 2/3 cup/150 ml plain yogurt

CHILLED YOGURT SOUP WITH CUCUMBER AND RAISINS

Serves: 4

Preparation: 25'

Level of difficulty: 1

- $^{1}/_{2}$ cup/125 ml heavy/double cream
- 2 cucumbers, peeled
- 1 quart/1 liter plain yogurt (thick Greek yogurt is ideal)
- 1 cup/250 ml ice water
- 4 leeks, white part only, very thinly sliced and separated into rings
- salt and freshly ground black pepper to taste
- 4 tbsp crushed ice cubes
- 4 tbsp golden raisins/sultanas
- 1 bunch fresh mint leaves, finely chopped

Beat the cream in a large bowl with an electric mixer at high speed until stiff. • Grate the cucumbers into a bowl (reserve a few slices to garnish), then squeeze out excess moisture. • Place the yogurt and ice water in a large bowl and stir in the cucumbers, leeks, and cream. Season with salt and pepper. • Ladle into individual bowls and place a little of the crushed ice at the center of each portion. • Garnish with the golden raisins and mint. • Serve immediately.

CREAM OF ZUCCHINI SOUP

Sauté the potatoes and onion in the butter in a large frying pan until lightly browned. • Add 1 cup (250 ml) of stock and let it reduce. • Cook the zucchini and zucchini flowers in a large saucepan with the oil and the remaining 1 cup (250 ml) stock for 10 minutes. • Season with salt and pepper. Transfer the cooked potato mixture and the zucchini mixture to a food processor or blender. Process until smooth. • Return to the saucepan and cook for 5 minutes more. • Swirl with the yogurt and garnish with the basil.
• Serve hot.

Serves: 4

Preparation: 10'

Cooking: 20'

Level of difficulty: 1

- 14 oz/400 g potatoes, peeled and finely chopped
- 1 onion, finely chopped
- 2 tbsp butter
- 2 cups/500 ml Vegetable Stock (see page 945)
- 1½ lb/750 g zucchini/ courgettes, cut in thin wheels
- 10 oz/300 g zucchini/courgette flowers, washed carefully and cut in half
- 2 tbsp extra-virgin olive oil
- salt and freshly ground black pepper to taste
- 1 tbsp plain yogurt
- fresh basil leaves, to garnish

CARROT AND CILANTRO SOUP

Sauté the onion in the oil with a pinch of salt in a large saucepan over medium heat for 5 minutes, or until tender. • Add the carrots, potatoes, celery, cilantro, parsley, and garlic. • Pour in the stock and simmer over low heat for 30 minutes, or until the carrots and potatoes are tender. • Process the mixture in a food processor or blender until smooth. • Return the soup to the saucepan and season with salt and pepper. If it is too thick, add a little water.
• Reheat over low heat. Stir in the crème fraiche.
• Ladle into soup bowls and serve hot.

The cilantro adds a sharp and tangy flavor to this rich-in-vitamin C soup.

246

Serves: 4–6

Preparation: 20'

Cooking: 35'

Level of difficulty: 2

- 1 large onion, finely chopped
- 2 tbsp extra-virgin olive oil
- salt and freshly ground black pepper to taste
- 1 lb/500 g carrots, peeled and chopped
- 3 medium potatoes, peeled and chopped
- 1 stalk celery, finely chopped
- 2–3 tbsp finely chopped fresh cilantro/coriander
- 2 tbsp finely chopped fresh parsley
- 1 clove garlic, peeled
- 1½ quarts/ 1.5 liters boiling Vegetable Stock (see page 945) or water
- 2 tbsp crème fraiche

GAZPACHO WITH YOGURT

Serves: 4

Preparation: 15' + 1 h to chill

Cooking: 5'

Level of difficulty: 1

- 1 clove garlic, finely chopped
- 1 onion, finely chopped
- 1 cup/250 g chopped tomatoes
- 1 cucumber, finely chopped
- 1 red bell pepper/ capsicum, seeded, cored, and finely chopped
- 1 green bell pepper/capsicum, seeded, cored, and finely chopped
- 2 cups/500 ml tomato juice
- 1 tbsp vinegar
- salt and freshly ground black pepper to taste
- 2 tbsp finely chopped parsley
- 2 scallions/spring onions, finely chopped
- 2 oz/60 g bread, cut into small cubes
- 1 tbsp extra-virgin olive oil
- 4 tbsp plain yogurt

Process the garlic, half the onion, half the chopped vegetables, and half the tomato juice in a food processor or blender until smooth.
• Stir in the remaining tomato juice and vinegar. Season with salt and pepper. • Add the parsley and scallions. • Refrigerate for 1 hour. • Sauté the bread in the oil in a small frying pan until golden brown and crisp all over. • Stir in the remaining chopped vegetables. • Drizzle with the yogurt and garnish with the croutons.

TOMATO AND YOGURT SOUP

B lanch the tomatoes in a large pot of salted boiling water for 1 minute. Drain, run under cold water, and peel. Chop coarsely with a knife and sieve to remove seeds. • Place the tomato in a medium saucepan over medium heat. Bring to a boil and season with salt and pepper. Add the oregano. • Stir in the yogurt until well blended, reserving 1 tablespoon to garnish. • Bring to a boil and cook over low heat for 10 minutes. • Serve in individual soup bowls, garnished with the basil and dotted with the extra yogurt. • Serve with freshly baked bread or warm toast.

Serves: 4

Preparation: 15'

Cooking: 15'

Level of difficulty: 2

- **3 lb/1,5 kg firm-ripe tomatoes**
- **salt and freshly ground black pepper to taste**
- **1 tsp dried oregano**
- **$^1/_2$ cup/125 ml plain yogurt + 2 tbsp to garnish**
- **4 leaves fresh basil, torn**

SMOOTH BEAN SOUP

Cook the beans in a large pot with enough water to cover for about 1 hour, or until tender. Season with salt. • Sauté the onion in 2 tablespoons of oil in a large saucepan until lightly browned. • Drain the beans. Add to the pan and cook for 3 minutes. • Pour in the water, partially cover, and cook for 75 minutes over medium-low heat. • Remove from heat and chop in a food processor until smooth. • Return the mixture to the saucepan and stir in the tomato concentrate. Cook for 5 minutes more. • Season with the salt and pepper and stir in the remaining oil. • Garnish with the sage and rosemary and serve hot.

Vegan

Serves: 6

Preparation: 20' + time to soak beans

Cooking: 2 h 20'

Level of difficulty: 2

- 2 lb/1 kg borlotti or red kidney beans, soaked overnight and drained
- salt and freshly ground black pepper to taste
- 1 onion, finely chopped
- 4 tbsp extra-virgin olive oil
- 3 quarts/3 liters water
- 2 tbsp tomato concentrate/puree
- fresh sage and rosemary, to garnish

COOL PEA CONSOMMÉ

Serves: 4

Preparation: 30'

Cooking: 35'

Level of difficulty: 2

- 1 scallion/spring onion, finely chopped (reserve a few rings to garnish)
- 2 tbsp extra-virgin olive oil
- 3 cups/375 g peas, hulled/shelled
- 1 quart/1 liter Vegetable Stock (see page 945)
- salt and freshly ground black pepper to taste
- ½ cup/125 ml light/single cream
- 1 tbsp cornstarch/ corn flour dissolved in 2 tbsp water
- 2 tbsp finely chopped basil

EGG CROUTONS

- 2 eggs, lightly beaten
- 6 tbsp light/single cream
- salt and freshly ground black pepper to taste

Sauté the scallion in the oil in a large saucepan over medium heat until softened. • Add the peas and pour in the stock. Season with salt and pepper. • Bring to a boil, cover, and cook for 15 minutes. • Stir in the cream and cornstarch mixture. Return to a boil and cook for 2 minutes, stirring constantly. • Add the basil and stir well. Remove from the heat and set aside. • Egg Croutons: Preheat the oven to 400°F/ 200°C/gas 6. • Butter a small square baking pan. • Beat the eggs and cream in a small bowl. Season with salt and pepper. • Pour into the prepared baking pan. • Bake for 12–15 minutes, or until set. • Cut into cubes. • Sprinkle the egg croutons into individual soup bowls and ladle over the soup. • Garnish with the reserved scallion rings and serve cold.

Refreshing and uplifting, serve this soup for brunch in the heat of summer.

PUMPKIN SOUP WITH AMARETTI

Sauté the onion in half the butter in a frying pan over low heat for 5 minutes, or until softened. • Add the pumpkin and sauté over medium heat for 3 minutes. • Pour in the stock and cook for about 15 minutes, or until the pumpkin has softened. • Transfer to a food processor or blender and process until smooth. • Pour the pumpkin cream into a large saucepan. Mix in the cream, sugar, and salt and bring to a boil. • Add the remaining butter and mix well. • Ladle into soup bowls and sprinkle with the crumbled amaretti cookies. Serve hot.

Serves: 4
Preparation: 30'
Cooking: 30'
Level of difficulty: 2

- 1 small onion, finely chopped
- 1 tbsp butter
- 1 lb/450 g pumpkin or winter squash, cleaned and diced
- 2 cups/500 ml boiling Vegetable Stock (see page 945)
- 1²/₃ cups/400 ml heavy/double cream
- 1 tsp sugar
- salt to taste
- 12 amaretti cookies, crumbled

CREAM OF MUSHROOM SOUP

Serves: 4

Preparation: 30' + 20' to soak

Cooking: 35'

Level of difficulty: 2

- ¾ oz/25 g dried porcini mushrooms
- 2 cups/500 ml warm water
- 1 onion, finely chopped
- 4 tbsp extra-virgin olive oil
- 1 lb/500 g white mushrooms, chopped
- 1 quart/1 liter Vegetable Stock (see page 945)
- 4 tbsp heavy/ double cream
- salt and freshly ground black pepper to taste
- croutons, to serve (optional)

Soak the dried porcini mushrooms in the warm water for 20 minutes. • Sauté the onion in the oil in a large frying pan over medium heat until lightly browned. • Add the mushrooms and sauté for 5 minutes. • Pour in the vegetable stock and dried mushrooms and their liquid. • Bring to a boil, then simmer for 30 minutes. • Remove from the heat and transfer to a food processor or blender. Process until smooth. • Return the mixture to the saucepan. Add the cream and season with salt and pepper. • Serve hot, with croutons, if liked.

COLD BELL PEPPER SOUP

C rumble 5 oz (150 g) of the bread into a large
bowl. Pour in the oil and add the garlic. Set
aside for 20 minutes. • Place the tomatoes,
cucumber, and bell pepper in a food processor or
blender along with the soaked bread mixture.
Process until very finely chopped. Transfer to a
large bowl. • Pour in the water and vinegar. Season
with salt and pepper. • Refrigerate for at least 2
hours, or until well chilled. • Cut the remaining
bread into cubes. • Garnish with the bread and
reserved tomatoes just before serving.

258

*Vegan

Serves: 4

Preparation: 30'+ 2 h
to chill

Level of difficulty: 1

- 6 oz/180 g day-old
  white bread
- ½ cup/125 ml
  extra-virgin olive
  oil
- 3 cloves garlic,
  peeled
- 1¾ lb/800 g firm-
  ripe tomatoes,
  peeled and cut into
  small cubes
- 1 large cucumber,
  peeled and cut into
  cubes
- 1 green bell
  pepper/capsicum,
  seeded, cored, and
  cut into cubes
  (reserve a few
  cubes to garnish)
- 1 cup/250 ml
  water
- 2 tbsp red wine
  vinegar
- salt and freshly
  ground black
  pepper to taste

FLOWER SOUP

S et aside a few flowers to garnish. Finely chop the remaining flowers. • Boil the chopped daisies in the stock for 10 minutes. • Sauté the leek in the oil in a large saucepan over medium heat for about 10 minutes, or until lightly browned. • Mix in the flower stock and mashed potato. • If the soup is too liquid, stir in enough of the flour and water mixture to thicken. • Season with salt and pepper. Cook for 10 minutes, stirring constantly. • Serve hot with the cubes of warm toast and the reserved petals of flowers.

For a pretty finish, be sure to garnish with some well-washed raw blossoms or petals.

260

*Vegan

Serves: 4

Preparation: 20'

Cooking: 25'

Level of difficulty: 1

- 4 oz/120 g edible flowers (daisies, cornflowers, mimosa, lilac, nasturtiums, pansies, roses)
- 1 quart/1 liter boiling Vegetable Stock (see page 945)
- white of 1 leek, thinly sliced
- 2 tbsp extra-virgin olive oil
- 1 large potato, boiled and mashed
- 1 tbsp all-purpose/ plain flour mixed in 3 tbsp water (optional)
- salt and freshly ground black pepper to taste
- cubes of toasted bread, to serve

GAZPACHO WITH BELL PEPPER

Serves: 4

Preparation: 20'

Level of difficulty: 1

- **2–3 thick slices day-old firm-textured bread**
- **4 tbsp extra-virgin olive oil + extra to serve**
- **2 tsp sherry wine vinegar or 1 tbsp white vinegar**
- **salt to taste**
- **6 large tomatoes, peeled and coarsely chopped**
- **1 red bell pepper/ capsicum, seeded and coarsely chopped**
- **1 large cucumber, peeled**
- **1 hard-boiled egg, shelled and coarsely chopped**
- **3 cloves garlic**
- **4 tbsp cold water (if needed)**
- **salt and freshly ground black pepper to taste**
- **croutons or squares of warm toast, to serve**

Soak the bread in the oil, vinegar, and salt for 15 minutes. • Place the tomatoes, bell pepper, cucumber, egg, garlic, and bread mixture in a food processor and chop until smooth. • If too dense, add the water. • Season with salt and pepper, drizzle with oil, and serve hot with the croutons or squares of warm toast.

RED LENTIL SOUP

Melt the butter in a large saucepan over medium heat. Sauté the onions for 8–10 minutes, or until lightly browned. • Stir in the lentils, stock, and tomato concentrate. Season with salt. • Cook for 25–30 minutes, or until the lentils are tender. • Remove from the heat and chop in a food processor until smooth. • Sprinkle with the parsley and serve with croutons on the side

Serves: 4

Preparation: 10'

Cooking: 40'

Level of difficulty: 1

- **2 tbsp butter**
- **2 medium onions, finely chopped**
- **2 cups/200 g red lentils, well-washed**
- **1 quart/1 liter Vegetable Stock (see page 945)**
- **1 tbsp tomato concentrate/puree**
- **salt to taste**
- **1 tbsp finely chopped parsley**
- **croutons, to serve**

RICE SOUP WITH EGGS AND LEMON

Serves: 6

Preparation: 15'

Cooking: 15–20'

Level of difficulty: 1

- **2 quarts/2 liters Vegetable Stock (see page 945)**
- **8 tbsp short-grain rice**
- **2 large eggs + 2 large egg yolks**
- **½ cup/125 ml fresh lemon juice**
- **salt and freshly ground white pepper to taste**

Bring the stock (reserving 1 cup/250 ml) to a boil in a large saucepan. • Add the rice. Partially cover and cook for 15–20 minutes, or until the rice is tender. • Beat the eggs, egg yolks, and lemon juice in a medium bowl until frothy. Season with salt and pepper. • Pour in the reserved stock. • Stir the egg mixture into the soup. Remove from the heat and beat until the eggs have thickened but are not scrambled. • Serve immediately.

CARROT SOUP WITH FRIED RICE

C ook the rice in a large pan of salted, boiling water for 12–15 minutes, or until tender. • Drain and spread out on a clean kitchen towel • Melt the butter in a large saucepan and sauté the onion and carrots until softened. • Pour in 1 cup (250 ml) of milk and season with salt and pepper. • Cover and cook over very low heat for 20 minutes, adding more milk if the vegetables begin to dry. • Transfer the soup to a food processor and process with the remaining milk and cream until smooth. Season with salt and nutmeg. • Heat the oil in a large frying pan and fry the rice, a little at a time, to keep the grains separate, until golden. • Drain on paper towels. • Garnish the soup with the fried rice and serve hot.

Serves: 4

Preparation: 25'

Cooking: 35–40'

Level of difficulty: 2

- **½ cup/100 g rice**
- **2 tbsp butter**
- **1 onion, finely chopped**
- **1 lb/500 g spring carrots, thinly sliced**
- **2 cups/500 ml milk**
- **salt and freshly ground black pepper to taste**
- **1 cup/250 ml heavy/double cream**
- **⅛ tsp freshly grated nutmeg**
- **2 tbsp extra-virgin olive oil**

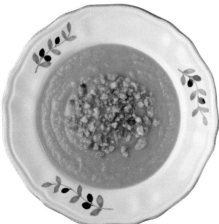

CREAM OF BARLEY SOUP

Serves: 4

Preparation: 25'

Cooking: 2 h

Level of difficulty: 1

- 1 quart/1 liter
  Vegetable Stock
  (see page 945)
- 1³/₄ cups/350 g
  pearl barley
- 1 stalk celery,
  finely chopped
- 1 cup/250 ml
  heavy/double
  cream
- salt and freshly
  ground black
  pepper to taste

Bring the stock to a boil in a large saucepan. Add the barley and celery. • Simmer over low heat for 25–30 minutes. • Remove from the heat and set aside 2 tablespoons of barley. Chop the rest in a food processor until smooth. • Heat the cream in a small saucepan to almost boiling.
• Stir in the barley purée with the reserved barley.
• Season with salt and pepper. Serve hot.

LENTIL SOUP

P lace the bulgur in a bowl and cover with cold water. Let stand for 30 minutes, or until the grains have softened. Drain well, squeezing out excess moisture. • Place the lentils in a large saucepan. Pour in enough water to cover and season with salt. Cook over medium heat for 30 minutes. • Add the bulgur wheat and cook for 30 minutes, or until the lentils and wheat are both tender. If the mixture dries out during cooking, add more hot water. Transfer to a large serving tureen. • Heat the oil in a large frying pan and sauté the onions and chile until golden brown. • Spoon the sautéed onions onto the soup. Spoon the hot tomato sauce into the center and add the yogurt. • Serve hot.

Serves: 4

Preparation: 40' + 30' to soak the bulgur

Cooking: 1 h

Level of difficulty: 1

- 1 cup/150 g bulgur wheat
- 1½ cups/150 g lentils
- salt to taste
- ½ cup/125 ml extra-virgin olive oil
- 2 large onions, finely chopped
- 1 red chile pepper, finely chopped
- 1 cup/250 ml store-bought or homemade Tomato Sauce (see page 951)
- ½ cup/125 ml plain yogurt

Serves: 6

Preparation: 15' +
time to soak beans

Cooking: 1 h 15'

Level of difficulty: 1

- 4 cups/400 g
  kidney beans
- 1⅓ cups/125 g
  green beans
- 2–3 medium
  potatoes, cubed
- 2–3 medium
  carrots, sliced
- 2–3 zucchini/
  courgettes, sliced
- 3 tomatoes, chopped
- 1 onion, chopped
- 4 quarts/4 liters
  water
- salt and freshly
  ground black
  pepper to taste
- 7 oz/200 g soup
  pasta
- ½ cup/125 ml
  Pesto (see page
  946)

MIXED VEGETABLE SOUP WITH BASIL

Soak the kidney beans in cold water for 12 hours. Drain. • Place the kidney, green beans, potatoes, carrots, zucchini, tomatoes, and onion in a large saucepan with the water. Season with salt and pepper. • Bring to a boil and cook, stirring often, over low heat for 1 hour. • Add the pasta and cook for 15 minutes more. • Spoon the pesto onto the soup. • Serve hot.

UKRAINIAN BORSCH

Place the beets, carrots, turnip, parsnip, celeriac, potato, cabbage, leeks, and onion in a large saucepan with the vegetable stock. • Bring to a boil. Cover and simmer for 35 minutes. • Stir in the tomato paste, peppercorns, bay leaf, vinegar, and sugar. • Simmer for 20 minutes, or until the vegetables are tender. • Grate in the reserved beet and cook for 5 minutes more. • Ladle into individual soup bowls and serve.

Traditionally topped with sour cream, Borsch is eaten in the cold months in Eastern Europe.

270

- 1 lb/500 g raw beets/red beet, peeled and cut in thin strips, reserving some beet to grate
- 2 carrots, cut in thin strips
- ½ medium turnip, cut in thin strips
- ½ medium parsnip, cut in thin strips
- 3½ oz/100 g celeriac or swede, cut in thin strips
- 1 potato, cut into thin strips
- 1 lb/500 g white cabbage, shredded
- whites of 2 leeks, finely chopped
- 1 red onion, finely chopped
- 2¼ quarts/2.25 liters Vegetable Stock (see page 945)
- 2 tbsp tomato paste
- 6 peppercorns
- 1 bay leaf
- 3 tbsp balsamic vinegar
- 1 tsp sugar

FAVA BEAN SOUP

B ring the water to a boil in a heavy-bottomed saucepan and add the beans. Partially cover, and simmer for about 3 hours over a low heat, stirring from time to time. Add the fennel and the chile pepper after $1^1/2$ hours. • After 2 hours, stir more frequently, crushing the beans as much as possible with a large wooden spoon. They should gradually turn into a coarse purée. Add a little boiling water if the soup becomes too thick.
• Season with salt only when the beans are cooked. • Place the toasted bread in heated soup bowls and drizzle with a little oil. Ladle the soup over the bread, drizzle with the remaining oil, and serve piping hot.

Serves: 4

Preparation: 35' + time to soak beans

Cooking: 3 h

Recipe grading: 1

- generous 1 quart/1.25 liters water
- $1^1/2$ cups/300 g dried fava beans/broad beans, soaked for 12 hours, drained and well rinsed
- small bunch of wild fennel, coarsely chopped
- $^1/2$ chile pepper, whole or crumbled, seeded
- salt to taste
- 4 slices of 2–3-day-old coarse white bread, toasted
- 4 tbsp extra-virgin olive oil

LEGHORN-STYLE MINESTRONE

Serves: 6–8

Preparation: 35' + time to soak beans

Cooking: 3 h 30'

Level of difficulty: 2

- 1 lb/500 g dried cannellini beans
- 12 oz/350 g Tuscan kale, shredded
- 1/2 cabbage, sliced
- 2 cloves garlic, finely chopped
- 2 tbsp parsley
- 2 tbsp basil
- 6 tbsp olive oil
- 1 onion, chopped
- 1 carrot, chopped
- 2 stalks celery, coarsely chopped
- 2 zucchini, chopped
- 2 potatoes, chopped
- 2 quarts/2 liters Vegetable Stock (see page 945)
- salt and pepper
- 1 1/2 cups/300 g rice
- 1/2 cup/60 g freshly grated Parmesan cheese

Soak the beans in cold water for 12 hours. Drain. • Cook the beans for 1 hour, or until tender. • Cook the Tuscan kale and cabbage in lightly salted water for 20–25 minutes. Drain, press out excess water, chop finely, and set aside. • Sauté the garlic, parsley, and basil in the oil in a large saucepan for 5 minutes. • Add the onion, carrot, celery, zucchini, potatoes, beans and their cooking liquid, Tuscan kale, and cabbage, stirring well. • Pour in the vegetable stock. Season with salt and pepper. • Cover and simmer over low heat for 2 1/2 hours. • Add the rice and cook for 20 minutes more. • Sprinkle with the Parmesan and serve hot.

MILLET AND WALNUT SOUP

Preheat the oven to 400°F/200°C/gas 6. •
Roast the walnuts on a baking sheet for 15
minutes. Rub off the outer skins. • Sauté the onion
and cabbage in the oil in a large saucepan over
medium heat for 5 minutes, or until softened.
• Add the millet, shelled walnuts, shoyu, and salt.
Pour in the water and cover the pan. • Cook for
30 minutes, stirring occasionally. • Serve in
individual soup bowls, sprinkled with the parsley.

274

Vegan

Serves: 4

Preparation: 30'

Cooking: 50'

Level of difficulty: 2

- ½ cup/60 g
  walnuts
- 1 small onion,
  finely chopped
- ¼ Savoy cabbage,
  finely shredded
- 4 tbsp extra-virgin
  olive oil
- 2 cups/400 g
  millet, washed
  and drained
- 2 tbsp shoyu (sweet
  soy sauce)
- ⅛ tsp salt
- 1¼ quarts/1.25
  liters water
- 1 tbsp finely
  chopped parsley

SPICED LENTIL SOUP

Sauté half the onion in 3 tablespoons of oil in a large saucepan over medium heat for 2–3 minutes, or until softened. • Add the cumin, coriander, red pepper flakes, and garlic and mix well. Cook for 2 minutes. • Add the lentils, carrot, and celery leaves, reserving a few to garnish.
• Pour in the stock and cook for 35–40 minutes, or until the lentils have broken down. • Add the lemon juice and season with salt and pepper. If the soup becomes too thick, add a little water to thin it. • Sauté the remaining onion in the remaining oil in a small frying pan for 5–10 minutes, or until very tender and golden brown. • Ladle the soup into serving bowls and garnish with the onions and reserved celery leaves.

Vegan

Serves: 4–6

Preparation: 20'

Cooking: 50–55'

Level of difficulty: 1

- 2 large onions, finely chopped
- 5 tbsp extra-virgin olive oil
- 1 tsp ground cumin seeds
- 1 tsp ground coriander
- ½ tsp red pepper flakes
- 3 cloves garlic, finely chopped
- 3¾ cups/375 g split red lentils
- 1 carrot, peeled and coarsely grated
- leaves from 1 head celery, coarsely chopped
- 2 quarts/2 liters Vegetable Stock (see page 945)
- juice of 1 lemon
- salt and freshly ground black pepper to taste
- celery leaves, to garnish

MIXED GREENS SOUP

Sauté the leek and wild fennel in half the oil in a large saucepan until softened. • Add the mixed greens and cover and cook for about 10 minutes. • Add the beans and water. Season with salt and pepper. Cover and cook for about 30 minutes over low heat. • Place the toast in individual soup bowls and pour the soup over the top. • Drizzle with the remaining oil, sprinkle with the Parmesan, and serve.

Serves: 4

Preparation: 20'

Cooking: 40'

Level of difficulty: 1

- **1 leek, thinly sliced**
- **3 stalks fresh wild fennel**
- **6 tbsp extra-virgin olive oil**
- **8 oz/250 g mixed greens (turnip, spinach, kale, or Swiss chard), shredded**
- **one 14-oz/400-g can cannellini beans**
- **2 cups/500 ml Vegetable Stock (see page 945)**
- **salt and freshly ground black pepper to taste**
- **6 large slices firm-textured bread, toasted**
- **$1/2$ cup/60 g freshly grated Parmesan cheese**

BAKED SOUP WITH PECORINO CHEESE

Serves: 6

Preparation: 5'

Cooking: 20'

Level of difficulty: 1

- 4 oz/125 g Pecorino cheese, thinly sliced
- 12 slices toasted bread
- 2 quarts/2 liters Vegetable Stock (see page 945)
- salt and freshly ground black pepper to taste

Preheat the oven to 400°F/200°C/gas 6. • Arrange alternating layers of Pecorino and toast in a large ovenproof baking dish. Finish with a layer of cheese. Season with salt and pepper • Pour the hot stock over top and bake for about 20 minutes. • Serve hot.

PANCOTTO WITH VEGETABLES

Soak the kidney beans in a large pot of cold water for 12 hours. • Drain and refill with fresh water. Add the salt and bring to a boil. • Simmer over low heat for 50–60 minutes, or until the beans have softened. • Sauté the onions in 4 tablespoons of oil in a large saucepan over medium heat for about 5 minutes, or until golden. • Add the potatoes, cabbage, tomatoes, and wild fennel. Cover and cook over medium heat for 10 minutes. • Pour in enough water to cover the vegetables. • Season with salt and cook for 20 minutes. • Add the beans and cook for 10 minutes more. • Cut the bread into small pieces and place in a large serving dish. • Pour the soup over the top and let it soak into the bread for 5 minutes. The bread should absorb the liquid but remain firm. • Drizzle with the remaining oil and serve hot.

Vegan

Serves: 4

Preparation: 40' + 12 h to soak

Cooking: 85–95'

Level of difficulty: 2

- 2 cups/200 g dried red kidney beans
- 1/4 tsp salt
- 4 onions, finely chopped
- 1/2 cup/125 ml extra-virgin olive oil
- 1 lb/500 g potatoes, cut into large chunks
- 1 Savoy cabbage, weighing about 1 lb/500 g, coarsely chopped and heart removed
- 6 firm-ripe tomatoes, coarsely chopped
- 2 sprigs dried wild fennel
- 2 cups/500 ml water + more as needed
- 6 slices day-old bread

MISO SOUP WITH FENNEL

*Vegan

Serves: 4–6

Preparation: 5'

Cooking: 25'

Level of difficulty: 1

- 14 oz/400 g fennel, thinly sliced
- 2 leeks, sliced
- 2 medium potatoes, peeled and cubed
- 1 large carrot, peeled and cut into thin batons
- 2 tbsp oil
- 1-inch/3-cm piece ginger, peeled and finely sliced
- 1 clove garlic, sliced
- ½ fresh green chile pepper, seeded and finely chopped
- 1 small fresh red chile pepper, seeded and chopped
- 1 tsp fennel seeds
- salt to taste
- 1½ quarts/1.5 liters water
- 3 tbsp miso
- 4 oz/125 g watercress, coarsely chopped
- 2 tbsp lemon juice
- 2 tbsp sugar

Sauté the fennel, leeks, potatoes, and carrot in the oil in a large saucepan over low heat for 2 minutes. • Add the ginger, garlic, chile peppers, and fennel seeds. Season with salt and sauté for 5 minutes. • Pour in the water and bring to a boil. Add the miso and simmer over low heat for 15 minutes, or until the vegetables are tender. • Add the watercress, lemon juice, and sugar and simmer for 3 minutes. • Serve hot.

LENTIL SOUP

Place the beans in a large saucepan with water. Cook for 30 minutes. Add the lentils and cook for 25–30 minutes more, or until the beans and lentils are tender. • Sauté the onion and caraway seeds in the oil in a large saucepan over medium heat until lightly browned. Season with salt and pepper. • Add the beans, lentils, and rice and cook for 12–15 minutes, or until the rice is tender. • Serve hot.

*Vegan

Serves: 4

Preparation: 25' + time to soak beans

Cooking: 1 h 20'

Level of difficulty: 2

- 1 cup/200 g dried black beans, soaked overnight and drained
- 1 cup/200 g dried garbanzo beans/ chick peas, soaked overnight and drained
- 1 cup/200 g lentils
- 2 quarts/2 liters water
- 1 small onion, finely chopped
- ½ tsp caraway seeds
- 4 tbsp extra-virgin olive oil
- salt and freshly ground black pepper to taste
- 1 cup/200 g rice

PORCINI MUSHROOM SOUP

Vegan

Serves: 4

Preparation: 20'

Cooking: 25'

Level of difficulty: 1

- 1¼ lb/600 g porcini mushrooms
- 2 cloves garlic, finely chopped
- 2 tbsp finely chopped parsley
- 3 tbsp extra-virgin olive oil
- ¾ cup/180 ml dry white wine
- 2 cups/500 ml water or Vegetable Stock (see page 945)
- 1 tsp dried calamint or thyme
- salt and freshly ground black pepper to taste
- 4 large slices firm-textured bread, toasted

Trim the mushrooms and rinse carefully under cold running water. Dry well and chop coarsely. • Sauté the garlic and parsley in the oil in a large frying pan until the garlic is pale gold. • Add the mushrooms and cook over high heat for 3–4 minutes. • Pour in the wine and cook until evaporated. • Lower the heat to medium and pour in the water. Season with the thyme, salt, and pepper and cook until the mushrooms are tender. Place a slice of toast in each serving bowl and pour the soup over the top. Serve hot.

FAVA BEAN SOUP

Serves: 4

Preparation: 10' +
time to soak beans

Cooking: 1 h 45'

Level of difficulty: 2

- 3½ cups/350 g
  dried fava/broad
  beans, soaked
  overnight and
  drained
- 1 onion, finely
  chopped
- 1 stalk celery,
  finely chopped
- 1 carrot, finely
  chopped
- 2 tbsp finely
  chopped marjoram
- 4 tbsp extra-virgin
  olive oil
- ¾ cup/200 g
  chopped tomatoes
- salt and freshly
  ground black
  pepper to taste
- 1 cup/250 ml
  boiling water
- ½ cup/50 g fresh
  fava/broad beans
- 4 slices day-old
  firm-textured
  bread, toasted

Cook the dried beans in salted, boiling water for 1 hour, or until tender. • Drain and set aside. • Sauté the onion, celery, carrot, and marjoram in the oil in a large saucepan over low heat until the vegetables have softened. • Add the tomatoes and cook over medium heat for 15 minutes. • Season with salt and pepper. Add the beans and pour in the water. • Bring to a boil and add the fresh beans. Simmer over low heat for 10–15 minutes, stirring often. • Place a slice of toast in each of 4 soup bowls. Ladle the soup over the top and serve hot.

BOILING VEGETABLE STOCK WITH EGG

Beat the eggs with a dash of salt and the nutmeg. Add the Parmesan and beat until smooth. • Pour the egg mixture into the boiling stock. Beat with a fork for 3–4 minutes over medium heat until the egg begins to cook and has formed lots of tiny lumps. • Serve immediately, with extra Parmesan to pass around separately.

288

- **5 eggs**
- **salt to taste**
- **¼ tsp grated nutmeg**
- **4–8 tbsp freshly grated Parmesan cheese + extra to serve**
- **1½ quarts/1.5 liters boiling Vegetable Stock (see page 945)**

YOGURT SOUP

- 2 quarts/2 liters Vegetable Stock (see page 945)
- 1 cup/200 g short-grain rice
- salt to taste
- ²/₃ cup/150 g butter
- ¾ cup/125 g all-purpose/plain flour
- 2 cups/500 ml plain yogurt
- 1 tbsp finely chopped mint
- 1 tbsp sweet paprika
- 1–2 tbsp extra-virgin olive oil

Reserve 1 cup (250 ml) of stock and bring the rest to a boil in a large saucepan. • Add the rice and season with salt. • Melt the butter in a small saucepan over low heat. Add the flour and stir until combined. • Pour in the reserved stock and bring to a boil. Stir the flour mixture into the rice and cook for 8–10 minutes more, or until the rice is tender. • Beat the yogurt and mint in a medium serving bowl until well blended. • Stir the paprika into the oil and drizzle over the soup.

• Transfer to a tureen or soup bowls and serve hot.

289

VEGETABLE SOUP WITH BEANS

If using dried beans, place in a large pan of cold water and soak for 12 hours. Drain well. • Blanch the tomatoes in boiling water for 30 seconds. Use a slotted spoon to remove them from the water. Slip off the skins and chop them coarsely. • Sauté the onion and celery in the oil in a large saucepan until softened. • Add the vegetables and beans and pour in the water. Bring to a boil. • Partially cover and cook for 20–30 minutes (for fresh beans) or 1 1/2 hours (for dried beans). • About 15 minutes before the soup is cooked, add the rice. Stir well and cook until tender. • Finely chop the garlic, parsley, and basil and add to the soup. • Transfer to a tureen or soup bowls and serve hot.

290

*Vegan

Serves: 6–8

Preparation: 20'

Cooking: 1 h 50'

Level of difficulty: 2

- 5 oz/150 g fresh hulled/shelled borlotti or red kidney beans or 1 cup/100 g borlotti or red kidney beans
- 7 oz/200 g firm-ripe plum tomatoes
- 1 large onion, finely chopped
- 3 1/2 oz/100 g celery, diced
- 4 tbsp extra-virgin olive oil
- 12 oz/350 g potatoes, peeled and diced
- 7 oz/200 g carrots, diced
- 5 oz/150 g zucchini/courgettes, diced
- 4 oz/100 g green beans, topped and tailed and diced
- 1 1/2 quarts/1.5 liters cold water
- 1 cup/200 g short-grain rice
- 1 clove garlic
- 1 bunch parsley
- 1 sprig basil

SPELT AND VEGETABLE SOUP

*Vegan

Serves: 6–8

Preparation: 30' +
time to soak beans

Cooking: 2 h 15'

Level of difficulty: 2

- 2 cups/200 g
  cannellini or white
  kidney beans,
  soaked overnight
  and drained
- 4 cloves garlic, 2
  lightly crushed, 2
  finely chopped
- 4 leaves fresh sage
- salt and freshly
  ground black
  pepper to taste
- 6 tbsp extra-virgin
  olive oil
- 1 onion, finely
  chopped
- 1 stalk celery,
  finely chopped
- 1 carrot, finely
  chopped
- 2 quarts/2 liters
  Vegetable Stock
  (see page 945)
- 6 tomatoes, peeled
  and finely chopped
- 8 oz/250 g fresh or
  frozen peas
- 2½ cups/250 g
  spelt

Place the beans, lightly crushed garlic, and sage in a large pot with enough water to cover. Bring to a boil and simmer for about 1 hour, or until the beans are tender. • Discard the garlic and sage and season with salt. • Drain the beans, reserving the cooking liquid. Place half the beans in a food processor and chop until smooth. •

Spelt is an ancient wheat with a rich nutty taste.

293

Sauté the chopped garlic in 4 tablespoons of oil in a large saucepan over medium heat for 2 minutes. Add the onion, celery, and carrot and sauté until softened. • Pour in the stock and add the tomatoes. Season with salt and pepper. Cover and simmer over medium heat for 30 minutes. • Add the spelt and cook for 20 minutes. • Stir in the peas, bean puree and reserved whole beans and cooking liquid. Simmer for 20 minutes more. • Drizzle with the remaining oil and serve hot.

LENTIL AND VEGETABLE SOUP

*Vegan

Serves: 4	
Preparation: 20'	
Cooking: 35–40'	
Level of difficulty: 1	

- 1 onion, finely chopped
- 2 cloves garlic, finely chopped
- 4 tbsp extra-virgin olive oil
- 5 cups/500 g Puy or green lentils
- 1 large firm-ripe tomato, peeled and coarsely chopped
- salt and freshly ground black pepper to taste
- 1 vegetable bouillon cube
- 1½ quarts/1.5 liters water
- 2 potatoes, diced
- 2 large carrots, diced

Sauté the onion and garlic in the oil in an earthenware pan over medium heat for 5 minutes until the garlic is pale gold. • Stir in the lentils and tomato. Season with salt and pepper and crumble in the bouillon cube. • Pour in the water and bring to a boil. Cover and simmer for 15 minutes. • Add the potatoes and

Tasty and nourishing, this hearty soup is ideal winter fare.

carrots and cook for about 15 minutes, or until the vegetables are tender. • Serve with pita bread.

SOUPS

CABBAGE AND LEEK SOUP

Preheat the oven to 375°F/190°C/gas 5. • Sauté the cabbage and leeks in the butter in a large saucepan over medium heat for 5 minutes. • Pour in the stock and bring to a boil. Cover and simmer over low heat for 20 minutes. • Toast the bread on an oiled baking sheet in the oven for 5–10 minutes, or until browned all over. • Ladle the soup into serving bowls and garnish with the croutons. • Serve hot.

296

Serves: 4
Preparation: 10'
Cooking: 30–35'
Level of difficulty: 1

- 1 lb/500 g Savoy cabbage, finely shredded
- whites of 3 leeks, thinly sliced
- 2 tbsp butter
- 2 cups/500 ml Vegetable Stock (see page 945)
- 2 slices whole-wheat or rye bread, cut into small cubes

WINTER VEGETABLE AND PASTA SOUP

Serves: 6

Preparation: 5'

Cooking: 30'

Level of difficulty: 1

- 1¼ quarts/1.25 liters Vegetable Stock (see page 945)
- 1 leek, thinly sliced
- 5 oz/150 g carrot, coarsely chopped
- 4 oz/125 g celery, coarsely chopped
- 8 oz/250 g cauliflower florets
- 8 oz/250 g tagliolini pasta
- 2 tbsp soy sauce
- salt and freshly ground black pepper to taste
- yolks of 4 hard boiled eggs, crumbled

Bring the stock to a boil in a large saucepan over medium heat. • Add the leek, carrot, celery, and cauliflower and simmer for 20 minutes. • Add the pasta and cook until al dente. • Stir in the soy sauce and season with salt and pepper. • Ladle into soup bowls and garnish with the crumbled egg yolk. • Serve hot.

*Vegan

Serves: 4–6

Preparation: 20' +
time to soak beans

Cooking: 1 h 10'

Level of difficulty: 1

- ½ cup/50 g garbanzo beans/ chick peas (reserve the cooking liquid)
- ½ cup/50 g dried borlotti beans
- ½ cup/50 g dried cannellini beans
- ½ cup/50 g lentils
- ½ cup/50 g spelt or pearl barley
- 1 onion, 1 carrot, 1 stalk celery, 4 leaves basil, 1 sprig parsley, and 1 leaf sage, finely chopped
- ½ cup/125 ml extra-virgin olive oil
- 1 cup/250 g peeled and chopped tomatoes
- 1 quart/1 liter Vegetable Stock (see page 945)
- salt and freshly ground black pepper to taste
- 10 oz/300 g croutons

BEAN SOUP WITH CROUTONS

Soak the garbanzo, borlotti, and cannellini beans in cold water for 12 hours. • Drain well and cook for about 1 hour, or until the beans are all tender. Drain. • Cook the lentils in a pan of salted, boiling water for about 30 minutes, or until tender. Drain and set aside. • Cook the spelt in a pan of salted, boiling water for the time indicated on the package, or until tender. Drain and set aside. • Sauté the onion, carrot, celery, parsley, and sage in the oil in a large frying pan over medium heat for 5 minutes, or until the onion is translucent. Season with salt and pepper. • Add the tomatoes, beans, lentils, spelt, and vegetable stock, and cook for 5–10 minutes. • Garnish with the croutons and serve hot.

SPINACH SOUP WITH GARBANZO BEANS

C ook the spinach with the water just clinging to the leaves in a large saucepan over medium heat for 3 minutes, or until wilted. • Remove from the heat and drain, squeezing with a fork to remove the excess moisture. Chop coarsely and set aside. • Fry the bread in 4 tablespoons of oil in a frying pan over medium heat for 5 minutes until crisp and golden. • Add the garlic, pine nuts, cumin, chile pepper, and oregano. Sauté for 2 minutes. • Transfer the mixture to a food processor or blender with the vinegar and water and chop until smooth. • Heat the remaining oil in a large frying pan over medium heat. Add the spinach and sauté for 2 minutes. Add the bread mixture, paprika, and the garbanzo beans. Cook over low heat for 5 minutes until all the ingredients are heated through. • Season with salt and pepper and serve hot.

Vegan

Serves: 6

Preparation: 30'

Cooking: 15'

Level of difficulty: 2

- 2 lb/1 kg spinach, tough stems removed
- 1 slice white bread, crusts removed and cut into small cubes
- 6 tbsp extra-virgin olive oil
- 3 cloves garlic, finely sliced
- 2 tbsp pine nuts
- 1 tsp cumin seeds, crushed
- 1 red chile pepper, seeded and finely sliced
- 1 tbsp finely chopped oregano
- 2 tbsp red wine vinegar
- 2 tbsp water
- 1 1/2 tsp sweet paprika
- 2 cups/400 g canned garbanzo beans/chick peas, rinsed and drained
- salt and freshly ground black pepper to taste

Serves: 4

Preparation: 30'

Cooking: 1 h

Level of difficulty: 1

- **5 tbsp extra-virgin olive oil**
- **2 onions, thinly sliced**
- **2 ½ cups/300 g fresh or frozen peas**
- **1¾ cups/200 g freshly hulled fava/broad beans**
- **1 medium carrot, sliced**
- **1 stalk celery, thinly sliced**
- **1 crumbled dried chile pepper**
- **12 oz/300 g trimmed young Swiss chard or spinach leaves, washed and shredded**
- **10 oz/300 g firm-ripe tomatoes, skinned and chopped**
- **1½ quarts/1.5 liters boiling water**
- **4 large fresh eggs**
- **freshly ground black pepper**
- **½ cup/60 g freshly grated parmesan or pecorino cheese**
- **4 slices firm-textured white bread, 2 days old**
- **1 clove garlic**

TUSCAN SOUP

Pour the oil into a large, heavy-bottomed saucepan. Add the onions, peas, fava beans, carrot, celery, chile pepper, and a dash of salt. • Sauté for about 10 minutes until tender and lightly browned. • Add the chard or spinach and the tomatoes and simmer for 15 minutes. • Pour in the boiling water and leave to simmer gently for 40 minutes, adding more salt if necessary. • Using a fork or balloon whisk, beat the eggs with salt, pepper, and the grated parmesan. • Toast the bread and when golden brown, rub both sides of each slice with the garlic. • Place a slice in each soup bowl or in individual straight-sided earthenware dishes, pour a quarter of the beaten egg mixture over each serving. Give the soup a final stir and then ladle into the bowls. • Serve immediately.

PASTA

PENNE WITH ASPARAGUS AND RICOTTA

Serves: 4–6

Preparation: 20'

Cooking: 15'

Level of difficulty: 1

- **2 bunches asparagus stalks**
- **1 onion, finely sliced**
- **1 tbsp extra-virgin olive oil**
- **2 tbsp water**
- **⅔ cup/150 g Ricotta cheese**
- **1 lb/500 g penne**
- **2 eggs, lightly beaten**
- **salt and freshly ground black pepper to taste**

Cook the asparagus in a large pot of salted, boiling water until tender. • Remove with a slotted spoon and set aside. • Cook the pasta in the boiling asparagus water until al dente. • Meanwhile, cook the onion with the oil and water in a small saucepan over medium heat for 5 minutes, or until softened. • Stir in the Ricotta. •

Asparagus is a good source of vitamin E and folate. It also has phytochemicals believed to prevent cancer.

Drain the pasta and return to the pan it was cooked in over low heat. • Stir in the beaten eggs and season with salt and pepper. Add the Ricotta mixture and asparagus. • Toss well and serve hot.

CAVATELLI WITH BEANS AND WHEAT

Cook the beans in a large pot of salted, boiling water with 1 clove of garlic, celery, and the coarsely chopped tomatoes until tender, about 1 hour. • Stir in 2 tablespoons of oil and set aside. • Cook the pearl barley in 3 cups (750 ml) salted water for 25–30 minutes, or until tender. Drain and set aside. • Finely chop the remaining clove of garlic. Sauté the basil and garlic in the remaining oil in a large frying pan until the garlic is pale gold. • Stir in the canned tomatoes and cook for about 20 minutes, or until the tomatoes have reduced. • Cook the pasta in a large pot of salted, boiling water until al dente. • Drain and add to the pan with the sauce. Mix in the beans and wheat. • Sprinkle with the Parmesan and serve hot.

Serves: 6–8

Preparation: 20'

Cooking: 1 h 40'

Level of difficulty: 2

- 2 cups/250 g dried beans, soaked overnight and drained
- 2 cloves garlic
- 1 stalk celery, finely chopped
- 2 firm-ripe tomatoes, coarsely chopped
- 1 cup/180 g pearl barley
- 4 tbsp extra-virgin olive oil
- 4 leaves fresh basil, torn
- 1 cup/250 g chopped tomatoes
- 1 lb/500 g cavatelli
- salt to taste
- ½ cup/60 g freshly grated Parmesan cheese

BAKED FUSILLI WITH CHEESE

Cook the pasta in a large pot of salted, boiling water until al dente. • Drain, reserving 4 tablespoons of the cooking water. • Preheat the oven to 350°F/180°C/gas 4. • Butter an ovenproof baking dish. • Mix the cream, the reserved cooking water, and eggs in a large bowl. Add the crumbled Feta, Gruyère, and flour. Season with salt and nutmeg. • Arrange the pasta in the prepared dish and pour in the egg mixture. Sprinkle with the Parmesan. • Bake for 30–35 minutes, or until golden. • Serve hot.

Serves: 4–6

Preparation: 20'

Cooking: 45–50'

Level of difficulty: 1

- 1 lb/500 g fusilli
- 1½ cups/375 ml heavy/double cream
- 3 eggs
- 12 oz/350 g Feta cheese, crumbled
- 1 cup/125 g freshly grated Gruyère cheese
- 3 tbsp all-purpose/ plain flour
- salt to taste
- ⅛ tsp freshly grated nutmeg
- ½ cup/60 g freshly grated Parmesan cheese

PENNE WITH GOAT'S CHEESE

Serves: 4–6

Preparation: 20'

Cooking: 20'

Level of difficulty: 1

- 1 lb/500 g penne
- 1 clove garlic, finely chopped
- 4 tbsp extra-virgin olive oil
- 1 1/2 lb/750 g cherry tomatoes, cut in half
- 12 black olives, pitted
- 1 tbsp capers in salt, rinsed of salt
- salt and freshly ground black pepper to taste
- 1 cup/250 g fresh, creamy goat's cheese (Caprino)
- 10 leaves fresh basil, torn

Cook the pasta in a large pot of salted, boiling water until al dente. • Sauté the garlic in the oil in a large frying pan over medium heat until pale gold. • Add the tomatoes, olives, and capers. Season with salt. Cook over high heat for 5 minutes, stirring often. • Drain the pasta, reserving 2 tablespoons of the cooking water. • Mix the Caprino with the reserved cooking water. Season with pepper. • Add the pasta to the pan with the tomatoes, stir in the goat's cheese, and basil, and toss gently. • Serve hot.

FARFALLINE WITH GRILLED VEGETABLES

Serves: 4–6

Preparation: 15'

Cooking: 20'

Level of difficulty: 1

- 8 oz/250 g zucchini/courgettes
- 1 eggplant/aubergine
- 10 oz/300 g cherry tomatoes
- 2 oz/60 g baby corn cobs
- 1 lb/500 g farfalline or tripolini
- 8 oz/250 g Mozzarella cheese, cut into small cubes
- 1–2 tbsp finely chopped mint, to garnish
- salt and freshly ground black pepper to taste
- 4 tbsp extra-virgin olive oil

Slice the zucchini and eggplant lengthwise into $1/4$-inch (5-mm) slices. • Place on a grill pan and grill for about 8 minutes, or until tender. • Cut into thin strips. • Blanch the tomatoes in boiling water for 1 minute. Slip off the skins. Chop coarsely. • Blanch the baby corn cobs in salted, boiling water for 1 minute. Drain and set aside. • Cook the pasta in a large pot of salted, boiling water until al dente. • Drain well and toss with the vegetables, Mozzarella, and mint. Season with salt and pepper and drizzle with the oil. Garnish with the mint. • Serve hot or at room temperature.

Grill the vegetables on an outdoor barbecue during the summer for extra flavor.

PENNE WITH BELL PEPPERS, EGGPLANT, AND ZUCCHINI

Cook the pasta in a large pot of salted, boiling water until al dente. • Drain and run under cold running water. Drain thoroughly and dry in a clean cloth. Place in a large serving bowl and toss with 2 tablespoons of oil. • Turn on the broiler (grill) and broil the bell peppers, turning them often, until the skins are blackened. Wrap in a brown paper bag or foil for 10 minutes. Take out of the bag or foil and remove the skins. Rinse carefully and dry well.
• Arrange the eggplants and zucchini in a grill pan and grill for about 8 minutes, or until tender.
• Chop all the vegetables coarsely. • Toss the pasta with the vegetables in a large salad bowl. Add the basil, mint, garlic, and ginger. Season with salt and pepper and drizzle with the remaining oil.
• Mix and let stand for 2 hours before serving.

*Vegan

Serves: 4–6

Preparation: 45' + 2 h to stand

Cooking: 30'

Level of difficulty: 2

- 1 lb/500 g penne
- 8 oz/250 g red bell peppers/ capsicums, seeded, cored, and quartered
- 8 oz/250 g eggplants/ aubergines, thinly sliced
- 8 oz/250 g zucchini/ courgettes, thinly sliced
- 4 leaves fresh basil, torn
- 1 tbsp finely chopped mint
- 1 clove garlic, finely chopped
- ½ tsp finely grated ginger
- salt and freshly ground black pepper to taste
- 6 tbsp extra-virgin olive oil

FARFALLE WITH BELL PEPPERS

Serves 4–6
Preparation: 35'
Cooking: 35'
Level of difficulty: 2

Turn on the broiler (grill) and broil the bell peppers, turning them often, until the skins are blackened. Wrap in a brown paper bag or foil for 10 minutes. Take out of the bag or foil and remove the skins. Rinse carefully and dry well. Cut into thin strips. • Cook the pasta in a large pot of salted boiling water until al dente. • Mix the Mozzarella, cherry tomatoes, garlic, capers, lemon zest, basil, and mint in a large serving bowl. Drizzle with the oil and season with salt and pepper. • Drain the pasta and add to the serving bowl. • Toss well and serve.

- 2 bell peppers/capsicums (1 red and 1 yellow), seeded, cored, and halved
- 1 lb/500 g farfalle
- 10 oz/300 g baby Mozzarellas, diced
- 7 oz/200 g cherry tomatoes, halved
- 1 clove garlic, finely chopped
- 2 tbsp salt-cured capers, rinsed
- grated zest of 1 lemon
- 2 sprigs each basil and mint, torn
- 6 tbsp extra-virgin olive oil
- salt and freshly ground black pepper to taste

316

Serves: 4–6	
Preparation: 15'	
Cooking: 20'	
Level of difficulty: 1	

- 1 medium onion, finely chopped
- 4 tbsp extra-virgin olive oil
- 1 lb/500 g coarsely chopped canned tomatoes
- salt and freshly ground black pepper to taste
- 3 oz/90 g almonds
- 4 thick slices day-old firm-textured bread, cut in cubes
- 1 lb/500 g bucatini
- 3/4 cup/75 g freshly grated Pecorino cheese

BUCATINI WITH ALMONDS

Sweat the onion in a frying pan with 1 tablespoon of oil for 10 minutes. • Add the tomatoes and season with salt and pepper. Cover and cook over low heat for 20–25 minutes. • Toast the almonds in a small frying pan over low heat. Remove from heat and chop coarsely. • Sauté the bread in a frying pan with the remaining oil until crisp and brown. • Cook the bucatini in plenty of salted, boiling water until al dente. Drain and transfer to a heated serving bowl. Pour the sauce over the top. Sprinkle with the almonds, bread, and Pecorino. Serve hot.

BAKED MACARONI CHEESE WITH PEAS

Serves: 6

Preparation: 30'

Cooking: 40'

Level of difficulty: 2

- 1 quantity Béchamel Sauce (see page 948)
- ¼ cup/30 g dried mushrooms, soaked in warm water and finely chopped (optional)

- 1 lb/500 g macaroni
- 6 tbsp butter
- 1¼ cups/150 g freshly grated Parmesan cheese
- 7 oz/200 g Mozzarella cheese, sliced
- 1⅓ cups/125 g frozen peas, thawed
- 4 tbsp milk
- 2 tbsp fine dry bread crumbs

Prepare the Béchamel sauce. • Mix in the mushrooms with their soaking liquid, if using. • Cook the pasta in a large pot of salted, boiling water until not quite al dente. • Drain and toss with 4 tablespoons of butter, 2 tablespoons of Parmesan, and one-third of the Béchamel. • Preheat the oven to 400°F/ 200°C/gas 6. • Butter a large baking dish. • Spoon half the pasta into the prepared baking dish and sprinkle with half the remaining Parmesan. • Top with the Mozzarella and peas. Cover with half the remaining Béchamel. Spoon the remaining pasta into the dish, sprinkle with the remaining Parmesan, and pour the remaining Béchamel over the top. • Drizzle with the milk, dot with the remaining butter and sprinkle with the bread crumbs. • Bake for 15–20 minutes, or until golden brown. • Remove from the oven and let rest for 10 minutes before serving.

BAKED MACARONI WITH BELL PEPPERS

Turn on the broiler (grill) and broil the bell peppers, turning them often, until the skins are blackened. Wrap in a brown paper bag or foil for 10 minutes. Take out of the bag or foil and remove the skins. Rinse carefully and dry well. Cut into thin strips. • Cook the pasta in a large pot of salted boiling water until not quite al dente. • Sauté 1 clove of garlic in the oil in a large frying pan over medium heat until pale gold. Remove from the heat. • Finely chop the remaining garlic and add to the pan with the capers, olives, bell peppers, parsley, and bread crumbs. Season with salt and pepper. Cook over low heat for 10 minutes, stirring occasionally. Add the oregano and remove from the heat. • Preheat the oven to 425°F/220°C/gas 7. • Butter a baking dish. • Drain the pasta and add to half the bell pepper mixture. • Spoon the pasta into the prepared baking dish. • Cover with the remaining bell pepper mixture and sprinkle with the Parmesan. • Bake for about 15 minutes, or until lightly browned and crisp on top. • Serve hot.

Serves: 4–6

Preparation: 35'

Cooking: 45'

Level of difficulty: 1

- 1½ lb/750 g red and yellow bell peppers/ capsicums, halved and seeded
- 1 lb/500 g macaroni or other tube pasta
- 2 cloves garlic, lightly crushed but whole
- 4 tbsp extra-virgin olive oil
- ¼ cup/50 g salt-cured capers, rinsed
- ½ cup/50 g black olives, pitted and coarsely chopped
- 2 tbsp finely chopped parsley
- 2 tbsp fine dry bread crumbs
- salt and freshly ground black pepper to taste
- 1 tbsp finely chopped oregano
- 1¼ cups/150 g freshly grated Parmesan cheese

SPAGHETTI WITH TOMATOES AND MOZZARELLA

Serves: 4–6

Preparation: 10'

Cooking: 15'

Level of difficulty: 1

- 1 lb/500 g spaghetti
- 1 lb/500 g cherry tomatoes, cut in half
- 7 oz/200 g Mozzarella cheese, cut into small cubes
- 2 tbsp finely chopped basil
- 1 tbsp finely chopped mint
- 1 clove garlic, finely chopped
- 6 tbsp extra-virgin olive oil
- salt and freshly ground black pepper to taste
- fresh basil leaves, to garnish

Cook the pasta in a large pot of salted, boiling water until al dente. • Drain and toss with the tomatoes, Mozzarella, basil, mint, garlic, and oil in a large bowl. Season with salt and pepper. • Transfer to serving dishes and garnish with the basil leaves. • Serve hot.

LINGUINE WITH PUMPKIN AND OLIVES

Preheat the oven to 400°F/200°C/gas 6. • Place the pumpkin on an ovenproof dish and roast for about 30 minutes, or until soft. Let cool slightly. Chop coarsely. • Sauté the onion in 2 tablespoons of oil in a large frying pan over medium heat for 5 minutes. • Add the pumpkin and sauté for 5–10 minutes, or until the pumpkin has broken down. • Season with salt and pepper and add the olives. • Cook the pasta in a large pot of salted, boiling water until al dente. • Drain, reserving 4 tablespoons of the cooking water. • Add the pasta and the reserved cooking water to the pan with the sauce. Toss gently and transfer to a serving dish. • Sprinkle with the pine nuts and drizzle with the remaining oil. • Serve hot.

Substitute the pumpkin with other squash for a variation on the color and presentation

324

*Vegan

Serves: 4–6	
Preparation: 10'	
Cooking: 25–30'	
Level of difficulty: 1	

- 1 lb/500 g pumpkin, peeled, seeded, and thinly sliced
- 1 onion, finely chopped
- 4 tbsp extra-virgin olive oil
- salt and freshly ground black pepper to taste
- scant 1 cup/80 g pitted and chopped black olives
- 1 lb/500 g linguine pasta
- ¼ cup/45 g pine nuts, chopped

SPINACH GNOCCHI WITH CHEESE SAUCE

Serves: 4–6	
Preparation: 50'	
Cooking: 50'	
Level of difficulty: 2	

- 3 large floury potatoes, peeled
- 1½ lb/750 g spinach, stems removed
- 1 cup/150 g all-purpose/plain flour
- 1 large egg yolk
- salt and freshly ground black pepper to taste
- generous 1½ cups/ 200 g freshly grated Taleggio or Fontina cheese
- ½ cup/125 ml milk
- 6 tbsp butter
- 6 leaves fresh sage
- 1 tbsp extra-virgin olive oil

Cook the potatoes in a large pot of salted, boiling water for about 20 minutes, or until tender. • Drain and mash in a large bowl. Let cool. • Cook the spinach in a large saucepan over low heat for 5 minutes, or until tender. Drain, squeezing out the excess water. • Process the spinach in a food processor or blender until puréed. • Mix the spinach purée into the potatoes. • Stir in the flour, egg yolk, and salt to make a smooth dough. • Flour your hands and shape the dough into "sausages" about ⅔ inch (1.5 cm) in diameter. Cut into ¾-inch (2-cm) lengths. Dust with flour to prevent them from sticking. • Melt the Taleggio or Fontina with the milk in a small saucepan over low heat, stirring constantly, for 5 minutes, to make a smooth cream. • Melt the butter with the sage in a small saucepan over medium heat for about 2 minutes, or until the butter begins to brown. • Cook the gnocchi in small batches in a large pot of salted boiling water with the oil for about 3 minutes, or until they bob to the surface. • Remove with a slotted spoon and transfer to a serving dish with the cheese sauce. Drizzle with the sage butter and season with salt and pepper. • Serve hot.

PASTA SHELLS WITH PEAS AND GREEN BEANS

Cook the pasta in a large pot of salted, boiling water for 5 minutes. • Add the green beans and peas. Cook for 5–7 minutes, or until the vegetables are tender and the pasta is al dente. • Drain and transfer to a serving dish. • Add the tomatoes, Pecorino, oil, marjoram, salt, and pepper. Toss well and serve hot.

Serves: 4–6

Preparation: 5'

Cooking: 15'

Level of difficulty: 1

- 1 lb/500 g large pasta shells
- 8 oz/250 g green beans, coarsely chopped
- 1 cup/125 g shelled peas
- 8 oz/250 g tomatoes, peeled, seeded, and coarsely chopped
- 1¼ cups/150 g freshly grated Pecorino cheese
- 3 tbsp extra-virgin olive oil
- 1 sprig marjoram, finely chopped
- salt and freshly ground black pepper to taste

HOMEMADE BASIL PASTA WITH TOMATOES AND OLIVES

Serves: 4

Preparation: 40' + 30'
  to rest the dough

Cooking: 10'

Level of difficulty: 2

- 1 bunch basil, torn
- 4 tbsp extra-virgin olive oil
- 1²/₃ cups/250 g all-purpose/plain flour
- 2 large eggs
- salt and freshly ground black pepper to taste
- 1 lb/500 g cherry tomatoes, halved
- 1 clove garlic, finely chopped
- 1 cup/100 g black olives, pitted

Process the basil with 1 tablespoon of oil in a food processor or blender until smooth. • Sift the flour into a bowl. Mix in the eggs, 1 tablespoon of the basil purée, and a pinch of salt to make a stiff dough. • Knead until smooth and elastic, 15–20 minutes. • Cover and let rest for 30 minutes. • Roll the dough out very thinly on a floured surface. Cut into ¹/₂-inch (1-cm) ribbons. • Sauté the tomatoes and garlic in the remaining oil in a large frying pan over medium heat for 5 minutes. • Cook the pasta in a large pot of salted, boiling water until al dente, about 3–4 minutes. • Drain and add to the pan with the sauce. Season with salt and pepper and add the olives. Toss carefully. • Transfer to a serving dish. Drizzle with the remaining oil and serve.

TORTIGLIONI WITH ZUCCHINI AND SAFFRON

Dredge the zucchini in the flour until well coated. • Heat the frying oil in a frying pan until very hot and fry the zucchini in small batches for about 5 minutes, or until crisp and golden. • Use a slotted spoon to remove them and drain on paper towels. Season with salt and keep warm in a warming oven. • Place the bread in a plastic bag and use a meat tenderizer to turn into coarse crumbs. • Sauté the garlic in the olive oil in a large frying pan over medium heat until pale gold. • Add the cherry tomatoes and sauté for 5 minutes. • Add the saffron, bread crumbs, and mint. Season with salt and cook over high heat for 1 minute. • Meanwhile, cook the pasta in a large pot of salted, boiling water until al dente. • Drain and add to the pan with the sauce. Sprinkle with the Parmesan, toss well, and serve hot.

Expensive and exotic, 225,000 stigmas from crocuses are needed to produce 1 lb (500 g) of saffron

332

Serves: 4–6
Preparation: 20'
Cooking: 25'
Level of difficulty: 2

- **14 oz/400 g zucchini/courgettes, cut into julienne sticks**
- **2 tbsp all-purpose/plain flour**
- **1 cup/250 ml olive oil, for frying**
- **salt to taste**
- **2 oz/60 g day-old bread, crusts removed**
- **1 clove garlic, lightly crushed but whole**
- **4 tbsp extra-virgin olive oil**
- **8 oz/250 g cherry tomatoes**
- **2 sachets saffron strands, crumbled**
- **1 sprig mint, finely chopped**
- **1 lb/500 g tortiglioni**
- **½ cup/60 g freshly grated Parmesan cheese**

TORTELLI WITH HERB SAUCE AND PINE NUTS

Serves: 6

Preparation: 15'

Cooking: 15'

Level of difficulty: 1

- 1 large bunch fresh mint
- 1 large bunch fresh basil
- 2 cloves garlic
- 1 cup/125 g freshly grated Parmesan cheese
- 6 tbsp extra-virgin olive oil
- 1 lb/500 g store-bought cheese-filled tortelli
- ½ cup/90 g pine nuts

Process the mint, basil, garlic, Parmesan, 5 tablespoons of oil, and salt in a food processor or blender until smooth. • Cook the pasta in a large pot of salted, boiling water until al dente. • Toast the pine nuts in a nonstick frying pan for 1 minute. • Drain the pasta and place in a heated serving bowl. Add the herb sauce, sprinkle with the pine nuts, and toss well. • Serve hot.

PASTA AND BEANS WITH CHERRY TOMATOES

Sauté the garlic in 4 tablespoons of oil in a frying pan until pale gold. Discard the garlic. • Add the tomatoes and sauté over high heat for 5 minutes. • Pour in the wine and cook until evaporated. • Cook the pasta in a large pot of salted, boiling water until not quite al dente. • Drain the beans and rinse under cold running water. Add to the tomatoes in the pan. • Drain the pasta and transfer to the pan with the beans. • Add the water and cook over high heat for 5 minutes, tossing continuously. Season with pepper and drizzle with the oil. • Garnish with the basil and serve hot.

Vegan

Serves: 4

Preparation: 20'

Cooking: 20'

Level of difficulty: 2

- 1 clove garlic, lightly crushed but whole
- 6 tbsp extra-virgin olive oil
- 12 oz/350 g cherry tomatoes, cut in quarters
- 4 tbsp dry white wine
- 10 oz/300 g small soup pasta
- 2 cups/250 g canned borlotti beans
- 1/2 cup/125 ml hot water
- salt and freshly ground black pepper to taste
- 1 sprig fresh basil, torn

FARFALLE WITH YOGURT SAUCE AND AVOCADO

Serves: 4–6

Preparation: 30'

Cooking: 20'

Level of difficulty: 1

- 2 cloves garlic, finely chopped
- 1 large onion, chopped
- 4 tbsp extra-virgin olive oil
- 1 tbsp dry white wine
- 1 lb/500 g farfalle
- 1 ripe avocado
- juice of 1 lemon
- 1 cup/250 ml plain yogurt
- salt and freshly ground black pepper to taste
- 1 red hot chile pepper, thinly sliced
- 1 celery heart, thinly sliced
- 1½ tbsp salt-cured capers, rinsed
- 1 tbsp finely chopped parsley

Sauté the garlic and onion in 2 tablespoons of oil in a frying pan over medium heat until the garlic is pale gold. • Add the wine and cook until evaporated. • Cook the pasta in a large pot of salted, boiling water until al dente. • Peel, pit, and dice the avocado. Drizzle with the lemon juice to prevent it from browning. • Beat the yogurt with the remaining oil in a large bowl. Season with salt and pepper. Add the chile pepper, celery, capers, and parsley. • Drain the pasta and toss in the yogurt sauce. Add the onion and avocado, toss again, and serve.

PASTA SHELLS WITH HERB CHEESE

Preheat the oven to 400°F/200°C/gas 6. • Cook the pasta in a large pot of salted, boiling water until not quite al dente. • Drain well and let dry on a kitchen towel. • Mix the Ricotta, mixed herbs, and oil in a large bowl. Season with salt and pepper.
• Spoon the mixture into the pasta shells. • Blanch the Swiss chard in salted boiling water for 1 minute. • Drain and chop finely. • Cook the chard in a large frying pan with the cream, 1 tablespoon of butter, and a pinch of salt until the cream begins to bubble.
• Spoon the mixture into an ovenproof dish. Arrange the filled pasta shells on top of the greens, dot with the remaining butter, and sprinkle with the Parmesan. • Bake for 10 minutes, or until the pasta and filling is beginning to brown. • Serve hot.

Serves:	4
Preparation:	30'
Cooking:	20'
Level of difficulty:	2

- **24 large pasta shells**
- **2 cups/500 g Ricotta cheese**
- **2 tbsp finely chopped mixed parsley, marjoram, and thyme**
- **1 tbsp extra-virgin olive oil**
- **salt and freshly ground black pepper to taste**
- **7 oz/200 g Swiss chard or spinach**
- **½ cup/125 g light/single cream**
- **2 tbsp butter**
- **1 cup/125 g freshly grated Parmesan cheese**

SPAGHETTI WITH VEGETABLE SAUCE

Serves: 4–6

Preparation: 20'

Cooking: 50'

Level of difficulty: 3

- 1 lb/500 g tomatoes, diced
- 1 eggplant/ aubergine, diced
- 1 yellow bell pepper/ capsicums, seeded, cored, and cut into strips
- 1 clove garlic, finely chopped
- 12 black olives, pitted
- 1 tbsp salt-cured capers, rinsed
- 1 handful fresh basil, torn
- 4 tbsp extra-virgin olive oil
- salt to taste
- 1 lb/500 g spaghetti
- ½ cup/60 g freshly grated Pecorino cheese

Sauté the tomatoes, eggplant, bell pepper, garlic, olives, capers, and basil in the oil in a large frying pan over medium heat for 5 minutes.
• Season with salt and cook over low heat for about 30 minutes, or until the vegetables have softened, stirring often. • Cook the spaghetti in a large pot of salted, boiling water until al dente.
• Add 4 tablespoons of the pasta cooking water to the vegetables. • Drain the pasta and add to the pan with the sauce. • Sprinkle with the Pecorino, toss gently, and serve hot.

343

PASTA

PENNE WITH TOFU

Cook the tofu in a saucepan of boiling water for 4 minutes. • Drain and process in a food processor or blender with the basil, parsley, almonds, oil, garlic, and salt until smooth.
• Cook the pasta in a large pot of salted, boiling water until al dente. • Drain and toss gently with the sauce.
• Serve hot.

344

Produced from dried soybeans, tofu is rich in protein, iron, and calcium

*Vegan*Vegan*

Serves: 4–6

Preparation: 15'

Cooking: 20'

Level of difficulty: 1

- 5 oz/150 g tofu (bean curd)
- 1 small bunch basil
- 1 small bunch parsley
- 1/3 cup/50 g blanched almonds
- 6 tbsp extra-virgin olive oil
- 2 cloves garlic
- salt to taste
- 1 lb/500 g whole-wheat penne

SPAGHETTI WITH CUCUMBER SAUCE

Vegan

Serves: 4–6

Preparation: 15'

Cooking: 20'

Level of difficulty: 1

- 1 onion, finely chopped
- 1 clove garlic, finely chopped
- 2 tbsp extra-virgin olive oil
- 4 medium cucumbers, sliced
- 4 tbsp dry white wine
- 2 tsp soy sauce
- 1 tbsp balsamic vinegar
- 1½ tsp sweet paprika
- salt and freshly ground white pepper to taste
- 1 lb/500 g spaghetti
- 4 large lettuce leaves

Sauté the onion and garlic in the oil in a large frying pan over medium heat until the garlic is pale gold. • Add the cucumbers and pour in the wine. Cook for 3–5 minutes, stirring constantly. • Add the soy sauce, balsamic vinegar, and 1 teaspoon of paprika. Season with salt and pepper. • Transfer the mixture to a food processor or blender and process until thick and smooth. • Cook the pasta in a large pot of salted, boiling water until al dente. • Drain well. • Arrange the lettuce on a large serving dish. Place the spaghetti on top of the lettuce. • Spoon the sauce into the center and sprinkle with the remaining paprika.

FARFALLE WITH BELL PEPPERS AND MUSHROOMS

S auté the bell peppers in 3 tablespoons of oil in a large frying pan over low heat for about 10 minutes, or until softened. • Add the tomatoes and season with salt. • Sauté the mushrooms in the remaining oil in a medium frying pan over medium heat for about 10 minutes, or until softened. • Add them to the bell pepper mixture. Cook over low heat for 5 minutes. • Stir in the cream, mix well, and remove from the heat. • Cook the pasta in a large pot of salted, boiling water until al dente. • Drain and add to the pan with the sauce. • Sprinkle with the Parmesan, toss gently, and garnish with the basil. • Serve hot.

Serves: 4–6	
Preparation: 30'	
Cooking: 30'	
Level of difficulty: 1	

- 1 yellow bell pepper/ capsicum, thinly sliced
- 1 red bell pepper/ capsicum, sliced
- 4 tbsp extra-virgin olive oil
- 4 tomatoes, peeled and coarsely chopped
- salt to taste
- 10 oz/300 g mushrooms, finely sliced
- ¾ cup/180 ml heavy/double cream
- 1 lb/500 g farfalle
- ½ cup/60 g freshly grated Parmesan cheese
- fresh basil leaves, to garnish

SPAGHETTI WITH ROSE AND SUNFLOWER PETALS

Serves: 4–6

Preparation: 20'

Cooking: 30'

Level of difficulty: 1

- **2 cloves garlic, finely chopped**
- **4 tbsp extra-virgin olive oil**
- **1½ cups/375 g chopped tomatoes**
- **petals from 1 sunflower, coarsely chopped (leave a few whole, to garnish)**
- **petals from 1 rose, coarsely chopped (leave a few whole, to garnish)**
- **1 small bunch basil, torn**
- **salt and freshly ground black pepper to taste**
- **4 tbsp dry white wine**
- **1 lb/500 g spaghetti**
- **½ cup/60 g freshly grated Parmesan cheese**
- **fresh basil leaves, to garnish**

Sauté the garlic in the oil in a large frying pan over medium heat until pale gold. • Stir in the tomatoes, chopped sunflower and rose petals, and basil. Season with salt and pepper. • Cook for 15 minutes, adding the wine as the mixture starts to dry out. • Meanwhile, cook the pasta in a large pot of salted boiling water until al dente. • Drain and add to the pan with the sauce. Sprinkle with the Parmesan and garnish with the basil and the reserved flower petals.
• Toss gently and serve hot.

Wash the petals gently but thoroughly before use.

WHOLE-WHEAT PENNE WITH WALNUTS

S auté the leeks in the oil in a large frying pan over medium heat for about 10 minutes, or until lightly browned. • Drain the mushrooms, reserving the water, and chop them finely. • Add the mushrooms to the leeks and cook for 5 minutes. • Pour in the mushroom water and cook until evaporated. • Stir in the cream and cook until it thickens slightly. Season with salt and pepper. • Meanwhile, cook the pasta in a large pot of salted, boiling water until al dente. • Drain and add to the pan with the sauce with the walnuts and chervil. • Toss gently and serve hot.

Serves:	4–6
Preparation:	25'
Cooking:	30'
Level of difficulty:	1

- whites of 2 leeks, cut in half lengthwise and thinly sliced
- 2 tbsp extra-virgin olive oil
- 2 tbsp dried mushrooms, soaked in warm water for 15 minutes
- ²⁄₃ cup/150 ml heavy/double cream
- salt and freshly ground black pepper to taste
- 1 lb/500 g whole-wheat/wholemeal penne
- 30 walnuts, shelled and chopped
- 1 tbsp finely chopped chervil

LUMACONI WITH BELL PEPPERS

*Vegan

Serves: 4–6

Preparation: 20'

Cooking: 30'

Level of difficulty: 1

- 1 medium onion, cut into rings
- 4 tbsp extra-virgin olive oil
- 1 red bell pepper/ capsicum, seeded, cored, and cut into thin strips
- 1 yellow bell pepper, seeded, cored, and cut into thin strips
- 1 lb/500 g lumaconi
- 1 tbsp finely chopped parsley
- 1 tbsp finely chopped mint
- 1 tbsp finely chopped basil
- salt and freshly ground black pepper to taste

Sauté the onion in the oil in a large frying pan over medium heat for 5 minutes, or until lightly browned. • Add the bell peppers and sauté for about 10 minutes, or until softened. • Meanwhile, cook the pasta in a large pot of salted, boiling water until al dente. • Drain and add to the pan with the sauce. • Add the parsley, mint, and basil. Season with salt and pepper. • Toss gently and serve immediately.

GRAPEFRUIT WITH PASTA AND CORN

Cut the grapefruit in half and remove the flesh. Wrap the empty skins in plastic wrap and refrigerate until ready to use. • Mix the corn, grapefruit flesh, oil, and mayonnaise in a large bowl. Season with salt and pepper. • Cook the pasta in a large pot of salted, boiling water until al dente. • Drain and run under cold running water. Drain well and dry on a clean cloth. • Add to the filling and toss gently. Add the basil. • Refrigerate for 1 hour. • Fill the empty grapefruit skins with the pasta mixture. • Garnish with the mint leaves and serve.

356

Serves: 4

Preparation: 25' + 1 h to chill

Cooking: 15'

Level of difficulty: 1

- **4 pink grapefruit**
- **1 cup/125 g canned corn/ sweetcorn**
- **2 tbsp extra-virgin olive oil**
- **1 tbsp mayonnaise**
- **salt and freshly ground white pepper to taste**
- **14 oz/400 g ditalini pasta**
- **1 bunch fresh basil, torn**
- **6 leaves fresh mint**

TAGLIOLINI WITH BEANS AND BROCCOLI

*Vegan

Serves: 4–6

Preparation: 30' + time to soak beans

Cooking: 30'

Level of difficulty: 1

- 10 oz/300 g dried beans, soaked overnight and drained
- salt to taste
- 1 bay leaf
- 10 tomatoes
- 2 cloves garlic
- 4 celery leaves
- 1 lb/500 g broccoli florets
- 1 lb/500 g tagliolini pasta
- 4 tbsp extra-virgin olive oil

Place the beans with salt, bay leaf, 1 tomato, 1 clove garlic, and half the celery leaves in a large pot with enough water to cover. Bring to a boil and simmer over medium heat for 50 minutes, or until tender. Drain, discarding the bay leaf and vegetables. • Cook the broccoli in a large pot of salted, boiling water until crunchy-tender. • Remove the broccoli with a slotted spoon and set aside. • Add the pasta to the broccoli cooking water and cook until al dente. • Sauté the remaining clove of garlic in the oil in a large frying pan until pale gold. • Chop the tomatoes and add to the pan. Season with salt and cook for about 10 minutes.• Drain the pasta well and fry a ladleful in 1 tablespoon of oil until crispy. Set aside. • Toss the remaining pasta with the broccoli and beans. • Remove from the heat. • Add the pasta, broccoli, and beans to the pan with the tomatoes and toss well. • Garnish with the fried pasta and serve hot.

PASTA WITH RICOTTA AND ARUGULA

C ook the pasta in a large pot of salted, boiling water until al dente. • Drain and run under cold running water. Drain well and dry on a clean cloth. • Transfer to a large serving bowl with the oil, garlic, tomatoes, olives, fresh Ricotta, and arugula. Toss well. • Sprinkle with the Ricotta Salata and refrigerate for 1 hour.

Serves: 4–6

Preparation: 10' + 1 h to chill

Cooking: 15'

Level of difficulty: 1

- 1 lb/500 g fusilli
- 6 tbsp extra-virgin olive oil
- 3 cloves garlic, finely chopped
- 6 ripe tomatoes, seeded and diced
- ½ cup/60 g black olives, pitted
- 1½ cups/375 g Ricotta cheese
- 2 oz/60 g arugula/ rocket, coarsely chopped
- 2 oz/60 g Ricotta Salata cheese, in flakes

FARFALLE WITH RADICCHIO AND GOAT'S CHEESE

Serves: 4–6

Preparation: 15'

Cooking: 15'

Level of difficulty: 1

- 1 onion, thinly sliced
- 7 tbsp extra-virgin olive oil
- 1 large head (or 2 small) red radicchio, cut in strips
- salt and freshly ground black pepper to taste
- 4 tbsp light beer
- ½ cup/125 g soft fresh Caprino or other goat cheese
- 2 tbsp milk
- 1 lb/500 g farfalle

Sauté the onion in 3 tablespoons of oil in a large frying pan until softened. • Add the radicchio and season with salt and pepper. Cook for 5 minutes. Pour in the beer and cook until evaporated. • Mix in the Caprino, softening the mixture with the milk. • Cook the pasta in a large pot of salted, boiling salted water until al dente. • Drain well and add to the pan with the sauce. • Toss for a few minutes, drizzle with the remaining oil, and serve.

PASTA SURPRISE

Cook the garbanzo beans in a large pot of boiling water for about 1 hour, or until tender. Drain and set aside. • Cook the lentils in a large pot of boiling water for about 30 minutes, or until tender. Drain and set aside. • Sauce: Sauté the onion and garlic in the oil in a large frying pan over medium heat for 5 minutes, or until the garlic is pale gold. • Stir in the tomatoes, red pepper flakes, and season with salt and pepper. Cook for 5 minutes. • Cook the rice in a large pot of salted boiling water for 12–15 minutes, or until tender. Drain. • Cook the two types of pasta separately in large pots of salted boiling water until al dente. Drain. • Heat the oil in a large frying pan until very hot. • Dip the onion rings in the egg, followed by the flour. • Fry the rings in small batches for 4–5 minutes, or until golden and crisp. • Layer the rice, pasta, garbanzo beans, and lentils on a serving dish. Drizzle with the sauce and arrange the onion rings around the edge of the plate. • Serve hot.

Serves: 8

Preparation: 45'

Cooking: 1 h 30'

Level of difficulty: 2

- 2 cups/250 g dried garbanzo beans/chickpeas, soaked overnight and drained
- 2 cups/200 g lentils

SAUCE

- 1 onion, finely chopped
- 1 clove garlic, finely chopped
- 2 tbsp extra-virgin olive oil
- ¾ cup/180 g peeled plum tomatoes, chopped
- ⅛ tsp red pepper flakes
- salt and freshly ground black pepper to taste

- 2 cups/400 g rice
- 10 oz/300 g small soup pasta
- 10 oz/300 g macaroni
- 2 tbsp extra-virgin olive oil
- 2 large onions, sliced into rings
- 2 large eggs, lightly beaten
- ⅓ cup/50 g all-purpose/plain flour

VEGETARIAN LASAGNA

Place the eggplant in a colander and sprinkle with salt. Let stand for 1 hour. • Blanch the lasagne sheets following the instructions on the package. Lay the sheets out in a single layer on a clean cloth. • Preheat the oven to 350°F/180°C/gas 4. • Butter a baking dish. • Sauté the garlic in the oil in a large frying pan over medium heat until pale gold. • Add the eggplant and sauté for 10 minutes. • Stir in the tomato sauce and basil. Cook for 5 minutes. • Spread two tablespoons of tomato sauce on the bottom of the prepared dish. Place the first layer of lasagna on top and cover with the sauce, low-fat Ricotta, and Ricotta Salata. Dot with the butter. • Cover with aluminum foil and bake for 30 minutes. • Remove the foil and bake for 10–15 minutes more. • Let stand for 10 minutes before serving.

364

Serves: 6

Preparation: 30' + 1 h to degorge eggplants

Cooking: 1 h

Level of difficulty: 2

- 1 eggplant/aubergine, coarsely chopped
- 1 tbsp coarse salt
- 1 lb/500 g store-bought lasagna sheets
- 1 clove garlic, finely chopped
- 6 tbsp extra-virgin olive oil
- 1 quantity Tomato Sauce (see page 951), make Spicy version, if liked
- 4 leaves fresh basil, torn
- 1¾ cups/400 g low-fat Ricotta cheese
- ½ cup/60 g freshly grated Ricotta Salata cheese
- 4 tbsp butter, cut into flakes

GRAINS

DATE AND ALMOND RICE

Bring 3 cups (750 ml) milk to a boil in a medium saucepan. • Add the rice and boil for 2 minutes, stirring constantly. • Lower the heat and cook, covered, for 15–20 minutes, or until the rice is tender. • Melt 4 tablespoons of butter in a medium frying pan over medium heat. Sauté the almonds for 4–5 minutes, or until the almonds are golden. • Add the raisins, dates, and sugar. Sauté for 5 minutes more. • Stir in the remaining milk and simmer for 15 minutes, or until the dates are plump and the milk has been absorbed. Season with salt. • Heat 1 tablespoon butter in a large Dutch oven or saucepan over low heat and spoon in half the rice. Cover with the date mixture and top with the remaining rice. • Dot with the butter and cover with a tight-fitting lid. • Cook over very low heat for 25–30 minutes, or until the rice is fluffy.

Serves: 4–6

Preparation: 15'

Cooking: 1 h 15'

Level of difficulty: 1

- 1 quart/1 liter milk
- 2½ cups/500 g Basmati rice
- ½ cup/125 g butter, cut up
- 1 cup/150 g blanched almonds, halved
- ½ cup/90 g raisins
- ½ cup/125 g dates
- 4 tbsp sugar

RISOTTO WITH TURNIPS AND TALEGGIO

Serves: 4

Preparation: 20'

Cooking: 30'

Level of difficulty: 2

- **1 small onion, finely chopped**
- **7 oz/200 g turnips, peeled and finely chopped**
- **2 tbsp butter**
- **1 tbsp extra-virgin olive oil**
- **1¹/₂ cups/300 g Italian risotto rice**
- **4 tbsp dry white wine**
- **3 cups/750 ml Vegetable Stock (see page 945)**
- **salt and freshly ground black pepper to taste**
- **5 oz/150 g Taleggio cheese, diced**

Sauté the onion and turnip in the butter and oil in a large frying pan for 10 minutes, or until softened. • Add the rice and cook for 2 minutes, stirring constantly. • Stir in the wine and when this has been absorbed, begin stirring in the stock, ¹/₂ cup (125 ml) at a time. • Add more stock and cook and stir until each addition has been absorbed, until the rice is tender, about 15–20 minutes. • Season with salt and pepper. Add the Taleggio and serve hot.

GREEN PAELLA

*Vegan

Serves: 4

Preparation: 20'

Cooking: 40'

Level of difficulty: 2

Wash the spinach and cook with just the water left clinging to its leaves for 5–7 minutes, or until wilted. • Drain, squeezing out any excess moisture. Chop coarsely. • Sauté the onions and garlic in the oil in a large frying pan over medium heat until the garlic is pale gold. • Add the pine nuts and chile and cook for 2 minutes. • Lower the heat and add the tomatoes and bell pepper. Cook for 6 minutes, stirring constantly. • Add the rice and sauté for 2 minutes. Season with salt and pepper. • Add the paprika, saffron water, and enough stock to cover the rice by about 1 inch (2.5 cm). Bring to a boil and simmer for about 15 minutes, or until the rice is tender and almost all the liquid has evaporated. Stir occasionally during the cooking time to prevent the rice from sticking to the pan. • Add the spinach and peas and mix well. Cook for 5 minutes, or until the peas are cooked. • Remove from the heat, cover, and let rest for 5 minutes. • Garnish with the peppers and serve.

Invest in a special paella pan to achieve the best results for this and a host of other paella recipes.

370

- 1 lb/500 g spinach
- 2 onions, sliced
- 3 cloves garlic, finely chopped
- 6 tbsp extra-virgin olive oil
- 2 tbsp pine nuts
- 1 dried red chile pepper, crumbled
- 8 oz/250 g tomatoes, peeled and chopped
- 1 large green bell pepper/capsicum, seeded, cored, and sliced
- 1¼ cups/250 g Italian risotto rice
- salt and freshly ground black pepper to taste
- 1 tsp sweet paprika
- ½ tsp saffron strands, soaked in boiling water for 15 minutes
- 2¾ cups/700 ml Vegetable Stock (see page 945)
- ¾ cup/90 g peas
- 7 oz/200 g Spanish piquillo peppers, sliced (optional)

SPICED RICE WITH TOFU

Serves: 4–6

Preparation: 20'

Cooking: 40'

Level of difficulty: 2

- 1/2 cup/125 g butter
- 2 1/4 cups/250 g Basmati rice
- 1/2 tsp saffron
- 3 cloves
- 1/2 stick cinnamon
- 3 cups/750 ml water
- salt to taste
- 1 onion, chopped
- 2 tbsp oil
- seeds from 4 cardamom pods
- 3 black peppercorns
- 1/2 tsp cumin seeds, crushed
- 1/2 green bell pepper, seeded, cored, and finely sliced
- 8 oz/250 g tofu, cut into small cubes
- 2 tbsp golden raisins/sultanas
- 2 tbsp chopped almonds
- 1 tbsp cashew nuts, halved (optional)
- 1 tbsp pistachios

Melt the butter in a large saucepan over medium heat. Add the rice and sauté for 2 minutes. • Add the saffron, cloves, and cinnamon. Pour in the water and season with salt. Cover and bring to a boil. Simmer over low heat for 20 minutes, stirring occasionally, until the rice has absorbed all the liquid. • Sauté the onion in the oil in a large frying pan over low heat until softened. • Add the cardamom, pepper corns, and cumin and cook for 30 seconds. • Add the bell pepper. Cook for 5 minutes. • Add the tofu, raisins, almonds, cashew nuts, and pistachios. Cook for 5 minutes more. • Add this mixture to the rice and mix well. Cover and let rest for 5 minutes. • Serve hot.

SPELT WITH EGGPLANT AND HERBS

C ook the spelt in a large pot of salted boiling water for 25 minutes. • Drain and let cool under cold running water. • Slice the eggplant into 12 thin slices. Place in a grill pan and grill for about 4 minutes on each side, or until tender. • Cut the lemon zest into very thin strips and mix half the zest with the spelt. • Add the herbs, garlic, oil, lemon juice, and chile powder. • Arrange the eggplant slices on a serving dish. Spoon the spelt into the center. Garnish with the remaining lemon zest and serve.

374

Vegan

Serves: 4

Preparation: 40'

Cooking: 35'

Level of difficulty: 1

- 1 cup/200 g quick-cooking spelt, rinsed
- 1 large eggplant/ aubergine
- zest and juice of ½ lemon
- 2 sprigs each of parsley, thyme, basil, and marjoram, finely chopped
- 1 clove garlic, finely chopped
- 4 tbsp extra-virgin olive oil
- ⅛ tsp chile powder

RICE WITH COCONUT MILK

S auté the onion, garlic, cloves, cinnamon, and garam masala in the ghee in a wok or large frying pan over medium heat until aromatic. • Add the rice. Season with salt. Cook for 3 minutes. • Pour in the coconut milk and cover and cook over low heat for 12–15 minutes, or until the rice is tender and all the liquid has been absorbed. • Remove and discard the cloves and serve hot.

Serves: 4

Preparation: 15'

Cooking: 25'

Level of difficulty: 1

- 1 tbsp finely chopped onion
- 1 clove garlic, finely chopped
- 5 cloves
- ½ stick cinnamon
- 1–2 tsp garam masala
- 2 tbsp ghee (clarified butter)
- 2 cups/400 g short-grain rice
- salt to taste
- 1 quart/1 liter coconut milk

RICE WITH YELLOW LENTILS

*Vegan

Serves: 4

Preparation: 25' + 2 h
  to soak

Cooking: 20'

Level of difficulty: 1

- 1 cup/200 g yellow
  lentils
- 1 large onion, finely
  chopped
- 1 tsp cumin seeds
- 5 tbsp extra-virgin
  olive oil
- 1 cup/200 g
  Basmati rice
- 4 cloves
- 1 stick cinnamon
- salt to taste
- 2½ cups/625 ml
  water

Soak the lentils for 2 hours in cold water.
• Drain and cook in salted, boiling water for 25 minutes. Drain and set aside. • Sauté the onion and cumin in the oil in a large frying pan over medium heat for 10 minutes, or until softened and golden. • Add the lentils, rice, cloves, and cinnamon. Season with salt. Pour in the water and bring to a boil. Cover and simmer over low heat for 10 minutes, or until the water has been absorbed and the rice is tender. • Serve hot.

BELL PEPPERS WITH MUSHROOM COUSCOUS

Preheat the oven to 400°F/200°C/gas 6. • Cut the bell peppers in half and remove the seeds and core. • Prepare the couscous according to the instructions on the package. • Sauté the mushrooms in the oil in a large frying pan over medium heat for 3 minutes. • Add the garlic, tomatoes, scallions, mint, and cilantro. Cook over low heat for 5 minutes. • Add the couscous and cook for 3 minutes. • Drizzle with the lemon juice and season with salt and pepper. Mix well and spoon the mixture into the bell peppers. Cover with aluminum foil and bake for 25–30 minutes, or until the bell peppers are tender. • Mix the yogurt and parsley in a small bowl. • Remove the bell peppers from the oven and garnish with the cilantro.
• Serve with the yogurt.

378

Serves:	4
Preparation:	15'
Cooking:	40'
Level of difficulty:	1

- 3 large red bell peppers/ capsicums
- 1 cup/150 g precooked couscous
- 7 oz/200 g mushrooms, coarsely chopped
- 4 tbsp extra-virgin olive oil
- 1 clove garlic, finely chopped
- 10 cherry tomatoes
- 6 scallions/spring onions, finely chopped
- 1 tbsp finely chopped mint
- 2 tbsp finely chopped cilantro/ coriander
- juice of ½ lemon
- salt and freshly ground black pepper to taste
- ¾ cup/180 ml plain yogurt
- 2 tbsp finely chopped parsley
- cilantro, to garnish

AROMATIC LEMON RICE

Serves: 4

Preparation: 20'

Cooking: 20'

Level of difficulty: 2

- **1 cup/200 g Basmati rice**
- **1²⁄₃ cups/400 ml water**
- **½ tsp ground turmeric**
- **⅛ tsp salt**
- **2 tbsp shredded coconut**
- **2 tbsp coconut milk**
- **4 tbsp butter**
- **4 tbsp oil**
- **1 green chile pepper, seeded and finely sliced**
- **seeds from 4 cardamom pods**
- **3 whole black pepper corns**
- **2 tbsp chopped almonds**
- **½ tsp cumin seeds**
- **½ tsp mustard seeds**
- **juice of ½ lemon**

Place the rice in a large saucepan with the water, turmeric, and salt. Bring to a boil, cover, and simmer over low heat for 10 minutes. • Remove from the heat and leave covered. • Soak the coconut in the coconut milk in a small bowl.

• Melt the butter in a small saucepan over medium heat. Add the oil, chile pepper, cardamom, pepper corns, almonds, cumin, and mustard seeds. Cook for 3–4 minutes, or until the mustard seeds begin to crackle. • Add this mixture to the rice. • Add the lemon juice and coconut and mix with a fork. Cook over low heat for 5 minutes, or until the rice is soft and fluffy. • Transfer to a serving dish and serve.

TOMATOES WITH COUSCOUS AND GRILLED VEGETABLES

Prepare the couscous according to the instructions on the package. • Thinly slice the zucchini and eggplant lengthwise. Grill the vegetables in a grill pan for about 10 minutes, or until tender. • Dice the grilled vegetables and season with salt and pepper. Drizzle with the oil and vinegar. • Place the couscous in a bowl with the vegetables, Feta, mint, and chives. Toss gently. Refrigerate for 1 hour. • Cut the tops off the tomatoes and use a teaspoon to hollow out the insides. Sprinkle the tomatoes lightly with salt and pepper and let stand upside down for 30 minutes to drain. • Fill with the couscous mixture.
• Serve at room temperature.

Serves: 4

Preparation: 30' + 1 h to chill and drain

Cooking: 15'

Level of difficulty: 1

- 1 cup/150 g precooked couscous
- 2 medium zucchini/courgettes
- 1 eggplant/aubergine
- salt and freshly ground black pepper to taste
- 4 tbsp extra-virgin olive oil
- 1 tbsp white wine vinegar
- 4 oz/125 g Feta cheese
- 2 tbsp finely chopped mint
- 2 tbsp finely chopped chives

BULGUR WHEAT WITH WALNUTS

*Vegan

Serves: 6

Preparation: 20' + 15' to soak

Level of difficulty: 1

S oak the bulgur wheat in warm water for 15 minutes. Drain, squeezing out the excess water. • Chop the walnuts coarsely with 1 teaspoon of salt on a chopping board. • Mix the bulgur wheat, walnuts, onion, tomatoes, and mint in a large bowl. Drizzle with the oil. • Refrigerate for 15 minutes. • Garnish with the mint and serve with garlic-flavored yogurt.

- 2 cups/250 g bulgur wheat
- 2⅓ cups/400 g shelled walnuts
- 1 tsp salt
- 1 onion, finely chopped
- 16 cherry tomatoes, halved
- 2 tbsp finely chopped mint + 1 sprig mint, to garnish
- 4 tbsp extra-virgin olive oil

Serves: 4

Preparation: 2'

Cooking: 13–15'

Level of difficulty: 1

- 2¼ cups/450 g short-grain rice
- 3 egg yolks
- ½ cup/125 ml light/single cream
- ⅓ cup/40 g freshly grated Parmesan cheese
- freshly ground white pepper to taste
- 2 tbsp butter

RICE WITH EGG AND PARMESAN

Cook the rice in a large pot of salted, boiling water for about 13–15 minutes, or until tender. • Beat the egg yolks, cream, Parmesan, and pepper in a medium bowl. • Drain the rice and transfer to a flameproof dish. • Pour the sauce over the hot rice and dot with the butter. • Stir over low heat until the eggs are cooked through. • Serve hot.

385

CURRIED RISOTTO

*Vegan

Serves: 4

Preparation: 20'

Cooking: 30–35'

Level of difficulty: 2

- 1 small onion, finely chopped
- $1/2$ stalk celery, finely chopped
- 3 tbsp extra-virgin olive oil
- $1^3/4$ cups/350 g Italian risotto rice
- 6 tbsp dry white wine
- 3 cups/750 ml boiling Vegetable Stock, + more if needed (see page 945)
- 1 tsp curry powder
- 2 tomatoes, peeled and finely chopped
- 2 tbsp finely chopped parsley
- salt and freshly ground black pepper to taste

Sauté the onion and celery in the oil in a large frying pan over medium heat for 5 minutes. • Stir in the rice. Cook for 2 minutes, stirring constantly. • Add the wine and cook until evaporated. • Begin stirring in the stock, $1/2$ cup (125 ml) at a time. Cook and stir until each addition has been absorbed, until the rice is tender, about 15–18 minutes. • When the rice is half cooked, add the curry powder, tomatoes, and parsley. Season with salt and pepper. • Serve immediately.

BROWN RICE WITH CARROTS AND OLIVES

Cook the rice in a large pan of boiling water with ¹/₂ teaspoon of salt for about 45 minutes, or until tender. • Drain and place in a serving dish. • Sauté the carrots in the oil in a large frying pan over low heat for about 20 minutes, or until they begin to break down. Add a little water during the cooking time if they begin to stick to the pan. Season with salt. • Top the rice with the carrots. Garnish with the parsley and olives. • Serve warm.

*Vegan

Serves:	6
Preparation:	20'
Cooking:	80'
Level of difficulty:	1

- 3 cups/600 g brown rice
- salt to taste
- 1 lb/500 g carrots, peeled and finely grated
- 2–4 tbsp extra-virgin olive oil
- 2 tbsp finely chopped parsley
- 1 oz/30 g black olives, cut in half

388

BULGUR PILAF WITH TOFU

Sauté the onion in the oil in a large frying pan over medium heat for about 5 minutes, or until softened. • Add the bulgur and sauté for 5 minutes. • Pour in the stock and season with the oregano and pepper. Bring to a boil. Cover and simmer over low heat for 15 minutes, or until the liquid has been absorbed. • Mix the tofu with the shoyu in a large bowl. • Add the bulgur and parsley. Sprinkle with sesame seeds and serve hot.

Vegan

Serves:	4
Preparation:	20'
Cooking:	30'
Level of difficulty:	1

- 1 small onion, finely chopped
- 3 tbsp extra-virgin olive oil
- 1 cup/150 g bulgur wheat
- 2 cups/500 ml Vegetable Stock (see page 945) or water
- ½ tsp dried oregano
- freshly ground black pepper to taste
- 8 oz/250 g tofu (bean curd)
- 2 tsp shoyu (sweet soy sauce) or 1 tbsp red miso
- 3 tbsp finely chopped parsley
- 2 tbsp sesame seeds

BAKED POLENTA WITH GREENS

Serves: 6

Preparation: 30'

Cooking: 55'–1 h 10'

Level of difficulty: 2

- 8 oz/250 g mixed vegetables (chicory, fennel, and spinach), washed
- 1 clove garlic, finely chopped
- 1 fresh hot chile pepper, finely chopped
- 4 tbsp extra-virgin olive oil
- 2$\frac{1}{2}$ quarts/2.5 liters water
- 2$\frac{2}{3}$ cups/400 g finely ground cornmeal
- 1–2 tbsp coarse sea salt
- 1 cup/125 g freshly grated Pecorino cheese

Preheat the oven to 350°F/180°C/gas 4. • Butter a baking dish. • Blanch the vegetables in salted, boiling water for 1 minute. Drain. • Sauté the garlic and chile in 2 tablespoons of oil in a large frying pan until the garlic is pale gold. • Add the vegetables. • Bring the water and coarse sea salt to a boil in a large pot. • Gradually sprinkle in the cornmeal, stirring constantly with a wooden spoon to prevent lumps from forming. • Continue cooking over medium heat, stirring almost constantly, for 45–50 minutes. • Spread a layer of the polenta in the prepared baking dish. • Arrange the vegetables on top with the cooking liquid and sprinkle with the Pecorino. Top with the remaining polenta. Drizzle with the remaining oil. • Bake for 10–15 minutes, or until golden. • Serve hot.

BAKED POLENTA WITH TASTY TOMATO TOPPING

Bring the water to a boil in a large pot. •
Gradually sprinkle in the cornmeal, stirring
constantly with a wooden spoon to prevent lumps
from forming. • Continue cooking over low heat,
stirring almost constantly, for 45–50 minutes.
• Drizzle a clean surface with cold water and turn
the hot polenta out onto it. Spread to about
$1/2$ inch (1 cm) thick and let cool. • Preheat the
oven to 400°F/200°C/gas 6. • Lightly oil a large
baking dish. • Sauté the garlic in the oil in a large
frying pan over medium heat until pale gold. • Add
the tomatoes and cook for 20 minutes, or until the
tomatoes have reduced. Season with salt and
pepper. • Use a glass or cookie cutter to cut out
disks of polenta about 2 inches (5 cm) in diameter.
• Arrange the polenta disks in the baking dish,
overlapping them slightly roof-tile fashion.
• Spoon the hot sauce over the top and sprinkle
with the Parmesan. • Bake for 10–15 minutes, or
until the cheese has melted. • Serve hot.

Serves: 4

Preparation: 20'

Cooking: 1 h

Level of difficulty: 1

- 1 lb/500 g finely ground cornmeal
- 1 quart/1 liter water
- 4 tbsp extra-virgin olive oil
- 2 cloves garlic, finely chopped
- 14 oz/450 g fresh or canned tomatoes, peeled and chopped
- salt and freshly ground black pepper to taste
- 1 cup/125 g freshly grated Parmesan cheese

POLENTA WITH MUSHROOM TOPPING

Bring the milk to a boil in a large saucepan.
• Gradually sprinkle in the cornmeal, stirring
constantly with a wooden spoon to prevent lumps
from forming. Continue cooking over medium heat,
stirring almost constantly, for 45–50 minutes.
• Sauté the mushrooms, shallots, and garlic in
2 tablespoons of butter in a large frying pan over
high heat for 2–3 minutes, or until the garlic is pale
gold. • Add the sage and mint and cook over low
heat for 5 minutes, or until the mushrooms are
tender and all the water they release has been
absorbed. Season with salt and pepper. • Pour the
polenta into a baking dish. Top with the mushroom
mixture and sprinkle with the Parmesan and
parsley. Dot with the remaining butter. • Turn on
the broiler (grill) to high setting. Broil for 2–3
minutes, or until golden brown. • Serve warm.

Serves: 6

Preparation: 15'

Cooking: 1 h

Level of difficulty: 1

- 2⅓ cups/580 ml milk
- 1 cup/150 g finely ground cornmeal
- 1 lb/500 g fresh porcini (or other) mushrooms, washed and thinly sliced
- 2 shallots, finely chopped
- 1 clove garlic, finely chopped
- 4 tbsp butter, melted
- leaves from 1 sprig sage, torn
- 3 leaves fresh mint, torn
- salt and freshly ground black pepper to taste
- 2 tbsp freshly grated Parmesan cheese
- 1 tbsp finely chopped parsley

SIMPLE BAKED POLENTA

Bring the water to a boil with the salt in a large pot. • Gradually sprinkle in the cornmeal, stirring constantly with a wooden spoon, to prevent lumps from forming. • Continue cooking over low heat for 45–50 minutes, stirring almost constantly. • Preheat the oven to 400°F/200°C/gas 6. • Turn the polenta onto a board and slice thickly. • Arrange the slices in layers in a baking dish. Pour the melted butter over the top and sprinkle with the Parmesan. • Bake for 8–10 minutes, or until golden. • Serve hot.

Serves: 6

Preparation: 40'

Cooking: 1 h

Level of difficulty: 2

- 2¹/₂ quarts/2.5 liters water
- 1 tbsp salt
- 1 lb/500 g finely ground cornmeal
- ¹/₂ cup/125 g butter, melted
- 1¹/₄ cups/150 g freshly grated Parmesan cheese

RICE WITH DATES AND ALMONDS

Serves: 4

Preparation: 10'

Cooking: 25–30'

Level of difficulty: 2

- 3½ cups/875 ml water
- 2½ cups/500 g Basmati rice
- ⅛ tsp salt
- 1 tsp saffron strands
- scant ½ cup/100 g butter, melted
- ½ cup/50 g chopped almonds
- 1 cup/200 g chopped pitted dates
- salt and freshly ground black pepper to taste

B ring the water to a boil in a large saucepan over medium heat. Add the rice and salt. Return to a boil. • Cover and simmer over low heat for 15 minutes. • Add the saffron and half the butter. • Cover the pan with a kitchen cloth. Finish cooking in the steam for 5–10 minutes, or until tender, over very low heat. • Melt the remaining butter into a small saucepan over medium heat. Add the almonds and dates and cook for 4 minutes. Season with salt and pepper. • Transfer the rice to a serving dish and garnish with the almonds and dates. • Serve hot.

ASPARAGUS RISOTTO

Serves: 6

Preparation: 30'

Cooking: 35–40'

Level of difficulty: 1

- 1¼ lb/600 g asparagus
- 4 tbsp butter, cut up
- 1¼ quarts/1.25 liters boiling Vegetable Stock (see page 945)
- 1 onion, finely chopped
- 2 cups/400 g Italian risotto rice
- 6 tbsp dry white wine
- 4 tbsp cream, boiling
- ½ cup/60 g freshly grated Parmesan cheese
- freshly ground white pepper to taste

Cut the tender tips away from the tougher bases of the asparagus stalks. Set aside the tips. • Chop the asparagus stalks coarsely. • Sauté the chopped asparagus in 2 tablespoons of butter in a large frying pan over low heat for 2–3 minutes. • Pour in 1 cup (250 ml) of stock and bring to a boil. Cook for about 15 minutes, or until the asparagus is very tender. • Transfer to a food processor or blender and process until smooth. Set aside in a bowl. • Sauté the onion in the remaining butter in a large saucepan over low heat for 5 minutes, or until softened. • Stir in the rice. Cook for 2 minutes, stirring constantly. • Stir in the wine and when this has been absorbed, begin stirring in the stock, ½ cup (125 ml) at a time. After about 10 minutes, add the asparagus purée and tips. Add more stock and cook and stir until each addition has been absorbed, until the rice is tender, about 15–18 minutes. • Add the cream and Parmesan, and season with pepper. • Serve hot.

RISOTTO WITH PEARS

P eel, core, and cube the pears. • Sauté the onion in the butter in a large frying pan until softened. • Stir in the rice and cook for 2 minutes. • Add the wine and cook until evaporated. • Add a ladleful of boiling stock and the pears. • Continue adding stock, 1/2 cup (125 ml) at a time, stirring often until each addition is absorbed, until the rice is tender, 15–18 minutes. Season with salt and pepper. • Add the Fontina and liqueur just before serving. • Stir well and serve hot.

| Serves: 4 |
| Preparation: 10' |
| Cooking: 25–30' |
| Level of difficulty: 2 |

- 4 medium pears
- 1 onion, finely chopped
- 2 tbsp butter
- 2 cups/400 g Italian risotto rice
- 1 cup/250 ml dry white wine
- 1½ quarts/1.5 liters Vegetable Stock (see page 945)
- salt and freshly ground black pepper to taste
- 3 oz/90 g Fontina cheese, diced
- 4 tbsp pear liqueur

*Vegan

Serves: 4

Preparation: 15'

Cooking: 20'

Level of difficulty: 1

RICE WITH OLIVES

- 1¾ cups/350 g Italian risotto rice
- ½ onion, sliced
- 4 tbsp olive oil
- 8 tbsp white wine
- 1 tbsp red wine vinegar
- 4 tomatoes, chopped
- juice of 2 lemons
- ½ chile pepper, crumbled
- 1 tsp finely chopped marjoram
- 4 leaves fresh basil
- 8 large black olives, pitted and cut into quarters

Cook the rice in a large pot of salted boiling water for 15–18 minutes, or until just tender.
• Drain the rice and transfer to a heated serving dish. • Sauté the onion in the oil in a large frying pan until softened. • Add the wine and vinegar and cook until evaporated. • Add the tomatoes, lemon juice, chile, marjoram, basil, and olives. Simmer over medium heat for 7–8 minutes, stirring occasionally. • Pour the sauce over the rice.
• Serve hot.

STRAWBERRY RISOTTO

Serves: 4

Preparation: 10'

Cooking: 25'

Level of difficulty: 2

- 1 small onion, cut in 4 or 6 pieces
- 2 tbsp extra-virgin olive oil
- 2 cups/400 g Italian risotto rice
- 4 tbsp white wine
- 1 quart/1 liter Vegetable Stock (see page 945)
- 12 oz/300 g strawberries
- 2 tbsp butter
- 1 tbsp freshly grated Parmesan cheese
- 2 tbsp light/single cream

Sauté the onion in the oil in a large frying pan over medium heat until softened. Discard the onion. • Add the rice and cook for 2 minutes, stirring constantly. • Pour in the wine and cook until evaporated. • Stir in $1/2$ cup (125 ml) of the stock. Cook, stirring often, until the stock is absorbed. Continue adding the stock, $1/2$ cup (125 ml) at a time, stirring often until each addition is absorbed, until the rice is tender, 15–18 minutes. • Wash, clean, and slice the strawberries, reserving 6 whole ones. Add the sliced strawberries to the rice 5 minutes before the end of cooking time. • Stir in the butter, Parmesan, and cream. • Garnish with the whole strawberries and serve.

MILANESE-STYLE RISOTTO

Sauté the onion in 2 tablespoons of butter in a large frying pan over medium heat until softened. • Stir in the rice and cook for 2 minutes, stirring constantly. • Pour in the wine and cook until evaporated. • Stir in $1/2$ cup (125 ml) of stock and cook, stirring often, until the stock is absorbed. • Continue adding the stock, $1/2$ cup (125 ml) at a time, stirring often until each addition is absorbed, until the rice is tender, 15–18 minutes. • Add the saffron and half the Parmesan. Season with salt. • Melt 4 tablespoons of butter in each of two 10-inch (25-cm) frying pans. • Divide the rice into two portions and flatten each one out to obtain two round cakes about 1 inch (2.5 cm) thick. • Cook in the frying pans over high heat for about 5 minutes, or until a crisp crust forms. • Turn them with the help of a plate. Melt the remaining butter in the pans and slip the rice back into the pans. • When both sides are crisp and deep gold, sprinkle with the Parmesan. Cut in half and serve.

Serves 4

Preparation: 20'

Cooking: 40'

Level of difficulty: 3

- 1 small onion, finely chopped
- $1/2$ cup/125 g butter
- 2 cups/400 g Italian risotto rice
- $1/2$ cup/125 ml white or red wine
- $11/2$ quarts/1.5 liters Vegetable Stock (see page 945)
- $1/2$ tsp powdered saffron
- $1/2$ cup/60 g freshly grated Parmesan cheese
- salt to taste

RISOTTO WITH RED ROSES

Serves: 4

Preparation: 20'

Cooking: 20'

Level of difficulty: 2

- 4 red roses (freshly opened buds)
- ½ cup/125 g butter
- 2 cups/400 g Italian risotto rice
- ⅛ tsp freshly grated nutmeg
- freshly ground black pepper to taste
- ½ cup/125 ml dry white wine
- 2 cups/500 ml Vegetable Stock (see page 945)
- 6 tbsp light/single cream
- 4 oz/125 g Emmental cheese
- few drops rose water

Check that the roses are perfectly clean, with no insects in among the petals. Pull off the petals, reserving 8 of the best to use as a garnish. (Keep these in a bowl of cold water). Divide the remaining petals, reserving the more brightly colored ones.
• Melt half the butter in a large frying pan and cook the less highly-colored petals until wilted. • Pour in the rice and cook for 2 minutes, stirring constantly. • Season with nutmeg and pepper. Pour in the wine and cook until evaporated. • Stir in ½ cup (125 ml) of the stock and cook, stirring often, until the stock is absorbed. • Continue adding the stock, ½ cup (125 ml) at a time, stirring often until each addition is absorbed, until the rice is tender, 15–18 minutes. • When the rice is about half cooked, add the reserved brightly colored rose petals. When the rice is tender, fold in the cream and remaining butter. Add the Emmental and rose water. • Transfer to a serving dish and garnish with the 8 reserved petals. • Serve hot.

PEAR AND GORGONZOLA RISOTTO

Serves: 4–6

Preparation: 20'

Cooking: 25'

Level of difficulty: 1

- 1 small onion, finely chopped
- ½ cup/125 g butter
- 2 cups/400 g Italian risotto rice
- 2 firm-ripe pears, finely chopped
- ½ cup/125 ml brandy
- 2 cups/500 ml Vegetable Stock (see page 945)
- 7 oz/200 g Gorgonzola cheese
- 4–6 walnuts, to garnish

Sauté the onion in 6 tablespoons of butter in a large frying pan over medium heat for about 5 minutes, or until softened. • Stir in the rice and pears and cook for 2 minutes. • Pour in the brandy and cook until evaporated. • Pour in ½ cup (125 ml) of stock. Cook for 10 minutes, adding more stock as the liquid begins to dry out. • Add the Gorgonzola and the remaining stock. Cook for about 5 minutes more, or until the rice is tender. • Stir in the remaining butter. • Serve on individual plates with a walnut in the center.

GRAPEFRUIT RISOTTO

Sauté the onions in the oil in a large frying pan over medium heat until softened. • Stir in the rice. Cook for 2 minutes, stirring constantly. • Stir in the grapefruit juice and when this has been absorbed, begin stirring in the stock, $1/2$ cup (125 ml) at a time. • After about 10 minutes, add the butter. • Add more stock and cook and stir until each addition has been absorbed, until the rice is tender, about 15–18 minutes. Season with salt and pepper. • Stir in the Parmesan and garnish with the parsley.

Try this unusual risotto, based on vitamin C- and potassium-rich grapefruit.

412

Serves: 4

Preparation: 20'

Cooking: 25–30'

Level of difficulty: 1

- 2 small onions, thinly sliced
- 3 tbsp extra-virgin olive oil
- 2 cups/400 g Italian risotto rice
- juice of 2 grapefruit
- 1¼ quarts/1.25 liters boiling Vegetable Stock (see page 945)
- 2 tbsp butter
- salt and freshly ground black pepper to taste
- 4 tbsp freshly grated Parmesan cheese
- 2 tbsp finely chopped parsley

CANTALOUPE RISOTTO

Serves: 4

Preparation: 25'

Cooking: 15–20'

Level of difficulty: 2

- 1 small cantaloupe/ rock melon
- 1 small onion, finely chopped
- 2 tbsp butter
- 1 quart/1 liter Vegetable Stock (see page 945)
- 1½ cups/300 g Italian risotto rice
- 4 tbsp brandy
- salt and freshly ground black pepper to taste
- 7 tbsp cream
- ½ cup/60 g freshly grated Parmesan cheese
- 1 bunch chives, snipped into small pieces

Cut the melon in half. Peel, remove the seeds, and chop the flesh coarsely. • Sauté the onion in the butter in a large frying pan over medium heat until softened. • Add 4 tablespoons of stock to prevent the onion from browning. Cook until the stock has evaporated completely. • Add the rice and cook for 2 minutes, stirring constantly. • Stir in the brandy and when this has been absorbed, begin stirring in the stock, ½ cup (125 ml) at a time. After about 10 minutes, add half the melon. • Add more stock and cook and stir until each addition has been absorbed, until the rice is tender, about 15–20 minutes. • Add the remaining melon. Season with salt and pepper. Add the cream, Parmesan, and chives. • Cover the pan with a lid and set the risotto aside for 5 minutes before serving.

Melons should be firm to the touch and give out a slightly fruity aroma.

GREEN RISOTTO

Wash the spinach and cook with just the water left clinging to its leaves for 5–7 minutes, or until wilted. • Drain, squeezing out any excess moisture. • Finely chop the spinach, onion, carrot, celery, and leeks. • Sauté the chopped vegetables with 2 tablespoons of butter over medium heat for 3 minutes. • Stir in the rice. Cook for 2 minutes, stirring constantly. • Begin stirring in the stock, $1/2$ cup (125 ml) at a time. Cook and stir until each addition has been absorbed, until the rice is tender, about 15–18 minutes. • Season with salt and pepper. Add the remaining butter, Parmesan, parsley, and basil. • Mix well and serve hot.

Serves: 4

Preparation: 20'

Cooking: 25–30'

Level of difficulty: 2

- **10 oz/300 g spinach, tough stalks removed**
- **1 small onion**
- **1 carrot**
- **1 stalk celery**
- **whites of 2 leeks**
- **6 tbsp butter**
- **1¾ cups/350 g Italian risotto rice**
- **1 quart/1 liter Vegetable Stock (see page 945)**
- **salt and freshly ground white pepper to taste**
- **3 tbsp freshly grated Parmesan cheese**
- **1 tbsp finely chopped parsley**
- **1 tbsp finely chopped basil**

BEANS & LENTILS

FAVA BEAN PURÉE

Place the fava beans and salt in a large pan of cold water and bring to a boil. Cook for about 1 hour, or until tender. • After the beans have been cooking for about 30 minutes, add the potatoes. • Drain the beans and potatoes and chop in a food processor with half the oil until smooth. • Spoon into a serving dish, drizzle with the remaining oil, and season with salt and pepper. • Serve hot or at room temperature.

Vegan

Serves: 4

Preparation: 20' + time to soak beans

Cooking: 1 h

Level of difficulty: 1

- 2 lb/1 kg dried fava/broad beans, soaked over night
- salt and freshly ground black pepper to taste
- 2 floury potatoes, peeled and coarsely chopped
- salt and freshly ground white pepper to taste
- ½ cup/125 ml extra-virgin olive oil

HOMEMADE BAKED BEANS WITH TOMATOES

*Vegan

Serves: 6

*Preparation: 20' +
time to soak beans*

Cooking: 1 h 45–50'

Level of difficulty: 1

- 5 cups/500 g large dried white beans, soaked overnight and drained
- ½ cup/125 ml extra-virgin olive oil
- 1 onion, finely chopped
- 3 cloves garlic, finely chopped
- 3 tomatoes, peeled, seeded, and finely chopped
- 3 tbsp finely chopped parsley
- salt and freshly ground black pepper to taste

Cook the beans in a large pot of boiling water for about 1 hour, or until tender. • Drain well. • Preheat the oven to 350°F/180°C/gas 4. • Place the oil, onion, garlic, tomatoes, and parsley in a large baking dish. Season with salt and pepper. Add the beans and mix well. • Bake for 45–50 minutes, or until the sauce is well cooked. • Serve hot.

SPLIT GREEN PEA PATTIES

Cook the split peas with the bay leaf in a large pot of salted boiling water for about $1^1/_2$ hours, or until very tender. • Drain, discarding the bay leaf. • Place the split peas in a medium bowl and mash with a fork. • Preheat the oven to 350°F/180°C/gas 4. • Butter a baking dish. • Add all the other ingredients except the oil to the split peas. Mix well.. • Form tablespoons of the mixture into 2-inch (5-cm) flat patties. • Arrange in a single layer in the prepared dish. • Drizzle with the oil and bake for 30 minutes, turning them halfway through, until browned all over. • Serve hot.

Vegan

Serves: 4

Preparation: 20'

Cooking: 90'

Level of difficulty: 1

- 1 cup/150 g split green peas
- 1 bay leaf
- 1 floury potato, peeled, boiled, and mashed
- 2 tbsp finely chopped celery leaves
- 1 carrot, peeled and finely grated
- 1 small onion, finely chopped
- 1 tsp finely chopped marjoram
- 1 tbsp finely chopped parsley
- 1/8 tsp freshly grated nutmeg
- 1/3 cup/50 g whole-wheat/wholemeal flour
- 4 tbsp extra-virgin olive oil

EGG-FREE VEGETABLE FRITTATA

Beat the garbanzo bean flour and water in a large bowl to make a smooth batter. • Add the zucchini, carrot, and tomatoes. Season with salt. • Lightly oil a large nonstick frying pan and warm over medium heat. • Pour the batter into the pan and cook for 5–7 minutes, or until golden brown. Turn and cook the other side for 5–7 minutes, or until golden brown all over. • Serve warm.

424

Vegan

Serves: 4	
Preparation: 10'	
Cooking: 10–15'	
Level of difficulty: 1	

- 1⅓ cups/200 g garbanzo bean/ chickpea flour
- 7 tbsp water
- 2 zucchini/ courgettes, finely grated
- 1 carrot, finely grated
- 2 tomatoes, coarsely chopped
- salt to taste

GARBANZO BEAN CREAM

Vegan

Serves: 4

Preparation: 20' +
    time to soak beans

Cooking: 2 h

Level of difficulty: 2

- 5 cups/500 g dried garbanzo beans/chick peas, soaked overnight and drained
- 1 clove garlic, finely chopped
- 2 tbsp extra-virgin olive oil
- juice of 1 lemon
- 1 tsp ground cumin
- salt to taste
- ½ tsp ground chile pepper
- fresh basil, to garnish

Cook the garbanzo beans in a large pan old salted water for about 1 hour, or until very tender. • Sauté the garlic in the oil in a large saucepan over low heat until pale gold. • Drain the garbanzo beans. Place in a food processor and process until smooth. • Mix in the lemon juice and cumin and season with salt. • Transfer to serving bowls and garnish with the chile pepper and basil. • Serve warm or at room temperature.

QUICK BEAN CHILE

Serves: 4
Preparation: 10'
Cooking: 25'
Level of difficulty: 1

Heat the oil and butter in a large saucepan over medium heat. Add the onions, chile peppers, ginger, cardamom, ground coriander, and garlic and sauté for 7–8 minutes. • Pour in tomato sauce and add the beans and bay leaf. Mix well and cook over medium-high heat for 15 minutes. Stir often to stop the mixture sticking to the pan. Season with salt and pepper. • Transfer to a serving dish and garnish with parsley and cilantro. Serve hot.

- 3 tbsp extra-virgin olive oil
- 2 tbsp butter
- 1 tbsp grated ginger
- seeds from 4 cardamom pods
- 1 tbsp ground coriander
- 5 cloves garlic, sliced
- 2 onions, chopped
- 2 fresh red chile peppers, sliced
- 1 cup/250 ml store-bought or home-made Tomato Sauce (see page 951)
- 2 cups/250 g canned garbanzo beans/chick peas, drained
- 2 cups/250 g red kidney beans
- 2 cups/200 g pinto beans, drained
- 1 bay leaf
- salt and freshly ground black pepper to taste
- 1 tbsp finely chopped parsley, to garnish
- 1 tsp finely chopped cilantro/coriander, to garnish

YELLOW SPLIT PEA PURÉE

Serves: 6

Preparation: 40' + 1 h
 to chill

Cooking: 2 h 30'

Level of difficulty: 2

- 3½ cups/350 g yellow split peas
- 1 onion, chopped
- 2 tbsp extra-virgin olive oil
- ½ tsp ground turmeric
- 4 tbsp butter
- 2 cloves garlic, finely chopped
- 2 scallions/spring onions, chopped
- 2 shallots, chopped
- 1 tbsp chopped mint
- ½ fresh green chile pepper, chopped
- ½ tsp red pepper flakes
- ½ tsp cumin seeds
- 1 tsp coriander seeds
- 2 tsp lemon juice
- 2 tsp lime juice
- salt and freshly ground black pepper to taste
- 1 small red chile pepper, thinly sliced

Place the split peas in a large saucepan and cover with water by about 1 inch (3 cm). Bring to a boil over medium heat and skim off any froth. • Add the onion, oil, and turmeric. Cover and simmer over low heat for about 2 hours, or until the peas are cooked and broken down. • Process in a food processor to eliminate any peas which remain whole. • Melt the butter in a small saucepan over low heat. Add the garlic, scallions, shallots, mint, and green chile pepper and sauté for 3 minutes. • Crush the red pepper flakes, cumin, and coriander seeds in a mortar and pestle. Mix with the lemon and lime juice in a small bowl to make a paste. Add to the sautéed mixture and cook for 3 minutes. • Add to the split peas, mix well, and simmer for 10 minutes. • Remove from the heat, season with salt and pepper, and let cool. • Transfer to a serving dish and refrigerate for 1 hour. • Garnish with the chile pepper and serve with warm bread.

Fiber-rich split peas are a great source of folate, potassium, and phosphorus.

429

LENTIL PÂTÉ

Soak the bread in the water and Port in a large bowl for 1 hour. • Drain, squeezing out the excess liquid. • Preheat the oven to 475°F/250°C/gas 9. • Butter an ovenproof baking dish. • Sauté the onions in the oil in a large frying pan over medium heat for about 10 minutes, or until softened. • Add the bread and cook over medium heat for 15 minutes, stirring constantly. • Add the parsley, bay leaves, salt, nutmeg, thyme, and coriander. Cook for 5 minutes, stirring well. • Process the lentils in a food processor or blender until puréed. Add the lentils to the sautéed mixture and mix well. Remove from the heat when the mixture is dense. Remove and discard the bay leaves. • Add the miso and sesame butter and stir for 5 minutes. • Pour the mixture into the prepared dish. • Bake for 40–45 minutes, or until firm to the touch. Slice and serve warm or at room temperature.

Vegan

Serves: 4

Preparation: 20' + 1 h to soak

Cooking: 1 h 15'

Level of difficulty: 1

- 8 oz/250 g day-old whole-wheat/wholemeal bread
- 4 tbsp warm water
- 4 tbsp Port or dry Marsala wine
- 2 onions, finely chopped
- 1 tbsp extra-virgin olive oil
- 2 cups/300 g cooked lentils, drained
- 3 tbsp finely chopped parsley
- 2 bay leaves
- $\frac{1}{2}$ tsp salt
- $\frac{1}{2}$ tsp freshly grated nutmeg
- $\frac{1}{2}$ tsp dried thyme
- $\frac{1}{2}$ tsp ground coriander
- 1 tbsp miso, preferably rice miso
- 1 tbsp sesame oil or tahini

430

LENTILS AND RICE
WITH TOMATO SAUCE

Vegan

Serves: 4

Preparation: 15'

Cooking: 1 h

Level of difficulty: 2

- 3½ cups/350 g lentils
- 1¼ cups/250 g short-grain rice

TOMATO SAUCE

- 1 large onion, finely sliced
- 1 clove garlic, finely chopped
- 4 tbsp extra-virgin olive oil
- 2 lb/1 kg tomatoes, peeled and finely chopped
- ⅔ cup/150 ml water
- 2 tbsp vinegar
- salt and freshly ground black pepper to taste

C over the lentils with boiling water in a large saucepan. Cook over low heat for about 30 minutes, or until the lentils are well cooked.
• Cook the rice in a large pot of salted, boiling water for about 15 minutes, or until tender.
• Tomato Sauce: Sauté the onion and garlic in the oil in a large saucepan over medium heat for 5 minutes. • Stir in the tomatoes and cook for 10–15 minutes, or until the tomatoes have reduced. • Add the water and vinegar and cook for 5–10 more minutes. Season with salt and pepper.
• Spoon a layer of lentils onto each of four serving dishes. Add a layer of rice and repeat the layering until all the rice and lentils are used. • Spoon the tomato sauce over the top.
• Serve warm.

LENTIL AND BARLEY BAKE

Cook the potatoes in a large pot of salted boiling water for about 20 minutes, or until tender.
• Drain and mash. • Cook the lentils and barley in a large pot of boiling water for 30 minutes, or until tender. • Drain well. • Preheat the oven to 350°F/ 180°C/gas 4. • Cook the carrot, onion, garlic, tomatoes, and herbs with the water in a medium saucepan over medium heat for about 15 minutes, or until the carrots are tender. • Add the flour and mix well. • Cook for 5 more minutes, or until the mixture thickens. Season with salt and pepper.
• Add the lentils and barley and mix well. • Spread the mixture in a baking dish and top with the mashed potatoes. • Bake for 30 minutes, or until browned. • Serve hot.

*Vegan

Serves: 4

Preparation: 10'

Cooking: 1 h 40'

Level of difficulty: 1

- **3 medium floury potatoes, peeled**
- **1 cup/100 g lentils**
- **½ cup/50 g pearl barley**
- **1 carrot, peeled and finely chopped**
- **1 onion, finely chopped**
- **1 clove garlic, finely chopped**
- **1 cup/250 g peeled tomatoes, seeded and coarsely chopped**
- **1 tbsp finely chopped parsley**
- **1 tbsp dried herbs (marjoram, rosemary, thyme, etc)**
- **1 cup/250 ml water**
- **1 tbsp all-purpose/ plain flour**
- **salt and freshly ground black pepper to taste**

BEANS COOKED IN A FLASK

*Vegan

Serves: 4

Preparation: 10'

Cooking: 3 h

Level of difficulty: 1

- 1¾ lb/800 g freshly hulled cannellini beans or 2 cups/350 g dried cannellini beans, soaked for 12 hours
- ½ cup/125 ml extra-virgin olive oil
- 2 cloves garlic, lightly crushed but whole
- 4 leaves fresh sage
- 2 cherry tomatoes, skins pricked with a fork
- salt and freshly ground black pepper to taste
- water, sufficient to fill the flask to three-quarters

Feed the beans into the flask. • Pour in the oil and add the garlic, sage, tomatoes, and salt and pepper. Top up with the water. • Cork up the flask tightly and place the bulbous end deep among the barely glowing embers of a wood fire to cook gently for several hours. • Tip the beans out of the flask. • Discard the garlic and sage and serve, with an extra drizzle of olive oil, salt, and freshly ground black pepper.

MEXICAN-STYLE BEANS

Sauté the onion in the oil in a large frying pan over medium heat for about 10 minutes, or until softened. • Add the chile and cumin and season with salt and pepper. Stir for 1 minute until the spices release their aroma. • Add the garlic, tomatoes, and lemon juice. Bring to a boil and cover and simmer over low heat for about 3 minutes, stirring occasionally. • Add the beans, cover, and cook over low heat for 25 minutes, stirring often, until the tomatoes are reduced.
• Pour into a heated serving dish. • Serve hot.

Vegan

Serves: 4

Preparation: 20'

Cooking: 40'

Level of difficulty: 1

- 1 onion, finely chopped
- 1 tbsp extra-virgin olive oil
- ½ tsp chile powder
- ½ tsp ground cumin seeds
- salt and freshly ground black pepper to taste
- 1 clove garlic, lightly crushed but whole
- 1 cup/250 g canned tomatoes
- juice of ½ lemon
- 14 oz/425 g canned red kidney beans or borlotti beans

BEANS WITH RADICCHIO

P lace the beans in a large pot with enough water to cover. Bring to a boil and simmer over low heat with the bay leaves for about 1 hour, or until tender. Season with salt. • Remove the beans with a slotted spoon and keep warm in a colander over the hot water. • Wash the radicchio, trim the roots, and pat dry with a clean tea towel. Cut each radicchio into 4–6long wedges. • Sauté the garlic in the oil in a medium frying pan until pale gold. • Remove from the heat and add the vinegar. Season with salt. • Arrange the radicchio on serving plates with the beans in the center. Drizzle with the sauce. • Season with pepper and serve.

*Vegan

Serves: 4–6

Preparation: 20' + time to soak beans

Cooking: 1 h

Level of difficulty: 1

- **14 oz/400 g white kidney beans, soaked overnight (if using dried beans, half the quantity)**
- **salt and freshly ground black pepper to taste**
- **2 bay leaves**
- **10 oz/300 g red radicchio or chicory**
- **4 cloves garlic, finely chopped**
- **6 tbsp extra-virgin olive oil**
- **4 tbsp strong white wine vinegar**

BEANS & LENTILS

BAKED BEANS WITH TOMATOES AND HERBS

Cook the beans in a large pan of salted water for 1 hour. • Drain well. • Preheat the oven to 400°F/200°C/gas 6. • Place the beans in a large baking dish. • Mix in the tomatoes, garlic, herbs, and oil. Season with salt and pepper. • Bake for 1 hour. • Serve hot.

Serve this nourishing dish on its own or with vegetarian sausages.

442

Vegan

Serves: 4

Preparation: 10' + time to soak beans

Cooking: 2 h

Level of difficulty: 1

- 4 cups/400 g cannellini or white kidney beans, soaked overnight and drained
- 1 lb/500 g peeled and chopped tomatoes
- 2 cloves garlic, lightly crushed but whole
- 2 tbsp finely chopped mixed fresh herbs (such as thyme, basil, and oregano)
- 6 tbsp extra-virgin olive oil
- salt and freshly ground black pepper to taste

STEWED
CURRIED
& BRAISED

CAPONATA WITH RICE

Sauté the eggplants and onion in 1 tablespoon of oil in a large frying pan over medium heat for 10 minutes, or until softened. • Add the celery, tomatoes, pear, olives, capers, and sugar. Season with salt and pepper. Add the water and vinegar. Simmer over low heat for about 15 minutes, or until all the vegetables have softened. • Cook the rice in a large pot of salted boiling water for 12–15 minutes, or until tender. • Drain and drizzle with the remaining oil. Stir in the basil. • Fill four small molds with the seasoned rice, pressing the rice down firmly. • Turn the rice out of the molds onto a serving dish and serve with the caponata.

*Vegan

Serves: 4–6

Preparation: 20'

Cooking: 30'

Level of difficulty: 1

- 2 eggplants/ aubergines, diced
- 1 small onion, coarsely chopped
- 3 tbsp extra-virgin olive oil
- 2 stalks celery, finely chopped
- 4 large tomatoes, coarsely chopped
- 1 firm-ripe pear, peeled and coarsely chopped
- 1 cup/100 g black olives
- 1 tbsp salt-cured capers, rinsed of salt
- 1 tbsp sugar
- salt and freshly ground black pepper to taste
- 4 tbsp water
- 2 tbsp vinegar
- 1 1/2 cups/300 g short-grain rice
- 1 tbsp finely chopped basil

POTATO, GREEN BEAN, AND TOMATO STEW

Vegan

Serves: 4–6

Preparation: 20'

Cooking: 25–30'

Level of difficulty: 1

- 12 oz/350 g potatoes, peeled and coarsely chopped
- 12 oz/350 g green beans, topped and tailed
- 1 onion, finely chopped
- 1 clove garlic, finely chopped
- 1 tbsp finely chopped parsley
- 4 tbsp extra-virgin olive oil
- salt and freshly ground black pepper to taste
- 3 large tomatoes, peeled and coarsely chopped

Cook the potatoes in salted boiling water for 15–20 minutes, or until almost tender. • Drain and set aside. • Blanch the green beans in salted boiling water for 5 minutes, or until almost tender. • Drain and chop into short lengths. • Sauté the onion, garlic, and parsley in the oil in a large frying pan over medium heat until the garlic is pale gold. Season with salt and pepper. Add the tomatoes and cook for 10 minutes. • Stir in the potatoes and green beans and tomatoes and cook for 10–15 more minutes. • Serve hot.

PINEAPPLE AND COCONUT CURRY

S pice Paste: Grind the chile peppers, coriander seeds, garlic, shallots, turmeric, and ginger root in a pestle and mortar until crushed. • Curry: Heat the oil in a large wok or frying pan and sauté the spice paste until aromatic. • Pour in the coconut milk and bring to a boil, stirring constantly. • Add the pineapple, star anise, cinnamon, cloves, nutmeg, lemongrass, and lime juice. Season with salt and pepper. Cook over medium heat until the pineapple is heated through, 5–7 minutes. • Stir in the coconut cream and cook for 2–3 minutes more. • Transfer to a heated serving dish. • Garnish with the fried shallots and serve hot with boiled rice.

*Vegan

Serves:	4–6
Preparation:	25'
Cooking:	20'
Level of difficulty:	1

SPICE PASTE
- 4–6 dried red chile peppers, crumbled
- 1 tsp coriander seeds
- 2 cloves garlic, finely chopped
- 6 shallots, chopped
- 1 tsp ground turmeric
- 1 tbsp finely grated ginger

CURRY
- 2 tbsp olive oil
- 3 cups/750 ml coconut milk
- 1 pineapple, cubed
- 2 star anise, chopped
- 1 stick cinnamon
- ¼ tsp ground cloves
- ⅛ tsp ground nutmeg
- 1 stalk lemongrass, finely chopped
- 1 tbsp lime juice
- salt and freshly ground black pepper to taste
- ½ cup/125 ml coconut cream
- 2 shallots, lightly fried, to garnish

Serves: 6

Preparation: 20'

Cooking: 45–50'

Level of difficulty: 1

- 2 cups/300 g small yellow lentils
- 2 onions, sliced
- 2 tomatoes, chopped
- 2 sprigs curry leaves
- ½ tsp ground turmeric
- 1 quart/1 liter water
- 1 tsp salt
- 1¾ lb/800 g mixed vegetables
- 2 tbsp tamarind paste
- 1 cup/100 g freshly grated coconut blended with 6 tbsp water
- ½ tsp sugar
- 1 tbsp chopped cilantro/coriander
- 2 tbsp extra-virgin olive oil
- 1 tsp mustard seeds
- 3–4 dried red chile peppers, crumbled

YELLOW LENTIL AND VEGETABLE CURRY

Cook the lentils, onions, tomatoes, curry leaves, turmeric, water, and salt in a large saucepan over medium heat for 20 minutes. • Add the vegetables that take longer to cook, such as carrots and potatoes, along with the tamarind paste, coconut, and sugar. Cook for 15 minutes, or until the vegetables are softening and the lentils have broken down. • Add the remaining vegetables and cilantro and cook for 10 minutes more. • Sauté the mustard seeds and chile peppers in the oil in a small saucepan until aromatic. • Add to the vegetable curry, stir well, and cook for 2 minutes more. • Serve hot.

451

CURRIED EGGPLANTS

Serves: 6

Preparation: 15'

Cooking: 35–40'

Level of difficulty: 1

- **⅛ tsp ground cinnamon**
- **1 tbsp ghee (clarified butter)**
- **2 onions, finely chopped**
- **1 bay leaf**
- **½ tsp chile powder**
- **½ tsp ground coriander**
- **⅛ tsp ground turmeric**
- **4 firm-ripe tomatoes, finely chopped**
- **1 eggplant/ aubergine, thickly sliced**
- **1 spicy fresh red chile pepper, sliced**
- **salt to taste**

Sauté the cinnamon in the ghee in a large frying pan over medium heat for 1 minute. • Add the onions and bay leaf and cook until the onions are golden. • Add the chile powder, coriander, and turmeric. Cook for 5 minutes. • Add the tomatoes, eggplant, and chile pepper. Season with salt. • Cook over low heat for 20–25 minutes, *Make ghee at home or buy it ready-made from an ethnic food store.* or until the vegetables are tender. • Serve hot.

453

SPICY EGGPLANT STEW

S team the eggplants over a large pot of boiling water for 20 minutes, or until tender. • Cook the tomatoes with the oil, garlic, paprika, cumin, and pepper in a medium saucepan over medium heat for about 20 minutes, or until the tomatoes have broken down. Season with salt. • Add the eggplants and cook over low heat for 15–20 minutes. • Drizzle with the lemon juice and a little extra oil. • Serve hot.

Vegan

Serves: 4

Preparation: 25'

Cooking: 55–60'

Level of difficulty: 1

- 2 lb/1 kg eggplants/ aubergines, unpeeled and cut into bite-sized chunks
- 1 lb/500 g tomatoes, peeled and coarsely chopped
- 5 tbsp extra-virgin olive oil
- 4 cloves garlic, finely chopped
- 1 tbsp sweet paprika
- 1 tsp cumin seeds
- 1/2 tsp ground black pepper
- salt to taste
- juice of 1 lemon

RED CABBAGE STEW

*Vegan

Serves: 4–6

Preparation: 15'

Cooking: 40'

Level of difficulty: 2

Heat the oil in a large saucepan over medium heat. Add the sugar and cook for 3–4 minutes, or until it begins to caramelize. • Add the onion and apples and cook for 10 minutes, or until the onion and apples begin to soften. • Add the red cabbage and vinegar and mix well. Season with salt and pepper. Stir in the cloves and bay leaves, adding enough stock to cover the bottom of the saucepan. Cover and cook over low heat for 30 minutes, or until the cabbage is very tender, stirring occasionally. • Add the bran, wine, and blueberry jelly, if using. • Sprinkle with the flour, mix well, and cook for 5 minutes. • Serve hot with boiled potatoes and Glazed Chestnuts (see page 83).

- 2 tbsp extra-virgin olive oil
- 1 tbsp sugar
- 1 onion, finely chopped
- 3 apples, peeled, cored, and coarsely chopped
- 2 lb/1 kg red cabbage, finely shredded
- 3 tbsp white wine vinegar
- salt and freshly ground black pepper to taste
- 4 cloves
- 2 bay leaves
- 1 cup/250 ml Vegetable Stock (see page 945)
- 1 tbsp bran
- ½ cup/125 ml dry red wine
- 1 tbsp blueberry jelly (optional)
- 1 tbsp all-purpose/ plain flour

Serves: 4

Preparation: 15'

Cooking: 35'

Level of difficulty: 1

- 1¼ lb/575 g green beans, topped, and tailed
- 1 clove garlic, finely chopped
- 1 onion or shallot, very thinly sliced
- 4 tbsp extra-virgin olive oil
- 1 tsp crushed fennel seeds
- 2 large ripe tomatoes, skinned, seeded, and diced
- salt and freshly ground black pepper to taste
- 1–2 tbsp hot water

FLORENTINE GREEN BEANS

C ook the beans in salted, boiling water until crunchy-tender. • Drain and set aside. • Sauté the garlic and onion in the oil in a large frying pan over medium heat until the garlic is pale gold. • Add the fennel seeds and tomatoes. Season with salt. Simmer over low heat for 4 minutes. • Add the green beans. Season with pepper and mix carefully. • Cover and cook for about 12 minutes, adding the water if the mixture starts to stick to the pan. • Serve hot.

POTATO CURRY

Wash the potatoes and cut in half. • Toast the cumin, fenugreek, and chile peppers in a nonstick frying pan for 2–3 minutes. • Add the onion and 1 tablespoon of ghee. Sauté over high heat for 2–3 minutes. • Remove from the heat and process in a food processor or blender with 2 tablespoons of water until smooth.

458

Pale orange fenugreek seeds have a bittersweet aftertaste that goes beautifully with potatoes.

• Melt the remaining ghee in a large frying pan and sauté the curry leaves and mustard seeds for 30 seconds. • Stir in the spice paste, potatoes, turmeric, coconut, and the remaining water. Season with salt. Cover and cook over low heat for 25–30 minutes, or until the potatoes are tender. • Serve hot.

Serves: 4

Preparation: 20'

Cooking: 35–40'

Level of difficulty: 2

- 1 lb/500 g new potatoes
- 1 tsp cumin seeds
- $\frac{1}{2}$ tsp fenugreek seeds
- 2 dried spicy red chile peppers
- 1 onion, finely sliced
- 3 tbsp ghee (clarified butter)
- 5 tbsp water
- 8 curry leaves
- 1 tsp mustard seeds
- $\frac{1}{2}$ tsp ground turmeric
- 1 tbsp desicated coconut
- salt to taste

CAULIFLOWER CURRY

Serves: 4

Preparation: 20'

Cooking: 20–25'

Level of difficulty: 1

- 1 onion, coarsely chopped
- 1 tbsp ghee (clarified butter)
- 2 tsp coriander powder
- 1 tsp cumin seeds
- 1 tsp chile powder
- ½ tsp ground turmeric
- 2 tsp garam masala
- 1 medium cauliflower, broken up into small florets
- juice of 1 lemon
- salt to taste
- 1 cup/250 ml water

Sauté the onion in the ghee in a large frying pan over medium heat for about 10 minutes, or until golden. • Add the coriander powder, cumin, chile, turmeric, and garam masala and cook for 2 minutes. • Add the cauliflower and drizzle with the lemon juice. Season with salt. • Add half the water, cover, and cook over low heat for 15–20 minutes, or until the cauliflower is tender. Add more water if the sauce dries out during cooking. • Serve hot.

CURRY WITH DHAL BALLS

Process the dhal, fresh chilies, and turmeric in a food processor to form a paste. • Season with salt and pepper and add the carrots. • Shape into balls or oblongs 1-inch (2.5-cm) in diameter and arrange in a steamer lightly greased with oil. • Steam for 10 minutes, then set aside. • Grind the dried chilies and fenugreek to a paste in a pestle and mortar. • Stir the ground spices into the tamarind water in a medium bowl. • Heat the oil in a small saucepan over medium heat. Add the cumin seeds, mustard seeds, and curry leaves and cook until aromatic. • Pour in the tamarind mixture and bring to a boil. Simmer for 20 minutes. • Add the dhal balls and simmer for 10 minutes more. • Serve hot.

*Vegan

Serves: 4

Preparation: 40'

Cooking: 45'

Level of difficulty: 1

- 10 oz/300 g Urad or blackgrain dhal, without the black skin, soaked in cold water for 3 hours and drained
- 2 small red chile peppers, chopped
- ½ tsp ground turmeric
- salt and freshly ground black pepper to taste
- 2 carrots, grated
- 6 dried red chile peppers, crumbled
- ¾ tsp ground fenugreek
- ½ cup/90 g tamarind pulp blended with 1 quart/1 liter water, strained
- 2 tbsp olive oil
- 1 tsp cumin seeds
- ½ tsp mustard seeds
- 6 curry leaves

*Vegan

Serves: 4–6

Preparation: 20'

Cooking: 35–45'

Level of difficulty: 1

- 3 tomatoes
- 2 onions, coarsely chopped
- 4 scallions/spring onions, bulbs only
- 6 tbsp extra-virgin olive oil
- 3 carrots, cut into rounds
- 3 zucchini/ courgettes, finely chopped
- $\frac{1}{8}$ tsp ground cinnamon
- 1 tsp cumin seeds
- $\frac{1}{8}$ tsp ground cloves
- 1 tbsp finely chopped mint
- 1 bunch mixed fresh herbs, finely chopped
- 2 cups/500 ml Vegetable Stock (see page 945)
- salt and freshly ground black pepper to taste

VEGETARIAN TAJINE

Preheat the oven to 350°F/180°C/gas 4.
• Blanch the tomatoes in salted boiling water for 1 minute. • Drain and slip off the skins. Remove the seeds and chop the flesh into small cubes.
• Sauté the onions and whole scallion bulbs in a tajine or a flameproof pot in 3 tablespoons of oil over medium heat until lightly browned. • Add the tomatoes, carrots, and zucchini. Cook for 10 minutes, stirring often. • Add the remaining oil, cinnamon, cumin seeds, cloves, half the mint, and the herbs. Pour in the stock and season with salt and pepper. • Cover with aluminum foil and bake for 35–45 minutes, or until the vegetables are tender. • Garnish with the remaining mint and serve hot.

463

PEAS IN CREAM SAUCE

Melt the butter and oil in a large saucepan over medium heat. Add the shallots, parsley, and mint and sauté for 5 minutes. • Add the peas and pour in the stock. • Lower the heat and cover and cook for about 15 minutes, adding more stock if the mixture begins to stick to the pan. • Use a slotted spoon to drain the peas, reserving the cooking juices in the pan. • Beat the eggs and cream in a medium bowl. Add the Parmesan and season with salt and pepper. • Add the cream mixture to the saucepan containing the reserved juices and mix well. • Cook over low heat for 5–10 minutes, or until slightly thickened. • Stir in the peas and serve hot.

Serves: 4

Preparation: 10'

Cooking: 30'

Level of difficulty: 1

- 4 tbsp butter
- 1 tbsp extra-virgin olive oil
- 3 shallots, finely chopped
- 1 tbsp finely chopped parsley
- ½ tsp finely chopped mint
- 3 lb/1.5 kg fresh peas, hulled/ shelled
- ⅔ cup/150 ml Vegetable Stock, boiling + more as needed
- 2 large eggs
- ½ cup/125 ml heavy/double cream
- ½ cup/60 g freshly grated Parmesan cheese
- salt and freshly ground white pepper to taste

MUSHROOM STEW WITH PARSLEY SAUCE

Serves: 6–8

Preparation: 20'

Cooking: 20'

Level of difficulty: 2

PARSLEY SAUCE
- 1 clove garlic, finely chopped
- 1 large bunch finely chopped parsley
- 1 tbsp torn basil
- 1 tsp finely chopped mint
- 4 tbsp dry white wine
- 3 tbsp water, + more as needed
- 1 tbsp salt-cured capers, rinsed (optional)
- salt and freshly ground black pepper to taste

MUSHROOM STEW
- 4 tbsp butter
- 2 cloves garlic, finely chopped
- 4 tbsp olive oil
- 2 lb/1 kg mushrooms, quartered
- 1 tbsp all-purpose/ plain flour
- juice of ½ lemon (optional)

Parsley Sauce: Mix the garlic, parsley, basil, mint, wine, water, and capers in a large bowl. Season with salt and pepper. • Mushrooms Stew: Melt the butter in a large frying pan over low heat. Add the garlic and sauté for 5 minutes, or until pale gold. • Add the oil and mushrooms and sauté over medium heat for 3–4 minutes, or until they begin to release their juices. Season with salt and pepper. • Cook over low heat for 8–10 minutes, or until the mushrooms are well cooked. • Add the flour and mix well. • Remove from the heat and stir in the parsley sauce. Mix well. Return to the heat and bring to a boil. • Simmer for 5 minutes, or until the sauce begins to thicken. Add the lemon juice and more water if the sauce has become too dense and begins to stick to the pan. • Serve hot.

CZECH SAUERKRAUT

Sauté the onion in the oil in a large saucepan over medium heat for 3 minutes until golden. • Add the garlic, apples, sauerkraut, cumin, and juniper berries. Mix well and add the water. • Cover and cook over low heat for 30 minutes, adding more water if it begins to dry out. • Season with salt and pepper. Add the wine and cook for 2 minutes. • Serve hot with slices of fresh bread.

Vegan

Serves: 4

Preparation: 10'

Cooking: 35'

Level of difficulty: 1

- 1 large onion, finely chopped
- 2 tbsp sunflower oil
- 1 head garlic, split into cloves, peeled but whole
- 3 apples, peeled, cored, and chopped
- 1¼ lb/575 g sauerkraut
- 1 tsp cumin seeds
- 6 juniper berries, crushed
- 4 tbsp hot water + more if needed
- salt and freshly ground black pepper to taste
- 4 tbsp dry white wine

SPICY BEAN CURD

Soak the dried mushrooms in warm water for 15 minutes. • Soak the bean curd strips in warm water for 15 minutes. • Chop the soaked bean curd finely and set aside. • Sauté the celery and garlic in the oil in a large wok or frying pan over medium heat for 3 minutes. • Add the mushrooms, soaked bean curd, and chile peppers and sauté for 3 minutes. • Stir in the bean curd, vegetable stock, soy sauce, sesame oil, and sugar. Cook for 5 minutes, or until the liquid has reduced slightly. • Mix the water and cornstarch in a small bowl. Stir into the wok to thicken the mixture. • Season with pepper, garnish with the parsley, and serve.

*Vegan

Serves: 6

Preparation: 20' + 30' to soak

Cooking: 10'

Level of difficulty: 1

- 2 tsp dried black mushrooms
- 2 tsp dried bean curd strips
- 2 stalks celery, finely chopped
- 2 cloves garlic, finely chopped
- 2 tbsp vegetable oil
- 2 red chile peppers, chopped
- 2 lb/1 kg bean curd or tofu, cut into small cubes
- 1½ cups/375 ml Vegetable Stock (see page 945)
- 1 tbsp soy sauce
- 1 tbsp sesame oil
- ½ tsp sugar
- 1 tbsp water
- 1 tsp cornstarch/ corn flour
- freshly ground black pepper to taste
- 1 tbsp finely chopped parsley

Serves: 6

Preparation: 20'

Cooking: 10'

Level of difficulty: 1

- 2 tbsp extra-virgin olive oil
- 2 lb/1 kg bean curd or tofu, cut into small cubes
- 2 scallions/spring onions, finely chopped
- 2 cloves garlic, finely chopped
- 1 tsp finely chopped fresh ginger
- 2 small red chile peppers, finely chopped
- 1 tbsp dry sherry
- 1½ tbsp soy sauce
- 1 cup/250 ml + 1 tbsp water
- ½ tsp salt
- 1½ tsp cornstarch/ corn flour

SWEET SPICY BEAN CURD

Heat the oil in a large wok or frying pan over medium-high heat. • Sauté the bean curd, half the scallions, 1 clove garlic, and ginger for 3 minutes. • Add the chile peppers and cook for 1 minute. • Stir in the sherry, soy sauce, 1 cup (250 ml) of water, and salt. Bring to a boil and cook for 3 minutes. • Mix the remaining water and cornstarch in a small bowl. Stir into the wok to thicken the mixture. • Sprinkle with the remaining scallion and garlic. • Transfer to a heated plate and serve hot.

SPICY POTATO CURRY

Serves: 4

Preparation: 20'

Cooking: 35'

Level of difficulty: 2

- 2 lb/1 kg potatoes, peeled and cut into bite-size pieces
- 2 scallions/spring onions, white and green parts separated, finely chopped
- 2 cloves garlic, finely chopped
- 1 fresh green chile pepper, seeded and finely chopped
- 1 tsp salt
- 2/3 inch/1½ cm fresh ginger, peeled and sliced
- seeds from 2 cardamom pods
- 2 tbsp extra-virgin olive oil
- 1 tbsp butter
- 1 stick cinnamon
- 2 large tomatoes, chopped
- 1 tsp mustard seeds
- 1 tbsp garam masala
- 1/2 cup/125 ml plain yogurt
- 1 tbsp finely chopped cilantro/ coriander

Cook the potatoes in a large pot of salted, boiling water for 15 minutes until almost tender. • Chop the white part of the scallions with the garlic, chile pepper, salt, ginger, and cardamom seeds in a food processor to make a paste. • Heat the oil and butter in a large frying pan over low heat. Add the spice paste and cook for 2 minutes. • Add the cinnamon, tomatoes, mustard seeds, and garam masala and cook for 5 minutes, stirring constantly. • Stir in the yogurt and cook for 2–3 minutes, or until the sauce has thickened slightly. • Add the potatoes and cook for 5–10 minutes, or until tender.

• Transfer to a serving dish. Garnish with the green part of the scallions and cilantro. • Serve hot.

Garam masala is a blend of ground spices found in well-stocked supermarkets.

473

BEAN CURD AND SPINACH MOLD

S oak the mushrooms in warm water for
15 minutes. • Drain and finely chop. • Rinse
the spinach thoroughly under cold running water
and dry well. • Remove the stems and finely chop
the leaves. • Cut the hard edges off the bean curd
and use a fork to mash the curd in a large bowl.
• Add the spinach, egg whites, sugar, 1 teaspoon
sesame oil, $1/2$ teaspoon salt, and pepper. Mash
until pureed. • Drizzle a 2-quart (2-liter) bowl with
the remaining sesame oil. • Spoon in the bean curd
puree. • Steam for 20 minutes over medium heat,
or until the bean curd does not stick to a chopstick
when pierced. • Carefully invert the mold and turn
the bean curd onto a serving plate. • Bring the
stock and remaining salt to a boil in a medium
saucepan. Add the mushrooms. • Mix the water
and cornstarch in a small bowl and
add to the stock to thicken. •
Pour this mixture over the
bean curd. Spoon
the mushrooms on
top and
around
the sides,
and serve hot.

Serves: 6

*Preparation: 20' + 15'
  to soak*

Cooking: 30'

Level of difficulty: 1

- 3 dried black
  mushrooms
- 10 oz/300 g fresh
  spinach leaves
- 4 lb/2 kg bean curd
  or tofu
- 2 egg whites
- 2 tsp sugar
- 1 tbsp + 1 tsp
  sesame oil
- $3/4$ tsp salt
- $1/2$ tsp freshly
  ground black
  pepper
- 1 cup/250 ml
  Vegetable Stock
- 1 tbsp water
- 1 tbsp cornstarch/
  corn flour

- **4 tbsp extra-virgin olive oil**
- **3 lb/1.5 kg eggplants/ aubergines, cut into small cubes**
- **2 lb/1 kg tomatoes, peeled, seeded, and finely chopped**
- **1 bay leaf**
- **1 tsp granulated sugar**
- **8 cloves garlic, finely chopped**
- **8 tbsp milk, boiling**
- **salt and freshly ground black pepper to taste**

EGGPLANT AND TOMATO STEW

Heat the oil in a large frying pan over medium heat. Sauté the eggplants for 5–7 minutes, or until tender. • Drain well, reserving the oil, and drain on paper towels. Set aside. • Reheat the oil in a casserole or saucepan over medium heat. Add the tomatoes and bay leaf and cook until the tomatoes have softened. • Stir in the sugar and garlic.
• Cook over low heat for 5–8 minutes. Remove from the heat and pour in the hot milk. Season with salt. • Run the cooked eggplants through a vegetable mill or chop in a food processor. Stir the eggplants into the tomato mixture. Season with pepper. • Cook over low heat for 15–20 minutes, or until well blended. • Serve hot.

475

STUFFED CABBAGE

Serves: 4–6

Preparation: 40'

Cooking: 60'

Level of difficulty: 2

Sauté the onion in half the butter and salt in a large saucepan over medium heat for 5 minutes, or until softened. • Add the garlic and cumin and sauté for 2 more minutes. • Add the mushrooms, paprika, and thyme. Cook over high heat for 5–7 minutes, or until the mushrooms have released all their liquid and it has evaporated. • Add 2 tablespoons of cream and the Emmental. Season with salt and pepper and remove from the heat. Let cool. • Blanch the cabbage leaves in a large pot of salted, boiling water for 3 minutes. • Drain well and flatten the leaves on a clean surface with a rolling pin. • Divide the filling evenly among the cabbage leaves, dropping it in the center of each leaf and folding over the edges to seal. • Melt the remaining butter in a casserole or flameproof pot over low heat. Add the tomato sauce, remaining cream, salt, and pepper to the stock and pour into the casserole. Place the stuffed cabbage leaves in the casserole, seam-side down, and cook for 30 minutes, adding more stock during the cooking time if they begin to dry out. • Add the potatoes to the pan 10 minutes before serving. • Garnish with the parsley and serve hot.

- 1 large onion, finely chopped
- 6 tbsp butter
- salt and freshly ground black pepper to taste
- 1 clove garlic, crushed
- ½ tsp cumin seeds, crushed
- 14 oz/400 g mushrooms, chopped
- 1 tsp paprika
- 1 tbsp finely chopped thyme
- 5 tbsp heavy/ double cream
- ½ cup/60 g freshly grated Emmental or Pecorino cheese
- 12 Savoy cabbage leaves, separated and tough white parts removed
- 1 cup store-bought or homemade Tomato Sauce (see page 951)
- 1 cup/250 ml Vegetable Stock + more if needed (see page 945)
- 1 tbsp finely chopped parsley, to garnish
- 2 lb/1 kg potatoes, boiled

Serves: 4
Preparation: 40' + 10' to marinate
Cooking: 20'
Level of difficulty:1

- 2 tbsp water
- 2 tbsp soy sauce
- 2 tsp cornstarch/ corn flour
- 1 tsp white wine
- 4 oz/125 g bean curd or tofu, coarsely chopped
- 6 tbsp extra-virgin olive oil
- 2 oz/60 g dried bean thread, soaked in warm water for 10 minutes and drained
- 2 oz/60 g yellow chive
- 4 oz/125 g fresh spinach leaves, stalks removed
- 6 scallions/spring onions, finely chopped
- 1 cup/250 ml Vegetable Stock (see page 945)
- ¾ tsp salt
- 4 oz/125 g bean sprouts
- 3 eggs, lightly beaten

CHINESE VEGETABLES WITH OMELET

Mix 1 tablespoon of water, 1 tablespoon of soy sauce, 1 teaspoon of cornstarch, and the white wine in a large bowl. Add the bean curd and let marinate for 10 minutes. • Stir in 1 tablespoon of oil. • Chop the soaked bean thread into short lengths. • Rinse the chive and spinach thoroughly under cold running water and dry well. Chop into short lengths. • Heat a large wok over medium heat and add 3 tablespoons of oil. • Sauté the bean curd for 3 minutes. Remove from the wok and set aside. • Sauté the chive and spinach for 3 minutes, or until slightly wilted. • Remove from the wok and set aside. • Add 1 tablespoon of oil and sauté the scallions until lightly browned. Add the bean thread, vegetable stock, remaining soy sauce, and ½ teaspoon salt. • Cook until the sauce has reduced. • Stir in the bean sprouts. Cook for 3 more minutes. • Add the bean curd mixture. Transfer to a serving dish. • Beat the eggs with the remaining water, cornstarch, and salt in a medium bowl until frothy. • Heat the remaining oil in a large frying pan over medium heat. • Pour in the beaten egg mixture, tilting the pan so that the batter thinly covers the bottom. • Cook until light golden brown on the underside. Use a large spatula to flip the omelet and cook until golden. • Drape the omelet over the top of the serving dish.
• Serve hot.

BEAN CURD WITH MUSHROOMS

H eat the frying oil in a wok until very hot. • Fry the bean curd in two batches for 5–7 minutes, or until golden brown all over. • Drain well on paper towels. • Sauté the scallions and ginger in the 3 tablespoons of extra-virgin oil in the wok over medium heat for 5 minutes. • Add the mushrooms and cook for 5 more minutes. • Stir in the bamboo shoots, vegetable stock, soy sauce, sesame oil, and the fried bean curd. Season with pepper.
• Bring to a boil and simmer for 3 minutes. • Add the bok choy and cook for 2 minutes more. • Mix the cornstarch and water in a small bowl. Stir into the wok to thicken the mixture. • Transfer to a heated serving dish and serve hot.

*Vegan

Serves: 6

Preparation: 20'

Cooking: 25'

Level of difficulty: 1

- 2 cups/500 ml olive oil, for frying
- 2 lb/1 kg bean curd or tofu, cut into small chunks
- 2 scallions/spring onions, thinly sliced
- 1 tbsp finely chopped fresh ginger
- 3 tbsp extra-virgin olive oil
- 1 lb/500 g button mushrooms
- 1/2 cup/125 g finely sliced bamboo shoots
- 1 cup/250 ml Vegetable Stock (see page 945)
- 2 1/2 tbsp soy sauce
- 1 tsp sesame oil
- freshly ground black pepper to taste
- 4 bok choy, cooked and cut in half
- 2 tsp cornstarch/ corn flour
- 1 tbsp water

ARTICHOKES PROVENÇAL STYLE

Remove the tough outer leaves from the artichokes by snapping them off at the base. Cut off the top third of the remaining leaves. Cut the artichokes in half, removing any fuzzy choke with a sharp knife. Rub with the lemon. • Sauté the onions and garlic in the oil in a large frying pan over medium heat until the garlic is pale gold. • Add the artichokes and pour in the wine. Cook for 7–10 minutes, or until the artichokes are tender, stirring often. • Season with salt and pepper. Add the thyme and bay leaf. • Cover and cook over low heat for 40–45 minutes, or until the artichokes are tender. • Arrange the artichokes on a serving plate and spoon the sauce over the top.

Vegan

Serves: 4–6

Preparation: 20'

Cooking: 1 h

Level of difficulty: 1

- 6 artichokes
- 1 lemon
- 2 onions, finely chopped
- 2 cloves garlic, finely chopped
- 4 tbsp extra-virgin olive oil
- 1 cup/250 ml dry white wine
- salt and freshly ground black pepper to taste
- 1 tsp finely chopped thyme
- 1 bay leaf

CAULIFLOWER WITH TOMATO AND FENNEL SEEDS

Vegan

Serves: 4–6

Preparation: 10'

Cooking: 45–50'

Level of difficulty: 1

- 2 cloves garlic, finely chopped
- 1 tsp fennel seeds
- 4 tbsp extra-virgin olive oil
- 4–6 peeled and chopped tomatoes
- 1 medium cauliflower
- salt and freshly ground black pepper to taste

Sauté the garlic and fennel seeds in the oil in a large frying pan over high heat until the garlic is pale gold. • Stir in the tomatoes and cook for 15 minutes. • Cut the cauliflower up into florets, removing the tough pieces of stalk. • Place the cauliflower in the tomato sauce and season with salt and pepper. • Cover and cook over medium heat until the cauliflower is tender. • Serve hot.

483

SWEET AND SOUR ARTICHOKES

Serves: 4

Preparation: 25'

Cooking: 40'

Level of difficulty: 1

- **8 very young fresh artichokes**
- **½ lemon**
- **2½ tbsp all-purpose/plain flour**
- **6 tbsp extra-virgin olive oil**
- **2½ tbsp finely chopped onion**
- **1 tbsp capers**
- **12 green olives, pitted and finely chopped**
- **1 small carrot, cut into small cubes**
- **2 stalks celery, finely chopped**
- **scant ½ cup/ 100 ml hot water**
- **salt and freshly ground black pepper to taste**
- **4 tomatoes**
- **4 tbsp red wine vinegar**
- **2½ tsp sugar**

Remove the outer leaves of the artichokes and the top third of the leaves. Remove the choke and peel the remaining stalk. Rub all over with the lemon to prevent discoloring. • Cut each artichoke lengthwise into six pieces. • Roll the artichokes in the flour. • Sauté the artichokes in the oil in a flameproof casserole over high heat for 3 minutes. • Remove the artichokes, letting the excess oil drain back into the casserole, and set aside. • Add the onion, capers, olives, carrot, celery, and hot water. Season with salt and pepper. Simmer over medium heat for 10 minutes. • Add the tomatoes and artichokes. Cover and simmer over low heat for 25 minutes. • Mix the vinegar and sugar and stir into the vegetables. Cook for 5 minutes more. • Serve warm or at room temperature.

STUFFED BRAISED ZUCCHINI

Trim the ends off the zucchini and cut in half lengthwise. Scoop out the centers and finely chop the flesh. • Mix the zucchini flesh, parsley, garlic, bread crumbs, Parmesan, egg, and milk in a medium bowl. • Spoon the mixture into the hollowed-out zucchini. • Sauté the scallion in the butter in a large frying pan over medium heat until softened. • Add the tomatoes and season with salt and pepper. • Arrange the zucchini in the pan with the tomato mixture. Pour in the water. • Braise over medium heat for 20 minutes. • Serve hot.

Serves: 4

Preparation: 20'

Cooking: 25'

Level of difficulty: 1

- **4 zucchini/ courgettes**
- **1 tbsp finely chopped parsley**
- **1 clove garlic, finely chopped**
- **½ cup/60 g fine dry bread crumbs**
- **½ cup/60 g freshly grated Parmesan cheese**
- **1 egg**
- **2 tbsp milk**
- **1 scallion/spring onion, finely chopped**
- **4 tbsp butter**
- **2 tbsp chopped tomatoes**
- **salt and freshly ground black pepper to taste**
- **1 cup/250 ml water**

BELL PEPPER AND POTATO STEW

*Vegan

Serves: 4–6

Preparation: 10'

Cooking: 35–40'

Level of difficulty: 1

- 2 medium potatoes, peeled and cut into small cubes
- 4 tbsp extra-virgin olive oil
- 1 large onion, finely chopped
- 1 red bell pepper, seeded and cut into small chunks
- 1 green bell pepper, seeded and cut into small chunks
- 1 eggplant/ aubergine, cut into small cubes
- 1 large zucchini/ courgette, cut into small cubes
- 4 large tomatoes, coarsely chopped
- salt and freshly ground black pepper to taste
- 4 tbsp water, if needed

Sauté the potatoes in the oil in a large frying pan or flameproof casserole over medium heat for 8–10 minutes, or until golden. • Add the onion and bell peppers and cook, stirring, for 8–10 minutes, or until the onion is lightly browned. • Add the eggplant and zucchini and cook for 5 minutes. • Stir in the tomatoes. • Season with salt and pepper. • Cook for 10–15 minutes more, or until the vegetables are tender, adding the water if the mixture begins to stick to the pan. • Serve hot.

VEGETABLE STEW

*Vegan

Serves: 6

Preparation: 15'

Cooking: 1 h 5'

Level of difficulty: 1

Sauté the onions in the oil in a large saucepan over medium heat for 5 minutes until translucent. • Add the eggplants, zucchini, bell peppers, tomatoes, bay leaf, thyme, and garlic. Season with salt and pepper. • Cover and cook over low heat for 1 hour. • Stir in the olives and garnish with the basil. • Serve hot.

- 2 onions, finely chopped
- ½ cup/125 ml extra-virgin olive oil
- 1 lb/500 g eggplants/ aubergines, cut into small cubes
- 1 lb/500 g zucchini/ courgettes, cut into small cubes
- 1 red or yellow bell pepper/capsicum, seeded and cut into thin strips
- 1 green bell pepper/capsicum, seeded and cut into thin strips
- 2 lb/1 kg tomatoes, peeled, seeded, and finely chopped
- 1 bay leaf
- 1 tbsp finely chopped thyme
- 2 cloves garlic, finely chopped
- salt and freshly ground black pepper to taste
- ½ cup/50 g black olives
- 1 tbsp torn basil

BABY ONIONS WITH HERBS AND WHITE WINE

Sauté the onions in the oil and butter in a large frying pan over high heat for about 10 minutes, stirring with a wooden spoon so that the onions brown evenly. Season with salt and pepper. • Pour in the wine and add the bay leaves and herbs. Partially cover and cook for 15 more minutes. • Uncover and cook until the sauce reduces by half. • Serve hot or at room temperature.

Serves: 4

Preparation: 10'

Cooking: 30'

Level of difficulty: 1

- 1³⁄₄ lb/800 g white baby onions, peeled
- 2 tbsp extra-virgin olive oil
- 3 tbsp butter
- salt and freshly ground black pepper to taste
- 2 cups/500 ml dry white wine
- 3 bay leaves
- 1 tbsp each finely chopped thyme, marjoram, and mint

FAVA BEAN AND PEA STEW

493

*Vegan

Serves: 4–6

Preparation: 15'

Cooking: 30'

Level of difficulty: 1

- 4 artichokes
- 1 lemon
- 1 small onion, finely chopped
- 4 tbsp extra-virgin olive oil
- 1 lb/500 g hulled/ shelled fava beans,
- 1 lb/500 g hulled/ shelled peas
- 1/8 tsp freshly grated nutmeg
- salt and freshly ground black pepper to taste
- 1 tbsp finely chopped mint
- 1 tsp sugar
- 1 tsp vinegar

Remove the outer leaves from the artichokes and trim the tops and stalks. Cut them in half and remove the choke. Cut the tender hearts in thin wedges. Rub all over with the lemon to prevent discoloring. • Sauté the onion in the oil in a large frying pan over medium heat for 3–4 minutes, or until softened. • Add the artichokes and cook for 5 minutes. • Add the fava beans, peas, and nutmeg. Season with salt and pepper and cook over medium-low heat for about 25 minutes, or until tender. • Stir in the mint, sugar, and vinegar a few minutes. • Serve at room temperature.

MUSHROOM STEW WITH PINE NUTS

*Vegan
Serves: 4
Preparation: 10'
Cooking: 25'
Level of difficulty: 1

F ry the potatoes and garlic in the oil and garlic in a large frying pan until the garlic is pale gold.
• Add the mushrooms and season with salt and pepper. Cover and cook for 5 minutes. • Uncover and let the moisture evaporate. Stir in the pine nuts and almonds and cook for 10 minutes. • Sprinkle with the mint just before removing from heat.
• Serve hot.

- 2 large potatoes, diced
- 2 cloves garlic, finely chopped
- 4 tbsp extra-virgin olive oil
- 1½ lb/750 g (fresh or frozen) white mushrooms, coarsely chopped
- salt and freshly ground black pepper to taste
- ⅔ cup/120 g pine nuts
- ½ cup/50 g slivered almonds
- 1 tbsp coarsely chopped mint

*Vegan

Serves: 6

Preparation: 15'

Cooking: 45'

Level of difficulty: 1

- 2 lb/1 kg onions, peeled and sliced
- ½ cup/125 ml extra-virgin olive oil
- 1 red bell pepper and 1 yellow bell pepper/capsicum, seeded, cored, and cut into small pieces
- 1¼ lb/600 g ripe tomatoes, blanched and peeled
- salt and freshly ground black pepper to taste

SAVORY ONIONS AND TOMATOES

Sauté the onions in the oil in a large frying pan until golden. • Add the bell peppers and cook for 10 minutes. • Coarsely chop the tomatoes and add to the pan. Season with salt and pepper. Simmer over low heat for 30 minutes, stirring occasionally. • Serve hot or at room temperature.

EGGPLANTS IN CHOCOLATE SAUCE

Fry the eggplants in $^1/_2$ cup (125 ml) of oil in a large frying pan over medium heat for 5–7 minutes, or until tender. • Drain on paper towels. • Sauté the onion, corn, and cinnamon in the remaining 1 tablespoon of oil in a large frying pan over low heat for 5 minutes. • Pour in $^3/_4$ cup (180 ml) of stock and add the almonds and parsley. Season with salt and green pepper and cook for 5 minutes. • Add the eggplants, cover, and cook for 5 minutes. • Dissolve the cocoa in the remaining stock and stir into the eggplants. Increase the heat and continue cooking for 5 minutes. • If the sauce is too thin, thicken it with the cornstarch. • Transfer to a heated serving dish and serve hot.

*Vegan

Serves: 4

Preparation: 45'

Cooking: 20'

Level of difficulty: 2

- 3 eggplants/ aubergines, thinly sliced
- $^1/_2$ cup/125 ml + 1 tbsp extra-virgin olive oil
- 1 onion, finely chopped
- 2 cups/200 g canned corn/ sweetcorn
- 1 tsp ground cinnamon
- 1 cup/250 ml Vegetable Stock (see page 945)
- $^1/_3$ cup/50 g finely chopped almonds
- 1 tbsp finely chopped parsley
- salt to taste
- 1 tsp freshly ground green peppercorns
- $^1/_3$ cup/50 g unsweetened cocoa powder
- 1 tsp cornstarch/ corn flour (optional)

Serves: 4–6

Preparation: 15'

Cooking: 25'

Level of difficulty: 1

- 1 lb/500 g green beans
- 4 tbsp extra-virgin olive oil
- 3 cloves garlic, finely chopped
- 1 tbsp salt-cured capers, rinsed of salt and finely chopped
- 10 walnuts, finely chopped
- 1 tsp chile paste
- 2 tsp black olive paste
- ½ tsp gomashio (Japanese salt and sesame mix)
- juice of ½ grapefruit

JAPANESE-STYLE BEAN STEW

Place the beans in a large pot with enough water to cover. Bring to a boil and simmer over low heat for 10 minutes. • Pour off most of the cooking water, leaving just enough to cover the beans. • Add the oil, garlic, capers, walnuts, and chile paste. Cook over low heat for about 15 minutes, or until the beans are tender. • Remove from the heat. Mix in the olive paste, gomashio, and grapefruit juice, and mix well. • Serve hot.

POTATO, PEA, AND TOMATO CURRY

Sauté the peas and potatoes in 4 tablespoons of butter in a large frying pan over medium heat for 10 minutes. • Transfer to a plate and keep warm. • Sauté the coriander, turmeric, chile peppers, ginger, and cumin seeds in the remaining butter in the same frying pan until aromatic. Season with salt. • Stir in the tomatoes, potatoes, and peas. Cook over medium heat until the tomatoes have broken down, about 20 minutes. • Stir in the yogurt and serve hot.

Serves: 4–6

Preparation: 15'

Cooking: 35'

Level of difficulty: 1

- **4 cups/500 g fresh peas, hulled/shelled**
- **12 oz/350 g potatoes, peeled and cut in small cubes**
- **¾ cup/180 g butter**
- **1 tbsp ground coriander**
- **1 tsp ground turmeric**
- **2 fresh red and green chile peppers, thinly sliced**
- **½ tsp fresh ginger, finely chopped**
- **½ tsp cumin seeds**
- **salt to taste**
- **12 oz/350 g tomatoes, peeled and coarsely chopped**
- **1 cup/250 ml plain yogurt**

AREZZO BEAN STEW

*Vegan

Serves: 4

Preparation: 25' +
time to soak beans

Cooking: 1 h

Level of difficulty: 2

- 14 oz/400 g firm-ripe tomatoes
- 2 cups/300 g dried beans, such as cannellini or borlotti, soaked overnight and drained
- 2 cloves garlic, lightly crushed but whole
- 1 bay leaf
- 1 quart/1 liter water
- salt and freshly ground black pepper to taste
- fresh basil, to garnish
- 4 tbsp extra-virgin olive oil

Blanch the tomatoes in salted boiling water for 1 minute. • Drain and slip off the skins. Remove the seeds and chop the flesh coarsely. • Place the beans in a large pan with the tomatoes, garlic, and bay leaf. • Pour in enough water to cover the beans completely and bring to a boil. Cover and cook over medium heat for about 1 hour. Season with salt halfway through the cooking. • Discard the garlic and bay leaf. • Garnish with the basil, season with pepper, and drizzle with the oil. • Serve hot.

STEWED ARTICHOKE HEARTS

Pour the oil into a large frying pan and add the parsley and garlic. Sauté over low heat for 5 minutes. • Add the artichoke hearts and season with salt and pepper. • Pour in enough water to cover the artichokes completely. Cover and cook over medium-low heat for 10 minutes. • Remove the lid, increase the heat and cook for 10 more minutes to reduce the cooking liquid. • Serve hot or at room temperature.

500

Vegan

Serves: 6

Preparation: 15'

Cooking: 25'

Level of difficulty: 1

- ½ cup/125 ml extra-virgin olive oil
- 2 tbsp finely chopped parsley
- 2 cloves garlic, finely chopped
- 12 fresh or frozen raw artichoke hearts
- salt and freshly ground black pepper to taste

SWEET AND SOUR VEGETABLES

*Vegan

Serves: 6–8

Preparation: 1 h +
   13 h to stand

Cooking: 50'

Level of difficulty: 1

- 2 lb/1 kg
  eggplants/
  aubergines, cut
  into small cubes
- 2 tbsp sea salt
- ⅔ cup/150 ml
  olive oil
- 4 tender stalks
  celery, cut into
  small lengths
- 1 large onion, thinly
  sliced
- 2 cups/500 ml
  sieved tomatoes
- 12 leaves fresh
  basil, torn
- 1 small firm pear,
  peeled, cored, and
  diced
- 1½ tbsp pickled
  capers, drained
- 20 green or black
  olives, pitted and
  chopped
- 3 tbsp pine nuts
- 2 tbsp sugar
- ½ cup/125 ml
  white wine vinegar
- 3 tbsp coarsely
  chopped almonds

Sprinkle the eggplants with the salt and let drain in a colander for 1 hour. • Fry the eggplant in ½ cup (125 ml) of oil in a large frying pan over medium heat for 10 minutes. • Drain and set aside. • Blanch the celery in salted boiling water for 5 minutes. • Drain and set aside. • Sauté the onion in the remaining oil in a large frying pan until golden. • Stir in the tomatoes and half the basil. Cook for 10 minutes. • Add the celery, pear, capers, olives, pine nuts, sugar, and vinegar. • Cook for 20 minutes, stirring occasionally. • Add the eggplant and remaining basil. Cook, stirring occasionally, for 10 minutes. • Remove from the heat and when the mixture is just warm, transfer to a serving dish. The eggplant should have absorbed most of the moisture. • Refrigerate for 12 hours or overnight. • Garnish with the basil and almonds. • Serve at room temperature.

ARTICHOKES WITH EGG AND LEMON SAUCE

Cut off the stalks and remove the lower, outermost leaves of the artichokes. Use kitchen scissors to snip off the top quarter from each of the remaining leaves. • Preparing one artichoke at a time, slice into quarters from top to bottom and, unless they are tiny artichoke buds, remove the hairy "choke" from the center. • Cut each quarter into 2–3 thin slices, dropping them immediately into a large bowl of cold water with 1 tablespoon of lemon juice to prevent them from turning black. • Drain well. • Melt the butter in a frying pan and add the well-drained artichoke slices. Season with salt and cook over medium heat for 20 minutes until tender. Stir and turn often, adding 1–2 tablespoons of hot water to keep them moist. • Beat the egg yolks, cream, cold water, and parsley in a small bowl. Season with salt and pepper. • Drizzle the remaining lemon juice over the artichokes and reduce the heat to very low. • Pour the egg mixture over the artichokes and stir. The egg mixture should turn creamy and thicken somewhat (this will only take about 2 minutes; do not allow the eggs to scramble). • Serve hot.

Serves: 4

Preparation: 10'

Cooking: 20–25'

Level of difficulty: 1

- **8 very young globe artichokes**
- **2–3 tbsp lemon juice**
- **4 tbsp butter**
- **salt and freshly ground white pepper to taste**
- **3 egg yolks**
- **2 tbsp light/single cream**
- **4 tbsp cold water**
- **1 tbsp finely chopped parsley**

CABBAGE CURRY

Chop the cabbage into wide strips. Wash and drain well. • Sauté the onion and garlic in the butter in a large frying pan over low heat for 5 minutes until softened. • Add the turmeric, chile, salt, garam masala, cabbage, and water. • Cook over medium heat for about 15 minutes, adding more water if the sauce dries out. • Cover and cook over low heat for 10 more minutes, or until the cabbage is tender. • Increase the heat and cook until the liquid has reduced by half.
• Serve hot.

Serves: 4

Preparation: 15'

Cooking: 30'

Level of difficulty: 1

- 1 cabbage, weighing about 2 lb/1 kg
- 1 onion, finely chopped
- 2 cloves garlic, finely chopped
- 2 tbsp butter
- 1 tsp ground turmeric
- 1/2 tsp chile powder
- 2 tsp salt
- 1 tbsp garam masala
- 1 cup/250 ml water + extra

BANANA CURRY

507

Serves: 4

Preparation: 20'

Cooking: 25'

Level of difficulty: 1

- **1½ lb/750 g unripe bananas**
- **4 tbsp butter**
- **1 clove garlic, finely chopped**
- **½ tsp ground turmeric**
- **½ tsp cumin seeds**
- **1 fresh spicy red chile pepper, thinly sliced**
- **1 tsp salt**
- **½ tsp garam masala**
- **1 tbsp milk**
- **1 tbsp fresh lemon juice**

Peel the bananas, remove the filaments, and chop into 1-inch (2.5 cm) rounds. • Melt the butter in a large frying pan and sauté the garlic, turmeric, and cumin seeds over medium heat until the garlic is pale gold. • Add the bananas, chile pepper, and salt. Cook over low heat for 5–7 minutes, or until the bananas have softened. • Add the garam masala and salt and mix well, taking care not to squash the bananas. • Drizzle with the lemon juice and cook over low heat for 10 minutes, or until the liquid has reduced by half. • Serve hot.

CURRIED TOFU

*Vegan

Serves: 4

Preparation: 5'

Cooking: 30'

Level of difficulty: 1

- 1 onion, finely chopped
- 1 clove garlic, finely chopped
- 3 tbsp extra-virgin olive oil
- 1 tsp curry powder
- salt to taste
- 6 tomatoes, peeled and chopped
- 14 oz/400 g tofu, cubed

Sauté the onion and garlic in the oil in a large frying pan over low heat until the garlic is pale gold. • Add the curry powder and season with salt. Cook for 1 minute. • Stir in the tomatoes and cook for about 5 minutes, or until they begin to break down. • Add the tofu and cook for 20 minutes. • Serve hot with vegetables as a main course or at room temperature as an appetizer.

STUFFED POTATOES

Use a sharp knife to hollow out the potatoes, leaving the sides 1 inch (2.5 cm) thick. Reserve the scooped-out potato. • Mix the oil, onion, the potato, three-quarters of the Parmesan, parsley, and salt and pepper in a large bowl. • Fill the potatoes with the stuffing and arrange them in a flameproof casserole. Pour in about 1 cup (250 ml) of water. Drizzle with the butter and sprinkle with the bread crumbs and the remaining Parmesan. Cook over medium heat for about 45 minutes, or until the potatoes are tender. • Turn the broiler (grill) to the high setting. Broil for 5–10 minutes, or until the potatoes are browned. • Serve hot.

Serves: 4–6

Preparation: 45'

Cooking: 50–55'

Level of difficulty: 2

- **10 large baking potatoes**
- **½ cup/125 ml extra-virgin olive oil**
- **1 onion, finely chopped**
- **4 cups/500 g freshly grated Parmesan or Cheddar cheese**
- **3 tbsp finely chopped parsley**
- **salt and freshly ground black pepper to taste**
- **2 tbsp butter, melted**
- **½ cup/60 g fine dry bread crumbs**

ARTICHOKE AND PEA STEW

*Vegan

Serves: 4

Preparation: 10'

Cooking: 35'

Level of difficulty: 1

- 8 medium artichokes
- juice of 1 lemon
- 1 onion, finely chopped
- 2 tbsp extra-virgin olive oil
- salt and freshly ground black pepper to taste
- 3 cups/375 g fresh hulled/shelled or frozen peas
- water (optional)

Clean the artichokes by trimming the tops and stalk. Remove all the tough outer leaves so that only the pale, inner part remains. Cut each artichoke in half and place in a large bowl of cold water with the lemon juice (this will stop them from discoloring). • Sauté the onion in the oil in a large frying pan over medium heat until golden. • Drain the artichokes and add them to the pan. Cook for 10 minutes. • Season with salt and pepper and add the peas. Cook over medium heat for about 15–20 minutes, or until the peas and artichokes are tender, adding water if the mixture begins to stick to the pan. • Serve hot or at room temperature.

CAULIFLOWER CREAM WITH SAFFRON MUSHROOMS

Place the onion in a medium bowl. Pour in the vinegar and let marinate for 20 minutes. • Cook the cauliflower in a large pot of salted, boiling water for 10 minutes, or until tender. • Drain and process in a food processor or blender until smooth. Set aside 4 tablespoons of the purée. • Add 2 tablespoons oil to the remaining purée and season with salt and pepper. • Sauté the mushrooms in the remaining oil in a large nonstick frying pan over medium heat for 10 minutes, or until tender. • Add the reserved cauliflower purée and saffron to the mushrooms and cook for 2 minutes. Place in a small serving dish. • Transfer the cauliflower purée to a serving dish. Drain the onions and arrange them around the edge of the puree. • Serve warm with the mushroom sauce.

Vegan

Serves: 4

Preparation: 10' + 20' to marinate onions

Cooking: 15'

Level of difficulty: 1

- 1 small red onion, finely sliced
- 6 tbsp white wine vinegar
- 1¾ lb/800 g cauliflower florets
- 4 tbsp extra-virgin olive oil
- salt and freshly ground black pepper to taste
- 4 oz/125 g mushrooms, finely chopped
- ⅛ tsp powdered saffron

BRUSSELS SPROUTS AND CHESTNUTS

Serves: 6

Preparation: 20'

Cooking: 45'

Level of difficulty: 1

- 1 lb/500 g dried chestnuts, soaked overnight and drained
- 1 quart/1 liter Vegetable Stock (see page 945)
- 2 lb/1 kg Brussels sprouts
- 1 wedge of lemon
- 6 tbsp butter
- salt to taste

Cook the chestnuts in the stock in a large saucepan over medium heat for about 30 minutes, or until tender. • Drain. • Cook the Brussels sprouts in a large pot of salted, boiling water with the lemon for 10–15 minutes, or until tender. • Drain well. • Melt the butter in a large saucepan. Add the chestnuts and the Brussels sprouts and sauté over high heat for 2–3 minutes. • Season with salt and serve hot.

PORCINI MUSHROOMS COOKED IN CREAM

S auté the mushrooms and garlic in the oil in a large frying pan over high heat for 5–7 minutes, or until the mushrooms are cooked and any liquid produced has evaporated. • Discard the garlic. Mix in the parsley and cream. Cook over low heat for about 10 minutes, or until the cream has thickened slightly. Season with salt and pepper. • Serve hot.

Serves: 4

Preparation: 5'

Cooking: 15–20'

Level of difficulty: 1

- 2 lb/1 kg fresh porcini mushrooms, thinly sliced
- 2 cloves garlic, lightly crushed but whole
- 3 tbsp extra-virgin olive oil
- 2 tbsp finely chopped parsley
- 1 cup/250 ml heavy/double cream
- salt and freshly ground black pepper to taste

GREEN BEANS WITH ASIAGO

Serves: 4

Preparation: 5'

Cooking: 20'

Level of difficulty: 1

- 1 onion, finely chopped
- 1 clove garlic, finely chopped
- 3½ tbsp butter
- 2 tbsp extra-virgin olive oil
- 12 oz/350 g green beans
- salt and freshly ground black pepper to taste
- 10 oz/300 g Asiago or Emmental cheese, cut into strips

Sauté the onion and garlic in the butter and oil in a large frying pan over medium heat for 3 minutes. • Add the green beans and season with salt and pepper. Cover and cook over low heat for about 15 minutes, or until the beans are tender, adding some water if the mixture begins to stick to the pan. • Add the cheese and cover and cook until the cheese has melted. • Serve hot.

SPICED BEANS WITH APPLE

Sauté the onion in the oil in a large frying pan over medium heat for 2–3 minutes, or until golden. • Add the spices and cook for 2 minutes, taking care not to allow the spices to burn. • Add the apples and sugar and cook for 5–10 minutes, or until the apples have softened. • Add the beans and just enough water to cover the base of the pan. Season with salt and pepper. Cover and cook for about 10 minutes. • Serve hot with Basmati or Thai rice.

Vegan

Serves: 2–4

Preparation: 5'

Cooking: 25'

Level of difficulty: 1

- 1 small onion, finely sliced
- 2 tbsp extra-virgin olive oil
- ½ tsp ground turmeric
- ½ tsp ground allspice
- ½ tsp ground cinnamon
- ½ tsp ground cumin
- 2 apples, cored and cut into bite-size pieces
- 2 tbsp sugar
- 2 cups/350 g canned cannellini or white kidney beans
- ½ cup/125 ml water + more as needed
- salt and freshly ground black pepper to taste

ONION AND ORANGE MARMALADE

*Vegan

Serves: 4

Preparation: 10'

Cooking: 20'

Level of difficulty: 2

- 2 lb/1 kg white onions, sliced
- 6 tbsp extra-virgin olive oil
- ⅓ cup/70 g granulated sugar
- 1¼ cups/310 ml fresh orange juice
- salt to taste

Place the onions in a bowl and cover with cold water until you are ready to use them. • Heat the oil over medium heat in a large nonstick frying pan. • Add the sugar and stir until completely dissolved, about 5 minutes. • Beat in the orange juice. • Drain the onions and add them to the pan. • Cook over medium heat for about 15 minutes, or until the onions are very tender and the mixture is glossy. Season with salt. • Serve warm.

Serve with raisin bread or over boiled new potatoes.

521

STIR-FRIED & SAUTÉED VEGETABLES

SAUTÉED PEAS WITH FENNEL SEEDS

Cook the peas in salted boiling water for 10–15 minutes, or until tender. • Drain well. • Sauté the onion in the oil in a large frying pan over low heat for 10 minutes, or until light golden brown. • Add the peas and fennel seeds. Season with salt and pepper. Sauté over high heat for 3–4 minutes. . • Sprinkle with the basil and parsley. • Serve hot.

*Vegan

Serves: 4

Preparation: 15'

Cooking: 20'

Level of difficulty: 1

- 1 lb/500 g hulled/shelled peas
- 1 onion, finely chopped
- 4 tbsp extra-virgin olive oil
- 1 tbsp fennel seeds, crushed
- salt and freshly ground white pepper to taste
- 1 tbsp torn basil
- 1 tbsp finely chopped parsley

PEAS SAUTÉED WITH BUTTER AND MINT

Cook the peas in salted, boiling water for 10–15 minutes, or until tender. • Drain well. • Place the peas in a frying pan with the butter and mint. Season with salt and pepper and sauté for 2–3 minutes. • Turn out onto a serving dish. Garnish with the mint leaves and serve hot.

Serves: 4–6

Preparation: 15'

Cooking: 20'

Level of difficulty: 1

- 1 lb/500 g hulled/ shelled peas
- 4 tbsp butter
- 4 tbsp finely chopped mint + extra leaves, to garnish
- salt and freshly ground white pepper to taste

CELERY WITH TOMATO AND MUSHROOM SAUCE

Vegan

Serves: 4–6

Preparation: 20'

Cooking: 45'

Level of difficulty: 1

- 1 lb/500 g celery stalks, leaves removed, cut into 3-inch/8-cm lengths
- juice of 1 lemon
- 8 oz/250 g mushrooms
- 1 small onion, finely chopped
- 4 tbsp extra-virgin olive oil
- 1 carrot, peeled and cut into julienne sticks
- 1 cup/250 g chopped tomatoes
- salt and freshly ground black pepper to taste
- 2 tbsp finely chopped parsley

Cook the celery in a large pot of salted, boiling water with half the lemon juice for 10–15 minutes, or until tender. Drain. • Soak the mushrooms in cold water with the remaining lemon juice for 5 minutes. • Drain and slice thinly. • Sauté the onion in the oil in a large saucepan over low heat for 2 minutes. • Add the carrot and mushrooms and cook for 5 minutes. • Add the tomatoes and season with salt and pepper. Cover and cook over low heat for 30 minutes, or until reduced, • Arrange the celery in a serving dish and pour the sauce over the top. • Sprinkle with the parsley and serve hot.

PIQUANT ONIONS AND TOMATOES

Peel the tomatoes, squeezing gently to remove as many seeds as possible. Chop coarsely.
• Sauté the bell pepper and chile pepper in the oil in a medium saucepan over high heat for 7–10 minutes, or until the bell pepper begins to soften.
• Add the tomatoes and onions. Season with salt, cover and cook for 35–40 minutes, or until the vegetables are tender. • Let cool completely.
• Sprinkle with the marjoram and serve.

Vegan

Serves: 4

Preparation: 20'

Cooking: 40–50'

Level of difficulty: 1

- **2 firm-ripe tomatoes**
- **½ red bell pepper, seeded, cored, and finely chopped**
- **1 small green chile pepper, seeded and finely sliced**
- **4 tbsp extra-virgin olive oil**
- **2 lb/1 kg onions, quartered**
- **salt to taste**
- **2 tbsp finely chopped marjoram**

SWEET AND SOUR BEETS

C ook the beets in salted, boiling water for
30–35 minutes, or until tender. • Cook the
onion in salted, boiling water for 5 minutes, or until
softened. • Drain and pat dry with paper towels.
• Peel the beets and dice them. • Sauté the beets
with the butter, water, vinegar, and sugar in a large
frying pan over low heat for 5 minutes. • Place the
beets on a serving plate and spoon the onions into
the center. • Serve warm.

Serves: 4

Preparation: 20'

Cooking: 40–55'

Level of difficulty: 2

- **1 lb/500 g red beets/beetroot**
- **1 onion, thinly sliced**
- **4 tbsp butter**
- **2 tbsp water**
- **1 tbsp red wine vinegar**
- **1 tbsp sugar**

CARROT AND SESAME STIR-FRY

Sauté the carrots in the oil in a large frying pan over medium heat for about 10 minutes, or until crunchy-tender. • Toast the sesame seeds in a small saucepan over medium heat for 5–10 minutes, shaking the pan to make sure they do not burn. • Toss the carrots with the sesame seeds and season with salt. • Serve hot.

*Vegan

Serves: 2–4
Preparation: 5'
Cooking: 15–20'
Level of difficulty: 1

- 6 large carrots, peeled and chopped
- 4 tbsp extra-virgin olive oil
- 1 tbsp sesame seeds
- salt to taste

BROCCOLI AND TOFU STIR-FRY

*Vegan

Serves: 2

Preparation: 5'

Cooking: 10'

Level of difficulty: 1

- 10 oz/300 g broccoli florets
- scant ½ cup/100 g tofu cubes
- salt and freshly ground black pepper to taste
- 2 tbsp soy sauce

Cook the broccoli in a large pot of salted, boiling water for 5 minutes, or until not quite al dente. • Drain well. • Sauté the broccoli and tofu in the oil in a large saucepan over medium heat for 3 minutes. Season with salt and pepper. • Drizzle with the soy sauce and serve hot.

SAUTÉED VEGETABLES WITH EGG WHITE OMELET

Serves: 6

Preparation: 20'

Cooking: 20'

Level of difficulty: 1

- 8 egg whites
- salt to taste
- 1 scallion/spring onion, finely chopped
- 3 tbsp butter
- 8 oz/250 g carrots, peeled and cut into thin sticks
- 1 cup/250 ml water
- 1 tbsp finely chopped thyme
- 1 tbsp finely chopped marjoram
- 2 tbsp extra-virgin olive oil
- 1 lb/500 g asparagus tips, cut in half
- 4 oz/125 g fresh fava/broad beans
- 1 tbsp finely chopped parsley
- 1 tbsp freshly grated Parmesan cheese

Beat the egg whites and $1/8$ teaspoon salt in a large bowl until stiff. • Sauté the scallion in 1 tablespoon of butter in a frying pan over medium heat until lightly browned. • Melt 1 tablespoon of butter in a large frying pan over medium heat. Pour in the beaten whites and cook until set. Turn out onto a board and cut into thin strips. • Sauté the carrots in the remaining butter in a frying pan over medium heat. Season with salt. • Pour in the water and cook for 8–10 minutes, or until tender. • Sauté the thyme and marjoram in the oil in a large pan until aromatic. • Add the asparagus and cook until tender. • Stir in the carrots, fava beans, and parsley. Cook for 1 minute. • Add the omelet strips and sprinkle with the Parmesan. • Serve hot.

RADICCHIO TREVISO-STYLE

Rinse the radicchio heads thoroughly under cold running water and dry well. • Trim off the end of the stalk and cut each head lengthwise into quarters. • Grease a large frying pan with 1 tablespoon of oil. • Place the radicchio pieces in the frying pan in a single layer. Drizzle with the remaining oil and season with salt and pepper. • Cook over low heat for 15–20 minutes, or until the radicchio is tender but still crisp. • Serve hot.

*Vegan

Serves: 6

Preparation: 20'

Cooking: 15–20'

Level of difficulty: 1

- 6 heads Treviso radicchio or red chicory
- 3–4 tbsp extra-virgin olive oil
- salt and freshly ground black pepper to taste

EGGPLANT WITH BASIL

Place the eggplant in a colander. Sprinkle with salt and drain for 1 hour. • Sauté the garlic and chile pepper in the oil in a wok or large frying pan over medium heat for 2 minutes. • Add the eggplant and sauté for 10 minutes, or until tender. • Add the soy sauce, sugar, vinegar, salt, and basil and mix well. • Drizzle with the sesame oil and serve hot.

538

*Vegan

Serves: 6

Preparation: 15' + 1 h to drain

Cooking: 12'

Level of difficulty: 1

- 1 lb/500 g eggplants/ aubergines, cut into bite-size chunks
- 1–2 tbsp coarse sea salt
- 1 tsp finely chopped garlic
- 1 tsp finely chopped red chile pepper
- 3 tbsp extra-virgin olive oil
- 2 tbsp soy sauce
- 1½ tbsp sugar
- 1 tbsp white wine vinegar
- ½ tsp salt
- 1 large bunch fresh basil, torn
- 1 tbsp sesame oil

*Vegan

Serves: 4

Preparation: 20'

Cooking: 10'

Level of difficulty: 1

- 1½ cloves garlic, 1 lightly crushed, ½ finely chopped
- 1 lb/500 g zucchini/ courgettes, cut into thin rounds
- 4 tbsp extra-virgin olive oil
- salt and freshly ground black pepper to taste
- 6 leaves fresh basil, finely chopped
- 2 leaves fresh mint, finely chopped

SAUTÉED HERBED ZUCCHINI

Sauté the crushed garlic and zucchini in 3 tablespoons of oil in a large frying pan over high heat for 10 minutes, or until the zucchini are lightly browned. • Season with salt and pepper and discard the garlic. • Mix the basil, mint, and finely chopped garlic in a small bowl with the remaining oil. • Add to the zucchini and remove from the heat. Mix well and serve hot.

GRILLED
VEGETABLES

BELL PEPPER, MUSHROOM, AND ZUCCHINI KEBABS

Serves: 6

Preparation: 30'

Cooking: 25'

Level of difficulty: 2

KEBABS

- 1 lb/500 g mushrooms, cut into large cubes
- 6 zucchini/ courgettes, coarsely sliced
- 3 bell peppers/ capsicums, seeded, cored, and coarsely chopped
- 3 onions, sliced
- 3 leaves fresh sage
- 12 cherry tomatoes
- salt to taste
- 6 tbsp extra-virgin olive oil

SAUCE

- 3 hard-boiled eggs
- 6 tbsp extra-virgin olive oil
- 1 tbsp chopped pickled gherkins
- 1 tbsp chopped capers
- 1 tbsp finely chopped parsley
- 1–2 tbsp vinegar
- salt and freshly ground white pepper to taste

Thread the vegetables onto wooden skewers, alternating slices of the mushrooms, zucchini, and bell peppers with pieces of onion, sage leaves, and tomatoes. Season with salt and brush with the oil. • Arrange the kebabs on a grill or barbecue for about 10–15 minutes, turning often, and basting with the oil, until the vegetables are tender. • Sauce: Separate the egg yolks from the whites. Use a fork to crush the yolks in a bowl with enough oil to make a creamy mixture. Mix in the gherkins, capers, parsley, and vinegar. Season with salt and pepper. • Finely chop the egg whites and add them to the sauce. • Serve the kebabs hot with the sauce on the side.

Soak wooden skewers in cold water before grilling to prevent them from burning.

GRILLED VEGETABLES WITH AÏOLI

Aïoli: Beat the egg yolks with the garlic in a medium bowl. Use a balloon whisk to gradually beat in the oil until the mixture is smooth and thick like mayonnaise. Season with pepper and add the lemon juice. Refrigerate until ready to use. • Grilled Vegetables: Wash, but do not peel the vegetables. Arrange them on a grill pan in batches and grill for until tender. • Let cool slightly. • Peel and chop the vegetables and transfer them to a serving plate. • Beat the oil, parsley, garlic, and pepper in a small bowl. Pour over the vegetables and serve with the aïoli as a dipping sauce.

544

Serves: 4

Preparation: 30'

Cooking: 35'

Level of difficulty: 1

AÏOLI
- **2 egg yolks**
- **2 cloves garlic, finely chopped**
- **1 cup/250 ml extra-virgin olive oil**
- **freshly ground pepper to taste**
- **1 tbsp fresh lemon juice**

GRILLED VEGETABLES
- **2 red and yellow bell peppers**
- **4 eggplants/ aubergines**
- **4 firm-ripe tomatoes**
- **4 onions**
- **4 tbsp extra-virgin olive oil**
- **2 tbsp finely chopped parsley**
- **1 clove garlic, lightly crushed but whole**
- **freshly ground pepper to taste**

GARLIC-MARINATED ZUCCHINI

Mix the oil, garlic, basil, chile powder, and salt in a small bowl. • Wash the zucchini, pat dry on paper towels, and slice finely lengthwise. • Brush with the marinade and let marinate for about 1 hour. • Drain the marinade from the zucchini slices. • Arrange the zucchini in small batches on a grill pan. Grill for about 8 minutes, or until tender, brushing with the marinade during cooking. • Transfer to a serving plate and serve hot.

*Vegan

Serves: 4

Preparation: 20' + 1 h to marinate

Cooking: 25'

Level of difficulty: 1

- **6 tbsp extra-virgin olive oil**
- **3 cloves garlic, finely chopped**
- **1 small bunch fresh basil, torn**
- **⅛ tsp mild chile powder**
- **⅛ tsp salt**
- **6 zucchini/ courgettes**

MARINATED EGGPLANTS

Vegan

Serves: 6

Preparation: 20' + 1 h
  to degorge
  eggplants +
  24 h to marinate

Cooking: 20'

Level of difficulty: 1

- 4 medium-large
  eggplants/
  aubergines
- salt to taste
- ½ cup/125 ml
  olive oil, for frying
- 2 cloves garlic,
  thinly sliced
- 8–10 leaves fresh
  sage
- good-quality wine
  vinegar, to serve

Trim, then wash and dry the eggplants. Slice them thinly lengthwise and arrange in layers in a colander, sprinkling each layer with salt. Cover with a plate. Place a weight on top and set aside for 1 hour. • Dry with paper towels. • Cook the eggplant in batches in a grill pan for 10 minutes, or until tender. • Arrange in layers in a deep dish, placing slices of garlic and sage leaves between the eggplant. • Pour in enough wine vinegar to completely cover the top layer. Let marinate for 24 hours.

GRILLED VEGETABLES

*Vegan

Serves: 4

Preparation: 15'

Cooking: 30'

Level of difficulty: 1

- 2 zucchini/
  courgettes, thickly
  sliced lengthwise
- 2 tomatoes, halved
- 2 onions, halved
- 2 eggplants/
  aubergines, thickly
  sliced lengthwise
- 6 tbsp extra-virgin
  olive oil
- 3 tbsp fresh lemon
  juice
- salt and freshly
  ground black
  pepper to taste

Arrange the vegetables in small batches on a grill pan and grill for about 8 minutes, or until tender. • Mix the oil and lemon juice in a small bowl. Season with salt and pepper and drizzle the dressing over the vegetables.

549

VEGETABLE KEBABS WITH MOZZARELLA

Arrange the zucchini and eggplant in a grill pan and grill for about 4 minutes, or until tender.
• Thread the vegetables onto wooden skewers alternating with the Mozzarella, tomatoes, and basil leaves. Season with salt and pepper and brush with the oil. • Cook on the grill for about 5 minutes, or until the cheese and tomatoes are heated through. • Serve hot.

Bocconcini (mini Mozzarella balls) can be found in Italian delicatessens.

Serves: 4

Preparation: 20'

Cooking: 25'

Level of difficulty: 1

- 2 zucchini/ courgettes, thickly sliced
- 1 medium eggplant/ aubergine, thickly sliced
- 8 baby Mozzarellas (bocconcini)
- 16 cherry tomatoes
- 8 leaves fresh basil
- salt and freshly ground black pepper to taste
- 1 tbsp extra-virgin olive oil

MIXED GRILLED VEGETABLES WITH CAPER SAUCE

*Vegan

Serves: 4

Preparation: 30' + 1 h to drain

Cooking: 30'

Level of difficulty: 2

- 8 oz/250 g eggplants/ aubergines
- 1 tbsp coarse salt
- 8 oz/250 g zucchini/ courgettes
- 8 oz/250 g onions
- 1 red radicchio, weighing about 7 oz/200 g
- 8 oz/250 g red bell peppers, seeded
- 4 tbsp extra-virgin olive oil
- salt and freshly ground black pepper to taste

CAPER SAUCE
- 2 oz/50 g capers
- 6 tbsp extra-virgin olive oil
- 1 tsp red wine vinegar
- 1 fresh red chile pepper, seeded
- 4 leaves fresh basil
- 1/8 tsp salt

Cut the eggplants into 1/4-inch (5-mm) thick slices without peeling them. Place in layers in a colander and sprinkle each layer with salt. Let drain for 1 hour. • Cut the zucchini and onions into 1/4-inch (5-mm) thick slices. • Wash the radicchio and divide into segments. • Cut the bell peppers into 1/4-inch (5-mm) strips. • Brush the vegetables with oil and season with salt and pepper. • Cook the vegetables in small batches in a grill pan for about 10 minutes, or until tender. • Transfer to a serving dish. • Caper Sauce: Process the capers, oil, vinegar, chile pepper, basil, and salt in a food processor or blender until smooth. • Serve the vegetables at room temperature with the sauce.

Capers are the unopened buds of shrubs native to the Mediterranean.

MIXED GRILLED VEGETABLES

Wash and chop the vegetables into large chunks. Brush with the oil and season with salt. • Cook the vegetables in small batches in a grill pan for about 10 minutes, or until tender. • Transfer to a serving plate and serve.

*Vegan

Serves: 4

Preparation: 10'

Cooking: 25'

Level of difficulty: 1

- **2 yellow bell peppers, seeded**
- **2 red radicchio**
- **3 firm-ripe tomatoes**
- **2 eggplants/ aubergines**
- **4 zucchini/ courgettes**
- **4 potatoes**
- **2 tbsp extra-virgin olive oil**
- **salt to taste**

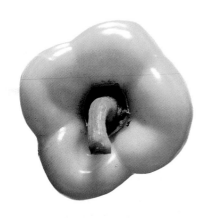

ZUCCHINI WITH ARUGULA PESTO

*Vegan

Serves: 4–6

Preparation: 25' + 1 h to marinate

Cooking: 30'

Level of difficulty: 1

- 1½ lb/750 g small zucchini/ courgettes
- 4 tbsp extra-virgin olive oil
- 2 tbsp cider vinegar
- 1 tbsp balsamic vinegar
- 1 clove garlic, thinly sliced
- salt and freshly ground black pepper to taste
- 4 oz/125 g arugula/rocket
- 6 tbsp pine nuts
- 4 tbsp raisins

Rinse the zucchini thoroughly under cold running water and dry well. • Trim the ends off the zucchini and cut lengthwise in very thin slices. • Place the zucchini in a small, shallow dish. Mix 2 tablespoons of oil, cider vinegar, balsamic vinegar, garlic, and salt and pepper in a small bowl. Pour the mixture over the zucchini. Let marinate for 1 hour. • Place 3 oz (90 g) of the arugula in a blender with 4 tablespoons of pine nuts and the remaining oil and chop until smooth. If the mixture is not liquid enough, add 1–2 tablespoons hot water. • Drain the zucchini, setting aside the marinade. • Heat a large grill pan over medium heat. Cook the zucchini in batches for 4–5 minutes each batch, or until lightly browned. • Arrange the remaining arugula on a serving platter and arrange the zucchini on top. Sprinkle with the remaining 2 tablespoons of pine nuts and the raisins. Season with salt and pepper and drizzle with the marinade. • Serve hot or at room temperature.

BAKED
VEGETABLES

EGGPLANT, BELL PEPPER, AND POTATO BAKE

Place the eggplant in a colander. Sprinkle with salt and let drain for 1 hour. • Rinse the eggplant and gently squeeze out excess moisture. Dry on a clean cloth. • Preheat the oven to 350°F/180°C/gas 4. • Heat the oil in a large frying pan until very hot and fry the eggplant in small batches for 5–7 minutes, or until tender. • Remove with a slotted spoon and drain on paper towels.
• Fry the potatoes in the oil for 5–7 minutes, or until golden. • Drain on paper towels. • Sauté the bell peppers and onion in 1 tablespoon of the extra-virgin oil in a small saucepan over low heat until softened. • Sauté the garlic in the remaining oil in a large frying pan until pale gold. • Stir in the tomatoes and cook for 15–20 minutes, or until the tomatoes have broken down. Add the basil.
• Add the fried eggplant, potatoes, bell peppers, and onions. Season with salt. Transfer to an earthenware casserole dish. • Bake for 10–15 minutes, or until lightly browned. • Serve hot.

*Vegan

Serves: 4

Preparation: 30' + 1 h to degorge eggplant

Cooking: 45–55'

Level of difficulty: 2

- 2 eggplants/aubergines, thinly sliced
- 1 tbsp coarse salt
- salt to taste
- 1 cup/250 ml olive oil, for frying
- 2 potatoes, peeled and cut into small sticks
- 2 bell peppers, seeded, cored, and coarsely chopped
- 1 onion, thinly sliced
- 2 tbsp extra-virgin olive oil
- 1 clove garlic, finely chopped
- 10 oz/300 g peeled and chopped tomatoes

BAKED MUSHROOMS WITH RICE

Serves: 6

Preparation: 25'

Cooking: 35–45'

Level of difficulty: 2

- 1 lb/500 g mixed mushrooms
- 2 cloves garlic, finely chopped
- 1 onion, finely chopped
- 4 tbsp extra-virgin olive oil
- 8 oz/250 g peeled plum tomatoes, coarsely chopped
- 1 tbsp finely chopped parsley
- 2¼ cups/450 g short-grain rice
- 2 eggs, lightly beaten
- 1 cup/125 g freshly grated Pecorino cheese
- 1 cup/125 g fine dry bread crumbs
- salt and freshly ground black pepper to taste

Preheat the oven to 400°F/200°C/gas 6.
• Butter a baking dish. • Clean the mushrooms, wiping them with a damp cloth. Slice thinly.
• Sauté the garlic and onion in 2 tablespoons of oil in a frying pan over low heat until the garlic is pale gold. • Add the mushrooms, tomatoes, and parsley. • Cook the rice in a large pot of salted, boiling water for 12–15 minutes, or until tender.
• Drain well and transfer to a large bowl. Mix in the eggs and half the Pecorino. • Spoon half of the rice mixture into the prepared baking dish. Top with half of the mushroom sauce. Cover with the remaining rice. Sprinkle with the bread crumbs and the remaining Pecorino. Season with pepper and drizzle with the remaining oil. • Bake for 15–20 minutes, or until golden on top. • Serve hot.

BAKED ZUCCHINI FLAN

Melt 2 tablespoons of butter with the oil in a large saucepan over low heat. Add the onion, garlic, parsley, and basil and cook for 5 minutes.
• Add the zucchini and season with salt and pepper. Cover and cook for about 20 minutes, adding 2–3 tablespoons of water if the mixture dried out too much. • Uncover, turn up the heat, and stir until the vegetables are coarsely mashed and any excess liquid has evaporated. • Preheat the oven to 350°F/180°C/gas 4. • Butter a $1^1/2$-quart (1.5-liter) ring mold. • Melt the remaining butter with the flour in a small saucepan over low heat. Cook for 1 minute, stirring constantly. • Remove from the heat and pour in half the hot milk. Return to the heat and cook until the mixture thickens. Gradually mix in the remaining milk, stirring constantly. Season with salt and pepper and add the nutmeg. • Cook for 5–10 minutes, stirring constantly, to make a creamy Béchamel sauce.
• Stir in the cooked vegetables and mix well.
• Add the eggs, beating until just blended. • Mix in the Parmesan. • Pour the mixture into the prepared mold. • Bake for about 1 hour, or until light gold and set. • Let cool for 15 minutes. • Turn out onto a serving dish and serve in slices.

Serves: 8

*Preparation: 15' + 15'
to rest*

Cooking: 1 h 45'

Level of difficulty: 2

- 4 tbsp butter
- 1 tbsp extra-virgin olive oil
- 1 onion, finely chopped
- 1 clove garlic, finely chopped
- 2 tbsp finely chopped parsley
- 1 tsp torn basil
- 2 lb/1 kg zucchini/ courgettes, finely chopped
- salt and freshly ground black pepper to taste
- 2 tbsp all-purpose/ plain flour
- generous ¾ cup/ 200 ml milk, boiling
- ¼ tsp freshly grated nutmeg
- 3 large eggs
- 3 tbsp freshly grated Parmesan cheese

VEGETABLE CRÊPES

Prepare the crêpe batter and refrigerate for
1 hour. • Filling: Sauté the mushrooms, celery,
carrots, leeks, and bell pepper in 2 tablespoons of
butter in a large frying pan over high heat for
5 minutes. Lower the heat and cook for 5 more
minutes. • Add the zucchini, crumble in the bouillon
cube, and season with pepper. Cook for 5–10
minutes, or until all the vegetables are tender.
• Pour in the cream and season with nutmeg.
Cook until the cream is heated through and slightly
thickened. • Preheat the oven to 400°F/200°C/
gas 6. • Butter a rectangular baking dish. • Melt a
little butter over medium heat in a small frying pan.
Spoon enough batter into the pan to cover the
base in a thin layer. Cook for 1–2 minutes, turn,
and cook for 1–2 minutes on the other side until
golden brown all over. • Stack the crêpes on a
plate. • Line the prepared dish with three crêpes
and spread about a quarter of the filling over the
top. Cover with another layer of crêpes and repeat
until all the ingredients are in the dish, finishing with
a layer of vegetables. • Sprinkle with the
Parmesan. • Bake for 15–20 minutes, or until
lightly browned. • Serve hot.

566

Serves: 4–6

Preparation: 20' + 1 h
to rest crêpe batter

Cooking: 1 h 10'

Level of difficulty: 2

- **1 quantity crêpes
  (see page 956)**

FILLING

- **7 oz/200 g
  mushrooms, sliced**
- **4 oz/125 g celery,
  finely sliced**
- **2 carrots, peeled
  and finely sliced**
- **2 leeks, sliced**
- **1 yellow bell
  pepper, finely
  sliced**
- **6 tbsp butter**
- **2 zucchini/
  courgettes, sliced**
- **1 vegetable
  bouillon cube**
- **freshly ground
  black pepper to
  taste**
- **2 cups/500 ml
  heavy/double
  cream**
- **¼ tsp freshly
  grated nutmeg**
- **generous ¾ cup/
  100 g freshly
  grated Parmesan
  cheese**

BAKED LEEKS

Preheat the oven to 350°F/180°C/gas 4.
• Butter a baking dish. • Remove the roots and green parts of the leeks and any tough outer leaves. Wash well to remove any dirt. • Cook the leeks in salted, boiling water for 10 minutes, or until tender. • Drain and transfer to the prepared baking dish. • Mix the Parmesan, bread crumbs, parsley, salt, and pepper in a small bowl and sprinkle over the leeks. Drizzle with the melted butter. • Bake for 10–15 minutes, or until golden.
• Serve hot.

Serves: 6

Preparation: 20'

Cooking: 25–30'

Level of difficulty: 1

- 2 lb/1 kg leeks
- 1 cup/125 g freshly grated Parmesan cheese
- 4 tbsp fine dry bread crumbs
- 1 tbsp finely chopped parsley
- salt and freshly ground black pepper to taste
- 4 tbsp butter, melted

BAKED RED LENTILS

*Vegan

Serves: 4

Preparation: 20'

Cooking: 1 h 15'

Level of difficulty: 1

- 2 cups/300 g red lentils
- 2 quarts/2 liters water
- 1 small bunch mixed aromatic herbs (such as parsley, cilantro/coriander, and thyme)
- 2 cloves garlic
- 1 small bunch parsley
- salt to taste
- ½ cup/60 g fine dry bread crumbs

Preheat the oven to 350°F/180°C/gas 4.
• Butter a 9-inch (23-cm) ovenproof baking dish. • Wash the lentils well and place in a large saucepan. Pour in the water and add the herbs. Cook over low heat for 25–30 minutes, or until tender. • Drain, discarding the herbs. Place in a food processor and chop with the garlic, parsley, and salt until puréed. Stir in the bread crumbs.
• Spoon the mixture into the prepared dish.
• Bake for 40–45 minutes, or until lightly browned. • Serve hot.

569

BAKED PUMPKIN WITH WINE

Serves: 4

Preparation: 10'

Cooking: 30'

Level of difficulty: 1

- **1 small pumpkin or winter squash, seeded and thinly sliced**
- **2 tbsp extra-virgin olive oil**
- **1 sprig rosemary, finely chopped, + extra leaves to garnish**
- **6 tbsp butter**
- **4 oz/125 g baby onions, peeled**
- **½ cup/125 ml dry white wine**
- **1 tbsp granulated sugar**
- **salt and freshly ground black pepper to taste**
- **2 amaretti cookies, crushed**

Preheat the oven to 400°F/200°C/gas 6. • Line a baking sheet with waxed paper. Arrange the pumpkin slices on the prepared sheet. Drizzle with the oil and bake for 20 minutes. • Sprinkle with the rosemary and bake for 5 more minutes. • Melt the butter over medium heat in a small saucepan. Add the onions and sauté for 5 minutes. • Pour in the wine and add the sugar. Cook for 5–10 minutes, or until the onions are tender and glossy. • Arrange the pumpkin on a serving plate. • Add the onions and season with salt and pepper. • Sprinkle with the crushed amaretti cookies and rosemary and serve.

Serve as a starter in the fall months leading up to Thanksgiving.

571

FAVA BEAN, ASPARAGUS, AND RICOTTA BAKE

Cook the fava beans in a large pot of salted, boiling water for 15–20 minutes, or until very tender. • Drain and set aside. • Cook the asparagus in a large pot of salted, boiling water for about 10 minutes, or until almost tender. • Drain and cut in half lengthwise. • Process three-quarters of the fava beans in a food processor with the cream, egg, Parmesan, salt, and pepper until puréed. • Mix the Ricotta, oil, salt, and pepper in a large bowl. • Preheat the oven to 400°F/200°C/ gas 6. • Warm a large roasting pan filled with 2 inches (4 cm) of water in the oven. • Line a 9-inch (23-cm) springform pan with aluminum foil. Arrange a layer of asparagus in the bottom of the pan. Cover with the Ricotta, followed by a layer of fava bean purée. Top with whole fava beans. Repeat until all the ingredients are in the dish. Cover with aluminum foil and place in the roasting pan filled with water. • Bake for 50 minutes. Remove from the oven and turn out onto a serving dish. • Serve hot or at room temperature.

Serves: 6	
Preparation: 25'	
Cooking: 1 h 30'	
Level of difficulty: 1	

- 1 lb/500 g fava/ broad beans
- 12 asparagus tips
- 4 tbsp heavy/ double cream
- 1 large egg
- 4 tbsp freshly grated Parmesan cheese
- salt and freshly ground black pepper to taste
- 1⅔ cups/400 g Ricotta cheese
- 2 tbsp extra-virgin olive oil

ASPARAGUS AND ALMOND GRATIN

Preheat the oven to 400°F/200°C/gas 6.
• Butter a baking dish. • Cook the asparagus in a large pot of salted, boiling water for 10 minutes, or until almost tender. • Drain and coarsely chop.
• Arrange the asparagus and zucchini in layers in the prepared baking dish. Sprinkle each layer with Parmesan and season with salt and pepper. Drizzle with the melted butter. • Beat the egg yolks and cream in a bowl until well blended. Pour the mixture over the vegetables. Sprinkle with the almonds.
• Bake for 10–15 minutes, or until set and lightly browned. • Serve hot.

Serves: 4

Preparation: 25'

Cooking: 20'

Level of difficulty: 1

- **14 oz/400 g asparagus tips**
- **1 zucchini/ courgette, thinly sliced**
- **6 tbsp freshly grated Parmesan cheese**
- **salt and freshly ground black pepper to taste**
- **2 tbsp butter, melted**
- **6 large egg yolks**
- **²⁄₃ cup/150 ml heavy/double cream**
- **4 tbsp slivered almonds**

BAKED CABBAGE AND POTATO ROLL

Cook the potatoes in a large pot of salted, boiling water for 15–20 minutes, or until tender. • Drain and mash. • Cook the carrots in a large pot of salted, boiling water for 8–10 minutes, or until tender. • Drain and add to the potatoes. • Cook the cabbage leaves in a large pot of salted, boiling water for 3–4 minutes, or until tender. • Drain and arrange the leaves overlapping in a rectangle on a clean cloth. Use a rolling pin to flatten them. • Mix the Fontina, butter, egg, half the Parmesan, parsley, and cumin into the mashed potatoes and carrots. Season with salt and pepper. • Spread the potato mixture evenly over the cabbage leaves. Roll them up tightly, using the cloth to help you. • Preheat the oven to 400°F/200°C/gas 6. • Butter a baking dish. • Slice the roulade 1 1/2-inch (4-cm) thick and arrange the slices in the prepared dish. Sprinkle with the remaining Parmesan. • Bake for 10–15 minutes, or until golden. • Serve hot.

Serves: 6
Preparation: 20'
Cooking: 45'
Level of difficulty: 1

- 2 lb/1 kg floury/ baking potatoes, peeled
- 14 oz/400 g carrots, scraped and thinly sliced
- 8–12 large Savoy cabbage leaves
- 8 oz/250 g Fontina or Emmental cheese, cut into small cubes
- 2 tbsp butter
- 1 large egg
- 2 tbsp freshly grated Parmesan cheese
- 2 tbsp finely chopped parsley
- 2 tsp ground cumin
- salt and freshly ground black pepper to taste

CABBAGE AND PUMPKIN TIMBALES

C ook the cabbage leaves in a large pot of salted, boiling water for 3–4 minutes, or until tender. • Drain and use a rolling pin to flatten them. • Oil 8 small timbale molds and line with a cabbage leaf. • Cook the potatoes in a large pot of salted, boiling water until tender. • Drain and chop finely. • Cook the pumpkin and leeks in a large pot of salted, boiling water until tender. • Drain. • Preheat the oven to 400°F/200°C/gas 6. • Warm a large roasting pan filled with 2 inches (4 cm) of water in the oven. • Sauté the potatoes, pumpkin, and leeks in the butter and oil in a large frying pan until browned. • Add the parsley. Season with salt and pepper. • Fill the molds with the vegetable mixture. Fold any excess cabbage leaf over the top. Place the molds in the pan. • Bake for 30 minutes. • Turn out onto serving dishes and serve hot.

Serves: 4–8

Preparation: 25'

Cooking: 1 h 15'

Level of difficulty: 1

- 8 whole Savoy cabbage leaves
- 1 lb/500 g floury potatoes, peeled
- 10 oz/300 g pumpkin, seeded and diced
- 7 oz/200 g leeks, finely sliced
- 4 tbsp butter
- 2 tbsp extra-virgin olive oil
- 3 tbsp finely chopped parsley
- salt and freshly ground black pepper to taste

CAULIFLOWER SOUFFLÉS WITH WATERCRESS SAUCE

Serves: 4

Preparation: 20'

Cooking: 1 h 25'

Level of difficulty: 2

- 1 lb/500 g cauliflower florets
- 2 cups/500 ml Béchamel sauce (see page 948)
- salt and freshly ground black pepper to taste
- 1 egg white

WATERCRESS SAUCE
- 4 oz/125 g watercress
- ¾ cup/180 ml heavy/double cream
- ¼ tsp freshly grated nutmeg

579

Preheat the oven to 350°F/180°C/gas 4.
• Butter four ¾-cup (180 ml) pudding molds.
• Warm a large roasting pan filled with 2 inches (5 cm) of water in the oven. • Cook the cauliflower in a large pot of salted, boiling water until tender.
• Drain and process in a food processor until smooth. • Gently fold the cauliflower and egg white into the Béchamel. • Spoon the mixture into the prepared molds. Place the molds in the roasting pan. • Bake for 1 hour. • Watercress Sauce: Process the watercress with the cream in a food processor until puréed. • Add the nutmeg and season with salt and pepper. Mix well. • Serve the timbales warm with the sauce.

BROCCOLI SOUFFLÉS

Serves: 6

Preparation: 20' +
time to make sauce

Cooking: 50'

Level of difficulty: 2

- 2½ lb/1.5 kg broccoli florets
- 2 tbsp butter
- 2 tbsp all-purpose/ plain flour
- 1 cup/250 ml hot milk
- salt and freshly ground black pepper to taste
- 2 large eggs, separated
- 1 quantity Tomato Sauce (see page 951)

Preheat the oven to 350°F/180°C/gas 4.
• Butter six ³/₄-cup (180-ml) pudding molds.
• Cook the broccoli in a large pot of salted, boiling water for 10 minutes, or until tender.
• Reserve 6 florets to garnish. Drain and process the remaining broccoli in a food processor or blender until smooth. • Melt the remaining butter with the flour in a small saucepan over low heat. Cook for 1 minute, stirring constantly. • Remove from the heat and pour in half the hot milk. Return to the heat and cook until the mixture thickens. Gradually mix in the remaining milk, stirring constantly. Season with salt and pepper. • Cook for 5–10 minutes, stirring constantly, to make a creamy Béchamel sauce. • Add the Béchamel to the broccoli purée. • Mix in the egg yolks and season with salt and pepper. • Beat the egg whites in a large bowl until stiff peaks form. Fold them into the broccoli mixture. • Pour the mixture into the prepared molds. • Bake for 30 minutes, or until well risen and browned on top. • Turn out onto serving dishes. Garnish with the reserved broccoli florets. Serve with the tomato sauce.

FILLED BELL PEPPERS

Cook the potatoes in a large pot of salted, boiling water for 15–20 minutes, or until tender. • Drain and cut into small cubes. • Preheat the oven to 450°F/220°C/gas 7. • Oil a roasting pan. • Finely chop 1 tomato and mix with the potatoes, celery, and zucchini in a large bowl. Mix in 6 tablespoons of oil, the garlic, basil, and 2 tablespoons of Parmesan. Season with salt.

• Spoon the filling into the bell pepper halves and arrange them in the roasting pan. Thinly slice the remaining tomato. Top each of the peppers with a slice of tomato and an olive. Sprinkle with oregano and the remaining Parmesan. Drizzle with the remaining oil. • Bake for 30–35 minutes, or until the bell peppers are well cooked. • Serve hot.

Serves: 6

Preparation: 15'

Cooking: 45–55'

Level of difficulty: 1

- 7 oz/200 g floury/ baking potatoes, peeled
- 2 large tomatoes
- 3 oz/90 g celery, finely chopped
- 10 oz/300 g zucchini/ courgettes, finely chopped
- ½ cup/125 ml extra-virgin olive oil
- 2 cloves garlic, finely chopped
- leaves from 1 sprig basil, torn
- 4 tbsp freshly grated Parmesan cheese
- salt to taste
- 3 yellow bell peppers, halved, seeded, and cored
- 2 tbsp green olives, pitted and halved
- 1 tsp dried oregano

TOMATO AND BREAD BAKE

Preheat the oven to 400°F/200°C/gas 6.
• Butter a deep 8-inch (20-cm) baking pan.
• Arrange the bread, tomatoes, and Emmental in layers in the prepared baking pan. • Beat the eggs, milk, and parsley in a large bowl. Season with salt and pepper. • Pour the mixture into the baking pan.

Ideal to use up leftover ingredients when you have no time to go to the supermarket.

• Bake for 20 minutes, or until set and golden. • Turn out onto a serving dish and serve hot.

584

Serves: 4

Preparation: 15'

Cooking: 20'

Level of difficulty: 1

- 4 slices whole-wheat bread, toasted and cubed
- 5 firm-ripe tomatoes, thinly sliced
- 5 oz/150 g Emmental or Gruyère cheese, thinly sliced
- 6 large eggs
- ⅔ cup/150 ml milk
- 1 tbsp finely chopped parsley
- salt and freshly ground black pepper to taste

POTATO AND VEGETABLE BAKE

Preheat the oven to 400°F/200°C/gas 6. • Line an 8-inch (20-cm) springform pan with waxed paper. • Sauté the onion in the oil in a large frying pan over medium heat until translucent. • Add the mixed vegetables and season with salt. Sauté over high heat for 5 minutes. • Cover and cook over low heat for 10 minutes more. • Blanch the potatoes in salted, boiling water for 1 minute. • Drain and pat dry with paper towels. • Use two-thirds of the potatoes to line the bottom and sides of the prepared pan, making a kind of "shell". • Mix the vegetables with the beaten eggs, Parmesan, marjoram, and a pinch of salt. • Spoon the mixture into the potato shell and cover with the remaining potatoes. Dot with the butter. • Bake for 50–60 minutes, or until lightly browned. • Serve warm.

Serves: 6

Preparation: 30'

Cooking: 1 h 15'

Level of difficulty: 2

- 1 large red onion, thinly sliced
- 3 tbsp extra-virgin olive oil
- 1 lb/500 g raw mixed vegetables
- salt to taste
- 1 lb/500 g potatoes, peeled and cut into thin sticks
- 2 eggs, lightly beaten
- 2/3 cup/80 g freshly grated Parmesan cheese
- 3 sprigs marjoram, finely chopped
- 1 tbsp butter, cut up

ROAST POTATOES
WITH MIXED HERBS

*Vegan

Serves: 6–8

Preparation: 15'

Cooking: 20'

Level of difficulty: 1

- 2½ lb/1.25 kg yellow-fleshed potatoes, peeled
- 1 bulb garlic
- 2 sprigs fresh thyme
- 2 sprigs fresh marjoram
- 2 sprigs fresh mint
- 4 tbsp extra-virgin olive oil
- salt and freshly ground black pepper to taste

Preheat the oven to 425°F/220°C/gas 7.
• Chop the potatoes into bite-size pieces and arrange them in a nonstick baking dish. • Add the cloves of garlic (with peel), thyme, marjoram, and mint. Drizzle with the oil and season with salt and pepper. • Roast for about 20 minutes, or until golden and tender, turning the potatoes occasionally. • Discard the garlic and season with salt and pepper. • Serve hot.

CARROT AND GREEN BEAN BAKE

Preheat the oven to 300°F/150°C/gas 2.
• Butter a deep 8-inch (20-cm) springform.
• Sauté the onion in 1 tablespoon of butter in a large frying pan until softened. • Bring the milk and cream to a boil in a small saucepan. Pour the mixture over the onion and add the parsley.
• Set aside for 15 minutes then chop in a food processor until smooth. • Steam the carrots and green beans until crunchy-tender. • Drain well.
• Sauté the green beans and garlic in 1 tablespoon of butter in a large frying pan over medium heat until the garlic is pale gold. • Arrange alternating layers of carrots and green beans in the prepared baking dish. • Beat the eggs and egg yolks, Parmesan, and cream and onion sauce in a large bowl until well blended. Season with salt and pepper. • Pour the mixture over the vegetables.
• Bake for 25–30 minutes, or until set and browned on top. • Serve hot.

Serves: 4

Preparation: 25'

Cooking: 50–55'

Level of difficulty: 2

- 1 small onion, finely chopped
- 2 tbsp butter
- 1 cup/250 ml milk
- ½ cup/125 ml heavy/double cream
- 1 tbsp finely chopped parsley
- 1 lb/500 g carrots, sliced lengthwise
- 10 oz/300 g green beans, topped and tailed
- 1 clove garlic, finely chopped
- 2 eggs + 2 egg yolks
- ⅔ cup/80 g freshly grated Parmesan cheese
- salt and freshly ground black pepper to taste

OREGANO-SPICED MIXED VEGETABLES

Serves: 4

Preparation: 25'

Cooking: 30'

Level of difficulty: 1

- **4 tbsp extra-virgin olive oil**
- **7 oz/200 g firm-ripe tomatoes**
- **7 oz/200 g waxy potatoes**
- **10 oz/300 g mixed cultivated mushrooms**
- **salt and freshly ground black pepper to taste**
- **1 tbsp dried oregano**

Preheat the oven to 325°F/170°C/gas 3. • Grease an ovenproof dish with 2 tablespoons of oil. • Cut the tomatoes into $1/2$-inch (1-cm) slices. • Peel the potatoes and slice them thinly. • Slice the mushrooms thinly lengthwise. • Arrange a layer of potatoes, mushrooms, and tomatoes on the bottom of the prepared dish. Season with salt and pepper and drizzle with the remaining oil. Sprinkle with the oregano. • Bake for 30 minutes. Set aside for a few minutes before serving.

STUFFED BAKED TOMATOES

Cut each tomato in half horizontally. Scoop out the flesh and sprinkle the tomato shells with salt. Let stand upside-down in a colander and let drain for 30 minutes. • Preheat the oven to 475°F/250°C/gas 8. • Process the garlic, two slices of bread, capers, bell peppers, and basil in a food processor or blender until finely chopped. Season with salt and pepper. • Fill the tomatoes with the chopped mixture. Crumble the remaining bread and sprinkle over the tops of the tomatoes. Sprinkle with the Parmesan and drizzle with the oil. • Bake for about 20 minutes, or until browned on top.
• Serve hot.

Serves: 4

Preparation: 30' + 30' to drain

Cooking: 20'

Level of difficulty: 2

- 4 large tomatoes, weighing about 5 oz/150 g each
- salt and freshly ground black pepper to taste
- 2 cloves garlic
- 4 slices white sandwich bread
- 2 tbsp salt-cured capers, rinsed
- 10 oz/300 g yellow bell peppers, halved, seeded, and cored
- 1 bunch fresh basil
- ½ cup/60 g freshly grated Parmesan cheese
- 4 tbsp extra-virgin olive oil

ASPARAGUS AND ZUCCHINI FLOWER BAKE

Preheat the oven to 350°F/180°C/gas 4.
• Butter a 9-inch (23-cm) ring mold. • Set aside the asparagus tips. Slice the stalks into rounds. • Cook the asparagus stalks in salted, boiling water until crunchy-tender. • Drain. • Sauté the asparagus stalks and shallot in 1 tablespoon of butter in a large frying pan until lightly golden. Season with salt and pepper.

Impressive and delicious, cook this for an elegant dinner party.

• Transfer to a food processor and process until smooth. • Mix the asparagus purée into the Béchamel with the egg yolks and Parmesan.
• Sauté the zucchini flowers in the remaining butter in a large frying pan until softened. • Use the flowers to line the prepared mold. • Pour the asparagus mixture into the mold. Fill a large roasting pan halfway with hot water and place the mold in the pan. • Bake for 90 minutes. • Turn out onto a serving dish and let cool completely.
• Blanch the snow peas, peas, and asparagus tips in salted, boiling water for 5–7 minutes, or until just tender. • Drain well and use them to garnish the center of the ring. • Serve warm.

Serves: 8

Preparation: 40'

Cooking: 1 h 40'

Level of difficulty: 3

- 1½ lb/650 g asparagus
- 1 shallot, finely chopped
- 2 tbsp butter
- salt and freshly ground black pepper to taste
- 2 cups/500 ml Béchamel Sauce (see page 948)
- 3 egg yolks, lightly beaten
- 4 tbsp freshly grated Parmesan cheese
- 8 zucchini/ courgette flowers
- 1¼ cups/150 g hulled/shelled peas
- 5 oz/150 g snow peas/mangetout

596

STUFFED BELL PEPPERS

Sauté the onions in the butter in a saucepan over low heat for 10–15 minutes, or until very soft and browned. • Add the rice, pine nuts, pumpkin and sunflower seeds, and raisins. Mix well. Add the water and bring to a boil. • Simmer for 8–10 minutes, or until the rice is not quite al dente. • Season with salt and pepper. Add the parsley, dill, and mint. Remove from the heat. • Preheat the oven to 350°F/180°C/gas 4. • Oil a large flameproof baking dish. • Spoon the filling into the bell peppers. Transfer to the baking dish. • Mix the tomato sauce with and paprika and gradually stir into the stock. Spoon over the bell peppers. Replace the tops on the peppers. • Bake for 30 minutes, or until the peppers are tender. • Carefully transfer the bell peppers to a serving dish with a slotted spoon. • Beat the flour, lemon juice, and egg yolks in a small bowl. Beat the mixture into the cooking juices in the baking pan over low heat. Simmer for 5 minutes, stirring often, until thickened. • Spoon the sauce over the bell peppers and garnish with the dill. • Serve hot.

Serves: 6

Preparation: 40'

Cooking: 1 h

Level of difficulty: 2

- 2 onions, chopped
- 4 tbsp butter
- 1 cup/200 g rice
- 1 tbsp pine nuts
- 2 tbsp pumpkin and sunflower seeds
- 2 tbsp raisins
- 1 cup/250 ml water
- salt and freshly ground black pepper to taste
- 3 tbsp finely chopped parsley
- 2 tbsp finely chopped dill
- 1 tbsp finely chopped mint
- 6 bell peppers, tops cut off and seeded
- 1 tbsp tomato sauce
- 1 tbsp paprika
- 1 cup/250 ml Vegetable Stock (see page 945)
- 2 tbsp all-purpose/ plain flour
- 2 tbsp lemon juice
- 2 large egg yolks
- salt and freshly ground black pepper to taste
- 1 small bunch dill, to garnish

ZUCCHINI AND ASPARAGUS LASAGNA

Serves: 4

Preparation: 25'

Cooking: 45'

Level of difficulty: 1

- 1¾ lb/800 g zucchini/ courgettes, cut into thin strips lengthwise
- 6 tbsp extra-virgin olive oil
- 1¾ cups/100 g fresh bread crumbs
- 1 clove garlic, finely chopped
- 2 tbsp butter, cut up
- 5 shallots, coarsely chopped
- 2 carrots, cut into small cubes
- 8 oz/250 g asparagus tips, finely chopped
- ¾ cup/180 ml heavy/double cream
- salt to taste
- 1 cup/125 g freshly grated Parmesan cheese

Preheat the oven to 400°F/200°C/gas 6. • Sauté the zucchini in 2 tablespoons of oil in a large frying pan over medium heat until lightly browned. • Set aside. • Sauté the bread crumbs and garlic in the same pan in 2 tablespoons of oil and 1 tablespoon of butter over medium heat until the garlic is pale gold. • Set aside. • Sauté the shallots and carrots in the remaining oil over medium heat until lightly browned. • Add the asparagus and cream and cook for 10 minutes. Season with salt. • Line a baking dish with a layer of the zucchini strips. Cover with a layer of the asparagus mixture and sprinkle with the bread crumbs and Parmesan. Repeat until all the ingredients are in the dish, finishing with a layer of bread crumbs and Parmesan. • Dot with the remaining butter. • Bake for 15–20 minutes, or until browned. • Serve hot.

VEGETABLE GRATIN

Preheat the oven to 350°F/180°C/gas 4.
• Butter a 12-inch (30-cm) baking dish.
• Arrange half the zucchini in a layer in the prepared dish. Top with half the tomatoes. Sprinkle with half the garlic and basil. Season with salt and pepper and drizzle with the oil. • Top with another layer of the remaining zucchini and cover with the remaining tomatoes. Sprinkle with the remaining garlic and basil. • Beat the egg and cream and season with salt and pepper. Pour over the vegetables. • Bake for 50–60 minutes, or until the vegetables are tender. • Serve warm.

Serves: 4

Preparation: 20'

Cooking: 50–60'

Level of difficulty: 1

- **6 zucchini/ courgettes, thinly sliced**
- **6 tomatoes, finely chopped**
- **6 cloves garlic, lightly crushed but whole**
- **1 cup/60 g finely chopped basil or parsley**
- **salt and freshly ground black pepper to taste**
- **4 tbsp extra-virgin olive oil**
- **1 egg**
- **1 cup/250 ml heavy/double cream**

BAKED RISOTTO-FILLED TOMATOES

Preheat the oven to 400°F/200°C/gas 6.
• Butter a shallow ovenproof dish into which the tomatoes will fit snugly. • Rinse and dry the tomatoes and cut a $^1/_2$-inch (1-cm) thick slice from the stalk end. Set these "lids" aside.
• Discard the flesh and seeds. • Sauté the onion in 2 tablespoons of butter in a large frying pan over low heat until transparent. • Add the rice and cook for 2 minutes, stirring constantly. • Begin stirring in the stock, $^1/_2$ cup (125 ml) at a time. Cook and stir until each addition has been absorbed, until the rice is tender, about 15–18 minutes. • Stir in the Parmesan and season with salt and pepper. • Stuff the tomatoes with the risotto and top each one neatly with its lid. • Beat the eggs lightly in a bowl and dip the stuffed tomatoes into the beaten egg. Coat with the bread crumbs. • Place the tomatoes in a single layer, lid-side uppermost, in the prepared baking dish. Top each tomato with a flake of butter.
• Bake for 25–30 minutes, or until golden. • Serve hot or at room temperature.

Serves: 4	
Preparation: 30'	
Cooking: 1 h	
Level of difficulty: 1	

- 8 medium tomatoes
- 1 tbsp very finely chopped onion
- 5 tbsp butter
- scant 1 cup/180 g Italian risotto rice
- 2 cups/500 ml boiling Vegetable Stock (see page 945)
- $^1/_2$ cup/60 g freshly grated Parmesan cheese
- salt and freshly ground black pepper to taste
- 2 eggs
- 1 cup/125 g fine dry bread crumbs

EGGPLANT WITH TOMATO SAUCE AND CHEESE

Cut the eggplant into quarters. Place in a colander. Sprinkle with salt and let drain for 1 hour. • Place the eggplant in a baking dish, cut-side up. • Preheat the oven to 300°F/150°C/gas 2. • Place the tomatoes, oil, capers, and basil in a small saucepan. Season with salt and pepper. Cook over medium heat until the sauce has reduced by half. • Spoon the sauce over the eggplant and sprinkle with the cheese. • Bake for 1 hour, or until the eggplants are tender. • Serve hot.

Serves: 4

Preparation: 30' + 1 h to degorge eggplants

Cooking: 1 h

Level of difficulty: 1

- **4 eggplants/ aubergines**
- **1 tbsp coarse salt**
- **1²/₃ cups/400 ml canned tomatoes**
- **4 tbsp extra-virgin olive oil**
- **1 tbsp salt-cured capers, rinsed of salt and chopped**
- **1 tbsp torn basil**
- **salt and freshly ground black pepper to taste**
- **2 oz/60 g Caciocavallo or Mozzarella cheese, diced**

ASPARAGUS SOUFFLÉ

Serves: 6

Preparation: 30'

Cooking: 20'

Level of difficulty: 3

- **12 asparagus stalks, boiled**
- **1 tbsp freshly grated Parmesan cheese**
- **3 eggs, separated + 1 egg yolk**
- **⅛ tsp freshly grated nutmeg**
- **1 cup/250 ml Béchamel Sauce (see page 948)**

Preheat the oven to 325°F/170°C/gas 3. • Butter six small soufflé dishes and sprinkle with semolina or bread crumbs. • Chop the asparagus stalks and set the tips aside. • Stir the chopped asparagus, Parmesan, egg yolks, and nutmeg into the Béchamel. • Beat the egg whites and salt in a large bowl until stiff. Gently fold them into the asparagus mixture. • Spoon the mixture evenly into the prepared dishes. • Bake for 20–25 minutes, or until risen and golden. • Garnish with the reserved asparagus tips and serve immediately.

BRIE AND VEGETABLE BAKE

Preheat the oven to 350°F/180°C/gas 4.
• Sauté the shallot in the oil in a large frying pan over medium heat until softened. • Add the zucchini, carrots, asparagus, and fava beans and cook for 5 minutes. Season with salt. • Oil two baking sheets. • Place the bread on the baking sheets and dust with the paprika. Toast in the oven until lightly browned. Set aside. • Mix the flour and milk in a small bowl. • Heat the cream and eggs in a medium saucepan over medium heat, stirring constantly. Add the milk mixture and stir until the sauce begins to thicken. • Line the base of a large baking dish with the toast and top with the Brie. Arrange the vegetables on top. • Pour in the sauce and sprinkle with the Parmesan. • Bake for 20–25 minutes, or until the vegetables are tender and the topping is nicely browned. • Serve hot.

608

Serves: 4

Preparation: 20'

Cooking: 40–45'

Level of difficulty: 1

- 1 shallot, finely chopped
- 4 tbsp extra-virgin olive oil
- 3 oz/90 g zucchini/ courgettes, cut into small cubes
- 3 oz/90 g carrots, cut into small cubes
- 3 oz/90 g asparagus tips, chopped
- 3 oz/90 g fresh fava/broad beans
- salt to taste
- 8–10 slices firm-textured bread
- 1 tsp paprika
- 1 tbsp all-purpose/ plain flour
- 6 tbsp milk
- 6 tbsp heavy/ double cream
- 2 eggs, beaten
- 5 oz/150 g Brie cheese, thinly sliced
- 1 cup/125 g freshly grated Parmesan cheese

SPINACH TIMBALES WITH WINE SAUCE

Serves: 6

Preparation: 45'

Cooking: 50'

Level of difficulty: 1

- **10 oz/300 g bread, cubed**
- **¾ cup/180 ml milk**
- **2½ lb/1.25 kg spinach leaves**
- **6 tbsp butter**
- **½ cup/60 g freshly grated Parmesan cheese**
- **2 eggs**
- **½ cup/50 g chopped almonds**
- **⅛ tsp nutmeg**
- **salt and freshly ground black pepper to taste**
- **7 oz/200 g carrots, cut in small cubes**

WHITE WINE SAUCE
- **1 cup/250 ml dry white wine**
- **1 shallot, chopped**
- **1¼ cups/310 ml light/single cream**
- **salt and freshly ground black pepper to taste**
- **¼ tsp paprika**
- **¼ tsp nutmeg**

P lace the bread in a medium bowl and pour the milk over the top. Let stand for 15 minutes, or until the milk has been absorbed. • Rinse the spinach under cold running water. Place in a saucepan and cook, with just the water clinging to its leaves, for 3 minutes. • Drain, press out excess moisture, chop coarsely, and set aside. • Sauté the spinach in 3 tablespoons of butter in a large frying pan over medium heat for 2 minutes.
• Process one-third of the spinach in a food processor with the soaked bread, Parmesan, eggs, almonds, remaining butter, and nutmeg until very finely chopped. Season with salt and pepper.
• Preheat the oven to 375°F/190°C/gas 5.
• Butter six small pudding molds. • Spoon the chopped spinach mixture into the bottom and up the sides of the molds. • Fill the center of the molds with the whole spinach leaves. Add the carrots and cover with the remaining spinach leaves. • Half-fill a large roasting pan with hot water and place the molds in the waterbath. • Bake for 50 minutes. • Remove the molds from the waterbath and set aside for 10 minutes. • Carefully invert the molds and turn out onto serving plates.
• White Wine Sauce: Bring the wine to a boil with the shallot. Simmer until the wine has reduced by half. • Stir in the cream and return to a boil. Cook until thick. • Season with salt and pepper and spoon over the timbales. • Dust with the paprika and nutmeg and serve.

TOMATO AND BELL PEPPER PÂTÉ

Blanch the tomatoes in a large pan of boiling water for 1 minute. • Drain and slip off the skins. Chop coarsely. • Cook the tomatoes in the oil in a large frying pan over medium heat for 10 minutes. • Turn on the broiler (grill) and broil the bell peppers, turning them often, until the skin blackens, about 15 minutes. • Let cool slightly and peel away the blackened skin. • Cut the bell peppers in half lengthwise and discard the stalks, seeds, and pulpy inner core. Rinse under cold running water to remove any remaining burnt skin and dry with paper towels. • Preheat the oven to 350°F/180°C/gas 4. • Oil a loaf pan. • Chop the tomatoes and bell peppers in a food processor with the eggs and egg yolks, basil, salt, and pepper. • Pour the mixture into the loaf pan. • Bake for 30–40 minutes, or until firm. • Set aside to cool. Refrigerate for at least 4 hours before serving.

Serves: 4

Preparation: 45' + 4 h to chill

Cooking: 40–50'

Level of difficulty: 1

- 1¾ lb/800 g ripe tomatoes
- 2 tbsp extra-virgin olive oil
- 2 large red bell peppers
- 2 eggs + 3 egg yolks
- 6 leaves fresh basil
- salt and freshly ground black pepper to taste

SWISS CHARD GRATIN

Serves: 4

Preparation: 30–35'

Cooking: 1 h

Level of difficulty: 2

- 2 lb/1 kg Swiss chard, tough stalks removed
- 1 cup/250 ml Béchamel Sauce (see page 948)
- 4 tbsp freshly grated firm cheese

Cook the chard in salted, boiling water for 10 minutes. • Use a slotted spoon to remove the chard. Peel the stalks, removing the tough fibers and chop coarsely. • Return to the water and boil for 15–20 minutes more, or until softened. • Drain well. • Preheat the oven to 400°F/200°C/gas 6. • Finely chop the Swiss chard greens. Add the stalks and arrange in an ovenproof dish. Pour the Béchamel sauce over the top and sprinkle with the cheese. • Bake for 20–25 minutes, or until the cheese is nicely browned. • Serve hot.

613

BELL PEPPERS BAKED WITH OLIVES AND ONION

Preheat the oven to 400°F/200°C gas 6.
• Place the bell peppers in a large baking dish. Sprinkle with the onions, olives, and capers. Drizzle with the oil and season with salt. • Bake for 25–30 minutes, or until the bell peppers are tender.
• Sprinkle with the oregano and serve hot.

*Vegan

Serves: 4–6

Preparation: 15'

Cooking: 25–30'

Level of difficulty: 1

- 3 lb/1.5 kg red bell peppers, seeded, cored, and cut into large chunks
- 1¾ lb/800 g onions, thickly sliced
- 20 green olives, pitted
- 2 tbsp capers in salt, rinsed
- 6 tbsp extra-virgin olive oil
- salt to taste
- 1 tbsp finely chopped oregano

BAKED MIXED VEGETABLES

Vegan

Serves: 6

Preparation: 15' + 1 h
to degorge eggplants

Cooking: 55–65'

Level of difficulty: 1

- 2 medium
  eggplants/
  aubergines, peeled
  and cut into cubes
- salt and freshly
  ground black
  pepper to taste
- 1 lb/500 g
  potatoes, peeled
  and cut into cubes
- 1 lb/500 g
  zucchini/
  courgettes, sliced
- 1 large red onion,
  cut into rings
- ½ cup/125 ml
  extra-virgin olive
  oil
- 2 tbsp finely
  chopped parsley
- 2 tbsp torn basil
- 2 lb/1 kg firm-ripe
  tomatoes, cut into
  small slices

Place the eggplant cubes in a colander. Sprinkle with salt and let drain for 1 hour. • Preheat the oven to 350°F/180°C/gas 4. • Set out a large roasting pan. • Mix the eggplants, potatoes, zucchini, onion, oil, parsley, and basil in a large bowl. Season with salt and pepper. • Place a layer of tomatoes in the pan, followed by the seasoned vegetables. Top with the remaining tomatoes. • Bake for 55–65 minutes, or until the vegetables are tender. If the tomatoes start to burn, cover with aluminum foil. • Serve hot.

RICE AND SPINACH RING

Preheat the oven to 350°F/180°C/gas 4.
• Butter a 10-inch (25-cm) ring mold. • Sauté the onion and leek in the oil in a large frying pan over medium heat for about 5–10 minutes, or until softened. • Add the spinach and chicory and cook for 15 minutes, or until tender. • Arrange a few leaves on the bottom of the mold. • Pour the water into the remaining spinach and chicory. Season with salt and bring to a boil. • Add the rice and cook for about 15 minutes, or until the rice is tender. • Drain and mix in the Parmesan and Béchamel. • Pour the mixture into the prepared mold, smoothing the top. • Bake for 20–25 minutes, or until lightly browned. • Turn out onto a serving dish and serve hot.

Serves: 6

Preparation: 45'

Cooking: 55–63'

Level of difficulty: 2

- 1 onion, finely chopped
- white of 1 leek, finely chopped
- 2 tbsp extra-virgin olive oil
- 12 oz/350 g young spinach leaves, finely shredded
- 5 oz/150 g chicory or green radicchio, finely shredded
- 3 cups/750 ml water
- 1/8 tsp salt
- 2 cups/400 g short-grain rice
- 1/2 cup/60 g freshly grated Parmesan cheese
- 2 cups/500 ml Béchamel Sauce (see page 948)

MUSHROOMS WITH BROCCOLI AND WALNUTS

*Vegan

Serves: 6

Preparation: 25'

Cooking: 40–50'

Level of difficulty: 2

- **12 large white mushrooms**
- **1 onion, finely chopped**
- **2 tbsp extra-virgin olive oil**
- **1 small head broccoli, cut into florets**
- **1 potato, peeled and coarsely chopped**
- **salt to taste**
- **water (optional)**
- **¹/₂ cup/50 g chopped walnuts**
- **¹/₄ tsp freshly grated nutmeg**

C lean the mushrooms. Remove the stalks and chop them finely. • Sauté the onion in the oil in a large frying pan over medium heat for 5–10 minutes, or until softened. • Add the broccoli, the mushroom stalks, and potato. • Season with salt and cook over medium heat for 20–25 minutes, adding water if the mixture starts to dry out. • Preheat the oven to 400°F/200°C/gas 6. • Transfer the vegetables to a food processor or blender and process with the walnuts and nutmeg until puréed. • Season the insides of the mushroom caps with salt and fill them with the vegetable purée. • Bake for 15–20 minutes, or until the filling has browned and the mushrooms have softened slightly. • Serve hot.

SPICY RICE AND LENTIL BURGERS

Preheat the oven to 375°F/190°C/gas 5.
• Oil a baking sheet. • Use your hands to mix
the rice, lentils, carrot, bread crumbs, peanut
butter, parsley, basil, oregano, paprika, and salt in
a large bowl to make a stiff dough. • Form the
mixture into burgers about 3 inches (8 cm) in
diameter and 1 inch (2.5 cm) thick. The mixture
will make 8–10 burgers. • Arrange on the prepared
baking sheet. • Bake for 15–20 minutes, or until
browned. • Heat the oil in a large frying pan until
very hot. Fry the burgers over medium heat for
2 minutes. Turn them and cook on the other side
for 2 minutes. • Serve hot with bread and salad.

Serves: 4

Preparation: 15'

Cooking: 19–24'

Level of difficulty: 1

- **1 cup/180 g cooked rice**
- **3 cups/300 g brown lentils, cooked and drained**
- **1 carrot, peeled and coarsely grated**
- **1 cup/125 g fine dry bread crumbs**
- **2 tbsp smooth peanut butter**
- **2 tbsp finely chopped parsley**
- **1 tsp dried basil**
- **1 tsp dried oregano**
- **1 tsp paprika**
- **¼ tsp salt**
- **6 tbsp sesame oil**

SPELT AND SPINACH PÂTÉ

Soak the spelt in warm water for 1 hour.
• Transfer to a saucepan with the stock, bay leaf, juniper berries, and soy sauce. Cover and simmer over medium heat for 1 1/2 hours.
• Preheat the oven to 350°F/180°C/gas 4.
• Oil a deep loaf pan. • Sauté the onion and sage in the oil in a large frying pan until softened.
• Add the brandy and cook until evaporated.
• Wash the spinach and place in a large saucepan with just the water still clinging to the leaves. Season with salt. Cook for 5–7 minutes, or until slightly wilted. • Remove from the heat, squeeze out the excess water, and chop finely. • Discard the bay leaf and juniper berries from the spelt and transfer to a food processor. Process until smooth.
• Add the spelt to the spinach and mix well. Mix in the flour, ginger, and pine nuts. Season with salt and pepper. • Spoon the mixture into the prepared pan. Place in a larger ovenproof container half filled with water. • Bake for 30 minutes, or until set.
• Let cool completely and let stand for at least 5 hours before serving.

*Vegan

Serves: 4

Preparation: 40' + 6 h to soak and stand

Cooking: 2 h 10'

Level of difficulty: 3

- 1 cup/100 g spelt
- 1 cup/125 ml Vegetable Stock (see page 945)
- 1 bay leaf
- 5 juniper berries
- 1 tbsp soy sauce
- 1 onion, finely chopped
- 1 leaf fresh sage
- 2 tbsp extra-virgin olive oil
- 4 tbsp brandy
- 1 lb/500 g spinach
- salt and freshly ground black pepper to taste
- 3 tbsp whole-wheat/wholemeal flour, toasted
- 1 tbsp finely grated ginger
- 1/4 cup/50 g crushed pine nuts

POTATO MOUSSAKA

*Vegan

Serves: 6–8

Preparation: 1 h

Cooking: 1 h

Level of difficulty: 2

Heat 2 tablespoons of oil in a large frying pan over medium heat. Sauté the onions for 8–10 minutes, or until lightly browned. • Add the tofu and season with salt and pepper. Sprinkle with the parsley and nutmeg. • Cook over low heat for 30 minutes until the tofu has softened and browned. • Preheat the oven to 350°F/180°C/gas 4. • Heat the remaining oil in a large deep frying pan until very hot. • Fry the potato slices, a few at a time, for 5–7 minutes, or until softened but not completely cooked. • Arrange a layer of potatoes in a baking pan and cover with a layer of tofu and tomatoes. Top with another layer of potatoes. Repeat until all the ingredients are used up, finishing with a layer of potatoes. • Pour in the water and cover with aluminum foil. • Bake for 45 minutes. • Remove the aluminum foil and bake for 15–20 minutes more, or until golden brown and crispy on top.

- 1 cup/250 ml extra-virgin olive oil
- 2 medium onions, finely chopped
- 8 oz/250 g ground/minced tofu
- salt and freshly ground black pepper to taste
- 1 tbsp finely chopped parsley
- 1/8 tsp freshly ground nutmeg
- 1 cup/250 ml water + more as needed
- 3 lb/1.5 kg potatoes, peeled, and cut into 1/2-inch/1-cm slices
- 2 lb/1 kg firm-ripe tomatoes, peeled and cut into cubes

Serves: 4–8

Preparation: 20' + 30'
to drain

Cooking: 50–60'

Level of difficulty: 2

- 8 large tomatoes
- salt and freshly
  ground black
  pepper to taste
- 6 tbsp extra-virgin
  olive oil
- 1 medium onion,
  finely chopped
- 1 clove garlic,
  finely chopped
- 1 cup/200 g short-
  grain rice
- 3 tbsp finely
  chopped mint
- 1 tbsp finely
  chopped parsley

RICE-STUFFED
TOMATOES

Cut the tops off the tomatoes and use a spoon
to scoop out the flesh. Reserve the flesh.
- Salt the interior of the tomatoes and place them
upside-down for 30 minutes in a colander.
- Preheat the oven to 375°F/190°C/gas 5.
- Set out a large baking dish. • Sauté the onion in
4 tablespoons oil in a large frying pan over medium
heat for 8–10 minutes, or until lightly browned. Add
the garlic and stir in the reserved tomato flesh.
- Cook for 15–20 minutes, or until the sauce has
reduced. • Season with salt and pepper. • Cook
the rice in a large pot of salted, boiling water for
8–10 minutes, or until the rice is almost tender.
- Drain well and add to the sauce. Cook for
5 minutes more. Remove from the heat and let
cool. • Sprinkle with the mint and parsley and
drizzle with 1 tablespoon of oil. • Stuff the
tomatoes, replace the tops, and arrange in
the dish. Drizzle with the remaining oil.
- Bake for 35–40 minutes, or until
well cooked. • Serve warm.

627

TURKISH BAKED EGGPLANT

*Vegan

Serves: 4

Preparation: 20' + 1 h

Cooking: 25–30'

Level of difficulty: 1

- 4 eggplants/ aubergines, cut in half
- salt to taste
- 4 cloves garlic, finely chopped
- 4 onions, thinly sliced
- 1 cup/250 ml extra-virgin olive oil
- 1 tbsp finely chopped parsley
- 2 large firm-ripe tomatoes, finely chopped

Make several deep cuts in the tops of the eggplants. Place in a colander and sprinkle with salt. Let drain for 1 hour. • Preheat the oven to 350°F/180°C/gas 4. • Sauté the garlic and onions in 2 tablespoons of oil in a large frying pan over medium heat for 8–10 minutes, or until lightly browned. • Season with salt. Add the tomatoes and cook for 15 minutes. • Heat the remaining oil in a large frying pan until very hot. • Fry the eggplants for 10–15 minutes, or until the flesh has softened.• Place the eggplants in a baking dish and fill with the onion mixture.• Bake for 25–30 minutes, or until tender. • Sprinkle with the parsley and serve hot.

BELL PEPPER AND EGGPLANT PURÉE

Preheat the oven to 400°F/200°C/gas 6.
• Arrange the bell peppers and eggplants in a baking pan. • Roast for 20 minutes, turning often, until the skins have blackened and the insides are tender. • Let cool completely. • Peel, removing the seeds, and chop coarsely. • Sauté the garlic in the oil in a large frying pan over medium heat for 2–3 minutes, or until pale gold. • Add the garlic to the bell pepper mixture. Season with salt and pepper and drizzle with the vinegar.
• Serve hot or at room temperature.

*Vegan

Serves:	4
Preparation:	15'
Cooking:	25'
Level of difficulty:	1

- 3 bell peppers, mixed colors
- 3 eggplants/ aubergines
- ½ cup/125 ml extra-virgin olive oil
- 3 cloves garlic, finely chopped
- salt and freshly ground black pepper to taste
- 2 tbsp white wine vinegar

*Vegan

Serves: 4

Preparation: 15'

Cooking: 30–35'

Level of difficulty: 1

- 1 medium green bell pepper
- 1 medium red bell pepper
- 1 medium yellow bell pepper
- 20 black olives, quartered
- 4 tbsp pine nuts
- 2 tbsp capers
- 10–12 leaves fresh basil, torn
- 6 tbsp extra-virgin olive oil
- salt to taste
- 4 tbsp fine dry bread crumbs

BAKED BELL PEPPERS

Preheat the oven to 350°F/180°C/gas 4. • Oil a large baking dish. • Slice the bell peppers from top to bottom into quarters. Remove the stalks and hard parts and the core and seeds. • Rinse the bell peppers and dry well. Cut into $1/2$-inch (1-cm) strips and transfer to a large bowl. • Add the olives, pine nuts, capers, and basil. • Add 5 tablespoons of oil and season with salt. Toss well. • Arrange the bell pepper mixture in the prepared baking dish, pressing down gently. • Sprinkle with the bread crumbs. • Bake for 30–35 minutes, or until the bell peppers are tender. • Serve warm.

631

ZUCCHINI AND ONIONS STUFFED WITH TOFU

Preheat the oven to 350°F/180°C/gas 4.
• Oil a baking dish. • Blanch the zucchini and onions in salted, boiling water for 5 minutes.
• Drain and use a spoon to scoop out the flesh from the center of the zucchini and onion halves.
• Arrange the zucchini and onions in the prepared baking dish. • Filling: Chop the tofu finely and mix with the rice, zucchini and onion flesh, garlic, soy sauce, and salt. • Spoon the filling into the hollows of the zucchini and onions. Sprinkle with the bread crumbs and oregano and drizzle with the oil.
• Bake for 40–45 minutes, or until browned on top and the vegetables are tender. • Serve warm or cold.

*Vegan

Serves: 2–4

Preparation: 25'

Cooking: 45–50'

Level of difficulty: 1

- 4 round zucchini/ courgettes, tops cut off
- 2 onions, cut in half

FILLING
- 4 oz/125 g tofu (bean curd) or ½ cup/100 g chopped seitan (wheat curd)
- ½ cup/80 g cooked rice
- 2 cloves garlic, finely chopped
- 1 tbsp soy sauce
- ½ tsp sea salt
- 3 tbsp whole-wheat/ wholemeal bread crumbs
- ¼ tsp dried oregano
- 1 tbsp oil

PUMPKIN BAKE

Preheat the oven to 400°F/200°C/gas 6.
• Cut the pumpkin in half and remove the seeds and peel. Cut into 2-inch (5-cm) lengths. • Transfer the pumpkin to a large baking dish with the bell peppers, onions, tomatoes, chile peppers, and garlic. • Drizzle with the oil and honey and sprinkle with the thyme and salt. • Bake for 50–60 minutes, or until the pumpkin is lightly browned, turning the vegetables for even baking. • Let cool for 5 minutes and serve with toasted bread.

Serves: 4–6

Preparation: 35'

Cooking: 50–60'

Level of difficulty: 2

- 1¼ lb/575 g pumpkin
- 4 bell peppers, seeded, cored, and cut into lengths
- 2 red onions, cut into quarters
- 16 cherry tomatoes
- 2 fresh red spicy chile peppers
- 4 cloves garlic, lightly crushed but whole
- 2 tbsp finely chopped thyme
- 5 tbsp extra-virgin olive oil
- 1 tbsp honey
- salt to taste

POTATOES BAKED IN SOUR CREAM

C ook the potatoes in their skins in salted, boiling water for 15–20 minutes, or until tender. • Drain well. Slip off their skins and slice thinly. • Preheat the oven to 350°F/180°C/gas 4. • Butter a baking dish and lay the slices of potato in the dish. • Pour in the sour cream. Sprinkle with garlic and herbs and top with the egg. • Bake for 20–25 minutes, or until golden. • Serve hot.

Serves: 4

Preparation: 20'

Cooking: 35–45'

Level of difficulty: 1

- 2 lb/1 kg potatoes
- ½ cup/125 ml sour cream
- 1 clove garlic, finely chopped
- 2 tbsp finely chopped mint
- 2 tbsp torn basil
- 2 hard-boiled eggs, thinly sliced

STUFFED MUSHROOMS

Preheat the oven to 350°F/180°C/gas 4.
• Oil an ovenproof dish just large enough to hold the mushrooms snugly. • Detach the stems from the mushrooms. Rinse the caps and stems under cold running water and dry with paper towels. Peel the caps and leave them whole.
• Chop the stems finely. Place in a bowl with the garlic, bread, and salt and pepper. Mix in the egg and egg yolk, Parmesan, oregano, parsley, marjoram, and 1 tablespoon of oil. • Use this mixture to stuff the mushrooms, pressing it in carefully with your fingertips. • Fill with the mushrooms and drizzle with the remaining oil.
• Bake for 30 minutes. • Serve hot or at room temperature.

Serves: 4

Preparation: 20'

Cooking: 30'

Level of difficulty: 2

- **12 fresh medium Caesar mushrooms**
- **1 clove garlic, finely chopped**
- **2 thick slices white bread, crusts removed, soaked in warm milk, and squeezed dry**
- **salt and freshly ground black pepper to taste**
- **1 egg + 1 egg yolk**
- **1½ cups/180 g freshly grated Parmesan cheese**
- **½ tsp dried oregano**
- **1 tbsp finely chopped parsley**
- **1 tbsp finely chopped marjoram**
- **4 tbsp extra-virgin olive oil**

BAKED EGGPLANTS WITH PARMESAN

Serves: 6

Preparation: 30' + 1 h
to degorge eggplants

Cooking: 1 h

Level of difficulty: 1

- 3 large eggplants/
  aubergines, peeled
  and cut into ¼-
  inch/5-mm slices
- 1 cup/150 g all-
  purpose/plain flour
- 4 eggs, lightly
  beaten
- 3 cups/750 ml
  olive oil, for frying
- 2 cups/500 ml
  Tomato Sauce (see
  page 951)
- 12 oz/350 g
  Mozzarella cheese
- 2½ cups/310 g
  freshly grated
  Parmesan cheese
- 2 tbsp butter

Place the eggplant slices in a colander and sprinkle with salt. Let drain for 1 hour. • Rinse the eggplant under cold running water and gently squeeze out extra moisture. • Preheat the oven to 350°F/180°C/gas 4. • Dredge the eggplant slices in the flour until well coated, then dip in the beaten eggs. • Heat the oil in a deep fryer or large frying pan until very hot. • Fry the eggplants in batches for 5–7 minutes, or until tender and well cooked. • Drain well on paper towels. • Spoon a layer of tomato sauce into a baking dish and cover with a layer of fried eggplants and Mozzarella. Sprinkle with the Parmesan. Repeat the layering process until all the ingredients are in the dish, finishing with a layer of tomato sauce and Parmesan. Dot with the butter. • Bake for 30–35 minutes, or until browned. • Serve hot.

FRIED
DISHES

ZUCCHINI FRITTERS

Cook the zucchini in salted, boiling water until almost tender. • Drain and let cool slightly. • Pat dry and chop finely. • Transfer to a large bowl and mix in the Pecorino, eggs, bread crumbs, parsley, mint, salt, and pepper. • Dust your hands with flour and shape the mixture into small balls about the size of golf balls. Roll them in bread crumbs until well coated. • Heat the oil in a large frying pan and fry the patties in small batches until golden and crisp. • Drain well and dry on paper towels. • Serve hot.

Serve these finger-licking bites with a glass of spumante or Champagne.

644

Serves: 6

Preparation: 20'

Cooking: 20'

Level of difficulty: 2

- 4 large zucchini/ courgettes
- 1 cup/125 g freshly grated Pecorino cheese
- 2 eggs
- 4 tbsp fine dry bread crumbs
- 2 tbsp finely chopped parsley
- 2 tbsp finely chopped mint
- salt and freshly ground black pepper to taste
- 2 cups/500 ml olive oil, for frying

FAVA BEAN FRITTERS

Cook the fava beans in a large pot of salted, boiling water for about 1 hour. Drain and remove the tough outer skins. • Sauté the onion in the butter and oil in a large frying pan over medium heat for 5 minutes, or until translucent. • Add the fava beans, bouillon cube, and nutmeg. Cook over low heat for 5 minutes. • Transfer to a food processor and process until smooth. Let cool. • Mix in the egg yolks and Parmesan. Season with salt and pepper and add the fennel. • Beat the egg whites until stiff and gently fold them into the bean mixture. • Heat the frying oil in a large frying pan until very hot and fry spoonfuls of the mixture in small batches for 3–4 minutes, or until golden all over. • Remove with a slotted spoon and drain on paper towels. • Garnish with the fennel and serve hot.

Serves: 4–6

Preparation: 45' + time to soak beans

Cooking: 1 h 35'

Level of difficulty: 2

- 12 oz/300 g dried fava/broad beans, soaked overnight and drained
- 1 small onion, finely chopped
- 1 tbsp butter
- 1 tbsp extra-virgin olive oil
- 1 vegetable bouillon cube, crumbled
- ¼ tsp freshly grated nutmeg
- 3 large eggs, separated
- ½ cup/60 g freshly grated Parmesan cheese
- salt and freshly ground black pepper to taste
- 2 tbsp finely chopped fennel, preferably wild
- 1 quart/1 liter sunflower oil, for frying
- 2–3 sprigs fennel, to garnish

PUMPKIN FRITTERS

Serves: 6

Preparation: 20'

Cooking: 30–35'

Level of difficulty: 2

- **10 oz/300 g pumpkin flesh**
- **3 eggs, separated**
- **1 cup/150 g all-purpose/plain flour**
- **1 amaretto cookie, crumbled**
- **2 tbsp freshly grated Parmesan cheese**
- **½ tsp baking powder**
- **¼ tsp freshly grated nutmeg**
- **½ tsp salt**
- **2 cups/500 ml olive oil, for frying**

Cook the pumpkin in salted, boiling water for 12–15 minutes, or until tender. • Drain and chop in a food processor until puréed. • Transfer to a large bowl and mix in 1 egg and 2 egg yolks, flour, the amaretto cookie, Parmesan, baking powder, and nutmeg. • Beat the egg whites until stiff and gently fold them into the pumpkin mixture. • Heat the oil in a large frying pan until very hot and fry tablespoons of the mixture in small batches until golden brown and crisp. • Remove with a slotted spoon and drain well on paper towels. • Serve hot.

FRIED POTATO BALLS

Cook the potatoes in their skins in salted, boiling water for 20–25 minutes, or until tender. Slip the skins off while hot and mash. • Place the mashed potato in a large bowl and mix in the butter, egg yolks, Parmesan, pine nuts, parsley, and salt. • Beat the egg whites in a medium bowl until frothy. • Shape tablespoons of the potato mixture into balls the size of marbles. • Dip in the egg white, then in the bread crumbs. • Heat the oil in a large frying pan until very hot and fry the potato balls in small batches for 5–7 minutes, or until golden. • Remove with a slotted spoon and drain well on paper towels. • Serve hot.

648

Serves: 6

Preparation: 25'

Cooking: 30'

Level of difficulty: 2

- 2 lb/1 kg floury potatoes
- ½ cup/125 g butter, cut up
- 3 eggs, separated
- 1 cup/125 g freshly grated Parmesan cheese
- 2 tbsp pine nuts, finely ground
- 1 tbsp finely chopped parsley
- salt to taste
- 1 cup/125 g fine dry bread crumbs
- 2 cups/500 ml olive oil, for frying

BREAD FRITTERS WITH KETCHUP

Serves: 4

Preparation: 20'

Cooking: 20'

Level of difficulty: 2

- **14 oz/400 g day-old bread, crumbled**
- **4 eggs**
- **1 cup/125 g freshly grated Pecorino cheese**
- **2 tbsp finely chopped parsley**
- **salt and freshly ground black pepper to taste**
- **2 cups/500 ml olive oil, for frying**
- **1 cup/250 ml ketchup or tomato sauce**
- **fresh basil**

Mix the bread, eggs, $1/2$ cup (60 g) of Pecorino, and parsley in a large bowl. Season with salt and pepper. • Shape the mixture into small fritters. • Heat the oil in a large frying pan until very hot and fry the fritters in small batches for 5–7 minutes, or until browned. • Remove with a slotted spoon and drain well on paper towels. • Arrange the fritters on a heated serving dish. • Heat the ketchup and pour it over the fritters. Sprinkle with the remaining Pecorino, sprinkle with the basil, and serve hot.

SAMOSAS

Cook the potato, peas, and mixed vegetables in a large pot of salted, boiling water for 5 minutes, or until crunchy-tender. • Drain, transfer to a large bowl, and set aside. • Mix in the onion, cilantro, garlic, lime juice, garam masala, ginger, chile, curcuma, and salt. • Unroll the puff pastry and cut into 4 x 6-inch (10 x 15-cm) strips. Place a little of the vegetable mixture in the center of each strip. • Fold the pastry strips into triangles and seal the edges with a little water. • Heat the oil in a deep frying pan until very hot and fry the samosas in small batches for 5–7 minutes, or until golden brown. • Serve hot.

Serves: 4

Preparation: 20'

Cooking: 20–25'

Level of difficulty: 2

- 1 potato, peeled and cut in small cubes
- 3 tbsp fresh or frozen peas, thawed if frozen
- 2 oz/60 g mixed diced cauliflower, carrots, and cabbage
- ½ onion, finely chopped
- 1 tbsp finely chopped cilantro/coriander
- 2 cloves garlic, finely chopped
- 2 tsp fresh lime juice
- 1 tsp garam masala
- ½ tsp grated fresh ginger
- ½ tsp green chile pepper
- ¼ tsp curcuma powder
- ¼ tsp salt
- 8 oz/250 g frozen puff pastry, thawed
- 2 cups/500 ml olive oil, for frying

FRIED VEGETABLES, INDIAN-STYLE

*Vegan

Serves: 4

Preparation: 20' + 30'
to stand

Cooking: 20'

Level of difficulty: 2

- ¾ cup/125 g
  garbanzo bean/
  chick pea flour
- 1 tsp red chile
  powder
- ¼ tsp baking
  powder
- ⅛ tsp salt
- 6 tbsp water
- juice of ½ lemon
- 5 oz/150 g
  potatoes, peeled
  and thinly sliced
- 5 oz/150 g onion,
  peeled and cut into
  rings
- 5 oz/150 g
  cauliflower, broken
  up into florets
- 5 oz/150 g
  eggplants/
  aubergines, thinly
  sliced
- 2 cups/500 ml oil,
  for frying

Sift the garbanzo bean flour, chile powder, baking powder, and salt into a large bowl. Beat in the water and lemon juice until smooth. Set aside for 30 minutes. • Heat the oil in a large frying pan until very hot. • Dip the chopped vegetables into the batter and drop them into the oil. Fry for 5–7 minutes, or until golden brown and crisp all over. • Drain well on paper towels. • Serve hot.

A favorite food at Holi parties in northern India to celebrate the end of winter.

ONION RINGS WITH BASIL

Soak the onions in cold water for 30 minutes. • Drain and dry on paper towels. • Sift 1 cup (150 g) of the flour into a large bowl. Stir in the cornstarch, parsley, and basil. Season with salt and pepper. • Sift the remaining flour into a separate bowl. Dip the onion rings in the plain flour, then in the milk, and finally in the seasoned flour. • Heat the oil in a large frying pan until very hot. Fry the onion rings for 5–7 minutes, or until crisp and golden. • Remove them with a slotted spoon and drain on paper towels. • Serve hot.

Serves: 4

Preparation: 20' + 30' to soak

Cooking: 7'

Level of difficulty: 2

- 2 large onions, cut into small rings
- 1²⁄₃ cups/250 g all-purpose/plain flour
- ¹⁄₃ cup/50 g cornstarch/corn flour
- 2 tbsp finely chopped parsley
- 3 tbsp finely chopped basil
- salt and freshly ground black pepper to taste
- 1 cup/250 ml milk
- 2 cups/500 ml olive oil, for frying

CHEESE CRISPS

Serves: 4

Preparation: 15'

Cooking: 20'

Level of difficulty: 1

- 1½ tbsp butter
- 3 eggs
- ¾ cup/90 g freshly grated Montasio or Pecorino cheese
- 2 tbsp freshly grated Parmesan cheese
- ⅛ tsp freshly grated nutmeg
- ⅛ tsp salt
- 1 cup/250 ml olive oil, for frying

Preheat the oven to 350°F/180°C/gas 4.
• Line a baking sheet with waxed paper. • Beat the butter, eggs, Montasio, Parmesan, nutmeg, and salt in a large bowl until creamy. • Pour the mixture onto the prepared baking sheet. Flatten to about ½ inch (1 cm) thick. • Bake for about 15 minutes, or until golden brown. • Let cool, then cut into squares. • Heat the oil in a large frying pan and fry the crisps for 5 minutes until golden brown.
• Serve with creamy vegetable soups.

CORN FRITTERS

Mix the flour, eggs, milk, corn, and Parmesan in a large bowl until well blended. Season with salt and pepper. • Heat the oil in a large frying pan until very hot and fry tablespoons of the corn mixture in small batches for 5–7 minutes, or until golden brown. • Remove with a slotted spoon and drain well on paper towels. • Serve hot.

658

Serves: 4

Preparation: 15'

Cooking: 20'

Level of difficulty: 2

- ²/₃ cup/100 g all-purpose/plain flour
- 2 eggs, lightly beaten
- ²/₃ cup/150 ml milk
- 3¹/₂ cups/350 g canned corn
- ³/₄ cup/90 g freshly grated Parmesan cheese
- salt and freshly ground black pepper to taste
- 2 cups/500 ml olive oil, for frying

LENTIL BURGERS

*Vegan

Serves: 4

Preparation: 20' + 30'
to cool

Cooking: 35'

Level of difficulty: 1

- **1 lb/500 g red lentils**
- **7 oz/200 g tofu, coarsely chopped**
- **salt to taste**
- **2 tbsp finely chopped parsley**
- **½ cup/60 g fine dry bread crumbs**
- **6 tbsp sunflower oil**

Cook the lentils in a large pot of salted, boiling water for about 30 minutes, or until tender. • Drain and process in a food processor with the tofu until finely chopped. Season with salt and add the parsley. Let cool slightly. • Shape the mixture into burgers about 3 inches (8 cm) in diameter and 1 inch (2.5 cm) thick. Dip each one in the bread crumbs. • Heat the oil in a large frying pan until very hot and fry the burgers in small batches for 3–4 minutes, or until browned. Turn and cook on the other side for 3–4 minutes, until browned all over. • Serve hot.

659

VEGETABLE PARCELS

Pastry: Sift the flour, baking powder, and salt into a large bowl. Mix in the ghee and enough milk to form a stiff dough. • Turn the dough out onto a lightly floured surface and knead until smooth. • Shape into small balls and cut them in half. • Filling: Cook the potato in a large pot of salted, boiling water for 8–10 minutes, or until tender. • Drain and set aside. • Sauté the onion and tomato in the ghee in a large frying pan over medium heat for 5 minutes, or until softened. • Mix in the garam masala, coriander powder, ginger, chile, and peas. • Add the potato and cook for 5 minutes. • Drizzle with the lemon juice. • Place a teaspoon of the filling in the center of each pastry half. Brush the edges with water and fold over to form a triangle. • Heat the oil in a deep frying pan until very hot and fry the parcels in small batches for 5–7 minutes, or until golden brown and crisp. • Remove with a slotted spoon and drain well on paper towels. • Serve hot.

660

Serves: 4

Preparation: 30'

Cooking: 30'

Level of difficulty: 2

PASTRY
- 1⅓ cups/200 g all-purpose/plain flour
- ½ tsp baking powder
- ⅛ tsp salt
- 1 tbsp ghee (clarified butter)
- 3 tbsp warm milk + more as needed

FILLING
- 1 potato, diced
- 1 small onion, finely chopped
- 1 tomato, chopped
- 2 tbsp ghee (clarified butter)
- 1 tbsp garam masala
- 1 tsp coriander powder
- 1 tsp grated fresh ginger
- ½ tsp chile powder
- ¾ cup/100 g peas
- 1 tbsp lemon juice
- 2 cups/500 ml peanut oil, for frying

ITALIAN-STYLE FRIED VEGETABLES

Serves: 4

Preparation: 25'

Cooking: 20–25'

Level of difficulty: 2

- 12 zucchini/ courgettes with flowers attached
- 12 asparagus stalks
- 1/3 cup/50 g finely ground cornmeal
- 2 cups/500 ml olive oil, for frying
- 6 frozen potato croquettes
- 6 triangles ready-made polenta
- 6 cauliflower florets, boiled until crunchy-tender
- 1/3 cup/50 g all-purpose/plain flour
- 4 eggs, lightly beaten
- 1 cup/125 g fine dry bread crumbs
- salt to taste

Remove the zucchini flowers and slice the zucchini thickly on a diagonal. • Dip the zucchini flowers, zucchini, and asparagus in the cornmeal. • Heat the oil in a large frying pan or deep fryer until very hot and fry the zucchini flowers, zucchini, and asparagus for 5–7 minutes, or until lightly golden. • Dip the potato croquettes, polenta triangles, and cauliflower in the flour, then in the beaten eggs, followed by the bread crumbs. Fry in small batches for 5–7 minutes, or until deep golden. • Remove with a slotted spoon and drain well on paper towels. • Season with salt. Arrange on a serving dish and serve with a dipping sauce.

663

SPICY FRIED PARCELS

Serves: 4

Preparation: 30' + 1 h
to rest

Cooking: 35'

Level of difficulty: 2

Dough: Sift the flour and salt into a large bowl. Mix in the butter and oil to make a smooth dough. • Shape into a ball, wrap in waxed paper, and let rest for 1 hour. • Filling: Cook the potatoes in salted, boiling water for 10 minutes. Drain. • Cook the onions, spices, oil, lemon juice, water, and salt in a large frying pan for 10 minutes. • Mash the potatoes. Add them to the onion mixture with the cilantro and mix well. • Roll the dough out thinly on a floured work surface. Cut out 4-inch (10-cm) rounds. • Drop a tablespoon of the filling into the center of each round. Fold in half and seal the edges well. • Heat the oil in a large frying pan until very hot and fry in small batches for 3–4 minutes on each side, or until golden all over. • Remove with a slotted spoon and drain on paper towels. • Serve hot.

DOUGH

- 1½ cups/225 g all-purpose/plain flour
- ½ tsp salt
- 4 tbsp butter
- ½ cup/125 ml olive oil

FILLING

- 1 lb/500 g potatoes, cut in small cubes
- 2 red onions, cut into thin wedges
- ½ tsp ground ginger
- ½ tsp ground cumin
- ½ tsp chile pepper
- ½ tsp ground cinnamon
- ¼ tsp ground cloves
- 4 tbsp extra-virgin olive oil
- 1 tbsp lemon juice
- 1 tbsp water
- ½ tsp salt
- 10–12 leaves fresh cilantro/coriander, torn
- 2 cups/500 ml olive oil, for frying

MEDITERRANEAN POTATO FRITTERS

Serves: 4

Preparation: 30' + 2 h 30' to rest

Cooking: 20'

Level of difficulty: 2

- **10 oz/300 g cherry tomatoes**
- **1 small bunch parsley, chives, basil, and marjoram, finely chopped**
- **1 clove garlic, thinly sliced**
- **salt and freshly ground black pepper to taste**
- **4 tbsp extra-virgin olive oil**
- **1 tbsp active dry yeast or ½ oz/ 15 g fresh yeast**
- **½ tsp sugar**
- **4 tbsp warm water**
- **1¾ lb/800 g floury potatoes**
- **1⅓ cups/200 g all-purpose/plain flour + more as needed**
- **2 tbsp butter, softened**
- **7 oz/200 g Mozzarella cheese, cut in small pieces**

Blanch the tomatoes in salted, boiling water for 30 seconds. Drain and peel. Squeeze out as many seeds as possible and chop finely. • Transfer to a large bowl with the herbs and garlic. Season with salt and pepper and drizzle with oil. Let marinate for 2 hours. • Dissolve the yeast with the sugar in 4 tablespoons of water and set aside for 15 minutes, until foamy. • Cook the potatoes in a large pot of salted, boiling water for about 20 minutes, or until tender. • Drain and mash. • Sift the flour and 1 teaspoon of salt into a medium bowl. Knead in the mashed potatoes, yeast mixture, and butter to make a stiff dough. If the dough is too soft, add more flour. Knead for about 10 minutes on a floured work surface. Cover and let rise for 30 minutes. • Shape into small balls and roll out into 4-inch (10-cm) rounds. • Heat the oil in a large frying pan until very hot and fry the fritters in small batches until golden and puffy. • Remove with a slotted spoon and drain well on paper towels. • Top with the marinated tomatoes and Mozzarella. • Serve immediately.

VEGETABLE TEMPURA

B atter: Beat the egg, water, and salt in a large bowl until well blended. • Gradually add the flour, mixing just enough to prevent any lumps from forming. • Refrigerate for at least 3 hours. • When the batter is well chilled, pour the oil into a deep-fryer. There should be about 3 inches (7 cm) of oil.

The secrets of good tempura lie in the temperature of the oil (325°F/170°C) and chilling the batter. • Place the pan over medium heat and heat the oil until very hot. • Dip the prepared vegetables in the batter, then fry them in the oil in small batches until golden brown and crispy. • Remove with a slotted spoon and drain well on paper towels. • Serve immediately with the soy sauce, horseradish sauce, and ginger and lemon sauce for dipping.

Serves: 4

Preparation: 45' + 3 h to chill

Cooking: 20'

Level of difficulty: 2

BATTER
- 1 egg
- 1 cup/250 ml water
- salt to taste
- 1¼ cups/180 g all-purpose/plain flour

VEGETABLES
- 4 artichokes, cleaned and cut into quarters
- 6 shallots, peeled and cut in 4 lengthwise
- 2 eggplants/aubergines, thickly sliced
- 2 large carrots, cut into small lengths
- 14 oz/400 g pumpkin, seeded, peeled, and sliced
- 3 cups/750 ml oil
- Soy sauce
- Horseradish sauce
- grated ginger mixed with fresh lemon juice

ZUCCHINI AND ONION FRITTERS

Serves: 4

Preparation: 30'

Cooking: 25'

Level of difficulty: 1

- 4 oz/125 g zucchini/courgettes
- ½ oz/15 g fresh yeast or 1 package (¼-oz/7-g) active dry yeast
- ½ cup/125 ml milk
- ¾ cup/125 g all-purpose/plain flour
- 1 egg, separated
- ¼ tsp salt
- 2 cups/500 ml olive oil, for frying
- 2 large onions, thinly sliced

Wash and dry the zucchini and coarsely chop. • Dissolve the yeast in 2 tablespoons of warm milk. Let stand for 10 minutes, until foamy. • Add the flour, egg yolk, and salt. Stir in the remaining milk. • Beat the egg white in a large bowl until stiff and fold it into the batter. • Heat the oil in a deep frying pan until very hot. Dip the zucchini and onions into the batter and fry in small batches until golden brown. Serve hot.

FRIED BEAN CURD

Coat the slices of bean curd with flour, then dip them in the egg. • Heat 2 tablespoons of oil in a large wok and place the bean curd in it. Fry over medium heat for about 1 minute, or until golden brown. Turn over, add 2 tablespoons of oil, and fry until golden brown. • Mix the sherry, salt, sesame oil, and stock in a small bowl. • Sprinkle the bean curd with the scallions, ginger, and sesame seeds and pour in the stock mixture. Pierce the bean curd with a fork. Lower the heat and cook until the liquid is absorbed by the bean curd.

Serves: 6

Preparation: 10'

Cooking: 10'

Level of difficulty: 1

- 2 lb/1 kg bean curd, cut in ½-inch/1-cm slices
- 1 cup/150 g all-purpose/plain flour
- 1 egg, lightly beaten
- 4 tbsp extra-virgin olive oil
- 1 tbsp sherry
- 1 tsp salt
- 1 tbsp sesame oil
- ½ cup/125 ml Vegetable Stock (see page 945)
- 1 tbsp finely chopped scallions/ spring onions
- 1 tbsp finely chopped ginger
- 2 tbsp toasted sesame seeds

VEGETARIAN SPRING ROLLS

Heat the extra-virgin oil in a wok and sauté the celery for 3 minutes. • Add the bean sprouts, black mushrooms, carrots, and bamboo shoots and stir-fry for 5 minutes. • Add the soy sauce, sesame oil, salt, and sugar. • Divide the filling into 12 equal portions. Wrap one portion of filling in each of the spring roll wrappers. • Mix the flour and water to form a smooth paste. Use the paste to seal the spring rolls. • Heat the oil to very hot in a large frying pan and fry the spring rolls until golden brown. • Remove with a slotted spoon and drain well on paper towels. • Serve immediately.

674

*Vegan

Serves: 6

Preparation: 30'

Cooking: 20'

Level of difficulty: 1

- 2 tbsp extra-virgin olive oil
- 1 stalk celery, finely chopped
- 4 oz/125 g mung bean sprouts
- 3 oz/90 g dried black Chinese mushrooms, cut in very thin strips
- 2 oz/60 g carrots, cut in very thin strips
- 2 oz/60 g bamboo shoots
- 1 tsp soy sauce
- 1 tsp sesame oil
- ½ tsp salt
- ½ tsp sugar
- 12 spring roll wrappers
- 1 tbsp all-purpose/ plain flour
- 1 tbsp water
- 1 quart/1 liter oil, for frying

*Vegan

Serves: 6

Preparation: 30'

Cooking: 30'

Level of difficulty: 1

- 1¼ cups/200 g raw peanuts
- 1 tsp coriander seeds
- 2 tsp finely chopped ginger
- 2 cloves garlic
- 1 tsp red pepper flakes (or 2 crumbled dried chilies)
- 1 tsp salt
- ½ tsp ground turmeric
- 1 cup/150 g rice flour
- ⅔ cup/100 g all-purpose/plain flour
- 1 cup/250 ml coconut milk
- 2 cups/500 ml oil, for frying

SPICY PEANUT FRITTERS

Place the peanuts in a wok and dry-fry over low heat for 5 minutes. Rub them to remove the skins and chop coarsely. • Process the coriander seeds, ginger, garlic, red pepper flakes, salt, and turmeric in a food processor or blender until smooth. • Sift both flours into a large bowl. Mix in the spice mixture and coconut milk, blending well. Add the peanuts. • Heat half the oil in a wok until very hot and fry tablespoons of batter in small batches until golden brown. • Remove with a slotted spoon and drain well on paper towels.

• Serve hot or at room temperature.

STUFFED FRIED ZUCCHINI FLOWERS

Serves: 4

Preparation: 10'

Cooking: 15'

Level of difficulty:1

- **20 fresh zucchini/ courgette flowers**
- **6 tbsp freshly grated Parmesan cheese**
- **1 cup/125 g fine dry bread crumbs**
- **1 tbsp finely chopped parsley**
- **3 eggs**
- **salt and freshly ground black pepper to taste**
- **1 cup/150 g all-purpose/plain flour**
- **1–2 cups/ 250–500 ml olive oil, for frying**

Rinse the flowers carefully under cold running water. Trim the stalks and dry the flowers carefully with paper towels. • Mix the Parmesan and bread crumbs in a large bowl. Add the parsley, 1 egg, and salt and pepper. • Use this mixture to carefully stuff the flowers. • Beat the remaining eggs and place them in a small bowl. Place the flour in a small bowl and dip the stuffed flowers first in the flour, followed by the egg. • Heat the oil in a large frying pan until very hot and fry the flowers in small batches until golden. • Remove with a slotted spoon and drain well on paper towels. • Season with salt and serve hot.

You will only be able to make this dish during the summer when fresh zucchini flowers are available.

RICE AND POTATO FRITTERS

C ook the potatoes in a large pot of salted, boiling water for 10 minutes. • Add the rice and cook for 15–18 minutes, or until the rice is tender. • Drain well and transfer to a large bowl. Let cool. • Mix in the Parmesan, parsley, garlic, eggs, salt, and pepper. • Form into small patties and roll the fritters in the flour. • Heat the oil in a large frying pan and fry in small batches for 5–7 minutes, or until golden brown all over. • Remove with a slotted spoon and drain well on paper towels. • Serve hot.

Serves: 6

Preparation: 15'

Cooking: 45'

Level of difficulty: 1

- 1 lb/500 g potatoes, peeled and cut into cubes
- 1 cup/200 g short-grain rice
- 4 tbsp freshly grated Parmesan cheese
- 1 tbsp finely chopped parsley
- 1 clove garlic, finely chopped
- 2 large eggs, lightly beaten
- salt and freshly ground black pepper to taste
- 2 cups/300 g all-purpose/plain flour
- 2 cups/500 ml olive oil, for frying

Serves: 4

Preparation: 15'

Cooking: 40'

Level of difficulty: 2

- 2 eggplants/
  aubergines
- 1 tbsp finely
  chopped parsley
- 10 leaves fresh
  basil, torn
- 1 clove garlic,
  finely chopped
- 4 tbsp freshly
  grated Parmesan
  cheese
- 2 large eggs, lightly
  beaten
- salt and freshly
  ground black
  pepper to taste
- 1 cup/125 g fine
  dry bread crumbs
- 2 cups/500 ml
  olive oil, for frying

SICILIAN-STYLE EGGPLANT FRITTERS

Preheat the oven to 400°F/200°C/gas 6. • Cut the eggplants in half lengthwise and place them on a baking sheet. • Bake for 15–20 minutes, or until tender and golden brown. Let cool and scoop out the flesh with a spoon, mashing it coarsely with a fork. • Mix the eggplant, parsley, basil, garlic, Parmesan, eggs, salt and pepper, and enough bread crumbs to make a firm mixture. Shape into balls the size of walnuts. Roll in the bread crumbs. • Heat the oil in a large frying pan until very hot and fry in small batches for 5–7 minutes, or until golden brown all over. • Remove with a slotted spoon and drain well on paper towels. Serve immediately.

FRIED FRESH SAGE LEAVES

Rinse the sage leaves under cold running water, then pat dry with paper towels. • Dredge the leaves in the flour. Dip in the egg and coat well with the bread crumbs. • Heat the oil in a large frying pan until very hot (test by dropping a leaf into the oil. If ready, it will sizzle sharply) and add half the leaves. They will turn golden brown almost immediately. Turn them once, then scoop them out with a slotted spoon. Drain on paper towels. Cook the remaining leaves. • Season with salt and serve hot.

Serves: 4

Preparation: 10'

Cooking: 1'

Level of difficulty: 1

- **40 large fresh sage leaves**
- **2 tbsp all-purpose/ plain flour**
- **1 large egg, beaten until foamy with a pinch of salt**
- **1½ cups/180 g fine dry bread crumbs**
- **2 cups/500 ml oil, for frying**
- **salt to taste**

MARINATED PUMPKIN

*Vegan

Serves: 6

Preparation: 20'

Cooking: 15' + 12 h
to marinate

Level of difficulty: 1

- 2 lb/1 kg pumpkin
- ⅔ cup/100 g all-purpose/plain flour
- 1 cup/250 ml oil, for frying
- 1 cup/250 ml red wine vinegar
- 1 clove garlic
- salt and freshly ground black pepper to taste
- 1 sprig fresh rosemary, finely chopped

Peel the pumpkin and remove the seeds and fibers. Cut into slices about $^1/_2$ inch (1 cm) thick. • Coat the pumpkin lightly with flour. Heat the oil in a large frying pan until very hot and fry the pumpkin in small batches until golden brown. • Remove with a slotted spoon and drain well on paper towels. • Bring the vinegar to a boil in a small saucepan with the garlic and a dash of salt and pepper. • Sprinkle a little salt over the fried pumpkin pieces and arrange in layers in a fairly shallow, straight-sided dish. Sprinkle with pepper and rosemary. • Pour the vinegar over the pumpkin slices, cover with a sheet of plastic wrap, and let marinate for 12 hours before serving.

FRIED ARTICHOKES

C lean the artichokes by trimming the tops and stalk (leave about $1^1/_2$ inches (4 cm) of stalk attached). Remove all the tough outer leaves so that only the pale, inner leaves and heart remain. Soak the cleaned artichokes in a bowl of cold water with the lemon juice. • Drain well and bang each artichoke down on the bench so that the leaves open out like flowers. • Heat the oil in a large frying pan until very hot. Fry the artichokes for about 15 minutes, or until tender. • Turn up the heat for 2–3 minutes and fry until golden brown. • Remove with a slotted spoon and drain well on paper towels. • Season with salt and serve hot.

*Vegan

Serves: 4
Preparation: 20'
Cooking: 15'
Level of difficulty: 1

- 8 large artichokes
- juice of 1 lemon
- 2 cups/500 ml oil, for frying
- salt to taste

MIXED FRIED VEGETABLES

Serves: 4

Preparation: 20'

Cooking: 50'

Level of difficulty: 1

- **6 medium zucchini/ courgettes**
- **2 large eggplants/ aubergines**
- **12 large zucchini/ courgette flowers**
- **2 cups/300 g all- purpose/plain flour**
- **4 eggs, beaten until foamy**
- **6 tbsp beer**
- **3 cups/750 ml oil, for frying**
- **salt to taste**

C ut the zucchini in half crosswise and cut each half in quarters lengthwise. Cut the eggplants in ¹/₄-inch (5-mm) thick slices and cut each slice in halves or quarters (depending on how big they are). • Trim the stems of the zucchini flowers and wash carefully. Drain on paper towels. • Heat the oil in a large frying pan until very hot. • Flour the vegetables, followed by the egg. • Fry the vegetables in small batches until golden brown. • Remove with a slotted spoon and drain well on paper towels. • Season with salt and serve hot.

TOMATO CROQUETTES

Blanch the tomatoes in boiling water for 1 minute. • Drain and slip off the skins. Remove the seeds, chop coarsely, and let drain. • Mix the Ricotta and egg yolks in a large bowl until smooth. • Add the tomatoes, parsley, nutmeg, salt, and pepper and mix well. • Form the mixture into croquettes of about 2 inches (4-cm) long and 1 inch (2.5-cm) thick. The mixture should be firm; if it is too runny, add 1–2 of tablespoons dry bread crumbs or freshly grated Parmesan cheese. • Roll the croquettes in the flour, dip them in the egg, and roll in the bread crumbs. • Heat the oil in a large frying pan until very hot and fry the croquettes in small batches for about 10 minutes, or until golden brown. • Remove with a slotted spoon and drain well on paper towels. • Serve hot.

686

Serves: 4

Preparation: 20'

Cooking: 40'

Level of difficulty: 2

- 1 lb/500 g ripe tomatoes
- 10 oz/300 g Ricotta cheese, crumbled
- 2 eggs, beaten until foamy, + 2 egg yolks
- 2 tbsp finely chopped parsley
- ¼ tsp freshly grated nutmeg
- salt and freshly ground black pepper to taste
- 1 cup/150 g all-purpose/plain flour
- 1 cup/125 g fine dry bread crumbs
- 2 cups/500 ml oil, for frying

EGGS

VEGETABLE FRITTATA

Break the eggs into a bowl and beat until frothy. Stir in the Pecorino and parsley. Season with salt and pepper. • Heat 2 teaspoons of the oil in a frying pan and sauté the diced vegetable for 8–10 minutes, or until tender. • Pour in the egg mixture and cook for 4–5 minutes, or until set on top. • Turn the frittata carefully and cook for 4 minutes more. It should be firm and lightly browned on both sides. • Peel and chop the tomatoes very finely. Place them in a bowl with the garlic and the remaining oil. Season with salt. • Transfer the frittata to a serving plate and cut into wedges. • Serve with the tomatoes.

Serves: 4

Preparation: 20'

Cooking: 15–20'

Level of difficulty: 1

- **6 eggs**
- **12 oz/350 g frozen diced vegetables, thawed**
- **4 tbsp freshly grated Pecorino Romano cheese**
- **1 tbsp finely chopped parsley**
- **salt and freshly ground black pepper to taste**
- **4 tbsp extra-virgin olive oil**
- **4 tomatoes**
- **1 clove garlic, finely chopped**

FRITTATA WITH MINT

Serves: 4

Preparation: 20'

Cooking: 10'

Level of difficulty: 1

- **6 eggs**
- **2 tbsp fine dry bread crumbs**
- **1 small bunch parsley, finely chopped**
- **25 leaves fresh mint, torn**
- **salt and freshly ground black pepper to taste**
- **1–2 tbsp extra-virgin olive oil**

Break the eggs into a bowl and beat until frothy. Stir in the bread crumbs, parsley, and mint. Season with salt and pepper. • Heat the oil in a large frying pan. Pour in the egg mixture and cook for 4–5 minutes, or until set on top. Turn the frittata carefully and cook for 4 minutes more. It should be firm and lightly browned on both sides. • Serve hot.

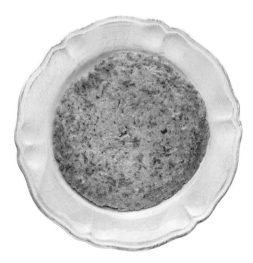

ONION AND PECORINO FRITTATA

C ook the onions with the oil and water in a large
frying pan over medium heat for 5 minutes.
• Beat the eggs in a medium bowl until frothy. Stir
in the Pecorino, basil, and salt. • Pour the egg
mixture into the pan and cook for 4–5 minutes, or
until set on top. Turn the frittata carefully and cook
for 4 minutes more. It should be firm and lightly
browned on both sides. • Sprinkle with the parsley
and serve hot.

692

Serves: 4–6

Preparation: 15'

Cooking: 15'

Level of difficulty: 1

- **8 small onions, thinly sliced**
- **3 tbsp extra-virgin olive oil**
- **1 tbsp water**
- **8 eggs**
- **5 oz/150 g mature Pecorino cheese, cut into flakes**
- **1 tbsp torn basil**
- **salt to taste**
- **1 tbsp finely chopped parsley**

TOMATO AND BELL PEPPER FRITTATA

Sauté the bell peppers and onion in the oil in a large frying pan over medium heat for about 10 minutes, or until the bell peppers and onions are tender. • Stir in the tomatoes and basil. Season with salt. • Beat the eggs in a medium bowl until frothy. Season with salt. • Pour the eggs into the frying pan. Stir well and cook until the eggs have set. • Turn on the broiler (grill) and broil the frittata for 3–4 minutes, or until the top is golden. • Serve hot.

Serves: 4

Preparation: 20'

Cooking: 25'

Level of difficulty: 1

- **12 oz/350 g mixed bell peppers/ capsicums, seeded, cored, and coarsely chopped**
- **1 onion, thinly sliced**
- **2 tbsp extra-virgin olive oil**
- **12 oz/350 g cherry tomatoes, coarsely chopped**
- **4 leaves fresh basil, torn**
- **salt to taste**
- **6 eggs**

STUFFED FRIED EGGS

Hard-boil 4 eggs and peel them. Cut in half lengthwise and remove the yolk. • Mash the yolks with the butter and capers in a small bowl. • Fill each half-egg with the mixture. Dip the eggs in the Béchamel, followed by the bread crumbs. • Heat the oil in a deep frying pan until very hot and fry the eggs in small batches for 5–7 minutes, or until golden and crisp. • Drain well on paper towels. • Serve hot.

Serves: 2–4

Preparation: 20'

Cooking: 10–15'

Level of difficulty: 1

- **5 eggs**
- **1 tbsp butter**
- **1 tbsp capers in salt, rinsed and chopped**
- **1 cup/250 ml Béchamel Sauce (see page 948)**
- **2 cups/250 g fine dry bread crumbs**
- **2 cups/500 ml olive oil, for frying**

BAKED EGGS WITH FONTINA

Serves: 4

Preparation: 15'

Cooking: 20–25'

Level of difficulty: 1

- **6 thin slices whole-wheat/wholemeal bread**
- **4 tbsp milk**
- **8 oz/250 g Fontina cheese, thinly sliced**
- **2 tbsp butter, cut into flakes**
- **6 eggs**

Preheat the oven to 350°F/180°C/gas 4.
• Butter an ovenproof baking dish. • Dip the bread in the milk and arrange in the prepared baking dish. • Top with half the Fontina and butter.
• Bake for 8–10 minutes, or until the bread is golden and the cheese is bubbling. • Break the eggs into the dish and cover each one with the remaining slices of Fontina. • Bake for 10–15 minutes, or until the egg white is cooked and the cheese has melted. • Serve hot.

ZUCCHINI AND MUSHROOM FRITTATA

Clean the mushrooms and wash away any dirt. Slice thinly. • Sauté the mushrooms and garlic in half the butter in a large frying pan over low heat for 20 minutes, or until tender. • Discard the garlic and add the zucchini and thyme. Season with salt and pepper. Cook for 10 minutes. • Break the eggs into a large bowl and beat until frothy. Stir in the Parmesan and milk. Season with salt and pepper. Pour over the mushrooms and zucchini and cook for 4–5 minutes, or until set. Sprinkle with the sesame seeds. • Turn the frittata carefully and cook for 4 minutes more. It should be firm and lightly browned on both sides. • Serve hot.

Serves: 4

Preparation: 25'

Cooking: 50'

Level of difficulty: 2

- **10 oz/300 g cultivated white mushrooms**
- **2 cloves garlic, lightly crushed but whole**
- **4 tbsp butter, cut up**
- **2 zucchini/ courgettes, thinly sliced**
- **1 sprig thyme, finely chopped**
- **salt and freshly ground black pepper to taste**
- **8 eggs**
- **1/3 cup/40 g freshly grated Parmesan cheese**
- **3 tbsp milk**
- **2 tbsp sesame seeds**

EGG CURRY

Serves: 2–4

Preparation: 20'

Cooking: 20–25'

Level of difficulty: 1

- 1 onion, finely chopped
- 1 tbsp ghee (clarified butter)
- 1 piece ginger, finely sliced
- 1 clove garlic, finely sliced
- 1 tsp salt
- 1 tsp garam masala
- 1 tsp coriander seeds
- ½ tsp chile powder
- 1 cup/250 g chopped tomatoes
- 1 small bunch fresh cilantro/coriander, finely chopped
- 4 hard-boiled eggs, peeled but whole

Sauté the onion in the ghee in a large frying pan over medium heat for about 10 minutes, or until golden brown. • Add the ginger, garlic, salt, garam masala, coriander seeds, and chile pepper and fry for 2 minutes. • Stir in the tomatoes and cook for 5 minutes. Add the cilantro. • Add the eggs and cook over low heat for 5 minutes, or until the sauce thickens. • Serve hot with boiled basmati rice.

EGGS AU GRATIN

Preheat the oven to 400°F/200°C/gas 6.
• Butter an ovenproof baking dish. • Melt the
butter in a medium saucepan over low heat. Add
the flour and mix to form a paste. • Pour in the
milk, stirring constantly. Bring to a boil and remove
from the heat. • Stir in half the Parmesan and
nutmeg. • Arrange layers of the cheese sauce,
Fontina, and eggs in the prepared dish, finishing
with the cheese sauce. Sprinkle with the remaining
Parmesan. • Bake for 10–15 minutes, or until
golden and bubbling. • Serve hot.

Serves: 4	
Preparation: 15'	
Cooking: 20–25'	
Level of difficulty: 2	

• 2 tbsp butter, cut
  up
• 2 tbsp flour
• 2 cups/500 ml milk
• ½ cup/60 g freshly
  grated Parmesan
  cheese
• ⅛ tsp freshly
  grated nutmeg
• 7 oz/200 g Fontina
  cheese, diced
• 8 hard-boiled eggs,
  thinly sliced

FRITTATA WITH VEGETABLES

VEGETABLES

- ½ cup/125 ml white wine vinegar
- 4 tbsp dry white wine
- 7 oz/200 g yellow, red and green bell peppers/capsicums, seeded, cored, and diced
- 1 small onion, diced
- 2 tbsp extra-virgin olive oil
- salt and freshly ground black pepper to taste

FRITTATA

- 2 tbsp extra-virgin olive oil
- 8 eggs
- 4 tbsp light/single cream
- 2 tbsp freshly grated Parmesan cheese
- salt and freshly ground black pepper to taste
- 10 oz/300 g mixed seasonal salad

Vegetables: Reserve 1 tablespoon each of the vinegar and wine. Bring the remaining vinegar and wine to a boil in a small saucepan. Add the bell peppers and onion and cook for 10–15 minutes.
- Drain and drizzle with the oil. Season with salt and pepper. • Frittata: Beat the eggs, cream, and Parmesan in a large bowl. Season with salt and pepper. • Heat the oil in a 9-inch (23-cm) frying pan over medium heat. Pour in the egg mixture and cook for 4–5 minutes, or until set on top. Turn the frittata carefully and cook for 4 minutes more. It should be firm and lightly browned on both sides.
- Cut into squares and serve on a serving dish with the vegetables and salad drizzled with the remaining oil and vinegar.

703

EGGS

BAKED WATERCRESS OMELET

Preheat the oven to 350°F/180°C/gas 4. • Oil a 9-inch (23-cm) pie plate. • Trim the watercress and rinse well under cold running water. Dry well. • Sauté the shallots in the oil in a large frying pan until translucent. • Add the watercress and season with salt and pepper. Cook for 10 minutes, stirring often. • Remove from the heat and chop coarsely. • Beat the eggs in a medium bowl. Season with salt and pepper. Stir in the Parmesan, parsley, and watercress mixture. • Pour the mixture into the prepared pie plate. • Bake for about 25 minutes, or until set. • Serve hot or at room temperature.

704

Serves: 4

Preparation: 10'

Cooking: 40'

Level of difficulty: 1

- 1 lb/500 g fresh watercress
- 2 shallots, finely chopped
- 2 tbsp extra-virgin olive oil
- salt and freshly ground black pepper to taste
- 5 eggs
- 2 tbsp freshly grated Parmesan cheese
- 4 tbsp finely chopped parsley

PANCAKES WITH CHEESE

Serves: 4–6	
Preparation: 5'	
Cooking: 25'	
Level of difficulty: 1	

- **3 eggs**
- **salt to taste**
- **1 cup/150 g all-purpose/plain white flour**
- **scant ½ cup/ 100 ml milk, warm**
- **4 tbsp butter**
- **1 cup/125 g freshly grated Pecorino Romano cheese**

Beat the eggs in a medium bowl. Season with salt. • Stir in the flour and milk to make a smooth batter. • Heat the butter or oil in a small frying pan until very hot. Add 1–2 tablespoons of batter and twirl the pan so that it spreads evenly across the bottom. Cook until brown, then toss to brown the other side. Repeat until all the batter is used up. • Sprinkle with the Pecorino and serve hot.

FRENCH-STYLE EGGS

Preheat the oven to 400°F/200°C/gas 6.
• Cut the tomatoes in half lengthwise. Butter an ovenproof baking dish and place a layer of tomatoes on the bottom. Season with salt.
• Cover with half the olives, half the eggs, half the parsley, and a pinch of salt. Top with a thin layer of leeks and half the Béchamel. • Repeat the layers until all the ingredients are used, finishing with the Béchamel. Dot with the butter. • Bake for 25–30 minutes, or until bubbling and lightly browned. • Serve hot.

Serves: 4

Preparation: 25'

Cooking: 25–30'

Level of difficulty: 1

- **10 firm-ripe tomatoes, peeled**
- **salt to taste**
- **12 black or green olives, pitted and finely sliced**
- **4 hard-boiled eggs, thinly sliced**
- **1 tbsp finely chopped parsley**
- **whites of 2 leeks, finely chopped**
- **2 cups/500 ml Béchamel Sauce (see page 948)**
- **2 tbsp butter, cut into flakes**

BAKED POTATO AND MUSHROOM FRITTATA

C ook the potatoes in a large pot of salted, boiling water for 15–20 minutes, or until tender. • Drain and slice thinly. • Preheat the oven to 350°F/ 180°C/gas 4. • Butter an 8-inch (20-cm) baking pan. • Sauté the onion in the oil and butter in a large frying pan over low heat for 4 minutes until transparent. • Add the mushrooms and herbs. Season with salt and pepper and cook for 5 minutes until the mushrooms are tender. • Beat the eggs and cream in a medium bowl. Season with salt and pepper. • Add the mushroom mixture and potatoes and mix well. • Pour into the prepared baking pan. • Bake for 15–20 minutes, or until golden brown and set. • Turn out onto a serving dish and let cool slightly. • Serve warm in slices.

Serve at lunch with a salad on the side.

708

Serves: 4

Preparation: 15'

Cooking: 40–45'

Level of difficulty: 2

- **14 oz/400 g waxy potatoes, peeled**
- **1 small onion, finely chopped**
- **3 tbsp extra-virgin olive oil**
- **1 tbsp butter**
- **4 small porcini mushrooms, thinly sliced**
- **¼ tsp finely chopped thyme**
- **¼ tsp finely chopped marjoram**
- **¼ tsp finely chopped rosemary**
- **2 tsp finely chopped parsley**
- **salt and freshly ground black pepper to taste**
- **4 eggs**
- **7 tbsp cream**

FRIED EGGS WITH BELL PEPPERS AND TOMATOES

Sauté the bell pepper and leek in 2 tablespoons of oil in a large frying pan over medium heat until crunchy-tender. • Add the tomatoes and season with salt and pepper. Cook for about 10 minutes, or until the tomatoes have broken down and the sauce has thickened slightly.
• Fry the eggs individually in the remaining oil in a large frying pan until cooked to your preference.
• Spoon the bell pepper sauce onto serving dishes and transfer an egg onto each dish. • Serve hot.

Serves: 4

Preparation: 5'

Cooking: 20'

Level of difficulty: 1

- 1 yellow bell pepper, seeded, cored, and finely sliced
- 1 leek, thinly sliced
- 3 tbsp extra-virgin olive oil
- 1²/₃ cups/400 g peeled tomatoes, finely chopped
- salt and freshly ground black pepper to taste
- 4 eggs

BAKED VEGETABLE AND OLIVE FRITTATA

Serves: 4

Preparation: 25'

Cooking: 45–50'

Level of difficulty: 2

- 2 red bell peppers
- 2 lb/1 kg firm-ripe tomatoes
- 4 small onions, thinly sliced
- 3 tbsp extra-virgin olive oil
- 1 small bunch aromatic herbs (oregano, basil, thyme, chervil), finely chopped
- salt to taste
- 4 eggs
- ½ cup/125 ml milk
- 1¾ cups/215 g freshly grated Gruyère cheese
- 1 cup/100 g black olives, pitted

Preheat the oven to 400°F/200°C/gas 6.
• Place the bell peppers and tomatoes on a plate in the microwave oven. Cook at high heat for 3 minutes. Peel them. • Cut the bell peppers into strips and the tomatoes into wedges. • Sauté the onions in the oil in a large frying pan over low heat for about 10 minutes, or until softened. • Add the tomatoes, bell peppers, and herbs. Season with salt. • Cook for 4 minutes. Transfer to a bowl. • Beat the eggs, milk, and Gruyère in a large bowl. Pour into the fried vegetables. • Pour the mixture into a baking dish and garnish with the black olives. • Bake for 25–30 minutes, or until set and golden on top. • Serve warm or cold.

Olives are low in calories and high in iron.

POLENTA SOUFFLÉ WITH PARMESAN SAUCE

Polenta Soufflé: Bring a large pot of water to a boil with the salt. • Gradually sprinkle in the cornmeal, whisking constantly to prevent any lumps from forming. Cook over medium heat for about 45 minutes, stirring constantly. • Remove from the heat and let cool to warm. • Preheat the oven to 400°F/200°C/gas 6. • Butter a soufflé mold and sprinkle with bread crumbs. • Beat the egg yolks in a medium bowl until pale and thick. • Beat the egg whites in a large bowl until stiff peaks form. • Gently fold the beaten egg yolks into the polenta, followed by the beaten whites. • Spread a quarter of the polenta mixture in the prepared mold and sprinkle with a third of the Parmesan. Repeat until the polenta has been used up, finishing with a layer of polenta. Sprinkle with the remaining Parmesan. • Bake for 20–25 minutes, or until risen and golden brown. • Sauce: Melt the Parmesan in the milk in a double boiler over barely simmering water. Beat well to make a smooth cream. • Serve the soufflé drizzled with the sauce.

Serves: 4	
Preparation: 40'	
Cooking: 1 h 15'	
Level of difficulty: 1	

POLENTA SOUFFLÉ
- ¾ cup/125 g finely ground cornmeal
- ⅛ tsp salt
- 1⅔ cups/400 ml water
- 3 eggs, separated + 3 egg whites
- 1¾ cups/215 g freshly grated Parmesan cheese

SAUCE
- 2⅓ cups/300 g freshly grated Parmesan cheese
- scant ½ cup/ 100 ml milk

FRITTATA RINGS WITH MIXED VEGETABLES

Slice the zucchini lengthwise. Drizzle with 1 tablespoon of oil and season with salt and pepper. • Arrange the zucchini on a greased grill pan and grill for about 4 minutes on each side, or until they take on blackened grill lines. • Beat the egg and egg yolks in a large bowl. Season with salt and pepper. • Ladle a quarter of the mixture at a time into a hot oiled frying pan to obtain four thin frittatas. Cook each frittata for 4–5 minutes, or until set on top. • Turn each frittata carefully and cook for 4 minutes more. They should be firm and lightly browned on both sides. • Arrange the zucchini slices on top with the Fontina and asparagus. Roll up and wrap individually in plastic wrap. • Refrigerate for 1 hour. • Slice the frittata rolls into rings and arrange on a bed of lettuce. • Drizzle with the remaining oil and season with salt. • Serve immediately.

Serves: 6

Preparation: 30' + 1 h to chill

Cooking: 20'

Level of difficulty: 2

- 2 zucchini/courgettes, weighing about 8 oz/250 g
- 4 tbsp extra-virgin olive oil
- salt and freshly ground white pepper to taste
- 1 egg + 3 egg yolks
- 3 oz/90 g Fontina cheese, thinly sliced
- 8 asparagus stalks, boiled
- 1 gem lettuce, to serve

THAI OMELET

Serves: 4

Preparation: 15'

Cooking: 20'

Level of difficulty: 2

- 1 clove garlic, finely chopped
- 1 onion, finely chopped
- 2 tbsp peanut oil
- 1 cup/250 g chopped tomatoes
- 2 tbsp finely chopped cilantro/coriander
- 1 tbsp soy sauce
- 8 eggs

Sauté the garlic and onion in 1 tablespoon of oil in a large frying pan over medium heat until the garlic is pale gold. • Add the tomatoes, cilantro, and soy sauce. Cook over medium heat for 10 minutes, or until the tomatoes have reduced. • Beat the eggs in a medium bowl. • Heat the oil in a large frying pan until hot. Pour in half the egg mixture and cook for 4–5 minutes, or until set on top. • Turn the omelet carefully and cook for 4 minutes more. It should be firm and lightly browned on both sides. • When the omelet is almost cooked, spoon half the tomato mixture into the center. Fold the sides in over the filling to make a square parcel. Cut into squares. Repeat with the remaining egg and tomato. • Serve hot.

717

BROCCOLI WITH EGGS

Serves: 4

Preparation: 30'

Cooking: 20'

Level of difficulty: 1

- 2 lb/1 kg broccoli, cut into florets
- 1 clove garlic, lightly crushed but whole
- ½ cup/125 ml extra-virgin olive oil
- 4 eggs
- 1 cup/125 g freshly grated Pecorino cheese
- salt and freshly ground black pepper to taste
- 1 fresh spicy red chile pepper, finely sliced, to garnish (optional)

Cook the broccoli in salted, boiling water for 8 minutes, or until crunchy-tender. • Drain, taking care not to break up the florets. • Sauté the garlic in 4 tablespoons of oil in a frying pan over medium heat until the garlic is pale gold. • Discard the garlic. • Add the broccoli to the oil and sauté for 5 minutes. • Beat the eggs and Pecorino in a medium bowl. Season with salt and pepper. • Heat the remaining oil in a frying pan until very hot and pour in the eggs. Stir with a fork until cooked and creamy. • Arrange the broccoli on a serving dish. Spoon the eggs over the top, garnish with the chile pepper, if liked, and serve hot.

EGGS WITH SPINACH CREAM

Serves:	4
Preparation:	10'
Cooking:	8–10'
Level of difficulty:	1

Preheat the oven to 350°F/180°C/gas 4.
• Use a small glass or cookie cutter to cut 8 disks out of the bread. Brush with the oil and place on a baking sheet. Toast for 8–10 minutes, or until nicely browned. • Wash the spinach under cold running water. Do not drain but place in a saucepan and cook, with just the water clinging to its leaves, for 3 minutes. • Drain, press out the excess water, and place in a food processor.
• Add the cream and Parmesan and process until smooth. Season with salt and pepper. • Use a teaspoon to remove the yolks from the eggs. Crumble and set aside. • Fill the eggs with the spinach cream. • Arrange the disks of toast on a serving dish. Place half an egg, filling-side up, on each toast. Sprinkle with the egg yolks and chives.

- 4–8 slices white sandwich bread
- 2 tbsp extra-virgin olive oil
- 8 oz/250 g spinach
- 1/2 cup/125 ml heavy/double cream
- 6 tbsp freshly grated Parmesan cheese
- salt and freshly ground black pepper to taste
- 4 hard-boiled eggs, shelled
- 2 tbsp finely chopped chives

EGGS WITH ZUCCHINI

Serves: 4–6
Preparation: 30'
Cooking: 5–7'
Level of difficulty: 1

- 12 oz/350 g zucchini/ courgettes
- 1 clove garlic, lightly crushed but whole
- 4 tbsp torn basil
- 6 tbsp extra-virgin olive oil
- salt and freshly ground black pepper to taste
- 6 hard-boiled eggs, shelled
- 1 bunch fresh salad greens
- 6 tbsp diced mixed bell peppers

Chop the zucchini into thin wheels. • Sauté the zucchini, garlic, and basil in 2 tablespoons of oil in a large frying pan over medium heat until the garlic is pale gold. Season with salt and pepper. • Remove the yolks from the eggs and place in a food processor or blender with the zucchini mixture. Chop until smooth. • Fill the egg whites with the mixture. • Arrange the salad greens on a serving dish and place the filled eggs on top. • Sprinkle with the bell peppers and drizzle with the remaining oil. • Season with salt and pepper and serve.

MINI PEA SOUFFLÉS

Serves: 4

Preparation: 30' + 30'
to chill

Cooking: 30–35'

Level of difficulty: 2

- 1½ cups/180 g fresh or frozen peas
- 2 tbsp butter
- 2 tbsp all-purpose/ plain flour
- 1 cup/250 ml milk
- salt to taste
- 2 tbsp freshly grated Parmesan cheese
- 6 egg whites
- 1 tbsp sugar

Cook the peas in a large pot of salted, boiling water until tender. • Drain, place in a food processor, and chop until smooth. • Melt the butter in a small saucepan and stir in the flour. • Gradually stir in the milk and bring to a boil. Cook, stirring constantly over low heat for 10 minutes. Season with salt. • Stir the sauce and Parmesan into the pea mixture and let cool. • Refrigerate for 30 minutes. • Preheat the oven to 400°F/200°C/ gas 6. • Butter and flour 4 individual soufflé molds. • Beat the egg whites with a pinch of salt until stiff peaks form. Beat in the sugar. • Gently fold the egg whites into the pea mixture. Spoon the mixture into the prepared molds. • Bake for 12–15 minutes, or until golden brown on top. • Serve hot.

BAKED POTATO FRITTATA

Preheat the oven to 375°F/190°C/gas 5. • Oil a 9-inch (23-cm) baking pan. • Cook the potato slices in a large pot of salted, boiling water for 8–10 minutes, or until tender. • Drain well and set aside. • Sauté the onion in the oil in a large frying pan over medium heat for 10 minutes, or until lightly browned. Season with salt. • Beat the eggs in a medium bowl. Mix in the potatoes, onions, and Parmesan. • Pour the mixture into the prepared pan. • Bake for 12–15 minutes, or until golden brown. • Serve hot or at room temperature.

Serves: 4

Preparation: 20'

Cooking: 30–35'

Level of difficulty: 2

- **10 oz/300 g potatoes, peeled and thinly sliced**
- **1 large red onion, coarsely chopped**
- **2 tbsp extra-virgin olive oil**
- **salt to taste**
- **4 eggs**
- **1 tbsp freshly grated Parmesan cheese**

ZUCCHINI OMELET

Rinse the zucchini under cold running water and dry with paper towels • Slice the zucchini into thin wheels and coat with flour, shaking off any excess. • Heat all but 2 tablespoons of the oil in a large frying pan over high heat until very hot. • Sauté the zucchini for about 8 minutes, or until lightly browned. • Drain well on paper towels. • Discard the oil and replace with the remaining oil. Arrange the zucchini in a single layer in the pan and return to medium-high heat. • Beat the eggs in a medium bowl. Season with salt and pepper. • Pour the egg mixture into the pan and cook for 4–5 minutes. • Turn on the broiler (grill) and broil the frittata for 3–4 minutes, or until the top is golden. • Turn out onto a heated serving dish and serve hot.

726

Serves: 4

Preparation: 10'

Cooking: 15–20'

Level of difficulty: 1

- **3 large zucchini/ courgettes**
- **½ cup/75 g all-purpose/plain flour**
- **½ cup/125 ml extra-virgin olive oil**
- **6 eggs**
- **salt and freshly ground black pepper to taste**

CHEESE

RICOTTA AND ZUCCHINI CRÊPES

Serves: 6	
Preparation: 45'	
Cooking: 30'	
Level of difficulty: 2	

C•rêpes: Mix the flour and milk in a large bowl.
• Add the eggs and beat until well blended.
• Beat in the thyme, marjoram, and parsley. Season with salt. • Melt the butter in a small frying pan over medium heat. • Pour in just enough batter to cover the bottom of the pan, tilting it so that it thinly covers the surface. • Cook until the crêpe is lightly gold on the underside. Use a large spatula to flip and cook the other side. Repeat until all the batter has been used. Stack the cooked crêpes one on top of another in a warm oven. • Preheat the oven to 400°F/200°C/gas 6. • Butter a large baking dish. • Ricotta Filling: Sauté the zucchini in the butter in a large frying pan over medium heat for 5–10 minutes, or until softened. • Add the zucchini flowers, Ricotta, pine nuts, and nutmeg. Cook for 3 minutes. • Place 2–3 tablespoons of filling in the center of each crêpe. Fold the crêpes in half and then in half again to form triangles. • Arrange the filled crêpes in the prepared baking dish. • Pour the cream over the top and sprinkle with the Parmesan.
• Cover with aluminum foil and bake for 10 minutes.
• Remove the foil and bake for 8–10 minutes more, or until the crêpes are crispy and and the cheese is golden brown.

CRÊPES
- 1⅔ cups/250 g all-purpose/plain flour
- 2 cups/500 ml milk
- 4 eggs
- 1 tbsp finely chopped thyme
- 1 tbsp finely chopped marjoram
- 1 tbsp finely chopped parsley
- ⅛ tsp salt
- 1 tbsp butter

RICOTTA FILLING
- 12 oz/350 g zucchini/courgettes, cut into rounds
- 2 tbsp butter
- 24 zucchini flowers, carefully washed
- 1⅔ cups/400 g Ricotta cheese
- ½ cup/60 g pine nuts, toasted
- ½ tsp freshly ground nutmeg
- 1¼ cups/310 ml cream
- 1 tbsp freshly grated Parmesan cheese

PANCAKES WITH TWO CHEESES

Pancakes: Mix the water and garbanzo bean flour in a small bowl until well blended. • Beat the eggs and milk in a large bowl until frothy. • Mix in the flour, butter, and garbanzo flour mixture until smooth. Season with salt. • Grease a small frying pan with oil. • Pour 2 tablespoons of the batter into the pan, tilting it so that the batter covers the surface. • Cook until the pancake is light golden on the underside. Use a large spatula to flip the pancake and cook until golden on the other side. Repeat until all the batter has been used. • Preheat the oven to 400°F/200°C/gas 6. • Butter a large baking dish. • Cheese Filling: Mix the Ricotta, goat cheese, 1/2 cup (60 g) of Parmesan, marjoram, parsley, and garlic in a large bowl. Season with salt and pepper. • Spread the pancakes with the filling and roll them up tightly. • Place the pancakes seam-side down in the baking dish. • Sprinkle with the remaining Parmesan and dot with the butter.
• Bake for 8–10 minutes, or until browned.
• Serve warm on a bed of arugula.

Serves: 6

Preparation: 40'

Cooking: 20'

Level of difficulty: 2

PANCAKES
- 2/3 cup/150 ml water
- 2/3 cup/100 g garbanzo bean/chickpea flour
- 2 eggs
- 6 tbsp milk
- 1/3 cup/50 g all-purpose/plain flour
- 1 tbsp butter, melted
- salt to taste

CHEESE FILLING
- 1 cup/250 g Ricotta cheese
- 2/3 cup/150 g creamy goat cheese
- 3/4 cup/90 g freshly grated Parmesan cheese
- 1 tbsp finely chopped marjoram
- 1 tbsp finely chopped parsley
- 1 clove garlic, finely chopped
- salt and freshly ground black pepper to taste
- 1 tbsp butter
- 1 bunch arugula/rocket, to serve

BAKED FENNEL
AND PARMESAN

Serves: 4

Preparation: 30'

Cooking: 40–50'

Level of difficulty: 2

- 6 large fennel bulbs
- 1 onion, thinly sliced
- 4 tbsp all-purpose/ plain flour
- ½ cup/125 g butter
- 4 tbsp heavy/ double cream
- salt and freshly ground black pepper to taste
- 1¼ cups/150 g freshly grated Parmesan cheese

Preheat the oven to 375°F/190°C/gas 5.
• Butter a baking dish. • Clean the fennel by removing the tough outer leaves. Trim the stalks and cut each bulb in half. • Cook the fennel in salted boiling water for 8–10 minutes, or until tender. • Drain well and pat dry with a clean cloth. Cut each half in 2 or 3 pieces. • Dip the fennel and onion in the flour. • Sauté the fennel and onion in 4 tablespoons of butter in a large frying pan over medium heat until golden. • Add the cream and season with salt and pepper. • Cover and cook over low heat for 12–15 minutes, or until the sauce has reduced. • Arrange the fennel and onion in layers with the sauce in the prepared baking dish. Sprinkle with the Parmesan and dot with the remaining butter. • Bake for 15–20 minutes, or until lightly golden. • Serve hot.

With its light aniseed taste, fennel is a cleansing and restorative vegetable.

MIXED CHEESE PIE

Serves:	4–6
Preparation:	1 h
Rising time:	1 h
Cooking:	25–30'
Level of difficulty:	1

Dough: Dissolve the yeast, milk, and sugar in a small bowl for 5 minutes, until foamy. • Sift the flour and salt into a bowl. Mix in the yeast mixture to make a firm dough. Knead until elastic. • Shape into a ball, place in an oiled bowl, and cover with a clean cloth. • Let rise for 1 hour, or until doubled in bulk. • Preheat the oven to 400°F/ 200°C/gas 6. • Butter a baking dish. • Roll the dough out on a lightly floured surface until large enough to cover the bottom and sides of the dish. • Filling: Mix the cheeses, flour, and milk in a saucepan. Season with pepper and cook over low heat until melted. • Beat in the egg yolks. • Beat the egg whites in a large bowl until stiff. • Fold the whites into the cheese filling. • Pour into the dough base. • Bake for 25–30 minutes, or until the filling is golden brown on top. • Serve hot.

DOUGH

- ½ oz/15 g fresh yeast or 1 package (¼-oz/7-g) active dry yeast
- 2 cups/500 ml warm milk
- 1 tsp sugar
- 1⅓ cups/200 g all-purpose/plain flour
- ¼ tsp salt

FILLING

- 8 oz/250 g mixed cheeses, such as Mozzarella, Provolone, and Fontina, cut into small cubes
- 2 tbsp all-purpose/ plain flour
- 1 cup/250 ml milk
- freshly ground black pepper to taste
- 3 eggs, separated

Serves: 4	
Preparation: 50'	
Cooking: 8–10'	
Level of difficulty: 1	

CRÊPES WITH CHEESE AND VEGETABLES

- 1 quantity Crêpes (see page 956)
- 1 carrot, cut into matchsticks
- 2 zucchini/ courgettes, cut into matchsticks
- white of 1 leek, very finely sliced
- 4 tbsp extra-virgin olive oil
- 1²/₃ cups/400 g Ricotta cheese
- 1 egg
- 1³/₄ cups/215 g freshly grated Pecorino cheese
- ³/₄ cup/90 g freshly grated Parmesan cheese
- 1 clove garlic, finely chopped
- 14 oz/400 g spinach leaves, blanched
- 3 tbsp heavy/ double cream
- freshly ground black pepper to taste

Prepare the crêpes • Preheat the oven to 400°F/200°C/gas 6. • Sauté the carrot, zucchini, and leek in 2 tablespoons of oil in a frying pan until golden. • Transfer to a baking dish. • Beat the Ricotta, egg, Pecorino, and ¹/₂ cup (60 g) of Parmesan in a large bowl. • Spread the mixture over the crêpes and roll up loosely. • Place half the crêpes on top of the vegetables. • Sauté the garlic in the remaining oil in a large frying pan until pale gold. • Add the spinach and sauté for 7 minutes. • Transfer to the baking dish and arrange the remaining crêpes on top. • Drizzle with the cream, season with pepper, and sprinkle with the remaining Parmesan. • Bake for 8–10 minutes, or until golden. • Serve hot.

CHEESE AND POTATO PIE

B oil the potatoes in their skins for 15–20 minutes, or until tender but still firm. • Drain well and let cool for 15 minutes. • Peel and let cool completely. • Preheat the oven to 400°F/200°C/gas 6. • Butter a baking dish. • Cut the potatoes into ¹/₂-inch (1-cm) slices and arrange in layers in the prepared baking dish. • Dot each layer with the butter and add the Parmesan. Season with salt and pepper. Pour in the milk. • Bake for 20–25 minutes, or until golden brown. • Serve hot.

Serves: 4

Preparation: 40'

Cooking: 35–40'

Level of difficulty: 1

- 1³/₄ lb/800 g potatoes
- ¹/₂ cup/125 g butter, cut up
- 8 oz/250 g Parmesan cheese, thinly sliced
- salt and freshly ground black pepper to taste
- 1 cup/250 ml milk

ASPARAGUS AND CHEESE SPIRALS

Serves: 4

Preparation: 45'

Cooking: 1 h

Level of difficulty: 3

- 1 quantity Crêpes (see page 956)

FILLING
- 14 oz/400 g fresh spinach leaves, stalks removed
- 1 lb/500 g tender asparagus spears
- ¾ cup/180 g creamy goat cheese
- 1 cup/250 g Ricotta cheese
- salt to taste
- ⅛ tsp freshly grated nutmeg
- ⅔ cup/150 ml light/single cream
- 1 tbsp butter, cut up
- ¾ cup/90 g freshly grated Parmesan cheese

Prepare the crêpes. • Filling: Cook the spinach and asparagus in salted boiling water until tender. Drain and chop finely. • Mix the spinach, asparagus, goat cheese, and Ricotta in a large bowl. Season with salt and nutmeg. • Spread the filling over the crêpes and carefully roll up. Cut each crêpe into 1 inch (2.5 cm) slices. • Butter a baking dish. • Place the slices of crêpe in the baking dish. • Drizzle with the cream, dot with the butter, and sprinkle with the Parmesan. • Bake for 15 minutes, or until browned. • Serve hot.

CANNOLI WITH HERB CHEESE

Serves:	6
Preparation:	30' + 30' to rest
Cooking:	20'
Level of difficulty:	3

Cannoli: Sift the flour and salt into a large bowl. • Use a pastry blender to cut in the butter until the mixture resembles coarse crumbs. • Mix in enough water to make a stiff dough. • Let rest for 30 minutes. • Roll the dough out thinly and cut out 12 squares. Brush with cold water. • Wrap around the cannoli molds, damp-side inward. • Heat the oil in a deep-fryer until very hot and fry the cannoli in small batches for 5–7 minutes, or until golden brown and crisp. • Drain on paper towels. Let cool slightly. • Slip off the molds and keep warm. • Herb Cheese Filling: Mix the Robiola, goat's cheese, mixed herbs, chile powder, and salt. • Beat the cream until stiff and fold into the cheese mixture. • Stuff the cannoli with the filling. • Serve immediately.

CANNOLI

- 1 cup/150 g all-purpose/plain flour
- 1/8 tsp salt
- 1 tbsp butter
- 4 tbsp water
- 2 cups/500 ml olive oil, for frying

HERB CHEESE FILLING

- 1 1/3 cups/330 g Robiola cheese
- 2/3 cup/150 g fresh goat's cheese
- 1 tbsp finely chopped parsley, thyme, marjoram, and chives
- 1/4 tsp chile powder
- 1/8 tsp salt
- 2/3 cup/150 g heavy/double cream

- 1 large bunch fresh basil
- ½ cup/125 ml extra-virgin olive oil
- 8 oz/250 g mixed salad greens, well-washed
- juice of 1 lemon
- salt and freshly ground black pepper to taste
- 4 small rounds of goat's cheese
- 4 slices firm-textured bread, toasted

WARM GOAT'S CHEESE WITH BASIL

C hop the basil in a food processor. Gradually pour in half the oil, pulsing until smooth.
• Transfer to a small bowl and let stand for 1 hour.
• Arrange the salad greens on individual serving plates. Drizzle with the lemon juice and remaining oil. Season with salt and pepper. • Heat a grill pan over medium heat. Cook the cheese for 5 minutes until soft and warmed through. • Arrange the cheese on top of the salad and serve with the toast. Drizzle with the basil dressing.

SAVORY CHEESECAKE

Serves: 8

Preparation: 40' + 3 h to chill

Cooking: 30–35'

Level of difficulty: 2

- 8 oz/250 g whole-wheat/wholemeal toast
- $^1/_2$ cup/125 g butter, cut up
- 4 tbsp cold water
- 1$^2/_3$ cups/400 g Ricotta cheese
- 1 cup/250 g soft fresh cheese
- $^1/_2$ cup/60 g freshly grated Parmesan cheese
- 3 eggs
- salt and freshly ground black pepper to taste
- 5 oz/150 g cherry tomatoes

Preheat the oven to 350°F/180°C/gas 4. • Place the toast in a plastic bag and use a bottle to crush it into fine bread crumbs. • Set aside 1 tablespoon of butter and melt the rest in a small frying pan over low heat. Add the bread crumbs and cook until the butter has been absorbed. Add the water. • Butter the base and sides of an 11-inch (28-cm) springform pan. Line the base with waxed paper. • Firmly press the bread crumb mixture into the base and sides to a thickness of $^1/_2$ inch (1 cm). • Beat the Ricotta, soft cheese, Parmesan, eggs, and salt and pepper in a large bowl until creamy. • Spoon the cream over the crumb base, smoothing the surface. Knock the pan on the surface two or three times to fill all the gaps. • Cut the tomatoes in half and arrange on the top of the cheesecake, pressing them in slightly. • Bake for 25–30 minutes, or until browned on top. • Let cool completely. • Refrigerate for 3 hours before serving.

CRUDITÉS WITH FRESH CHEESE

Preheat the oven to 425°F/220°C/gas 7.
• Line a baking sheet with waxed paper.
• Cut the vegetables into equal-sized sticks.
Arrange them around the edges of individual
serving plates. Season with salt and drizzle with
the oil. • Place the cheeses on a baking sheet.
• Bake for about 5 minutes, or until warm and
slightly melted. • Arrange one form of cheese in
the center of each plate with the crudités.
Season with black pepper and serve immediately.

744

Serves: 6

Preparation: 15'

Cooking: 5'

Level of difficulty: 1

• 1½ lb/750 g mixed
  fresh vegetables,
  such as mixed bell
  peppers, halved,
  and celery,
  carrots, or fennel

• salt and freshly
  ground black
  pepper to taste

• 2 tbsp extra-virgin
  olive oil

• 6 small fresh
  cheeses (such as
  goat's cheese or
  Tomini)

SEMOLINA, SPINACH, AND FONTINA SANDWICHES

Serves: 4–8
Preparation: 40'
Cooking: 20'
Level of difficulty: 3

- 2 cups/500 ml milk
- salt to taste
- 1 cup/150 g semolina
- 2 egg yolks
- 1 tbsp freshly grated Parmesan cheese
- 7 oz/200 g Fontina or Cheddar cheese, thinly sliced
- 1 tbsp extra-virgin olive oil
- 1 clove garlic, finely chopped
- 10 oz/300 g spinach leaves, boiled and finely chopped

Bring the milk to a boil with the salt in a large pan. • Gradually sprinkle in the semolina, stirring constantly with a balloon whisk to prevent any lumps from forming. Cook over low heat, stirring almost constantly for 10 minutes.
• Remove from the heat and mix in the egg yolks, Parmesan, and salt. • Pour the mixture onto an oiled work surface, spreading it 1 inch (2.5 cm) thick. Let cool completely. • Cut into $2^1/_2$-inch (6-cm) rounds. • Use a $2^1/_2$-inch (6-cm) cutter to cut the cheese into eight rounds. Grate the remaining cheese. • Sauté the garlic in the oil in a large frying pan until pale gold. • Add the spinach and sauté over high heat for 2–3 minutes. • Toast the little disks of semolina in a frying pan over high heat. • Stack them, filling with alternate layers of spinach and grated cheese. Top with the rounds of cheese. • Use toothpicks to fasten the sandwiches. • Place under a broiler (grill) until golden. • Serve hot.

Serve these eyecatching little sandwiches as an appetizer or snack.

SALADS

SPINACH AND WATERCRESS SALAD

S oak the raisins in the lemon juice for 5 minutes. • Wash the spinach and watercress and dry well. Place in a large salad bowl. • Add the carrots, walnuts, raisins, and lemon juice. Season with salt and drizzle with the oil. • Toss well and serve immediately.

750

Peppery and pungent, the watercress adds a sharpness to this salad.

*Vegan

Serves: 4

Preparation: 15'

Level of difficulty: 1

- 1 tbsp golden raisins/sultanas
- 2 tbsp fresh lemon juice
- 1 lb/500 g baby spinach leaves
- 4 oz/125 g watercress, stems removed
- 2 carrots, scraped and coarsely grated
- ½ cup/50 g chopped walnuts
- salt to taste
- 4–6 tbsp extra-virgin olive oil

STRAWBERRY AND CUCUMBER SALAD

Place the strawberries in a large bowl and drizzle with the balsamic vinegar. • Mix the yogurt and mint in a medium bowl. Stir in the oil and season with salt. Refrigerate until ready to use. • Wash the salad and dry well. Place in a salad bowl. Arrange the rice on top of the salad, followed by the strawberries and cucumber. • Spoon the yogurt sauce over the top. Season with pepper and serve.

Serves: 4

Preparation: 20'

Level of difficulty: 1

- 10 oz/300 g strawberries, washed, hulled, and thinly sliced
- 1 tbsp balsamic vinegar
- 1 cup/250 ml low-fat yogurt
- 1 tbsp finely chopped mint
- 3 tbsp walnut oil
- salt and freshly ground pink (or black) pepper to taste
- 7 oz/200 g mixed salad greens
- ½ cup/100 g cooked brown rice
- 1 cucumber, thinly sliced

PINEAPPLE AND CANTALOUPE SALAD

Peel the cantaloupe and cut in half. Cut the flesh of one half into small cubes and thinly slice the other half. • Slice the pineapple thinly. • Place the pineapple slices on serving plates and place the cantaloupe slices on top. Arrange the green beans, cantaloupe cubes, tomatoes, and bell pepper on top. • Dressing: Process the lemon juice, oil, parsley, and Tabasco sauce in a food processor or blender until well blended. Season with salt.
• Pour the dressing over the salad and serve.

*Vegan

Serves: 4–6

Preparation: 20'

Level of difficulty: 1

- 1 small cantaloupe/rock melon, cut in half
- 1 small pineapple, skin removed
- 7 oz/200 g green beans, cooked and cut in short lengths
- 12 cherry tomatoes, cut in half
- 1 green bell pepper/capsicum, seeded, cored, and cut in small squares

DRESSING
- juice of 1 lemon
- 1/2 cup/125 ml extra-virgin olive oil
- 1 small bunch parsley
- 3 drops Tabasco sauce
- salt to taste

MANDARIN, APPLE, AND TOMATO SALAD

Serves: 4

Preparation: 20'

Level of difficulty: 1

- **3 endive hearts, well-washed**
- **1 cup/250 ml sour cream**
- **juice of 1 lemon**
- **juice of ½ orange**
- **7 oz/200 g tomatoes, cut into small cubes**
- **5 oz/150 g tart apples, peeled, cored, and cut into small cubes**
- **2 mandarins, peeled and cut into small cubes**
- **1 scallion/spring onion, finely chopped**
- **1 tbsp finely chopped parsley**

Discard any damaged or discolored outer leaves from the endives. Reserve 12–15 attractive outer leaves and coarsely chop the remainder.
• Arrange the outer leaves like the spokes in a wheel on a large serving plate. • Place the sour cream, lemon juice, orange juice, chopped endives, tomatoes, apples, mandarins, scallion, and parsley in a medium bowl and toss well.
• Spoon the mixture into the center of the plate and serve.

ORANGE AND ARTICHOKE SALAD

C lean the artichokes by trimming the stalks and cutting off the top third of the leaves. Remove the tough outer leaves by pulling them down and snapping them off at the base. Cut the artichokes in half and use a sharp knife to remove any fuzzy core. Cut the artichokes into thin wedges. • Place the artichokes in a large salad bowl and drizzle with half the lemon juice. • Add the oranges, Pecorino, and parsley. • Drizzle with the oil and remaining lemon juice and season with salt and pepper.
• Toss well and serve.

Serves: 4

Preparation: 20'

Level of difficulty: 1

- **6 artichokes**
- **juice of 1 lemon**
- **2 oranges, peeled and cut into segments**
- **3 oz/90 g Pecorino Romano cheese, flaked**
- **1 tbsp finely chopped parsley**
- **6 tbsp extra-virgin olive oil**
- **salt and freshly ground black pepper to taste**

COUSCOUS SALAD

Prepare the couscous according to the instructions on the package. • Wash the vegetables and chop them all into small cubes. • Place in a large salad bowl and mix in the couscous. • Drizzle with the oil and lemon juice. Season with salt and add the mint. • Toss well and serve.

*Vegan

Serves: 4

Preparation: 15'

Level of difficulty: 1

- 10 oz/300 g pre-cooked couscous
- 14 oz/400 g mixed vegetables (bell peppers/capsicum, scallion/spring onion, tomatoes, cucumber, zucchini/courgettes)
- ½ cup/125 ml extra-virgin olive oil
- juice of ½ lemon
- salt to taste
- fresh mint, finely chopped

FENNEL, RUSSIAN-STYLE

Clean the fennel bulbs by trimming the stem and removing any blemished outer leaves. Cut in half and then into thin wedges. • Process the pear, cucumber, almonds, mint, vinegar, and oil in a food processor or blender until smooth. Season with salt and pepper. • Arrange the fennel on a serving plate and spoon the sauce over the top. • Garnish with the flaked almonds and serve.

*Vegan

Serves: 2

Preparation: 10'

Level of difficulty: 1

- 2 bulbs fennel
- 1 pear, peeled and cored
- 1 cucumber, peeled and chopped
- ⅓ cup/50 g blanched almonds
- fresh mint leaves
- 2 tbsp cider vinegar
- 2 tbsp extra-virgin olive oil
- salt and freshly ground black pepper to taste
- flaked almonds, to garnish

LEMON AND MINT SALAD

*Vegan

Serves: 4–6

Preparation: 20' + 2 h
   to chill

Level of difficulty: 1

- 2 lb/1 kg lemons
- 6 tbsp extra-virgin olive oil
- salt and freshly ground black pepper to taste
- 1 bunch mint, separated into leaves
- 1 green chile pepper, thinly sliced
- 1 red chile pepper, thinly sliced

P eel the lemons, removing all the white pithy skin beneath the skin. Cut into small cubes. • Place the lemon cubes in a salad bowl and drizzle with the oil. • Season with salt and pepper. Sprinkle with the mint leaves and chile peppers. • Refrigerate for at least 2 hours before serving.

MIXED VEGETABLE AND MAYONNAISE SALAD

Top and tail the beans and chop into $1/4$-inch (5-mm) pieces. • Peel the carrots and potatoes and chop into $1/4$-inch (5-mm) cubes. • Add 1 tablespoon of vinegar to a saucepan of salted, boiling water. Add the potatoes and cook for about 5 minutes, or until tender. • Drain and set aside to cool. • Add the peas, green beans, carrots, and remaining vinegar to another saucepan filled with salted, boiling water. Cook for about 5 minutes, or until the vegetables are tender. • Drain and set aside to cool. • Slice the gherkins into $1/4$-inch (5-mm) thick wheels. • When the vegetables are cool, place them in a large bowl. Mix in the gherkins and capers. Season with salt and pepper, drizzle with the oil, and mix gently. • Add the mayonnaise. • Arrange on a large serving plate and pipe mayonnaise around the edge in a decorative manner. Garnish with the snow pea and lemon wedges. • Refrigerate for 15 minutes before serving.

Serves: 4–6

Preparation: 15' + 15' to chill

Cooking: 15'

Level of difficulty: 1

- 6 oz/180 g green beans
- 2 large carrots
- 2 large potatoes
- 2 tbsp white wine vinegar
- 6 oz/180 g fresh or frozen peas
- 8 pickled gherkins
- 1 tbsp pickled capers, drained
- salt and freshly ground white pepper to taste
- 4 tbsp extra-virgin olive oil
- $1/2$ cup/125 ml mayonnaise
- 1 snow pea/ mangetout pod, to garnish
- lemon wedges, to garnish

766

SUMMER SALAD

Vegan

Serves: 4

Preparation: 30'

Cooking: 5–10'

Level of difficulty: 1

- 5 oz/150 g green beans, topped and tailed
- 1 bunch arugula/ rocket
- 2 peaches, pitted and cut in 8
- 2 small fennel bulbs, cut into small pieces
- 5 oz/150 g bell peppers/ capsicums, mixed colors, seeded, cored, and cut into thick strips
- juice of 1 lemon
- 6 tbsp extra-virgin olive oil
- salt and freshly ground black pepper to taste

Cook the green beans in a large pot of salted boiling water for 5–10 minutes, or until just tender. • Drain well and let cool completely.
• Rinse the arugula thoroughly under cold running water and dry well. • Arrange the arugula leaves in a fan shape around the outer edge of the plate. Place the peach slices on top so that you can still see the arugula. Place the green beans in a circle overlapping the peaches, followed by the fennel.
• Arrange the bell peppers in the center. • Drizzle with the lemon juice and oil. Season with salt and pepper and serve.

APPLE, RASPBERRY, AND WALNUT SALAD

Arrange the slices of apple around the outer edge of a large serving plate. Drizzle with half the lemon. • Rinse the lettuce thoroughly under cold running water and dry well. • Coarsely chop the lettuce and place in the center of the plate. Sprinkle with the Parmesan, raspberries, and walnuts. • Drizzle with the remaining lemon juice and oil. Season with salt and pepper and serve.

770

Serves: 4

Preparation: 15'

Level of difficulty: 1

- **2 large green apples, cored and thinly sliced**
- **1 small curly-leaved lettuce**
- **4 oz/125 g Parmesan cheese, flaked**
- **½ cup/125 g raspberries**
- **½ cup/50 g walnuts, shelled**
- **juice of 1 lemon**
- **4 tbsp extra-virgin olive oil**
- **salt and freshly ground white pepper to taste**

EXOTIC SALAD WITH YOGURT

Rinse the lettuce thoroughly under cold running water and dry well. Coarsely chop the lettuce and place in a salad bowl with the coconut, cantaloupe, and bell pepper. • Dressing: Beat the yogurt, oil, chile pepper, and coriander seeds in a small bowl until smooth and well blended. • Drizzle the dressing over the salad and serve.

Serves: 4

Preparation: 20'

Level of difficulty: 1

- **1 crisp lettuce**
- **flesh of ½ fresh coconut, cut into small pieces**
- **½ cantaloupe/ rock melon, cut into small pieces**
- **½ red bell pepper, seeded, cored, and cut into small pieces**

DRESSING
- **scant 1 cup/200 ml plain yogurt**
- **6 tbsp extra-virgin olive oil**
- **1 small red chile pepper, thinly sliced**
- **¼ tsp ground coriander seeds**

WARM POTATO SALAD

Place the potatoes in a large pot filled with the boiling stock and red wine vinegar. Cover and cook for 10–15 minutes, or until almost tender.
• Add the green beans and cook for 5 minutes, or until tender. • Dressing: Place the vinegar, olive oil, sesame oil, stock, and mustard seeds in a small container with a screw top. Shake well. • Drain the potatoes and green beans and arrange on 4 individual serving plates. Drizzle with the dressing. Sprinkle with the chives and scallions and serve.

*Vegan

Serves: 4

Preparation: 15'

Cooking: 15–20'

Level of difficulty: 1

- 14 oz/400 g small salad potatoes, such as Charlottes, cut in half
- 1¼ cups/310 ml boiling vegetable stock (see page 945)
- 1 tbsp red wine vinegar or sherry
- 8 oz/250 g green beans, topped and tailed

DRESSING
- 2 tbsp sherry vinegar
- 2 tbsp extra-virgin olive oil
- 2 tbsp sesame oil
- 1 tbsp vegetable stock
- 1 tbsp mustard seeds
- 1 tbsp finely chopped chives
- 2 scallions/spring onions, finely chopped

*Vegan

Serves: 4

Preparation: 5'

Level of difficulty: 1

AVOCADO SALAD

- 1 large ripe avocado, pitted, peeled, and cut into small cubes
- juice of ½ lemon
- salt to taste
- 1–2 heads of Belgian endive, shredded
- 1 cup/100 g canned corn/ sweetcorn
- 1 sprig fresh basil, torn
- 1 sprig fresh parsley, coarsely chopped
- 4 whole lettuce leaves
- 6 tbsp extra-virgin olive oil

Drizzle the avocado with lemon juice to prevent it from browning. Season with salt. • Gently toss the avocado with the Belgian endive, corn, basil, and parsley in a large bowl. • Arrange the lettuce leaves on a serving dish and spoon the salad into them. • Drizzle with the oil and serve immediately.

TOMATOES FILLED WITH ARUGULA AND PESTO

C ut the tomatoes in half and squeeze out as many of the seeds as possible. • Sprinkle lightly with salt and place upside-down in a colander to drain for 30 minutes. • Process the parsley, basil, pine nuts, oil, capers, lemon juice, and salt in a food processor or blender until smooth. • Garnish the tomatoes with the arugula and spoon the pesto over the top. • Serve.

776

Vegan

Serves: 4–6

Preparation: 20' + 30' to drain

Level of difficulty: 1

- 8–12 small salad tomatoes
- salt to taste
- 1 small bunch parsley
- 4 leaves fresh basil
- 4 tbsp pine nuts
- 4 tbsp extra-virgin olive oil
- 1 tbsp capers
- 1 tbsp fresh lemon juice
- 1 lb/500 g arugula/rocket

SPELT WITH VEGETABLES AND SUN-DRIED TOMATO PESTO

Cook the eggplants, bell peppers, and zucchini in batches in a grill pan for about 10 minutes each batch, or until tender. • Chop all the vegetables coarsely. • Place the spelt in a large bowl with the chopped vegetables. Drizzle with the oil and season with salt and pepper. • Toast the pine nuts in a frying pan over high heat until lightly golden. • Process the pine nuts, sun-dried tomatoes, and oil in a food processor until puréed. • Add the oregano and pour over the salad. • Toss gently. Cover and set aside for 1 hour before serving.

778

Vegan

Serves: 4

Preparation: 25' + 1 h to stand

Cooking: 15'

Level of difficulty: 1

- 10 oz/300 g eggplants/ aubergines, bell peppers and zucchini/ courgettes
- 1½ cups/300 g cooked spelt or pearly barley
- 4 tbsp extra-virgin olive oil
- salt and freshly ground black pepper to taste
- 2 tbsp pine nuts
- 3½ oz/100 g sun- dried tomatoes
- 1 tsp dried oregano

SWEET AND SOUR SALAD

Cook the cardoon in a large pot of salted, boiling water for 20 minutes. • Add the cauliflower and artichokes and cook for 5 minutes. • Add the celery and fennel and cook for 5 minutes. Drain and let cool completely. • Sauté the onion in the oil in a small frying pan over medium heat for 2 minutes. Add the water, cover, and cook over low heat for 10 minutes. • Add the sugar and cook for about 10 minutes, or until the sugar begins to caramelize. • Add the vinegar and tomato paste. Cook for 4 minutes. • Add the capers, olives, and raisins. Season with salt and remove from the heat. • Arrange the orange and lemon slices on a serving dish. Arrange the vegetables over the oranges and lemons and drizzle with the sauce. • Serve warm.

.

*Vegan

Serves: 4–6

Preparation: 20'

Cooking: 1 h

Level of difficulty: 2

- ½ cardoon, tough stalks removed and coarsely chopped
- ½ small cauliflower, cut into florets
- 2 artichoke hearts, cut into quarters and finely sliced
- 6 stalks celery, thinly sliced
- 2 fennel bulbs, thinly sliced
- 1 small onion, finely chopped
- 2 tbsp extra-virgin olive oil
- 2 tbsp water
- 1 tbsp sugar
- 4 tbsp white wine vinegar
- 1 tbsp tomato paste/concentrate
- 2 tbsp salt-cured capers, rinsed of salt
- 2 tbsp black olives
- 2 tbsp golden raisins/sultanas
- ⅛ tsp salt
- 1 orange, washed and finely sliced
- 1 lemon, washed and finely sliced

CARROT AND BEAN SPROUT SALAD

Serves: 2–4

Preparation: 5'

Level of difficulty: 1

Toss the carrots, bean sprouts, and yogurt in a large bowl. Season with salt and pepper.

• Arrange the lettuce leaves in a serving dish and spoon the salad over the top.

- **3 carrots, scraped and coarsely grated**
- **1 cup/200 g bean sprouts**
- **1 cup/250 ml plain yogurt**
- **salt and freshly ground black pepper to taste**
- **4 large lettuce leaves**

782

Serves: 6	
Preparation: 20'	
Cooking: 45–60'	
Level of difficulty: 1	

- 1¾ lb/800 g beets/beetroot
- 1 egg yolk
- 1 tbsp fresh lemon juice
- salt and freshly ground black pepper to taste
- ½ cup/125 ml extra-virgin olive oil
- 1 tsp dry mustard powder
- 4 tbsp light/single cream
- 3 onions, finely chopped
- 2 tbsp finely chopped dill

RUSSIAN BEET SALAD

Preheat the oven to 400°F/200°C/gas 6.
• Place the beets on a baking sheet. • Bake for 45–60 minutes, or until tender. • Remove from the oven and let cool completely. • Peel and cut into thin strips. Arrange on 6 individual serving plates.
• Beat the egg yolk and lemon juice until frothy. Season with salt and pepper. • Transfer to a food processor or blender and gradually add the oil, pulsing until smooth and well blended. • Stir in the mustard, cream, onions, and dill and season with the salt and pepper. • Pour over the beets, toss well, and serve.

ARUGULA BREAD SALAD

S lice the bread thinly and toast on both sides under the broiler (grill). • Rub all over with the garlic, let cool, and cut into cubes. • Place the tomatoes in a colander set over a bowl and sprinkle with salt. Let drain for 15 minutes. • Mix the lemon juice, 5 tablespoons of oil, the basil, and salt and pepper in a small bowl. • Place all the ingredients in a salad bowl. • Pour the oil dressing over the top and toss well. • Let stand for 30 minutes before serving.

This salad comes from Tuscany, where yesterday's bread is often used as a base for soups and salads.

784

- 14 oz/400 g rustic farmhouse bread, preferably saltless
- 1 clove garlic
- 4 large firm-ripe tomatoes, coarsely chopped
- salt and freshly ground black pepper to taste
- juice of 1 lemon
- 5 tbsp extra-virgin olive oil
- 1 small bunch fresh basil, torn
- 1 red onion, coarsely chopped
- 1 cucumber, peeled and diced
- 1 green celery heart, coarsely chopped
- 30 black olives, pitted and chopped
- 1 bunch arugula/ rocket

ORANGE SALAD

*Vegan

Serves: 4

Preparation: 10'

Level of difficulty: 1

Peel the oranges, taking care to remove all the white pith. • Slice thinly and place in a salad bowl. Sprinkle with a little salt, then add the olives and onion. • Drizzle with the oil and season with a generous grinding of pepper. Serve as a starter.

- **4 juicy oranges**
- **salt and freshly ground black pepper**
- **10 black olives, pitted and cut in half**
- **1 small white onion, thinly sliced**
- **4–6 tbsp extra-virgin olive oil**

786

*Vegan

Serves: 4

Preparation: 10'

Cooking: 15–20'

Level of difficulty: 1

- 14 oz/400 g small yellow potatoes, peeled
- 2 cups/500 ml boiling vegetable stock (see page 945)
- 1 tbsp white wine vinegar
- 8 oz/250 g green beans, topped and tailed

DRESSING
- 2 tbsp white wine vinegar
- 2 tbsp extra-virgin olive oil
- 2 tbsp sesame oil
- 1 tbsp finely chopped chives
- 1 tbsp vegetable stock
- 1 tbsp whole-grain mustard

- 1 tbsp chopped chives, to garnish
- 2 scallions/spring onions, chopped, to garnish

WARM POTATO SALAD

Place the potatoes in a medium pot filled with the boiling stock and white wine vinegar. Cover and cook for 10–15 minutes, or until almost tender. • Add the green beans and cook for 5 minutes, or until tender. • Dressing: Put all the ingredients for the dressing in a jar with an airtight seal and shake well. • Drain the potatoes and green beans and transfer to a large salad bowl. Drizzle with the dressing. • Garnish with chives and scallions and serve warm.

SEASONAL SALAD WITH TOMATOES

Place the lettuce in a salad bowl. Sprinkle with the Feta, tomatoes, green beans, and olives.
• Dressing: Beat the garlic, vinegar, and oil in a small bowl until well blended. Season with salt and pepper. • Drizzle the dressing over the salad and toss well.

Serves: 6

Preparation: 20'

Level of difficulty: 1

• 1 crisp lettuce, well-washed and coarsely chopped
• 5 oz/150 g Feta cheese, cut into small cubes
• 10 cherry tomatoes, cut in half
• 10 oz/300 g green beans, cooked
• ½ cup/50 g black olives, pitted

DRESSING
• 2 cloves garlic, finely chopped
• 1 tbsp vinegar
• 6 tbsp extra-virgin olive oil
• salt and freshly ground black pepper to taste

CABBAGE AND CARROT SALAD

*Vegan

Serves: 6

Preparation: 15'

Level of difficulty: 1

- 1 small cabbage, finely shredded
- 4 small carrots, finely shredded

DRESSING
- 1 clove garlic, finely chopped
- ½ cup/125 ml extra-virgin olive oil
- 2 tbsp fresh lemon juice

Toss the cabbage and carrots together in a large bowl. • Dressing: Mix the garlic, oil, and lemon juice in a small bowl. • Pour over the carrot and cabbage mixture and toss well. Serve.

PEAR AND BELL PEPPER SALAD

C lean the bell peppers by removing the stalk,
seeds, and core. • Rinse under cold running
water, drain, and dry well. Cut in short, thin strips.
• Rinse the pears. Peel, core, and cut into match-
size sticks. Drizzle with the lemon juice.• Place the
pear and bell peppers in a salad bowl. Add the
garlic (if using), salt, pepper, parsley, and oil.
• Toss gently and serve. • Arrange on
serving plates.

792

Vegan

Serves: 4–6

Preparation: 15'

Level of difficulty: 1

- **3 medium bell
  peppers (mixed
  colors)**
- **2 large ripe pears**
- **juice of 1 lemon**
- **1 clove garlic,
  finely chopped
  (optional)**
- **salt and freshly
  ground black
  pepper to taste**
- **1 tbsp finely
  chopped parsley**
- **4 tbsp extra-virgin
  olive oil**

SPINACH AND AVOCADO SALAD

Serves: 4

Preparation: 10'

Level of difficulty: 1

- 2 tbsp finely chopped parsley
- 1 tsp whole-grain mustard
- 5 tbsp extra-virgin olive oil
- salt and freshly ground black pepper to taste
- 7 tbsp cream
- 7 oz/200 g fresh baby spinach leaves
- 1 large ripe avocado, peeled, pitted, and sliced

Mix the parsley, mustard, and oil in a small bowl. Season with salt and pepper. Add the cream and beat until smooth and glossy. • Toss the spinach, avocado, and dressing in a large salad bowl. Drizzle with the dressing and serve.

Avocados are not only great tasting, they are also rich in potassium and vitamin A.

TOFU AND TOMATO SALAD

Arrange the bread in a large salad bowl. Top with the tomatoes, cucumbers, tofu, onion, olives, and basil. • Refrigerate for at least 30 minutes. • Mix the lemon juice, oil, and salt in a small bowl. Pour over the salad, toss well, and serve.

*Vegan

Serves: 4

Preparation: 10' + 30' to chill

Level of difficulty: 1

- 6 slices toasted bread, preferably unsalted
- 1 lb/500 g cherry tomatoes, cut into quarters
- 4 cucumbers, peeled and thinly sliced
- 14 oz/400 g tofu (bean curd), diced
- 1 large red onion, thinly sliced
- 1 cup/100 g pitted black olives
- 6 leaves fresh basil, torn
- 2 tbsp fresh lemon juice
- 6 tbsp extra-virgin olive oil
- salt to taste

GREEN BEAN AND HAZELNUT SALAD

Preheat the oven to 350°F/180°C/gas 4.
• Steam the green beans for 20–25 minutes, or until crunchy-tender. • Drain and let cool completely. • Toast the hazelnuts and pine nuts on a baking sheet in the oven for 5–10 minutes, or until lightly browned. • Let cool completely. • Wash and dry the arugula. Finely chop and arrange in a salad bowl. • Cut the beans into short lengths and add to the arugula. • Coarsely chop the hazelnuts and sprinkle over the salad. • Mix 4 tablespoons of oil, the vinegar, and salt in a small bowl and drizzle over the salad. • Chop the tomato coarsely and drizzle with the remaining oil. Season with salt.
• Arrange the salad on individual serving plates with the chopped tomato in the center.
• Garnish with the toasted pine nuts.

*Vegan

Serves: 4

Preparation: 20'

Cooking: 25–35'

Level of difficulty: 1

• 1 lb/500 g green beans, topped and tailed
• ½ cup/80 g shelled hazelnuts
• 1 tbsp pine nuts
• 1 bunch arugula/ rocket
• 2 tbsp best-quality balsamic vinegar
• 6 tbsp extra-virgin olive oil
• 1 firm-ripe tomato, finely chopped
• salt to taste

CUCUMBER AND RICOTTA SALAD

Serves: 4

Preparation: 25' + 2 h
to stand

Cooking: 1'

Level of difficulty: 1

Cut the cucumber in half lengthwise, remove the seeds, and slice the flesh thinly. • Blanch the cucumber in salted, boiling water for 1 minute. • Mix the vermouth, tarragon, dill, chives, pepper, mustard powder, and salt in a small bowl. • Drain the cucumber and place in the marinade. • Cover with plastic wrap and leave in a cool place for 2 hours. • Mix in the Ricotta and serve.

- 1 cucumber
- 2 tbsp red vermouth
- 1 tbsp finely chopped tarragon
- 1 tbsp finely chopped dill
- 1 tbsp finely chopped chives
- ½ tsp ground black pepper
- ½ tsp mustard powder
- ¼ tsp salt
- 1½ cups/350 g Ricotta cheese

*Vegan

Serves: 4

Preparation: 25'

Cooking: 30'

Level of difficulty: 2

- 1 cup/200 g pearl barley
- 12 oz/350 g firm-ripe tomatoes
- 3 oz/90 g pitted and chopped black olives
- 10 oz/300 g white mushrooms, coarsely chopped
- 1 bunch fresh basil, torn
- 4–6 tbsp extra-virgin olive oil
- salt and freshly ground black pepper to taste

BARLEY AND MUSHROOM SALAD

Cook the barley in salted, boiling water for 25–30 minutes, or until tender. • Blanch the tomatoes in boiling water for 1 minute. • Drain and slip off the skins. Squeeze out the seeds and chop the flesh coarsely. • Drain the barley and pass under cool running water. • Drain well and dry on a clean cloth. Transfer to a large salad bowl. • Add the tomatoes, olives, mushrooms, and basil. Drizzle with the oil and season with salt and pepper. Toss well and serve.

MIXED VEGETABLE SALAD

Rinse and drain the lettuce, arugula, and mushrooms. • Break the lettuce into bite-size pieces. • Sauté the bread cubes in the butter in a small frying pan until golden and crispy. • Arrange the lettuce and arugula in a large salad bowl and place the mushrooms and olives on top. • Arrange the bell pepper and carrot around the edge of the salad. • Sprinkle with the walnuts and pine nuts. • Mix the lemon juice and oil in a small bowl. Season with salt and pepper. Drizzle over the salad. • Sprinkle with the bread cubes and serve.

Serves: 4
Preparation: 20'
Cooking: 5'
Level of difficulty: 1

- 1 lettuce
- 7 oz/200 g arugula/rocket
- 4 oz/100 g chanterelle mushrooms
- 2 slices white sandwich bread, crusts removed and cut into small cubes
- 1 tbsp butter
- ½ cup/50 g pitted green olives
- 1 yellow bell pepper, seeded and cut into julienne strips
- 3 carrots, cut into julienne strips
- 2 tbsp shelled walnuts, crumbled
- 2 tbsp pine nuts
- 2 tbsp fresh lemon juice
- 6 tbsp extra-virgin olive oil
- salt and freshly ground black pepper to taste

TOMATO AND MIXED RAW VEGETABLES

Serves: 4–6

Preparation: 15'

Level of difficulty: 1

- **14 oz/400 g Mozzarella cheese**
- **4–6 large red tomatoes**
- **1 cup/250 g mixed raw vegetables (zucchini, carrots, celery, bell peppers, onion), cut in small cubes**
- **1 tbsp pickled capers, drained**
- **salt and freshly ground black pepper to taste**
- **4 tbsp extra-virgin olive oil**
- **8 leaves fresh basil, torn**

Cut the Mozzarella into ¼-inch (5-mm) thick slices and arrange on a flat serving dish.
• Cut the tomatoes in slices of the same width and place over the Mozzarella. • Place the mixed vegetables in a bowl with the capers, salt, pepper, and oil. Toss well and sprinkle over the Mozzarella and tomato. • Garnish with the basil and serve.

NORTH AFRICAN SALAD

S oak the scallions in a bowl of iced water for
10 minutes to lose their pungent flavor.
• Drain and slice in thin rings. • Wash and chop the
arugula and place in a large bowl. • Add the
radishes, oranges, olives, scallions, and walnuts.
• Dressing: Beat the orange juice and oil with a
pinch of salt and pepper. Add the lemon juice,
orange flower water, and cinnamon and mix until
blended. • Drizzle over the salad and serve.

*Vegan

Serves: 4

Preparation: 20'

Level of difficulty: 2

• 3 scallions/spring
  onions, white parts
  only
• 1 bunch arugula/
  rocket
• 1 bunch radishes,
  washed and thinly
  sliced
• 3 oranges, peeled
  and thinly sliced
• ²⁄₃ cup/60 g pitted
  black olives
• 15–20 shelled
  walnuts, coarsely
  chopped

DRESSING
• 4 tbsp fresh orange
  juice
• 4–6 tbsp extra-
  virgin olive oil
• salt and freshly
  ground black
  pepper to taste
• juice of 1 lemon
• 1 tbsp orange
  flower water
• ¹⁄₈ tsp ground
  cinnamon

AVOCADO AND APPLE SALAD

Mix the oil and apple vinegar in a small bowl. Season with salt and pepper. • Peel the avocado and chop coarsely. Arrange in a salad bowl and pour over the dressing. • Peel and chop the apple and add to the avocado. Cover with plastic wrap (cling film) and refrigerate for 1 hour. • Serve chilled.

*Vegan

Serves: 2–4

Preparation: 15' + 1 h to chill

Level of difficulty: 1

- 4 tbsp extra-virgin olive oil
- 1 tbsp apple vinegar
- salt and freshly ground black pepper to taste
- 1 large firm-ripe avocado, cut into quarters
- 1 Granny Smith apple

ORANGE AND OLIVE SALAD

*Vegan

Serves: 4

Preparation: 15' + 10'
to stand

Level of difficulty: 1

- 4 ripe, juicy
  oranges
- 10 green or black
  olives, pitted and
  cut into quarters
- white of 1 leek,
  thinly sliced into
  rings
- 1 tbsp finely
  chopped parsley
- 4 tbsp extra-virgin
  olive oil
- salt and freshly
  ground black or
  white pepper to
  taste

Peel the oranges, removing all the white pith and skin. Slice thinly. • Place the oranges in a salad bowl and add the olives, leek, parsley, and oil. Season with salt and pepper. • Toss gently and let stand for 10 minutes before serving.

809

GRILLED EGGPLANT, BELL PEPPER, AND TOMATO SALAD

Clean the bell peppers by removing the core and seeds and cut into small strips.
• Cook in a grill pan and grill for about 5 minutes, turning often, until tender. Set aside. • Cut the eggplants into ¹/₂-inch (1-cm) thick slices. Grill for about 5 minutes, or until tender. • Peel the tomatoes, cut them in half, and grill until lightly cooked. • Place the grilled vegetables in a salad bowl. Add the garlic and season with salt and pepper. Add the basil and drizzle with the oil.
• Serve hot or at room temperature.

*Vegan

Serves: 6

Preparation: 10'

Cooking: 45'

Level of difficulty: 1

- 4 bell peppers, mixed colors
- 2 large eggplants/ aubergines
- 8 ripe tomatoes
- 3 cloves garlic, finely chopped
- salt and freshly ground black pepper to taste
- 6 leaves fresh basil, torn
- ¹/₂ cup/125 ml extra-virgin olive oil

RICE SALAD WITH OLIVES AND RAISINS

C ook the rice in a large pot of salted, boiling water for about 15 minutes, or until tender but still firm. • Drain and pass under cold running water for 30 seconds to stop the cooking process. Drain again and dry on a clean cloth. Transfer to a large salad bowl.

812

Ideal for picnics and outdoor dining.

• Drizzle with the oil and lemon juice. Season with pepper. • Add the remaining ingredients and toss well.

Serves: 4

Preparation: 15'

Cooking: 15'

Level of difficulty: 1

- 1½ cups/300 g short-grain rice
- 6 tbsp extra-virgin olive oil
- 2 tbsp fresh lemon juice
- salt and freshly ground white pepper to taste
- 4 medium tomatoes, diced
- 2 stalks celery, sliced
- 6 pickled gherkins, sliced
- 8 small white pickled onions, quartered
- 1 tbsp pickled capers, drained
- 10 green olives in brine, pitted and quartered
- 2 tbsp golden raisins/sultanas, rinsed and drained
- 4 oz/125 g Parmesan cheese, flaked

CARROT AND LEEK SALAD

*Vegan

Serves: 4

Preparation: 20' + 1 h to chill

Level of difficulty: 1

Drizzle the carrots with the lemon juice in a medium bowl. Add the leeks. • Dressing: Mix the olive oil, vinegar, brown sugar, garlic, sesame oil, and ginger in a small bowl. Season with salt and pepper. • Pour the dressing over the salad and toss well. • Refrigerate for at least 1 hour. • Serve with breadsticks or freshly baked bread.

- 1 3/4 lb/800 g carrots, finely grated
- juice of 1 lemon
- 7 oz/200 g leeks, very finely sliced

DRESSING
- 6 tbsp extra-virgin olive oil
- 2 tbsp white wine vinegar
- 1 tsp brown sugar
- 1 clove garlic, finely chopped
- 1 tbsp sesame oil
- 2 tbsp crystallized ginger, cut into small cubes
- salt and freshly ground black pepper to taste

GRILLED SALAD

- **6 green bell peppers**
- **4 large ripe tomatoes**
- **4 cloves garlic, lightly crushed but whole**
- **1 fresh red chile pepper, finely chopped (optional)**
- **4 hard-cooked eggs, 3 mashed + 1 cut into quarters**
- **2 stalks celery, finely chopped**
- **1 sprig parsley, finely chopped**
- **1 tbsp capers**
- **1 tbsp finely chopped cilantro/ coriander**
- **3 tbsp extra-virgin olive oil**
- **1 tbsp fresh lemon juice**
- **1 cup/100 g black olives, to garnish**

Grill the bell peppers, tomatoes, garlic, and chile pepper, if using, on the barbecue or a grill pan for 12–15 minutes, or until the skins of the bell peppers are blackened. • Seal the bell peppers in a paper bag for 5 minutes to make it easier to remove the skins. Peel the bell peppers and tomatoes while still warm. Cut away the tough parts and remove the seeds. • Coarsely mash the bell peppers, chile pepper, tomatoes, and garlic. Add the mashed hard-cooked eggs, celery, parsley, capers, and cilantro. • Mix the oil and lemon juice in a small bowl. Drizzle over the vegetables. • Garnish with the hard-cooked egg quarters and olives.

815

BEET AND POTATO SALAD

SALADS

Boil the beets in their skins in a large pot of salted, boiling water until tender, 30–60 minutes, depending on their size. Drain well and let cool enough to handle. Slip off the skins and thinly slice. • Boil the potatoes in their skins in a large pot of salted, boiling water for 20–25 minutes. Drain well, let cool enough to handle, then slip off the skins. • Place the potatoes in a large bowl and mash until smooth. Mix in the garlic, oil, and lemon juice. Season with salt and pepper. • Arrange the beets, overlapping them in a decorative manner, on a serving plate. • Spoon the potatoes into the center. • Refrigerate for 30 minutes before serving.

*Vegan

Serves: 6

Preparation: 15' + 30' to chill

Cooking: 1 h 30"

Level of difficulty: 1

- 2 lb/1 kg beets/beetroot
- 1 lb/500 g potatoes, boiled and peeled
- 4 cloves garlic, finely chopped
- 1 tbsp extra-virgin olive oil
- 4 tbsp fresh lemon juice or white wine vinegar
- salt and freshly ground black pepper to taste

816

ARTICHOKE SALAD

*Vegan

Serves: 4

Preparation: 10' + 10'
to soak

Level of difficulty: 1

- **4 large fresh artichokes**
- **juice of 2 lemons**
- **1 tsp salt**
- **1/2 cup/125 ml extra-virgin olive oil**
- **freshly ground black pepper to taste**
- **2 tbsp finely chopped parsley**
- **2 tbsp finely chopped mint**

Clean the artichokes by removing all the tough outer leaves and trimming the tops and stalks. Remove the fuzzy inner choke and cut into thin wedges. Soak in a bowl of cold water with the juice of 1 lemon for 10 minutes to prevent discoloring. • Dissolve the salt in the remaining lemon juice. Add the oil, pepper, parsley, and mint and beat vigorously with a whisk to emulsify. • Drain the artichokes and dry on a clean cloth. • Place in a salad bowl. Pour the dressing over the top and toss well. • Serve immediately.

WINTER SALAD WITH GORGONZOLA DRESSING

Clean the fennel by discarding the tough outer leaves, then cut the bulbs in half. Wash under cold running water, drain, and dry well. Cut into $1/8$-inch (3-mm) thick slices. • Trim the carrots and cut in julienne strips. • Trim the celery, removing the tough outer leaves and stringy filaments. Cut the stalks in thin slices. • Wash the apple and cut in thin wedges. • Place the vegetables and apple in a salad bowl with the garlic. Season with salt, pepper and drizzle with the lemon juice and 2 tablespoons of oil. • Melt the Gorgonzola slowly with the remaining oil over very low heat in a heavy-bottomed saucepan, stirring continuously. • When barely lukewarm and creamy, pour over the vegetables. • Sprinkle with the parsley and serve.

Serves: 6

Preparation: 15'

Cooking: 10'

Level of difficulty: 1

- 2 fennel bulbs
- 2 carrots
- 1 bunch celery
- 1 Granny Smith apple
- 1 clove garlic, finely chopped
- salt and freshly ground black pepper to taste
- 1 tbsp fresh lemon juice
- 6 tbsp extra-virgin olive oil
- 6 oz/180 g Gorgonzola cheese, diced
- 1 tbsp finely chopped parsley

818

TOMATO AND MOZZARELLA PASTA SALAD

Serves: 4

Preparation: 10'

Cooking: 15'

Level of difficulty: 1

- 1 lb/500 g plain, whole-wheat/ wholemeal, or colored penne pasta
- 4 tbsp extra-virgin olive oil
- 4 large ripe tomatoes
- 2 cloves garlic, finely chopped
- 2 tbsp finely chopped parsley
- salt and freshly ground black pepper to taste
- 14 oz/400 g Mozzarella cheese
- 6 leaves fresh basil, torn

Cook the pasta in a large pot of salted, boiling water until al dente. • Drain well. • Transfer to a large salad bowl and toss vigorously with half the oil. Let cool. • Cut the tomatoes into bite-size pieces and add to the pasta. • Mix the garlic and parsley with the remaining oil and salt and add to the pasta. Garnish with the basil. • Slice the Mozzarella thinly and place on top of the salad. Season with pepper and serve.

WHEAT AND BARLEY SALAD

C ook the wheat berries in salted, boiling water
for 1 hour until tender. • Drain. • Bring
2 cups (500 ml) of water to a boil and season
with salt. Add the barley and cover and cook for
about 30 minutes, or until tender. • Drain the
wheat berries and barley, leaving a small amount of
liquid. Transfer to a salad bowl. • Blanch the
green beans in salted, boiling water for 5 minutes.
• Drain and add to the grains. • Sauté the garlic
and parsley in the oil in a small saucepan until the
garlic is pale gold. • Pour the flavored oil over the
grains. Season with salt and pepper, toss well,
and serve.

*Vegan

Serves: 4

Preparation: 25'

Cooking: 1 h

Level of difficulty: 2

- ¾ cup/150 g
  wheat berries
- ¾ cup/150 g pearl
  barley
- salt and freshly
  ground black
  pepper to taste
- 7 oz/200 g green
  beans, topped and
  tailed
- 1 clove garlic,
  finely chopped
- 1 tbsp finely
  chopped parsley
- 4 tbsp extra-virgin
  olive oil

GARDEN VEGETABLES

Remove the tough outer leaves from the artichoke hearts by pulling them down and snapping them off. Cut the heart in half and place in cold water with lemon juice. • Place the celery hearts, cauliflower, carrots, zucchini, onions, and mushroom caps in a bowl. Drain the artichoke hearts and add to the other vegetables. • Pour the oil and vinegar into a large saucepan and add the garlic and salt. • Wrap the fresh herbs and peppercorns in a muslin (cheesecloth) pouch and add to the pan. • Transfer the vegetables to the pan and pour in the boiling water. Simmer for 5 minutes. • Drain the vegetables, reserving the cooking liquid. • Return to the pan and cook over low heat until reduced by half. • Place the vegetables in a bowl. Pour over the reserved liquid. • Let cool completely. • Refrigerate for 2 hours before serving.

Vegan

Serves: 6

Preparation: 30' + 2 h to chill

Cooking: 30'

Level of difficulty: 1

- 6 artichoke hearts
- juice of 1 lemon
- 2 celery hearts
- 10–14 oz/ 300–400 g cauliflower florets
- 2 carrots, sliced
- 2 zucchini/ courgettes, cut into sticks
- 2 onions, quartered
- 8 mushroom caps
- 4 tbsp olive oil
- 2 tbsp white wine vinegar
- 1 clove garlic, finely chopped
- ¼ tsp salt
- 4 black peppercorns
- 1 bay leaf
- 1 sprig parsley
- 1 sprig thyme or basil
- 1 quart/1 liter boiling water

POTATO AND CHARD BREAD SALAD

*Vegan

Serves: 4

Preparation: 20'

Cooking: 15'

Level of difficulty: 1

- 2 cloves garlic, finely chopped
- 4 tbsp extra-virgin olive oil
- 3 potatoes, peeled and diced
- salt and freshly ground black pepper to taste
- 1 fresh hot chile pepper, finely chopped
- 2 tbsp hot water
- 14 oz/400 g Swiss chard or spinach, finely shredded
- 7 oz/200 g day-old bread, broken up into pieces

Sauté the garlic in 3 tablespoons of oil in a large frying pan until pale gold. • Add the potatoes and season with salt. • Add the chile pepper and water. Cook over low heat for about 10 minutes, or until the potatoes are tender. • Cook the Swiss chard in salted, boiling water for 5–7 minutes, or until wilted. Drain. • Add to the potatoes with the bread. Mix well and return to the heat. Season with salt and pepper. Drizzle with the remaining oil and serve hot.

AVOCADO AND MANDARIN SALAD

Toss the radicchio and onion in a salad bowl. Arrange the avocado and mandarins on top in a decorative manner. • Mix the oil, mustard, vinegar, and salt and pepper in a small bowl. • Drizzle the dressing over the salad. Sprinkle with the pumpkin seeds. • Serve immediately.

Vegan

Serves: 4

Preparation: 10'

Level of difficulty: 1

- 1 head red radicchio or chicory, finely shredded
- 1 red onion, very finely sliced
- 1 large ripe avocado, peeled, pitted, and cut into cubes
- 2 mandarins, peeled and cut into segments
- 4–6 tbsp extra-virgin olive oil
- 1 tbsp Dijon mustard
- 1 tbsp red wine vinegar
- salt and freshly ground black pepper to taste
- 1 tbsp pumpkin seeds, toasted

WARM VEGETABLE SALAD

Preheat the oven to 400°F/200°C/gas 6.
• Bake the onions whole in their skins for
40 minutes. • Peel and cut into segments.
• Cook the potatoes in a large pot of salted,
boiling water for 15–20 minutes, or until tender.
• Drain and cut into bite-size pieces. • Cook the
broccoli in a large pot of salted, boiling water for
5–7 minutes, or until tender. Drain. • Place the
onions, potatoes, and broccoli in a large salad
bowl. • Add the parsley and oil. Season with salt
and pepper and toss well. • Serve warm.

*Vegan

Serves: 6

Preparation: 15'

Cooking: 60–67'

Level of difficulty: 1

- 4 large onions
- 4 large potatoes, peeled
- 1½ lb/650 g broccoli florets
- 3 tbsp finely chopped parsley
- 6 tbsp extra-virgin olive oil
- salt and freshly ground black pepper to taste

SPRING VEGETABLES

Serves: 2–4
Preparation: 15'
Cooking: 5–8'
Level of difficulty: 1

Layer the vegetables in a casserole, starting with the lettuce, then the scallions, snow peas, asparagus, artichokes, and peas. Sprinkle each layer with parsley, mint, and lemon zest. Season with pepper. Dot with the butter and pour in two-thirds of the stock. • Bring to a boil over medium heat and simmer for 5–7 minutes, or until the vegetables are crunchy-tender. Add more stock if the vegetables begin to dry out. • Transfer to a warm serving dish, drizzle with lemon juice, and serve with the yogurt.

- 2 small heads lettuce, coarsely shredded
- 4 scallions/spring onions, cut into short lengths
- 8 snow peas/mangetout
- 4 oz/125 g asparagus spears, cut in half
- 2 artichoke hearts preserved in oil, drained and quartered
- 2 cups/250 g peas
- 1 tbsp finely chopped parsley
- 1 tbsp finely chopped mint
- 1 tsp grated lemon zest
- freshly ground black pepper to taste
- 4 tbsp butter
- 7 tbsp vegetable stock, boiling, + more as needed
- juice of ½ lemon
- ½ cup/125 ml plain yogurt

PICKLED RED CABBAGE AND FENNEL SALAD

Serves: 4

Preparation: 20'

Cooking: 10–15'

Level of difficulty: 1

- 3 slices whole-wheat (wholemeal) bread, cubed
- 4 tbsp extra-virgin olive oil
- 1 tbsp fennel seeds
- salt and freshly ground black pepper to taste
- 1 1-lb/500-g jar pickled red cabbage, drained
- 4 scallions/spring onions, sliced
- 1 green and 1 yellow bell pepper/ capsicum, seeded, cored, and sliced
- $\frac{1}{2}$ fennel, sliced
- 2 tbsp pumpkin seeds
- 1 tsp cumin seeds
- salt and freshly ground black pepper to taste
- juice of $\frac{1}{2}$ lemon
- $3\frac{1}{2}$ oz/100 g Emmental cheese, cubed
- $3\frac{1}{2}$ oz/100 g smoked cheese, cubed
- 4 large lettuce leaves

Preheat the oven to 400°F/200°C/gas 6.
• Mix the bread with 2 tablespoons of oil and fennel seeds in a large bowl. Season with salt and pepper. • Transfer to a baking sheet and bake for 10–15 minutes, or until browned and crisp, turning halfway through the cooking time. • Remove from the oven and let cool. • Mix the pickled cabbage, scallions, bell peppers, and fennel in a large salad bowl. Add the pumpkin and cumin seeds. Season with salt and pepper. Drizzle with the remaining oil and lemon juice and mix well. • Add the cheeses.
• Arrange the lettuce leaves on a serving dish and place the mixed salad on top. Sprinkle with the croutons and serve.

AUSTRIAN SAUERKRAUT SALAD

S prinkle the onion with salt and let rest for
30 minutes. • Rinse to remove the salt and
drain well. This process gives the onions a milder
flavor. • Place the onion, sauerkraut, and apples in
a large bowl and mix with the lemon juice to
prevent them from blackening. • Add the bell
pepper and carrots. • Dressing: Shake the vinegar,
oil, and crème fraiche in a jar with an airtight seal
until well blended. Season with salt, pepper, and
sugar. Reseal and shake well. • Drizzle over the
salad, add the wine, and toss well. Let the salad
absorb the dressing for 30 minutes before serving.

834

Serves: 4

*Preparation: 10' + 60'
to rest*

Level of difficulty: 1

- **1 onion, thinly sliced**
- **¼ tsp salt**
- **1 lb/500 g sauerkraut, drained and coarsely chopped**
- **3 apples, peeled, cored, and cut into bite-size pieces**
- **1 tbsp fresh lemon juice**
- **1 green bell pepper, seeded, cored, and sliced**
- **2 carrots, peeled and shredded**

DRESSING
- **2 tbsp white wine vinegar**
- **4 tbsp extra-virgin olive oil**
- **4 tbsp crème fraiche**
- **salt and freshly ground black pepper to taste**
- **1 tsp sugar**
- **1 tbsp dry white wine (optional)**

SWEDISH POTATO SALAD

Mayonnaise: Beat the egg yolk in a small bowl until pale and creamy. • Add 1 tablespoon of oil and beat until well blended. • Add 1 tablespoon of the vinegar mixture, beating constantly. • Repeat this process, adding only 1 tablespoon of oil or water at a time, until all the ingredients are used. This is a slow process. If you add too much oil or water at any one time, the mayonnaise will separate and curdle. Season with salt and pepper. • Cook the potatoes in a large pot of salted, boiling water for 15–20 minutes, or until tender. • Drain and let cool. Cut into small cubes. • Gently toss the potatoes, gherkins, onion, nutmeg, and curry powder in a large salad bowl. • Add the mayonnaise and mix gently. • Refrigerate for 1 hour before serving. • Garnish with the eggs.

836

Serves: 6–8

Preparation: 1 h 10' + 1 h to chill

Cooking: 15–20'

Level of difficulty: 3

MAYONNAISE
- 1 egg yolk
- scant 1½ cups/ 350 ml sunflower or peanut oil
- 2 tbsp white wine vinegar mixed in ⅔ cup/150 ml warm water
- salt and freshly ground white pepper to taste

- 2¼ lb/1.25 kg potatoes, peeled
- 6 small pickled gherkins, finely chopped
- 1 large onion, finely chopped
- 1 tsp freshly grated nutmeg
- ¼ tsp curry powder
- 8 hard-boiled eggs, shelled and coarsely chopped

WINTER SALAD WITH VINAIGRETTE

C ook the cauliflower in a large pot of salted, boiling water for 10 minutes, or until tender.
• Drain and let cool. • Cook the artichokes in a large pot of salted, boiling water for 15–20 minutes, or until tender. • Drain and let cool.
• Beat the oil, vinegar, and salt in a small bowl.
• Toss the cauliflower, artichokes, apple, celery, and endive in a large salad bowl. Drizzle with the vinaigrette and season with pepper.

838

*Vegan

Serves: 6

Preparation: 5'

Cooking: 25–30'

Level of difficulty: 1

- 14 oz/400 g cauliflower florets
- 6 artichoke hearts, cut into segments
- ⅔ cup/150 ml extra-virgin olive oil
- 3 tbsp cider vinegar
- salt and freshly ground black pepper to taste
- 1 red apple, cored and thinly sliced
- 2 stalks celery, finely chopped
- 1 head curly endive, torn

*Vegan

Serves: 4

Preparation: 5' + 30'
to absorb

Level of difficulty: 1

- 1 lb/500 g
  sauerkraut,
  drained and
  coarsely chopped
- 2 pickled
  cucumbers, cut
  into small cubes
- 1 gherkin, cut into
  small cubes
- 2–3 pickled red and
  yellow roast bell
  peppers, thinly
  sliced
- 1 onion, finely
  sliced
- 1 tbsp corn oil
- 2 tbsp extra-virgin
  olive oil
- 1/8 tsp sugar
- salt and freshly
  ground white
  pepper to taste

SERBIAN
SAUERKRAUT SALAD

Place the sauerkraut, cucumbers, gherkin, bell peppers, and onion (reserving a few slices for garnish) in a large salad bowl. Add both oils and sugar. Season with salt and pepper. • Toss and let the salad absorb the dressing for 30 minutes.
• Garnish with the reserved onion and serve.

RUSSIAN BEET SALAD

Preheat the oven to 400°F/200°C/gas 6.
• Roast the beets for 50 minutes, or until tender. • Remove from the oven and let cool. Cut into thin strips. • Beat the egg yolk, lemon juice, and mustard in a small bowl. Season with salt and pepper. • Add the oil, 1 tablespoon at a time, beating constantly until blended. • When all the oil is incorporated, add the crème fraiche, shallots, and dill, and mix well. • Arrange the beets in a large salad bowl, pour over the sauce, and serve.

Serves: 6

Preparation: 20'

Cooking: 50'

Level of difficulty: 2

- 1¼ lb/575 g white beets
- 1 large egg yolk
- 1 tbsp fresh lemon juice
- 1 tsp mustard
- salt and freshly ground black pepper to taste
- ½ cup/125 ml extra-virgin olive oil
- 3 tbsp crème fraiche
- 1 oz/30 g shallots, finely chopped
- 2 tbsp finely chopped dill

FRUIT AND VEGETABLE SALAD

Serves: 6

Preparation: 15'

Level of difficulty: 1

- 3 lettuce hearts
- 1 grapefruit
- 1 Golden Delicious apple
- 1 tbsp capers
- 1 cup/100 g black olives, pitted
- 8 oz/250 g Gruyère cheese, cut into small cubes
- 1 cup/125 ml extra virgin olive oil
- juice of ½ lemon
- salt and freshly ground black pepper to taste

Wash, drain, and chop the lettuce coarsely.
• Peel the grapefruit, taking care to remove all the bitter white pith beneath the skin, and chop coarsely. • Peel, core, and chop the apple. • Mix together in a salad bowl with the capers, olives, and Gruyère. • Drizzle with the oil and lemon juice. Season with salt and pepper. • Toss well and serve.

DESSERTS

FRUIT BASKETS IN CHILLED PORT CREAM

Baskets: Mix the honey, butter, flour, and sugar in a large bowl. Refrigerate for 30 minutes.
• Port Cream: Bring the brown sugar, Port, and water to a boil in a small saucepan. Simmer over low heat for 10 minutes until syrupy. Let cool.
• Process three-quarters of the strawberry and melon with the port cream in a blender until smooth. • Refrigerate for 1 hour. • Preheat the oven to 325°F/170°C/gas 3. • Line a cookie sheet with parchment paper. • Shape teaspoons of the wafer mixture into small balls. Flatten on the prepared cookie sheet. • Bake for 8–10 minutes, or until golden brown. • Working quickly, remove from the sheet and drape over oiled glasses. Let cool completely. • Chop the reserved fruit and place in the baskets. Spoon the port cream into serving dishes. Place a basket in each one and serve.

Serves: 4

Preparation: 30' + 1 h 30' to chill

Cooking: 15'

Level of difficulty: 3

BASKETS
- 2 tbsp clear honey
- 2 tbsp butter, melted
- 2 tbsp all-purpose/ plain flour
- ½ cup/100 g granulated sugar

PORT CREAM
- 2 tbsp brown sugar
- 2 tbsp Port
- 7 tbsp water

- 8 oz/250 g strawberries
- 1 ripe melon, peeled and cut into bite-size pieces

Serves: 4

Preparation: 30' +
12 h to chill

Level of difficulty: 2

- 4 eggs, separated
- ½ cup/100 g granulated sugar
- grated zest of 1 lemon
- juice of 2 lemons
- 1 tbsp agar-agar
- 1 cup/250 ml heavy/double cream
- 1 lemon, very thinly sliced, to decorate

LEMON MOUSSE

Beat the egg yolks, sugar, and lemon zest in a large bowl with an electric mixer at high speed until creamy. • Place the lemon juice and agar-agar in a small saucepan and mix well to prevent any lumps from forming. Set aside for 5 minutes. • Place the gelling mixture over low heat and cook until it has dissolved completely. • Remove from the heat and mix into the egg yolk mixture. • With mixer at high speed, beat the cream in a large bowl until stiff. • Beat the egg whites in a separate large bowl until stiff. Fold the cream and beaten whites into the egg yolk mixture. • Pour into a serving bowl and refrigerate overnight. • Decorate the mousse with the slices of lemon.

CARAMELIZED ORANGES

issolve the sugar in the cold water in a large heavy-based saucepan over low heat. When the sugar has dissolved completely, bring the mixture to a boil. Boil for about 15 minutes, or until the syrup has become a light caramel color. • Pour 2 inches (4 cm) of cold water into a large roasting pan. Remove the saucepan with the sugar from the heat and place it in the cold water to stop the cooking process. • Add the hot water immediately, taking care as the hot sugar will spark. Mix well. • Arrange the oranges on a serving plate. • Pour the caramel over the oranges and let cool.

*Vegan

Serves: 6–8

Preparation: 5'

Cooking: 15'

Level of difficulty: 2

- 2 cups/400 g granulated sugar
- 1¼ cups/310 ml cold water
- 1¼ cups/310 ml hot water
- 8 oranges, peeled and thinly sliced

CARAMELIZED GRAPES

*Vegan

Serves: 4

Preparation: 25'

Cooking: 15'

Level of difficulty: 2

- **2 bunches large, seedless white grapes**
- **½ cup/125 ml water**
- **2½ cups/500 g granulated sugar**
- **½ tsp cream of tartar**

Use a pair of scissors to snip the grapes from the bunch, leaving a little of the stem attached. • Wash well and dry on paper towels. Insert a toothpick in each grape next to the stem. • Pour the water into a small saucepan and add the sugar and cream of tartar. • Bring to a boil and simmer over low heat until it forms a syrup. To test: drop a little syrup onto a plate; it should form soft balls. • Remove from the heat and dip in the grapes one by one. • Let the grapes set on a lightly buttered dish, keeping them well-spaced.

STRAWBERRY MOUSSE WITH KIWI SAUCE

Oil six small straight sided glasses. Use sweet almond oil if possible, or sunflower oil.
• Process the strawberries (reserving 1 to garnish), $^1/_3$ cup (70 g) of sugar, and vanilla in a food processor or blender until puréed. • Warm 3 tablespoons of liqueur in a small saucepan over low heat. Add the agar-agar and stir until completely dissolved. • Add the gelling mixture to the strawberry purée and mix well. • Beat the cream in a large bowl until stiff. • Gently fold the cream into the strawberry mixture. • Pour into the prepared glasses, cover with plastic wrap, and refrigerate for about 3 hours. • Process the kiwifruit, remaining sugar, and remaining liqueur in a blender until puréed. • Run a knife around the edge of each glass and turn out onto serving dishes. Drizzle with the sauce, garnish with slices of the reserved strawberry, and serve.

Serves: 6

Preparation: 30' + 3 h to chill

Level of difficulty: 2

- **12 oz/350 g fresh strawberries, preferably wild, hulled and chopped**
- **½ cup/100 g granulated sugar**
- **1 tsp vanilla extract**
- **4 tbsp fruit liqueur**
- **1 tbsp agar-agar powder or flakes**
- **1 cup/250 ml heavy/double cream**
- **2 kiwifruit, peeled and chopped**
- **1 tbsp lemon juice**

BANANA AND GORGONZOLA DIP

Peel the bananas and place them in a large bowl. Add the Gorgonzola and rum and use a fork to mash them until smooth and well blended. • Refrigerate for 30 minutes. • Garnish with the figs and serve with crackers or breadsticks to finish a meal.

Serves: 4

Preparation: 20' + 30' to chill

Level of difficulty: 1

- 2 large, firm-ripe bananas
- 1 cup/250 g sweet Gorgonzola cheese
- 4 tbsp dark rum
- fresh figs, sliced, to garnish

PEAR AND LEMON CREAM

Serves: 4

Preparation: 30' + 2 h
to chill

Cooking: 15–20'

Level of difficulty: 2

- **4 soft pears, peeled and thinly sliced**
- **¼ cup/50 g raw sugar**
- **2 egg whites**
- **1 level tsp agar-agar**
- **grated zest and juice of 1 lemon**
- **⅔ cup/60 g finely chopped toasted hazelnuts**
- **1 lemon, finely sliced, to decorate**

Cook the pears with the sugar in a large pan for 10–15 minutes, or until very soft. • Let cool. • Melt the agar-agar with the lemon zest and juice and 2 tablespoons of the pear cooking liquid in a small saucepan over low heat for 2 minutes, stirring constantly. • Chop the pears and remaining cooking liquid in a food processor until smooth. Add the gelling mixture and let stand until almost set. • Beat the egg whites in a large bowl with an electric mixer at high speed until stiff. • Fold into the puréed pears with half the hazelnuts. • Pour the mixture into four ramekins or custard cups. • Refrigerate for at least 2 hours. • Turn out onto serving dishes and decorate with the remaining hazelnuts and lemon..

853

EGGPLANT TIRAMISÙ

Serves: 6

Preparation: 25' + 60'
to soak + 2 h
to chill

Cooking: 30'

Level of difficulty: 2

- 2 lb/1 kg
  eggplants/
  aubergines, sliced
  ½-inch/1-cm thick
  lengthwise
- 1 tbsp coarse salt
- 2 cups/500 ml
  olive oil, for frying
- 3 cups/750 ml milk
- 2 egg yolks
- ¾ cup/150 g
  granulated sugar
- ½ cup/75 g all-
  purpose/plain flour
- 1 tsp vanilla extract
- generous ½ cup/
  100 g finely
  chopped candied
  peel
- ½ cup/75 g
  unsweetened
  cocoa powder

Place the eggplant in a colander and sprinkle with salt. Let stand for at least 1 hour. • Drain and pat dry with paper towels. • Butter a deep 8-inch (20-cm) square dish. • Heat the oil in a large frying pan until very hot and fry the eggplants over medium heat for 5–7 minutes, or until tender. • Drain well on paper towels. • Beat the egg yolks and ½ cup (100 g) of sugar in a large saucepan until pale and thick. • Mix in ⅓ cup (50 g) of flour until well blended. • Pour in 2 cups (500 ml) of milk and the vanilla. Place the pan over low heat and cook, stirring constantly, for 10–15 minutes, or until thick. • Remove from the heat and add the candied peel. • Mix the cocoa, remaining flour, and sugar in a small saucepan. Gradually mix in the remaining milk, beating constantly to prevent any lumps from forming. • Cook over low heat for about 10 minutes, stirring constantly, until the mixture thickens. • Spread a layer of custard on the bottom of the dish. Cover with a layer of eggplant and chocolate cream; Repeat this layering process until all the ingredients are in the dish. • Refrigerate for 2 hours before serving.

WARM ORANGE SOUFFLÉ

P lace the orange in a small saucepan and cover with boiling water. Cook over medium heat for about 30 minutes, or until the liquid is reduced by half. • Drain and cover with cold water. • Return to the heat and cook for about 30 minutes, or until the liquid is reduced by half again. • Drain and repeat the process again. • Drain and let the orange cool completely. • Preheat the oven to 325°F/170°C/gas 3. • Beat the egg yolks, $^1/_2$ cup (100 g) of sugar, and vanilla in a large bowl until pale and creamy. • Cut the orange flesh into pieces and chop in a food processor until puréed. • Fold the orange purée into the beaten egg yolks, followed by the flour, potato starch, butter, and orange liqueur. • Beat the egg whites in a large bowl until stiff. • Gradually add $^2/_3$ cup (140 g) of sugar, beating until all the sugar is blended and the mixture is thick and glossy. • Gently fold the yolk mixture into the beaten whites. • Butter six ramekins or soufflé molds. Sprinkle the remaining sugar into the ramekins, coating the insides evenly. Spoon in the mixture and bake for about 45 minutes. • Turn out onto serving dishes. • Dust with the confectioners' sugar and decorate with a cherry and slices of orange. Serve warm.

Serves:	6
Preparation:	45'
Cooking:	2 h 15'
Level of difficulty:	3

- 1 large orange, washed
- 4 large egg yolks
- 1$^1/_3$ cups/270 g granulated sugar
- 1 tsp vanilla extract
- 2 tbsp all-purpose/ plain flour
- 1 tbsp potato starch
- 2 tbsp butter, melted
- 4 tbsp orange liqueur
- 2 large egg whites
- $^1/_8$ tsp salt

- candied cherries, halved, to decorate
- 4 tbsp confectioners'/ icing sugar, to dust
- 1 orange, thinly sliced, to decorate

ICE CREAM-FILLED FIGS

Cut the figs in half and use a teaspoon to remove the flesh. • Stir the flesh into the ice cream in a medium bowl. • Spoon the ice cream into the fig skins. • Freeze for about 30 minutes, or until firm. • Beat the cream and confectioners' sugar in a large bowl with an electric mixer at high speed until stiff. • Decorate the figs with the cream. Sprinkle with the pine nuts and dust with the cocoa. • Serve immediately.

Serves: 6

Preparation: 20' + 30' to freeze

Level of difficulty: 1

- **12 firm-ripe green figs**
- **2 cups/500 g vanilla ice cream, softened**
- **1 cup/250 ml heavy/double cream**
- **1 tbsp confectioners'/ icing sugar**
- **4 tbsp pine nuts, toasted**
- **1 tbsp sweetened cocoa powder**

FRESH FRUIT SALAD WITH VERMOUTH

Serves: 2–4

Preparation: 15' + 1 h to chill

Level of difficulty: 1

- 2 oranges
- 1 pink grapefruit
- 2 bananas, thinly sliced
- 2 kiwifruit, thinly sliced
- juice of ½ lemon
- 2–4 tbsp raw sugar
- ⅛ tsp ground cinnamon
- ½ cup/100 ml sweet white vermouth
- whipped cream, to serve

Peel the orange and grapefruit and chop into small pieces. • Mix with the sliced banana and kiwifruit. • Add the lemon juice, sugar, cinnamon, and vermouth. • Refrigerate for about 1 hour. • Serve with whipped cream.

SEMOLINA PUDDING WITH FRUIT COMPOTE

P lace all the fruit in a large saucepan over low heat and pour in the wine. Add the cinnamon and 1 tablespoon of confectioners' sugar. Cook for 20 minutes, stirring occasionally. • Remove from the heat and discard the cinnamon. • Bring the milk to a boil with the vanilla, butter, and salt in a large saucepan over medium heat. Lower the heat and discard the vanilla pod. • Gradually sprinkle in the semolina, whisking constantly to prevent lumps from forming. • Add the remaining sugar and cook for 15 minutes, stirring constantly, until the semolina has thickened. • Butter a 2-quart (2-liter) ring mold. • Pour the semolina into the prepared mold and let cool for 15 minutes. • Turn out the semolina onto a serving dish and arrange the fruit in the center. Serve warm.

860

Serves: 4

Preparation: 30'

Cooking: 40'

Level of difficulty: 2

- 1 apple, peeled, cored, and chopped into bite-size pieces
- 1 pear, peeled, cored, and chopped into bite-size pieces
- 1 orange, peeled and sliced
- 4 kumquats, sliced
- 6 prunes, pitted and halved
- 6 apricots, pitted and halved
- 1 cup/250 ml fruity red wine
- 1 stick cinnamon
- $\frac{1}{3}$ cup/50 g confectioners'/icing sugar
- $1\frac{1}{4}$ quarts/1.25 liters milk
- 1 vanilla pod
- 1 tbsp butter
- $\frac{1}{8}$ tsp salt
- $1\frac{1}{3}$ cups/250 g semolina

FROZEN STRAWBERRY PLATTER

862

Granita: Dissolve the sugar in the water in a small saucepan over medium heat. Bring to a boil and simmer over low heat for 5 minutes.
• Process with the strawberries and lemon juice until smooth. • Pour into a bowl and freeze for 3–4 hours, stirring from time to time to break up the ice crystals. • Jell-o: Bring the honey, sugar, water, and agar-agar to a boil in a small saucepan over low heat. • Transfer to a blender with the strawberries and chop until smooth. • Pour into a freezerproof container and refrigerate for 4 hours, or until set. • Toss the remaining strawberries with the mint, brown sugar, and lime juice in a large bowl. • Spoon the strawberries into 4 small glasses. • Spoon the granita into 4 small glasses. Arrange a glass of strawberries, a glass of granita, a slice of jelly, and a spoonful of ice cream on 4 serving dishes. • Garnish with mint leaves and serve.

Serves: 4

Preparation: 25' + 4 h to freeze and set

Cooking: 10'

Level of difficulty: 2

GRANITA
• 2 tbsp sugar
• 6 tbsp water
• 4 oz/125 g strawberries, hulled
• juice of ½ lemon

JELL-O
• 2 tsp honey
• 1 tsp sugar
• 6 tbsp water
• 2 tsp agar-agar
• 5 oz/150 g strawberries, hulled

• 10 strawberries, hulled and cut into quarters
• 1 sprig mint, finely chopped + extra to garnish
• 1 tsp brown sugar
• juice of ½ lime
• 5 oz/150 g best-quality strawberry ice cream

ICED CHERRY SOUFFLÉS

Beat the cream in a large bowl until stiff and refrigerate until ready to use. • Take four 3-inch (8-cm) soufflé dishes. Wrap a strip of waxed paper around the outside of each one (the strip should be twice the height of the dish and slightly longer than the circumference). • Process the cherries in a food processor or blender until puréed and place in a large bowl. • Stir the egg whites, cream of tartar, and sugar in a double boiler over barely simmering water. Cook over low heat, beating constantly with an electric mixer at low speed until the whites register 160°F (80°C) on an instant-read thermometer. • Beat at high speed until stiff peaks form. Gently fold the beaten whites into the cherry purée, followed by $^3/_4$ cup (180 ml) of cream. • Spoon the mixture into the soufflé dishes, smoothing the surface. • Freeze for 6 hours. Remove from the refrigerator at least 30 minutes before serving. • Remove the paper. Pipe the cream around the edge of each portion. Decorate with the cherries and serve.

Serves: 4

Preparation: 1 h + 6 h 30' to freeze

Level of difficulty: 2

- 1½ cups/375 g heavy/double cream
- 5 oz/150 g ripe cherries, pitted + 4 whole cherries, to decorate
- 4 egg whites
- ¼ tsp cream of tartar
- ¾ cup/150 g granulated sugar

ICE CREAM WITH THREE SAUCES

Serves: 6

Preparation: 1 h + 6 h 30'

Level of difficulty: 2

STRAWBERRY SAUCE
- 12 oz/350 g strawberries, washed and hulled
- ¼ cup/50 g granulated sugar
- juice of ½ lemon
- 4 tbsp Maraschino liqueur

KIWI SAUCE
- 3 kiwifruit, peeled
- ¼ cup/50 g granulated sugar
- 1 tbsp lemon juice

PASSIONFRUIT SAUCE
- 3 passionfruit
- ¼ cup/50 g granulated sugar
- juice of ½ lemon

- 10 oz/300 g vanilla ice-cream
- 10 oz/300 g lemon ice-cream

Strawberry Sauce: Process the strawberries in a food processor or a blender until smooth.
• Bring the sugar and water to a boil in a small saucepan and cook for 8 minutes, or until the sugar has dissolved completely. • Add the puréed strawberries and cook until the sauce thickens.
• Remove from the heat and let cool. Mix in the lemon juice and Maraschino. • Kiwi Sauce: Process the kiwifruit in a food processor or blender with the sugar and lemon juice. • Passionfruit Sauce: Halve the 3 passionfruit, scrape out the flesh and seeds, and place them in a bowl. Add the sugar and lemon juice. Use a wooden spoon to mix well. • Serve the three sauces chilled with the ice cream.

MELON SORBET WITH PORT

Cut the melons in half horizontally. Remove and discard the seeds. Use a spoon to take out the flesh. Place in a bowl and set aside. • When the melon halves are cleaned, place them in the freezer. • Process the melon flesh in a food processor or blender with the confectioners' sugar, egg white, and Port. • Spoon the purée in ice cube trays and freeze for about 3 hours. • Before serving, return the melon ice cubes to the blender and process until finely chopped. • Pour the sorbet into the melon halves. Garnish with the mint and serve on dessert plates.

Serves: 4

Preparation: 20' + 3 h to freeze

Level of difficulty: 2

- **2 small melons**
- **1¼ cups/175 g confectioners'/icing sugar**
- **1 egg white**
- **4 tbsp Port**
- **4 sprigs fresh mint, to garnish**

WATERMELON BASKET WITH ICE CREAM

Use a sharp knife to cut out two semi-circles from the watermelon leaving a strip in the center. The watermelon should look like a basket with a handle. • Remove the flesh from underneath the strip and from the remaining melon with a melon-baller, taking care not to damage the skin. Place the melon balls in a bowl with the strawberries. Sprinkle with sugar and stir carefully. Refrigerate until ready to serve. • Place the watermelon basket on a serving dish and cut a zigzag pattern around the edge. • Just before serving, fill with balls of the two types of ice cream, melon balls, and strawberries.

A summertime treat for adults and children alike!

870

Serves: 8

Preparation: 30'

Level of difficulty: 2

- 1 watermelon, weighing about 4 lb/2 kg
- 1½ lb/750 g strawberries, washed and hulled
- 4 tbsp sugar
- 1 lb/500 g lemon ice cream
- 1 lb/500 g pistachio ice cream

COUSCOUS WITH HONEY AND POMEGRANATE

Serves: 6

Preparation: 5' + 15' to cool

Cooking: 5'

Level of difficulty: 1

- 1 lb/500 g instant couscous
- scant 1 cup/225 ml honey
- 1 cup/100 g chopped walnuts
- grated zest of 1½ oranges
- 1 tsp ground cinnamon
- seeds of 2 pomegranates

Prepare the couscous according to the instructions on the package. • Place the couscous in a large bowl. Mix in the honey, walnuts, orange zest, cinnamon, and half of the pomegranate seeds. Mix well and let cool completely. • Transfer to a serving dish and decorate with the remaining pomegranate seeds.

APRICOTS WITH MASCARPONE

874

Dissolve the sugar in the water in a large saucepan over low heat and bring to a boil. • Add the apricots and cook for 10–15 minutes, or until the apricots are tender and a syrup has formed. • Add the lemon juice and remove from the heat. • Use a slotted spoon to transfer the apricots to a plate and let cool. • Cut open each apricot and fill with the Mascarpone. • Arrange the stuffed apricots on a serving dish. Drizzle with the syrup and sprinkle with the pistachios.

Serves: 6–8

Preparation: 30'

Cooking: 10–15'

Level of difficulty: 1

- 3 cups/600 g granulated sugar
- 3 cups/750 ml water
- 2¾ cups/500 g dried apricots, soaked overnight and drained
- 1 tbsp fresh lemon juice
- 2 cups/500 g Mascarpone cheese
- 2 cups/200 g chopped pistachios

COUSCOUS WITH DATES AND ALMONDS

Prepare the couscous according to the instructions on the package. • Transfer to a large bowl and stir in the oil and salt. • Stir in the orange flower water, 1 tablespoon of confectioners' sugar, dates, pistachios, and almonds. Mix well and transfer to a serving dish. • Dust with the remaining confectioners' sugar and cinnamon just before serving.

876

Vegan

Serves: 6
Preparation: 30'
Cooking: 50'
Level of difficulty: 2

- 1 lb/500 g instant couscous
- 6 tbsp almond oil
- 1/8 tsp salt
- 2 tbsp orange flower water
- 2 tbsp confectioners'/icing sugar
- 1/2 cup/100 g chopped dates
- 1/2 cup/100 g chopped pistachios
- 1 cup/100 g chopped almonds
- 2 tsp ground cinnamon

CHILLED RICOTTA WITH FRUIT

Place the Ricotta and honey in a food processor or blender and process until well blended.
• Butter a 10-inch (25-cm) baking pan. • Pour the Ricotta mixture into the prepared pan and refrigerate for at least 3 hours. • Cut the fruit into bite-size pieces and mix with the sugar and lemon juice in a large bowl. • Turn the Ricotta out onto a large serving plate and top with the fruit salad.
• Serve in slices.

Serves: 4

Preparation: 20' + 3 h to chill

Level of difficulty: 1

- 3¼ cups/810 g Ricotta cheese
- generous ¾ cup/ 200 g honey
- 2 kiwifruit, peeled
- 6 strawberries
- 1 banana, peeled
- 1 orange, peeled
- juice of 1 lemon
- 2 tbsp granulated sugar

BAKED PLUM DELIGHT

Preheat the oven to 325°F/170°C/gas 3.
• Butter an ovenproof baking dish large enough to hold all the plums. • Wash the plums, cut them in half, and remove the pits. • Place the plums in the prepared dish, pitted-side up. • Sprinkle with the sugar and drizzle with the lemon juice and water. Cover with aluminum foil and bake for 35–40 minutes, or until tender but still holding their shape. • Serve warm with whipped cream.

Serves: 6

Preparation: 15'

Cooking: 35–40'

Level of difficulty: 1

- **1¾ lb/750 g plums**
- **¾ cup/150 g granulated sugar**
- **juice of 1 lemon**
- **3 tbsp water**
- **whipped cream, to serve**

880

MELONS ON ICE

*Vegan

Serves: 4

Preparation: 25' + 2 h to chill

Level of difficulty: 1

- 2 cantaloupe/rock melons
- ½ cup/125 ml dry Port
- crushed ice, to serve

Cut the melons in half horizontally. Remove the seeds. • Use the melon baller to remove the flesh from each half and place the balls in a large bowl. Remove all the remaining flesh on the inside of the skins. Pour the Port over the melon balls and mix well. • Refrigerate for at least 2 hours. • Use an ice crusher or put the ice cubes in a tea towel and crush well with a meat tenderizer. Place the crushed ice in individual bowls. • Place the empty melon halves on top of the ice and fill with the melon balls. Pour the remaining marinade over each melon half. Serve immediately.

BLACKBERRY BREAD PUDDING

Preheat the oven to 350°F/180°C/gas 4.
• Set out a 1 quart (1 liter) fluted soufflé dish.
• Heat the milk in a small saucepan. Place the bread in a large bowl and pour in the milk. Beat with an electric mixer at medium speed until fairly smooth. • Add the eggs, beating until just blended. • Beat in 1/2 cup (100 g) of sugar, the brandy, and salt. Mix well. • Stir in the blackberries. • Place the remaining sugar and water in a small saucepan and cook and stir over medium-low heat until the sugar has dissolved. Continue cooking, without stirring, until pale gold. Remove from the heat and sprinkle with the lemon juice. Pour into the soufflé dish. Turn the dish quickly to coat the sides. • Spoon the blackberry mixture into the dish and bake for 35–40 minutes, or until firm to the touch. • Turn out of the dish onto a serving plate and decorate with blackberries.

Serves: 4
Preparation: 30'
Cooking: 35–40'.
Level of difficulty: 2

• 2 cups/500 ml milk
• 14 oz/400 g day-old soft bread, torn into pieces
• 3 large eggs
• 1 1/4 cups/250 g granulated sugar
• 2 tbsp brandy
• 1/4 tsp salt
• 3 cups/400 g blackberries, mashed + extra, to decorate, rinsed and well dried
• 2 tsp cold water
• 1 tsp fresh lemon juice

884

EASY LIME CHEESECAKE

Serves: 4–6

Preparation: 25' + 5 h to chill

Level of difficulty: 1

CRUMB BASE
- ¾ cup/100 g graham cracker crumbs/crushed digestive biscuits
- 2 tbsp brown sugar
- 4 tbsp butter, melted

LIME FILLING
- 1⅔ cups/400 ml sweetened condensed milk
- 1 cup/250 ml cream cheese, softened
- ½ cup/125 ml light/single cream
- 2 tbsp grated lime zest
- 4 tbsp lime juice

TOPPING
- ¾ cup/180 ml heavy/double cream
- ripe fresh fruit, to decorate

Butter a 9-inch (23-cm) springform pan. • Crumb Base: Mix the crumbs, sugar, and butter in a small bowl. • Press into the bottom of the prepared pan. • Refrigerate for 1 hour. • Lime Filling: Beat the condensed milk, cream cheese, cream, and lime zest in a large bowl with an electric mixer at low speed until creamy. • Beat in the lime juice. • Spoon the filling into the crust. • Refrigerate for 4 hours. • Loosen and remove the pan sides. • Topping: Beat the cream in a large bowl until stiff. • Spread the cream over the filling and decorate with the fruit.

APPLE FRITTERS

Serves: 6

*Preparation: 20' + 1 h
30' to rest the
dough*

Cooking: 15'

Level of difficulty: 1

- **2 tbsp active dry
  yeast**
- **½ cup/125 ml milk**
- **3⅓ cups/500 g all-
  purpose/plain flour**
- **⅛ tsp salt**
- **8 oz/250 g apples,
  peeled, cored, and
  coarsely chopped**
- **2 cups/500 ml oil,
  for frying**
- **4 tbsp granulated
  sugar**
- **2 cups/500 ml
  plain yogurt**
- **4 tbsp clear honey**

Mix the yeast and milk in a small bowl. Let stand for 15 minutes, until foamy. • Sift the flour and salt into a large bowl. Mix in the yeast mixture and apples to make a soft dough. • Cover and let rise for about 90 minutes. • Roll the dough out on a floured surface to 1 inch (2.5 cm) thick. Cut out 4-inch (10-cm) rounds. • Heat the oil in a deep-fryer until very hot and fry in small batches for 5 minutes, or until golden brown all over. • Remove with a slotted spoon and drain well on paper towels. • Sprinkle with the sugar. • Serve hot with the yogurt and honey in separate bowls.

CAKES & COOKIES

CHERRY SHORTCAKE

Preheat the oven to 325°F/170°C/gas 3.
• Butter a 9¹/₂-inch (24-cm) baking pan. • Sift the flour, baking powder, and salt into a medium bowl. • Beat the butter and sugar in a large bowl until creamy. • Add the eggs and milk, beating until just blended. • Mix in the dry ingredients and vanilla extract. • Pour the batter into the prepared pan. • Bake for 30–35 minutes, or until golden and springy to the touch. • Cool in the pan for 5 minutes. Turn out onto a rack and let cool completely. • Slice it in half horizontally and spread one half with the preserves. • Sandwich the cake together and place on a serving plate. • Dust with the confectioners' sugar and decorate with the cherries just before serving.

Serves: 8

Preparation: 30' + 60' to cool

Cooking: 35'

Level of difficulty: 2

- 1²/₃ cups/250 g all-purpose/plain flour
- 2 tsp baking powder
- ¹/₈ tsp salt
- ²/₃ cup/150 g butter, softened
- ³/₄ cup/150 g granulated sugar
- 4 large eggs
- 6 tbsp milk
- 1 tsp vanilla extract
- ³/₄ cup/180 g cherry preserves:
- 2 tbsp confectioners'/ icing sugar
- about 20 fresh or canned cherries, pitted and halved, to decorate

Serves: 4

Preparation: 65' + 2 h to freeze

Cooking: 1 h

Level of difficulty: 3

CAKE
- 8 large eggs, separated
- 1½ cups/300 g granulated sugar
- 2 cups/300 g all-purpose/plain flour

FILLING
- 4 egg yolks
- 4 tbsp milk
- ½ tsp cinnamon
- 1 tsp vanilla extract
- 16 cherries, pitted
- scant ⅔ cup/140 g granulated sugar
- 2 cups/500 ml cream

SYRUP
- 1⅔ cups/400 ml fruity red wine
- ¾ cup/180 ml Port
- 2 sticks cinnamon
- 3 tbsp sugar

MERINGUE
- 4 large egg whites
- ½ cup/100 g sugar
- ⅔ cup/100 g confectioners'/icing sugar
- scant ½ cup/100 ml Alchermes liqueur
- sprigs of fresh mint

CHERRY MERINGUE DESSERT

Preheat the oven to 350°F/180°C/gas 4.
• Cake: Butter two 8-inch (20-cm) baking pans.
• Beat the 8 egg yolks with the first measure of sugar in a large bowl until pale and creamy. Fold in the flour. • Beat the egg whites until stiff and fold into the mixture. • Spoon the batter into the prepared pans. • Bake for 30–35 minutes, or until golden. • Turn out onto a rack to cool.
• Filling: Beat the 4 egg yolks in a large bowl until frothy. • Warm the milk with the cinnamon and vanilla in a small saucepan over low heat. Add the cherries and sugar and cook until the cherries are tender. • Pour over the yolks and beat until cooled.
• Beat the cream in a large bowl until stiff and fold into the mixture. Spoon into an 8-inch (20-cm) pan and freeze for 2 hours. • Syrup: Warm the wine, Port, and cinnamon in a small saucepan over low heat. Add the sugar and cook until dissolved. Bring to a boil and simmer over low heat for 20 minutes.
• Meringue: Beat the egg whites until soft peaks form. • Add the sugar and confectioners' sugar and beat until stiff. • Place a layer of cake on a serving plate and drizzle with half the syrup. Cover with the frozen cherry layer and top with the second layer of cake. Drizzle with the remaining syrup. • Spread the meringue over the top. Brown the meringue under a hot broiler (grill) for 5 minutes or decorate using a chef's blowtorch. Garnish with the mint and serve.

UPSIDE-DOWN CHERRY TART

Sift the flour into a bowl. Stir in the sugar.
• Use a pastry blender to cut in $^1/_3$ cup
(80 g) of the butter. • Add the egg yolks and lemon
zest to make a smooth dough, kneading as little as
possible so as not to melt the butter. • Shape into
a ball, wrap in plastic wrap, and refrigerate for
30 minutes. • Preheat the oven to 400°F/200°C/
gas 6. • Wash, dry and pit the cherries and cut
them in half. • Use the remaining butter to grease
an 11-inch (28-cm) springform pan. Sprinkle with
the confectioners' sugar to evenly cover the
bottom of the pan. Arrange the cherries in the
prepared pan, cut-side down. • Roll the dough out
on a lightly floured surface to make an 11-inch
(28-cm) round. Gently place the dough gently on
top of the cherries. • Bake for 20–25 minutes,
or until the pastry is lightly browned. Cool in the
pan for 5 minutes. • Carefully turn out, cherry-side
up, onto a serving dish and let cool completely.
• Beat the cream in a large bowl until stiff. • Spoon
the cream into a pastry bag fitted with a small
star tip and pipe the cream decoratively on
top of the tart.

Serves: 6–8

Preparation: 40' + 30'
  to chill

Cooking: 20–25'

Level of difficulty: 2

- 1$^1/_3$ cups/200 g all-
  purpose/plain flour
- $^1/_3$ cup/70 g
  granulated sugar
- $^1/_2$ cup/125 g
  butter, softened
- 2 egg yolks
- grated zest of 1
  lemon
- 14 oz/400 g ripe
  cherries, stems
  removed
- $^1/_2$ cup/75 g
  confectioners'/
  icing sugar
- $^3/_4$ cup/200 ml
  heavy/double
  cream

STRAWBERRY AND PEACH STRUDEL

Preheat the oven to 350°F/180°C/gas 4.
• Butter and flour a baking sheet. • Lay a clean cloth on a work surface and sprinkle with flour. Unfold or unroll the sheets of pastry on top of the cloth. Brush each one with the melted butter and apricot preserves. • Arrange the prepared fruit in the center of the pastry. Sprinkle with the pine nuts, bread crumbs, lemon zest, and sugar.
• Roll up the pastry and tuck in the ends to seal to prevent the filling from leaking out during cooking. • Carefully transfer the strudel to the prepared sheet and brush all over with milk.
• Bake for 45–50 minutes, or until lightly browned.
• Dust with the confectioners' sugar and serve hot.

Serves: 6–8
Preparation: 45'
Cooking: 45–50'
Level of difficulty: 3

• 10 oz/300 g frozen phyllo pastry, thawed
• 1 tbsp butter, melted
• 1 cup/150 g apricot preserves:
• 14 oz/400 g strawberries, washed, hulled, and thinly sliced
• 4 peaches, pitted and thinly sliced
• 4 tbsp pine nuts
• 1/3 cup/50 g fine dry bread crumbs
• grated zest of 1 lemon
• 1 tbsp sugar
• 4 tbsp milk
• 1/2 cup/75 g confectioners'/ icing sugar, to dust

RASPBERRY TART

Pastry: Sift the flour, confectioners' sugar, and salt into a large bowl. • Use a pastry blender to cut in the butter until the mixture resembles coarse crumbs. • Stir in the hazelnuts and vanilla. • Mix in enough of the beaten egg yolk to make a stiff dough. • Shape the dough into a ball, wrap in plastic wrap, and refrigerate for 30 minutes.
• Raspberry Filling: Cook the raspberries with the sugar in a medium saucepan until the fruit has softened and resembles jam. • Preheat the oven to 400°F/200°C/gas 6. • Set out a 12-inch (30-cm) springform pan. • Roll the dough out to a $^1/_4$ inch (5 mm) thick. Fit into the pan, trimming the edges if needed. Line the pastry with waxed paper and fill with dried beans or pie weights. Prick all over with a fork, pinching the edges. • Bake for 20 minutes, then remove the paper with the beans or weights.
• Spoon in the raspberry filling. Decorate with the raspberries. • Dust with the confectioners' sugar and serve.

Serves: 8

Preparation: 40' + 30' to chill

Cooking: 20'

Level of difficulty: 2

PASTRY
- 1$^2/_3$ cups/250 g all-purpose/plain flour
- $^3/_4$ cup/125 g confectioners'/ icing sugar
- $^1/_8$ tsp salt
- $^2/_3$ cup/150 g butter
- 1$^1/_3$ cups/130 g chopped hazelnuts
- 1 tsp vanilla extract
- 2 egg yolks, lightly beaten

FILLING
- 10 oz/300 g fresh raspberries + extra to decorate
- 1 cup/200 g granulated sugar

- $^1/_3$ cup/50 g confectioners'/ icing sugar, to dust

898

LEMON TART
WITH STRAWBERRIES

Serves: 8

Preparation: 50' + 30'
to chill

Cooking: 40'

Level of difficulty: 2

PASTRY
- 3⅓ cups/500 g all-purpose/plain flour
- ⅛ tsp salt
- ¼ cup/50 g granulated sugar
- ⅛ tsp freshly grated nutmeg
- ¾ cup/180 g butter
- 7 tbsp milk

LEMON FILLING
- 1 egg and 5 egg yolks
- ½ cup/100 g granulated sugar
- 4 tbsp butter
- grated zest of 1 lemon
- 3 tbsp lemon juice

- 10 oz/300 g strawberries, washed and hulled
- ⅓ cup/50 g confectioners'/icing sugar, to dust

Pastry: Sift the flour and salt into a large bowl. Stir in the sugar and nutmeg. • Use a pastry blender to cut in the butter until the mixture resembles coarse crumbs. • Mix in enough milk to make a smooth dough. • Shape the dough into a ball, wrap in plastic wrap, and refrigerate for 30 minutes. • Preheat the oven to 350°F/180°C/gas 4. • Set out a 12-inch (30-cm) springform pan or pie plate. • Roll the dough out to ¼ inch (5 mm) thick. Fit into the pan, trimming the edges if needed. Line the pastry shell with waxed paper and fill with dried beans or pie weights. • Bake for 40 minutes, then remove the paper with the beans. • Lemon Filling: Beat the egg, egg yolks, and sugar in a double boiler over barely simmering water until well blended. Cook over low heat, stirring constantly with a wooden spoon, until the mixture lightly coats a metal spoon or registers 160°F (80°C) on an instant-read thermometer. • Stir in the butter and lemon zest and juice. • Immediately plunge the pan into a bowl of ice water and stir until cooled. Pour the filling into the pastry base. • Arrange the strawberries on top of the tart. • Dust with the confectioners' sugar and serve.

BANANA CAKE WITH PASSIONFRUIT FROSTING

Preheat the oven to 350°F/180°C/gas 4.
• Butter a 9-inch (23-cm) cake pan and line with waxed paper. • Sift the flour, baking powder, baking soda, and ginger into a medium bowl. • Beat the butter and brown sugar in a large bowl with an electric mixer at high speed until creamy.

902

Adding the passionfruit pulp to the frosting gives this cake that little something extra.

• Add the eggs, beating until just blended. • Mix in the dry ingredients, mashed banana, sour cream, and milk. • Spoon the batter into the prepared pan. • Bake for 40–50 minutes, or until a toothpick inserted into the center comes out clean. • Cool the cake in the pan for 10 minutes. Turn out onto a rack and let cool completely. • Passionfruit Frosting: Beat the confectioners' sugar, passionfruit pulp, and butter in a double boiler over barely simmering water until creamy. • Spread evenly over the top and sides of the cake.

Serves: 6

Preparation: 30'

Cooking: 40–50'

Level of difficulty: 1

- 1²⁄₃ cups/250 g all-purpose/plain flour
- 2 tsp baking powder
- 1 tsp baking soda
- 1 tsp ground ginger
- ½ cup/125 g butter, softened
- ¾ cup/150 g firmly packed light brown sugar
- 3 large eggs
- 10 oz/300 g very ripe bananas, mashed
- ½ cup/125 ml sour cream
- 4 tbsp milk

PASSIONFRUIT FROSTING

- 1²⁄₃ cups/250 g confectioners'/icing sugar
- 3 tbsp passionfruit pulp
- 1 tbsp butter, softened

PINEAPPLE AND GINGER CAKE

Serves: 8

Preparation: 25'

Cooking: 40–45'

Level of difficulty: 1

- 1½ cups/225 g all-purpose/plain flour
- 2 tsp baking powder
- 1 tsp ground ginger
- ⅛ tsp salt
- ½ cup/125 g butter
- 1 cup/200 g granulated sugar
- 2 eggs
- ⅔ cup/80 g sweetened shredded coconut
- 4 oz/125 g canned pineapple, undrained and broken up
- pieces of candied ginger, to decorate

PINEAPPLE FROSTING
- 2 tbsp butter
- 1½ cups/225 g confectioners'/icing sugar
- 1 tsp ground ginger
- 4 tbsp pineapple juice

Preheat the oven to 325°F/170°C/gas 3. • Butter a 10½-inch (26-cm) springform pan and line with waxed paper. • Sift the flour, baking powder, ginger, and salt into a medium bowl. • Beat the butter and sugar in a large bowl with an electric mixer at high speed until creamy. • Add the eggs, beating until just blended. • Mix in the dry ingredients, coconut, and pineapple. • Spoon the batter into the prepared pan. • Bake for 40–45 minutes, or until a toothpick inserted into the center comes out clean. • Cool in the pan for 10 minutes. Turn out onto a rack and let cool completely. • Pineapple Frosting: Beat the butter, confectioners' sugar, and ginger in a small bowl. Gradually beat in the pineapple juice to make a smooth frosting. • Spread the frosting over the cake and decorate with candied ginger.

WALNUT AND CARROT CAKE

Preheat the oven to 350°F/180°C/gas 4.
• Butter a 9-inch (23-cm) springform pan.
• Sift the flour, baking powder, cinnamon, baking soda, ginger, nutmeg, cloves, and salt into a large bowl. • Beat the butter and sugar in a large bowl with an electric mixer at high speed until creamy.
• Add the eggs and vanilla, beating until just blended. • Mix in the dry ingredients, carrots, walnuts, and raisins. • Spoon the batter into the prepared pan. • Bake for 45–55 minutes, or until a toothpick inserted into the center comes out clean. • Turn out onto a rack and let cool completely. • Frosting: Beat the cream cheese, confectioners' sugar, butter, and lemon juice and lemon zest to make a spreadable consistency. • Spread the frosting over the cake and decorate with the walnuts.

Serves: 6

Preparation: 40'

Cooking: 45–55'

Level of difficulty: 1

- 2⅓ cups/350 g all-purpose/plain flour
- 2 tsp baking powder
- 2 tsp ground cinnamon
- 1 tsp baking soda
- 1 tsp ground ginger
- ½ tsp ground nutmeg
- ¼ tsp ground cloves
- ⅛ tsp salt
- ¾ cup/180 g butter, softened
- 1½ cups/300 g granulated sugar
- 4 large eggs
- 1 tsp vanilla extract
- 14 oz/400 g finely shredded carrots
- 1¼ cups/100 g chopped walnuts
- ¼ cup/50 g raisins

FROSTING

- 1 cup/250 g cream cheese, softened
- 2⅓ cups/350 g confectioners'/icing sugar
- 4 tbsp butter
- 2 tsp lemon juice
- 1 tbsp finely grated lemon zest
- halved walnuts, to decorate

APPLE AND RAISIN CAKE

Serves: 6
Preparation: 25'
Cooking: 1 h 15'
Level of difficulty: 1

Preheat the oven to 350°F/180°C/gas 4.
• Butter a 9-inch (23-cm) square pan. • Sift the flour, baking powder, cinnamon, nutmeg, baking soda, and salt into a large bowl. • Mix in the brown sugar, eggs, butter, and vanilla extract until well blended. • Add the apples, raisins, and walnuts. • Spoon the batter into the prepared pan. • Bake for 60–75 minutes, or until a toothpick inserted into the center comes out clean. • Cool completely in the pan.

- 1½ cups/225 g all-purpose/plain flour
- 2 tsp baking powder
- 1 tsp ground cinnamon
- 1 tsp ground nutmeg
- ½ tsp baking soda
- ⅛ tsp salt
- 1⅓ cups/270 g firmly packed light brown sugar
- 3 large eggs
- 4 tbsp butter, softened
- ½ tsp vanilla extract
- 2 apples, grated
- 1 cup/180 g golden raisins/sultanas
- 1 cup/100 g chopped walnuts

Serves: 6	
Preparation: 25'	
Cooking: 1 h 15'	
Level of difficulty: 1	

CARAMELIZED PEARS

- 8 small firm pears, peeled, cored, and halved
- 2 tbsp water
- 4 tbsp lemon juice
- 2 tbsp butter
- ½ cup/100 g granulated sugar

CAKE

- 1½ cups/225 g all-purpose/plain flour
- 1 tsp baking powder
- 1 tsp ground ginger
- 1 tsp chile powder
- ⅛ tsp salt
- ½ cup/125 g butter
- ¾ cup/150 g granulated sugar
- 2 tbsp finely grated lemon zest
- 2 eggs
- ½ cup/125 ml yogurt

PEAR AND YOGURT CAKE

Preheat the oven to 375°F/190°C/gas 5. • Butter a 9-inch (23-cm) baking pan. • Caramelized Pears: Place the pears in a bowl with water and lemon juice for 5 minutes. • Drain well. • Melt the butter and sugar in a large saucepan over medium heat and add the pears. Cook for 15–20 minutes, stirring often, until the pears are caramelized. • Let cool slightly. • Cake: Sift the flour, baking powder, ginger, chile powder, and salt into a medium bowl. • Beat the butter, sugar, and lemon zest in a large bowl until creamy. • Add the eggs, beating until just blended. • Mix in the dry ingredients and yogurt. • Place the pears (round part down) in the pan. Pour any remaining cooking liquid over the top. • Spoon the batter over the pears. • Bake for 45–55 minutes, or until springy. • Cool in the pan for 5 minutes. • Turn out onto a serving plate.

ZUCCHINI AND APRICOT CAKE

Serves:	6
Preparation:	25'
Cooking:	40–50'
Level of difficulty:	1

Preheat the oven to 350°F/180°C/gas 4.
• Butter a 9-inch (23-cm) cake pan and line with waxed paper. • Sift both flours, baking powder, baking soda, and salt in a medium bowl. • Beat the butter, brown sugar, and lemon zest and juice in a large bowl with an electric mixer at high speed until creamy. • Add the eggs one at a time, beating until just blended after each addition. • Stir in the zucchini and apricots, followed by the dry ingredients and milk. • Spoon the batter into the prepared pan. • Bake for 40–50 minutes, or until a toothpick inserted into the center comes out clean. • Cool in the pan for 10 minutes. Turn out onto a rack and let cool completely. • Fruit Frosting: Place the apricots in a heavy-bottomed saucepan with the water. Bring to a boil over medium heat. Simmer over low heat for about 10 minutes, or until the apricots have softened. • Remove from the heat and let cool. Beat the cream cheese, confectioners' sugar, and lemon juice to make a spreadable frosting. Mix in the apricots. • Spread the frosting over the top and sides of the cake.

Zucchini provide a natural sweetness and moistness to basic cakes.

- 1 cup/150 g all-purpose/plain flour
- ½ cup/75 g whole-wheat flour
- 1 tsp baking powder
- 1 tsp baking soda
- ⅛ tsp salt
- ½ cup/125 g butter, softened
- ¾ cup/150 g brown sugar
- 1 tbsp lemon zest
- 1 tsp lemon juice
- 2 eggs
- 1 cup/125 g grated zucchini/courgettes
- 4 tbsp finely chopped dried apricots
- 4 tbsp milk

FRUIT FROSTING
- 6 tbsp finely chopped dried apricots
- ½ cup/125 ml water
- 1 cup/250 g cream cheese, softened
- 1 cup/150 g confectioners'/icing sugar
- 2 tbsp lemon or lime juice

CARROT, DATE, AND WALNUT CAKE

Serves: 6–8

Preparation: 20'

Cooking: 50–60'

Level of difficulty: 1

- 1½ cups/225 g all-purpose/plain flour
- 2 tsp baking powder
- 1½ tsp chile powder
- ½ tsp baking soda
- ⅛ tsp salt
- ½ cup/125 g butter
- ¾ cup/150 g granulated sugar
- 2 eggs
- ½ tsp vanilla extract
- 8 oz/250 g finely shredded carrots
- ⅔ cup/120 g chopped dates
- 1 cup/100 g chopped walnuts

Preheat the oven to 350°F/180°C/gas 4.
• Butter a 10½-inch (26-cm) ring mold.
• Sift the flour, baking powder, chile powder, baking soda, and salt into a medium bowl.
• Beat the butter and sugar in a large bowl with an electric mixer at high speed until creamy.
• Add the eggs and vanilla, beating until just blended. • Mix in the carrots, dates, and walnuts, followed by the dry ingredients. • Spoon the batter into the prepared mold. • Bake for 50–60 minutes, or until a toothpick inserted into the center comes out clean. • Cool in the pan for 15 minutes. • Turn out onto a rack and let cool completely.

APPLE AND CINNAMON STREUSEL CAKE

Serves: 6

Preparation: 30'

Cooking: 40–50'

Level of difficulty: 2

- **3 medium apples (weighing 1 lb/ 500 g in total)**
- **2 tbsp brown sugar**
- **4 tbsp lemon juice**
- **2⅓ cups/350 g all-purpose/plain flour**
- **2 tsp baking powder**
- **⅛ tsp salt**
- **¾ cup/180 g butter, softened**
- **¾ cup/150 g granulated sugar**
- **2 eggs**
- **¾ cup/180 ml milk**

CINNAMON STREUSEL
- **1 cup/150 g all-purpose/plain flour**
- **½ cup/100 g brown sugar**
- **1 tbsp ground cinnamon**
- **6 tbsp butter, in pieces**
- **⅔ cup/100 g chopped walnuts**

Preheat the oven to 350°F/180°C/gas 4. • Butter a 9-inch (23-cm) square pan and line with waxed paper. • Peel and core the apples and slice them thinly. • Place the apples, brown sugar, and lemon juice in a medium saucepan over medium-low heat and bring to a boil. • Cover and simmer over low heat for about 10 minutes, or until the apples have softened. • Drain the apples. • Sift the flour, baking powder, and salt into a medium bowl. • Beat the butter and sugar in a large bowl with an electric mixer at high speed until creamy. • Add the eggs, beating until just blended. • Mix in the dry ingredients and milk. • Spoon two-thirds of the batter into the prepared pan. Spoon the cooked apples over the top. Cover with the remaining mixture. • Cinnamon Streusel: Mix the flour, brown sugar, and cinnamon. Use a pastry blender to cut in the butter until the mixture resembles coarse crumbs. Add the walnuts and sprinkle over the cake. • Bake for 40–50 minutes, or until a toothpick inserted into the center comes out clean. • Let cool completely in the pan.

RED CURRANT CAKE

Preheat the oven to 350°F/180°C/gas 4.
• Butter a deep 8-inch (20-cm) cake pan.
• Sift the flour, baking powder, and salt into a medium bowl. • Beat the butter and sugar in a large bowl with an electric mixer at high speed until creamy. • Add the eggs and vanilla, beating until just blended. • Mix in the dry ingredients and currants. • Spoon the batter into the prepared pan. • Bake for 1 hour 20 minutes, or until a toothpick inserted into the center comes out clean. • Cool in the pan for 5 minute. • Turn out onto a rack and let cool completely. • Dust with the confectioners' sugar before serving.

Serves: 6

Preparation: 20'

Cooking: 1 h 20'

Level of difficulty: 1

- **2 cups/300 g all-purpose/plain flour**
- **2 tsp baking powder**
- **⅛ tsp salt**
- **⅔ cup/150 g butter, softened**
- **¾ cup/150 g granulated sugar**
- **4 large eggs**
- **½ tsp vanilla extract**
- **¾ cup/140 g red currants**
- **⅓ cup/50 g confectioners'/icing sugar, to dust**

ORANGE AND CARROT CAKE

Serves: 6

Preparation: 20'

Cooking: 40–50'

Level of difficulty: 1

- 1½ cups/225 g all-purpose/plain flour
- 2 tsp baking powder
- 1 tsp ground nutmeg
- 1 tsp ground cinnamon
- ½ tsp baking soda
- ⅛ tsp salt
- ½ cup/125 g butter
- 1 cup/200 g granulated sugar
- 3 eggs
- 10 oz/300 g finely shredded carrots
- 1 cup/100 g chopped walnuts

ORANGE CREAM CHEESE FROSTING

- ½ cup/125 g cream cheese, softened
- 1 tbsp finely grated orange zest
- 1 tbsp orange juice
- 1½ cups/225 g confectioners'/icing sugar

Preheat the oven to 350°F/180°C/gas 4.
• Sift the flour, baking powder, nutmeg, cinnamon, baking soda, and salt into a medium bowl. • Butter a 9-inch (23-cm) cake pan and line with waxed paper. • Beat the butter and sugar in a large bowl with an electric mixer at high speed until creamy. • Add the eggs one at a time, beating until just blended after each addition. • Mix in the dry ingredients, carrots, and walnuts. • Spoon the batter into the prepared pan. • Bake for 40–50 minutes, or until a toothpick inserted into the center comes out clean. • Turn out onto a rack and let cool completely. • Orange Cream Cheese Frosting: Beat the cream cheese, confectioners' sugar, and orange zest and juice to make a spreadable frosting. • Spread the frosting over the top of the cake.

ORANGE AND NUT LOAF

Plump the raisins in the water in a small bowl for 20 minutes. Drain well and pat dry with paper towels. • Preheat the oven to 350°F/180°C/gas 4. • Butter an 8¹/₂ x 4¹/₂-inch (21 x 11-cm) loaf pan. Line with foil, letting the edges overhang. Butter the foil. • Sift the flour, baking powder, and salt into a large bowl. • Gradually beat in the milk, egg, butter, marmalade, brandy, and orange zest. • Stir in the hazelnuts, almonds, and raisins. • Spoon the batter into the prepared pan. • Bake for 45–55 minutes, or until a toothpick inserted into the center comes out clean. • Cool the loaf on a rack for 10 minutes. Using the foil as a lifter, remove the loaf from the pan. Carefully remove the foil. • Cool the loaf completely on a rack. • Serve with extra marmalade to spread.

Serves: 6

Preparation: 20' + 20' to soak

Cooking: 45–55'

Level of difficulty: 1

- ³/₄ cup/120 g raisins
- 1 cup/250 ml warm water
- 1¹/₂ cups/225 g all-purpose/plain flour
- 1¹/₂ tsp baking powder
- ¹/₄ tsp salt
- ¹/₂ cup/125 ml milk
- 1 large egg, lightly beaten
- 6 tbsp butter, melted
- 6 tbsp orange marmalade
- 2 tbsp brandy
- 2 tbsp grated orange zest
- ¹/₂ cup/50 g chopped hazelnuts
- 2 tbsp chopped almonds

Serves: 6

Preparation: 15' + 30'
to soak

Cooking: 40–50'

Level of difficulty: 1

- ¾ cup/120 g
  raisins
- 1½ cups/375 ml
  warm water
- 1½ cups/225 g all-
  purpose/plain flour
- 1½ tsp baking
  powder
- ¼ tsp salt
- ½ cup/100 g
  granulated sugar
- ½ cup/125 ml milk
- 1 large egg, lightly
  beaten
- 4 tbsp butter,
  melted
- ¾ cup/75 g
  chopped hazelnuts
- ½ cup/50 g
  chopped almonds
- 2 tbsp mixed
  chopped nuts, to
  decorate

RAISIN-NUT LOAF

Plump the raisins in the water in a small bowl for 30 minutes. • Drain well and pat dry with paper towels. • Preheat the oven to 350°F/180°C/gas 4. • Butter an 8½ x 4½-inch (21 x 11-cm) loaf pan. Line with aluminum foil, letting the edges overhang. Butter the foil. • Sift the flour, baking powder, and salt into a large bowl. • Beat in the sugar, milk, egg, and butter. Stir in the hazelnuts, almonds, and raisins. • Spoon the batter into the prepared pan. • Bake for 40–50 minutes, or until a toothpick inserted into the center comes out clean. • Cool in the pan on a rack for 10 minutes. Using the foil as a lifter, remove the loaf from the pan. Carefully remove the foil and let cool completely. Decorate with the chopped nuts.

SPICY CARROT AND RAISIN LOAF

Preheat the oven to 350°F/180°C/gas 4.
• Butter an 8¹/₂ x 4¹/₂-inch (21 x 11-cm) loaf pan. Line with foil, letting the edges overhang. Butter the foil. • Place the eggs, baking soda, chile powder, and carrots in a blender and process until the carrots are finely chopped. • Add the butter and sugar and pulse until smooth. • Transfer to a large bowl and mix in the whole-wheat flour, baking powder, salt, raisins, and milk. • Spoon the batter into the mold. • Bake for 45–55 minutes, or until a toothpick inserted into the center comes out clean.
• Cool the loaf on a rack for 10 minutes. Using the foil as a lifter, remove the loaf from the pan. Carefully remove the foil. • Cool the loaf completely on a rack.

Serves: 4–6

Preparation: 15'

Cooking: 45–55'

Level of difficulty: 1

- **2 eggs**
- **¹/₂ tsp baking soda**
- **1 tsp chile powder**
- **2 large carrots, sliced into rounds**
- **6 tbsp butter, melted**
- **³/₄ cup/150 g raw sugar**
- **1¹/₄ cups/180 g whole-wheat/ wholemeal flour**
- **1 tsp baking powder**
- **¹/₈ tsp salt**
- **²/₃ cup/120 g golden raisins/ sultanas**
- **4 tbsp milk**

SWEET TOMATO CAKE

Serves: 8

Preparation: 15'

Cooking: 1 h

Level of difficulty: 1

- 3⅓ cups/500 g all-purpose/plain flour
- 2 tsp baking powder
- 1½ tsp ground cinnamon
- 1½ tsp freshly grated nutmeg
- ⅛ tsp salt
- 4 tbsp butter, softened
- 1½ cups/300 g granulated sugar
- zest of 1 lemon
- 1 cup/180 g golden raisins/sultanas
- 3 oz/90 g tomatoes, peeled and finely chopped

Preheat the oven to 325°F/170°C/gas 3. • Butter a 9-inch (23-cm) cake pan. • Sift the flour, baking powder, cinnamon, nutmeg, and salt into a large bowl. • Beat the butter and sugar in a large bowl with an electric mixer at high speed until creamy. • Mix in the dry ingredients, lemon zest, raisins, and tomatoes. • Spoon the batter into the prepared pan. • Bake for 1 hour, or until golden and well risen. • Let cool completely.

PISTACHIO CAKE

Preheat the oven to 350°F/180°C/gas 4.
• Butter a 9-inch (23-cm) springform pan.
• Plunge the pistachios into a saucepan of boiling water for 30 seconds. Drain. Rub dry with a clean kitchen towel, then carefully peel off the inner skins. • Place the pistachios and sugar in a food processor and chop finely. • Transfer to a large bowl and stir in the egg yolks, lemon zest, cornstarch, baking powder, baking soda, and salt.
• Beat the egg whites in a medium bowl with an electric mixer at high speed until stiff peaks form. Use a large rubber spatula to fold them into the batter. • Spoon the batter into the prepared pan.
• Bake for 25–35 minutes, or until a toothpick inserted into the center comes out clean. • Cool the cake in the pan for 10 minutes. Loosen and remove the pan sides and let the cake cool completely on a rack.

Serves: 6

Preparation: 40'

Cooking: 25–35'

Level of difficulty: 1

- 1½ cups (225 g) pistachios
- 1 cup (20 g) granulated sugar
- 3 large eggs, separated
- 2 tbsp grated lemon zest
- ⅓ cup/50 g cornstarch (cornflour)
- 1 tsp baking powder
- ½ tsp baking soda
- ¼ tsp salt

APPLE PECAN CAKE

Serves: 6

Preparation: 20'

Cooking: 40–50'

Level of difficulty: 1

- 1⅓ cups/200 g all-purpose/plain flour
- ⅓ cup/50 g custard powder
- 1 tsp baking powder
- ½ tsp baking soda
- ¼ tsp salt
- ½ cup/125 g butter, softened
- 1 cup/150 g confectioners'/icing sugar
- 2 large eggs
- ½ cup/50 g chopped pecans
- 2 large apples, peeled, cored, and thinly sliced
- 2–3 tbsp apricot jam or preserves:
- 1 tbsp brandy

Preheat the oven to 350°F/180°C/gas 4. • Butter and flour a 9-inch (23-cm) springform pan. • Sift the flour, custard powder, baking powder, baking soda, and salt into a medium bowl. • Beat the butter and confectioners' sugar in a large bowl with an electric mixer at medium speed until creamy. • Add the eggs, beating until just blended. • With mixer at low speed, gradually beat in the pecans and dry ingredients. • Spoon the batter into the prepared pan. • Arrange the apple slices over the batter. • Bake for 40–50 minutes, or until a toothpick inserted into the center comes out clean. • Cool the cake in the pan on a rack for 10 minutes. Loosen and remove the pan sides and let cool completely. • Warm the jam and brandy in a small saucepan. Drizzle over the cake and serve.

UPSIDE DOWN LEMON POLENTA CAKE

Preheat the oven to 350°F/180°C/gas 4.
• Butter and flour a 9-inch (23-cm) springform pan. • Heat 1¼ cups (310 ml) water and ¾ cup (150 g) sugar in a large saucepan over medium heat until the sugar has dissolved. Bring to a boil and cook and stir for 5 minutes, or until the syrup begins to thicken.
• Add the lemons and simmer for about 8 minutes, turning once, until the lemon peel is tender. • Using tongs, remove the lemon slices from the syrup and press them, overlapping, onto the bottom and sides of the prepared pan. • Return the syrup to medium heat and stir in the remaining 4 tablespoons of water. Simmer until the syrup is light gold. Carefully spoon the syrup over the lemon slices in the pan. • Stir together the flour, polenta, ground almonds, baking powder, and salt in a medium bowl. • Beat the butter, remaining sugar, lemon zest, and lemon extract in a large bowl with an electric mixer at medium speed until creamy. • Add the eggs, beating until just blended. • Gradually beat in the dry ingredients, alternating with the sour cream and lemon juice. • Spoon the batter into the prepared pan. • Bake for 50–60 minutes, or until a toothpick inserted into the center comes out clean.
• Cool the cake in the pan for 15 minutes. Loosen and remove the pan sides. Invert onto a serving dish. Serve warm.

Sumptuous and irresistible, you will be called on to bake this cake time and time again.

Serves: 6

Preparation: 30'

Cooking: 50–60'

Level of difficulty: 1

- 1½ cups/375 ml water
- 1¾ cups/350 g granulated sugar
- 3 large lemons, thinly sliced
- 1 cup/150 g all-purpose/plain flour
- ¾ cup/125 g polenta or yellow cornmeal
- ½ cup/75 g finely ground almonds
- 1 tsp baking powder
- ¼ tsp salt
- ½ cup/125 g butter, softened
- 1 tbsp grated lemon zest
- 1 tsp lemon extract
- 3 large eggs
- 6 tbsp sour cream
- 4 tbsp lemon juice

PINEAPPLE UPSIDE-DOWN CAKE

Serves: 6

Preparation: 20'

Cooking: 40–50'

Level of difficulty: 1

- ½ cup/125 g butter, softened
- 12 walnut halves, broken
- 9 rings drained canned pineapple
- ⅔ cup/140 g granulated sugar
- 2 large eggs
- 1½ tsp baking powder
- 1 tsp vanilla extract
- ¼ tsp salt
- 1½ cups/225 g all-purpose/plain flour
- ½ cup/125 ml milk

Preheat the oven to 350°F/180°C/gas 4.
• Melt 4 tablespoons of butter and pour into a 9-inch (23-cm) round cake pan. Sprinkle in the walnuts. Arrange the pineapple rings in the pan, cutting to fit. • Beat the sugar, remaining butter, and eggs in a medium bowl with an electric mixer at medium speed until just blended. • Beat in the baking powder, vanilla, and salt. Gradually beat in the flour, alternating with the milk. The batter should be smooth and quite sticky. • Spoon the batter over the pineapple. • Bake for 40–50 minutes, or until a toothpick inserted into the center comes out clean. • Cool the cake in the pan for 20 minutes. Invert onto a serving plate and serve.

SUNFLOWER CARROT CAKE

Serves: 6–8

Preparation: 20'

Cooking: 70–80'

Level of difficulty: 1

- 2½ cups/375 g all-purpose/plain flour
- 2½ tsp baking powder
- 1 tsp ground ginger
- 1 tsp ground nutmeg
- ½ tsp baking soda
- ½ tsp salt
- 1 cup/250 ml vegetable oil
- 1¼ cups/250 g brown sugar
- 3 large eggs
- 3 cups/300 g grated carrots
- 1 cup/100 g chopped hazelnuts
- 2 tbsp sunflower seeds

FROSTING

- 8 oz/250 g cream cheese, softened
- 2 tbsp butter
- 1 tbsp grated orange zest
- 1½ cups/225 g confectioners'/icing sugar

Preheat the oven to 350°F/180°C/gas 4. • Butter and flour a 10-inch (25-cm) springform pan. • Sift the flour, baking powder, ginger, nutmeg, baking soda, and salt into a large bowl. • Beat the oil, brown sugar, and eggs in a large bowl with an electric mixer at high speed until creamy. • Beat in the carrots, hazelnuts, sunflower seeds, and the dry ingredients. • Spoon the batter into the prepared pan. • Bake for 70–80 minutes, or until a toothpick inserted into the center comes out clean. • Cool in the pan for 10 minutes. Loosen and remove the pan sides. Invert the cake onto a rack. Loosen and remove the pan bottom and let cool completely. • Frosting: Beat the cream cheese, butter, and orange zest in a medium bowl until fluffy. Beat in the confectioners' sugar. Spread the cake with the frosting.

ALMOND CRESCENTS

Beat the egg white and confectioners' sugar in a large bowl until stiff. Mix in the almonds, chocolate, and butter to form a stiff dough. • Shape the dough into a ball, wrap in plastic wrap, and refrigerate for 1 hour. • Preheat the oven to 400°F/200°C/gas 6. • Line a baking sheet with waxed paper. • Shape teaspoons of the dough into small half-moon shapes. Arrange on the prepared sheet. • Bake for 15–20 minutes, or until golden brown. • Let cool completely. • Topping: Melt the chocolate in a double boiler over barely simmering water. Dip each cookie in the chocolate. • Sprinkle with the pistachios and let the chocolate set.

Serves: 10

Preparation: 1 h 10' + 1 h to chill

Cooking: 20'

Level of difficulty: 2

- **1 egg white**
- **1⅓ cups/200 g confectioners'/ icing sugar**
- **2 cups/200 g finely chopped almonds**
- **5 oz/150 g semisweet/dark chocolate, finely grated**
- **⅔ cup/150 g butter, softened**

TOPPING
- **1½ lb/650 g semisweet/dark chocolate, coarsely chopped**
- **½ cup/50 g finely chopped pistachios**

MARZIPAN COOKIES

Chop the almonds in a food processor or blender until finely ground. • Transfer to a large bowl and mix in the sugar. • Beat the confectioners' sugar and water in a medium bowl until a thick paste has formed. Mix into the almond mixture. • Roll out the marzipan on a work surface dusted with confectioners' sugar. Shape into a ball. Let rest for 30 minutes. • Break off pieces of dough and form into balls the size of marbles. • Roll in the pine nuts and dust with the remaining confectioners' sugar.

Deliciously chewy little cookies. Equally good with coffee at afternoon tea or after dinner with a liqueur.

938

*Vegan

Serves: 10

Preparation: 30' + 30' to rest

Level of difficulty: 1

- generous 2½ cups/ 400 g blanched almonds
- 1 cup/150 g confectioners'/ icing sugar
- 3 tbsp warm water
- 1 cup/100 g chopped pine nuts
- ⅓ cup/50 g confectioners' sugar, to dust

SESAME COOKIES

Serves: 6–8

Preparation: 30' + 30' to rest the dough

Cooking: 15'

Level of difficulty: 1

- 1⅔ cups/250 g all-purpose/plain flour
- 2 tsp baking powder
- ⅛ tsp salt
- ½ cup/125 g butter, melted
- ½ cup/100 g granulated sugar
- 4 tbsp water, + more as needed
- 2½ cups/250 g sesame seeds

Preheat the oven to 350°F/180°C/gas 4. • Set out two cookie sheets. • Sift the flour, baking powder, and salt into a medium bowl.
• Beat the butter and sugar in a large bowl with an electric mixer at high speed until creamy. • Mix in the dry ingredients and enough water to make a smooth dough. • Shape the dough into a ball, wrap in plastic wrap, and refrigerate for 30 minutes.
• Shape the dough into balls the size of walnuts.
• Put the sesame seeds in a small bowl and roll each ball of dough in it. • Transfer to a baking sheet, spacing them 2 inches (5 cm) apart. Flatten the cookies with a fork. • Bake for 10–15 minutes, or until golden brown, rotating the sheets halfway through for even baking. • Let cool completely.

BASIC
RECIPES

VEGETABLE STOCK

*Vegan

*Makes: about 1½
  quarts/1.5 liters*

Preparation: 15'

Cooking: 1 h

Level of difficulty: 1

- 2 tbsp extra-virgin
  olive oil
- 1 medium onion,
  cut in quarters
- 1 carrot, peeled
  and cut in 4 pieces
- 1 leek, trimmed
  and cut in 4 pieces
- 2 celery stalks with
  their leaves, cut
  into 4 pieces
- 1 small tomato,
  halved
- 6 sprigs parsley
- 5 whole black
  peppercorns
- 1 clove
- 1 bay leaf
- ½ tsp salt
- 2 quarts/2 liters
  boiling water

Heat the oil in a medium saucepan. Add the onion, carrot, leek, celery, tomato, and parsley. • Cover and sauté over low heat for about 5 minutes. • Add the pepper corns, clove, and bay leaf. Season with salt. • Pour in the water, cover, and simmer over low heat for about 1 hour. • Strain through a fine mesh strainer and discard the vegetables.

PESTO

Place the basil, pine nuts, garlic, oil, salt, and pepper in a food processor or blender and chop until smooth. • Transfer the mixture to a medium bowl and stir in the cheese and water. The amount of water required will vary according to how you intend to use the pesto.

Makes: 1 generous cup/250–300 ml

Preparation: 10'

Level of difficulty: 1

- 2 cups/45 g fresh basil leaves
- 2 tbsp pine nuts
- 2 cloves garlic
- $^1/_2$ cup/125 ml tbsp extra-virgin olive oil
- 4 tbsp freshly grated Parmesan cheese
- about 2 tbsp boiling water
- salt and freshly ground black pepper to taste

BÉCHAMEL SAUCE

Melt the butter in a medium saucepan over low heat. Add the flour and cook for 3 minutes, stirring constantly. • Remove the pan from the heat and add the milk all at once. Stir well then return to the heat. Season with the salt and pepper and add the nutmeg, if liked. • Bring to a boil and cook for about 10 minutes, stirring constantly. If any lumps form, beat with a wire whisk until smooth.

Makes: 3 cups/ 750 ml

Preparation: 5'

Cooking: 15'

Level of difficulty: 1

- **3 tbsp butter**
- **3 tbsp all-purpose/ plain flour**
- **3 cups/750 ml milk**
- **salt and freshly ground black pepper to taste**
- **$\frac{1}{2}$ tsp freshly grated nutmeg (optional)**

TOMATO SAUCE

Vegan

Makes: about 3 cups/
750 ml

Preparation: 10'

Cooking: 1 h

Level of difficulty: 1

- 4–5 cloves garlic, finely chopped
- 6 tbsp extra-virgin olive oil
- 2 tbsp finely chopped oregano
- 1 tbsp finely chopped marjoram
- 1 tbsp finely chopped basil
- 2 lb/1 kg tomatoes, peeled and chopped
- 2 oz/60 g sun-dried tomatoes, finely chopped
- salt and freshly ground black pepper to taste

SPICY TOMATO SAUCE
- 2 fresh red chile peppers, seeded and finely sliced

Sauté the garlic in 4 tablespoons of oil in a large saucepan over low heat for 2–3 minutes until pale gold. • Add the oregano, marjoram, basil, and tomatoes, squashing them with a wooden spoon. Mix in the sun-dried tomatoes and season with salt and pepper. • Partially cover and simmer for 45 minutes over low heat, stirring occasionally. • This versatile sauce is delicious with pasta, but can also be spooned over boiled rice (try it with brown rice), potatoes, polenta, spelt or pearl barley. It is a good basic sauce for baked dishes, such as lasagne, and many others. If you cook it for 20–30 minutes longer, reducing it to a thick, almost-paste-like sauce (take care it doesn't burn), it can be spread on toast and served as is.

For a hot and spicy version of this tasty sauce, add 2 or more finely chopped red chile peppers together with the herbs.

PIZZA DOUGH

P lace the fresh or active dry yeast in a small
bowl. If using fresh yeast, crumble it with your
fingertips. • Add half the warm water and stir until
the yeast has dissolved. • Set the mixture aside for
15 minutes. It will look creamy when ready. Stir
well. • Place the flour in a large bowl and sprinkle
with the salt. • Make a hollow in the center and
pour in the yeast mixture, the remaining water, and
any other ingredients listed in the recipe. Use a
wooden spoon to stir the mixture. Stir well until the
flour has almost all been absorbed. • Knead the
dough following the instructions for bread dough
on the next page (954). • To shape the pizza, place
the dough in the pizza pan and use your fingertips
to press it out, stretching it as you go, until it
covers the pan. Set aside for 10 minutes before
adding the topping. This will give the dough time to
regain some volume and will make the crust lighter
and more appetizing. • To make calzones, proceed
as for pizza, giving the dough a round shape. Place
the topping on one half of the disk only, leaving a
1-inch (2.5-cm) border around the edge. Fold the
other half over the filling and press the edges
together with your fingertips to seal.

Makes: one (12-inch/ 30-cm pizza)

Preparation: 30'

Rising time: 1 h 30'

Level of difficulty: 1

- **1 oz/25 g fresh yeast or 2 ($^1/_4$-oz/ 7-g) packages active dry yeast**
- **about $^2/_3$ cup/150 ml warm water**
- **3 cups/450 g all-purpose/plain flour + $^1/_2$ cup/75 g to sprinkle work surface**
- **$^1/_2$ tsp salt**

BREAD DOUGH

Place the yeast in a small bowl. Add the sugar and half the warm water and stir until dissolved. • Set aside for 15 minutes. It will look creamy when ready. Stir well. • Place the flour in a large bowl and sprinkle with the salt. • Make a hollow in the center and pour in the yeast mixture and remaining water. Stir until the flour has been absorbed. • **Kneading**: Sprinkle a work surface, preferably made of wood, with a little flour. • Place the dough on the work surface. Curl your fingers around it and press together to form a compact ball. • Press down on the dough with your knuckles to spread it a little. Take the far end of the dough, fold it a short distance toward you, then push it away again with the heel of your palm. Flexing your wrist, fold it toward you again, give it a quarter turn, then push it away. Repeat, gently and with the lightest possible touch, for 8–10 minutes. When the dough is firm and no longer sticks to your hands or the work surface, lift it up and bang it down hard against the work surface a couple of times. This will develop the gluten. The dough should be smooth and elastic, show definite air bubbles beneath the surface, and spring back if you flatten it with your palm. • Place in a large, lightly oiled bowl and cover with a cloth. Set aside to rise. The dough should double in volume. • To test if ready, poke your finger gently into the dough; if the impression remains, then it is ready. Remember that yeast is a living ingredient, affected by temperature and humidity, among other things. Some days it will take longer to rise than others.

Preparation: 30'

Rising time: 1 h 30'

Level of difficulty: 1

BASIC FOCACCIA

- 1 oz/25 g fresh yeast or 2 (^{1}/4-oz/ 7-g) packages active dry yeast
- 1 tsp sugar
- about ^{3}/4 cup/ 200 ml warm water
- 3^1/3 cups/500 g all-purpose/plain flour + ^{1}/2 cup/75 g to sprinkle work surface
- ^{3}/4 tsp salt

BASIC BREAD

- 1 oz/25 g fresh yeast or 2 (^{1}/4-oz/ 7-g) packages active dry yeast
- 1 tsp sugar
- about 1^1/2 cups/ 350 ml warm water
- 5 cups/750 g all-purpose/plain flour + ^{1}/2 cup/75 g to sprinkle work surface
- 1 tsp salt

954

CRÊPES

Sift the flour and salt into a medium bowl.
• Beat in the eggs and sugar. • Pour in the
milk gradually, followed by the melted butter. Beat
the batter until smooth, then set aside to rest for
1 hour. • Brush a small, heated frying pan with the
remaining butter, and add a small ladleful of batter.
Spread evenly by tipping the pan, so that it forms
a thin film. Cook each crêpe on both sides, taking
care not to let them color too much. When the
edges curl slightly, it is done. • If not using
immediately, crêpes can be stored in the
refrigerator, piled one on top of the other
in a covered container.

Makes: 12 crêpes

Preparation: 15' + 1 h to rest

Cooking: 25'

Level of difficulty: 1

- 1 cup/150 g all-purpose/plain flour
- salt to taste
- 2 eggs
- 1 teaspoon sugar
- 1 cup/250 ml milk
- 2 tbsp butter, melted, + extra, to grease the pan

BASIC PASTRY RECIPES

S ift the flour and salt into a large bowl. If making sweet pastry, stir in the sugar at this stage. • Use a pastry blender to cut in the butter until the mixture resembles fine crumbs. Add enough water, and the egg yolks, if making the egg pastries, and knead quickly with your hands to form a fairly stiff dough. • Gather the crumbs and shape into a ball. Wrap in plastic wrap (cling film) and chill in the refrigerator for 1 hour. • Use as indicated in the recipes.

F ood processor version: Place the flour, salt, and sugar, if using, in the bowl of a food processor and pulse a few to times to add air. • Add the butter, and pulse briefly to cut into the flour. • Add the water and egg yolks, if using, and pulse rapidly until the mixture is crumbly, but no longer. • Gather the crumbs and shape into a ball. Wrap in plastic wrap (cling film) and chill in the refrigerator for 1 hour. • Use as indicated in the recipes.

Makes: pastry for a 10–12-inch/ 26–30-cm pan

Preparation: 15' + 1 h to chill

Level of difficulty: 1

SHORT CRUST PASTRY
- 2 cups/300 g all-purpose/plain flour
- ½ tsp salt
- ½ cup/125 g butter, cut up
- 4–6 tbsp ice water

SHORT CRUST EGG PASTRY
- 2 cups/300 g all-purpose/plain flour
- ½ tsp salt
- ½ cup/125 g butter, cut up
- 2–4 tbsp ice water
- 2 egg yolks

SWEET EGG PASTRY
- 2 cups/300 g all-purpose/plain flour
- ½ tsp salt
- ½ cup/125 g butter, cut up
- 2–4 tbsp ice water
- 2 egg yolks
- 2–3 tbsp granulated sugar

INDEX

A

Almonds
– Almond crescents, 936
– Asparagus and almond gratin, 575
– Bucatini with almonds, 317
– Couscous with dates and almonds, 876
– Date and almond rice, 368
– Leek and almond quiche, 112
– Rice with dates and almonds, 399

Apples
– Apple and cinnamon streusel cake, 915
– Apple and raisin cake, 908
– Apple fritters, 886
– Apple pecan cake, 929
– Apple, raspberry, and walnut salad, 770
– Avocado and apple salad, 808
– Mandarin, apple, and tomato salad, 757
– Pancakes with walnuts, Pecorino, and apple, 32
– Spiced beans with apple, 518

Artichokes
– Artichoke and fava bean quiche, 105
– Artichoke and pea stew, 511
– Artichoke quiche, 117
– Artichoke salad, 817
– Artichokes Provençal style, 482
– Artichokes with egg and lemon sauce, 504
– Fried artichokes, 682
– Italian savory pie with artichokes, 111
– Jerusalem artichoke pie, 113
– Orange and artichoke salad, 758
– Stewed artichoke hearts, 500
– Sweet and sour artichokes, 485
– Zucchini and artichoke quiche, 137

Arugula
– Arugula and creamy cheese pizzas with walnuts, 65
– Arugula bread salad, 785
– Pasta with Ricotta and arugula, 360
– Tomatoes filled with arugula and pesto, 776
– Zucchini with arugula pesto, 557

Asparagus
– Asparagus and almond gratin, 575
– Asparagus and cheese spirals, 739
– Asparagus and goat's cheese mini quiches, 61
– Asparagus and orange crostoni, 53
– Asparagus and zucchini flower bake, 597
– Asparagus in a crust, 88
– Asparagus risotto, 401
– Asparagus soufflé, 607
– Fava bean, asparagus, and Ricotta bake, 572
– Penne with asparagus and Ricotta, 307
– Zucchini and asparagus lasagna, 601

Avocados
– Avocado and apple salad, 808
– Avocado and mandarin salad, 826
– Avocado salad, 775
– Farfalle with yogurt sauce and avocado, 339
– Spinach and avocado salad, 795

961

C

E

Eggplant

Eggs

969

P

975